WITHDRAWN

ENGINEERING
INTELLIGENT
SYSTEMS

ENGINEERING INTELLIGENT SYSTEMS

Concepts, Theory, and Applications

Robert M. Glorioso
Fernando C. Colón Osorio

Digital Press

Printed in the U.S.A.

1st Printing, July 1980

Documentation Number: EY-AX011-DP

Library of Congress Cataloging in Publication Data

Glorioso, Robert M.
  Engineering intelligent systems.

  A revision of Engineering cybernetics, published in 1975.
  Includes bibliographies and index.
  1. Cybernetics. 2. Information theory. 3. Computer engineering. I. Colón Osorio, Fernando C., 1949-   joint author. II. Title.
  Q310.G45 1980   001.53   80-16896
  ISBN 0-932376-06-1.

Trademarks

Digital Equipment Corporation: DEC, DECUS, PDP, UNIBUS, VAX, DECnet, DECsystem-10, DECSYSTEM 20, DECwriter, DIBOL, EduSystem, IAS, MASSBUS, PDT, RSTS, RSX, VMS, VT.

CREDITS

Figure 1.1a   Courtesy Digital Equipment Corporation.

Figure 1.1b   Courtesy Digital Equipment Corporation.
Continued on page 465

DEDICATION

To
Nan and Mickey,
Dee and Scott

Robert M. Glorioso

To
My mother, Lucía, my father, Monserrate,
my brothers, Luis and Pedro, and
my dear niece, Teresita

Fernando C. Colón Osorio

Contents

Preface to
Engineering Intelligent Systems: Concepts, Theory, and Applications

This book is a revised, updated and expanded version of *Engineering Cybernetics* by Robert M. Glorioso and published by Prentice-Hall in 1975. In the last five years the combinations of our understanding of cybernetic systems and the technology needed to make them real has afforded us the opportunity to build some sophisticated yet practical systems. Semiconductor technologists have continued to provide exponentially growing functionality at a nearly constant cost, while computer technologists have created new software systems and computer networks. Simultaneously, satellites are providing wide-band inexpensive communications; artificial intelligence researchers have begun to get exciting results in the area of computer vision and the representation of knowledge; while at the same time the highly interdisciplinary area of robotics has made great strides making possible the ever expanding application of robots to industry. It is with this backdrop that we have undertaken this book.

First, we have attempted to correct all the errors, type, conceptual or otherwise, in the original book. Experience indicates that this process is asymptotic; however, our goal has been to get as close as is possible to the limiting and escapable value of zero. This of course leads to another problem found in the development of large software systems, that is, changes usually introduce errors of their own even into the cleanest of documents. Thus, we have tried to divide the new material into modules so that we can debug easily. In the final analysis there are sure to be errors and we ask you, our readers, to communicate those you find to us so we may correct subsequent printings.

The major changes from the original book are primarily in the later chapters although notation changes (to more current or better accepted forms) and some additional material have been included in almost all of the original chapters. Several new chapters have been added to reflect either new results in topics treated in the original work such as Chapter 6, Stochastic Automata Models, and Chapter 9, Stochastic Automata Models in Computer and Communications Networks, or to add material, not covered previously such as Chapter 14, Computer Vision, and Chapter 15, Robotics.

Computer Vision and Robotics, Chapters 14 and 15, have emerged as practical areas of endeavor since 1975 and the principles and applications of both areas are included here. These last two chapters have a particular emphasis on applications of Vision and Robotics in an industrial environment.

The production of this book could not have occured without the help, advice and consent of many people. In particular we thank the people at Digital Press for their cooperation and tolerance of our continual revision of the schedule and Gordon Bell, Jim Bell, Walt Kohler, Cliff Anderson and our other colleagues at Digital who made suggestions or provided moral support. Also our special thanks to the reviewers of our manuscript for their invaluable comments and suggestions.

Robert M. Glorioso
Fernando C. Colón Osorio
Maynard, Mass.

Preface to
Engineering Cybernetics

This book was developed for a one semester course given in the Electrical and Computer Engineering Department at the University of Massachusetts, Amherst. This course serves as a senior elective as well as an introduction for both Engineering and Computer Sciences graduate students to advanced work in artificial intelligence, pattern recognition, adaptive control, adaptive communications, and system design. Although some junior level students have successfully completed this course, it has been a popular course for seniors following an introductory course in computers and switching theory. Thus the prerequisites for this course are switching theory, a reasonable background in probability or random signal theory, and some familiarity with computer programming.

The various disciplines which together are generally referred to as cybernetics, including adaption, learning, self-organization, self-repair, game playing by machines, pattern recognition, and artificial intelligence have been generating interest for the past two decades. It is one purpose of this book to explore these concepts under one cover and present a framework wherein these topics can be united. Another purpose is to present some of the applications of cybernetics which have emerged thus far. Finally, the student is provided with some of the background necessary to carry out further work in these areas.

No work of this kind happens spontaneously but grows from one's interest in the subject and from interaction and discussions with colleagues and friends. I would like to acknowledge the following individuals for their special contributions. First, my colleagues at the U.S. Army Electronics Command at Fort Monmouth, N.J., where first thoughts of the book originated, especially Messrs. J. C. Dunn, G. R. Grueneich, W. Huber and W. Rothamel. Mssrs. M. A. Arbib, L. E. Franks, L. O. Gilstrap, A. Ginsburg, and W. Kilmer each suggested material that was included in the text. Finally, I thank my wife, Dee and son, Scott, for their patience and understanding without which this text could not have come to pass.

Robert M. Glorioso
Amherst, Mass.

ENGINEERING
INTELLIGENT
SYSTEMS

1

Computers and Intelligence

During the last twenty years the area which is broadly defined as artificial intelligence has emerged from the disciplines of computer science and cybernetics. This base of knowledge, coupled with today's technology, now allows the engineer to design intelligent systems to solve complex problems.

We have gathered key topics from these and other areas which have been, or which we expect to be, useful tools for the design engineer. Thus, we have not included some of the more esoteric work whose promise for application appears remote.

Since the area of cybernetics is at the root of many of the topics in this book, we begin by tracing the origins of the discipline. The word "cybernetics" was coined by Norbert Wiener in 1948 in his book of the same name [1]. "Cybernetics" was derived from the Greek word for "steersman," whose Latin derivative means "governor." Wiener defined cybernetics to include control and communications, "whether in the machine or in the animal." Subsequent use of the word has led to its application to concepts of artificial intelligence as well as to all types of feedback control systems.

Since the word "cybernetics" was coined, a great deal of theoretical work has been carried out on the basic concepts of control and communications, often with emphasis on their relation to biological systems in general and brains in particular [2, 3, 4]. Other work has been of an applied nature; it is this area which is treated here.

Many of the theories put forth in the area of cybernetics have also found application in real physical systems. These systems, such as the control of rocket motors for launching satellites and spaceships, use engineering design approaches that encompass many of the concepts that have emerged from cybernetics. It is the design of systems using adaptive, learning, and self-repairing concepts which is of interest in this book.

Since the first notions of systems exhibiting adaptive, learning, or self-repairing behavior were introduced, and throughout the years since, engineers lacked the technology to implement most of the notions. Specifically, the two items generally needed to implement them were stable, high gain amplifiers and the ability to execute algorithms and make state-dependent decisions. The solutions to both problems have occurred as a result of the semiconductor revolution. The amplifier problem was the first to be solved; and reasonably priced, high gain, stable operational amplifiers

(a)

Figure 1.1. Powerful microcomputers in small packages such as these produced by Digital Equipment Corporation, allow "intelligence" to be built into products such as automobiles, machine tools, and robots that execute complex control tasks. (a) DEC 11/23 CPU boards, containing all the

have been available for a decade. The second problem has only recently been solved with the advent of microprocessors and the evolution of solid-state memory technology. This technology has provided the breakthrough needed to engineer cybernetic systems.

COMPUTERS—A TOOL FOR ENGINEERING INTELLIGENT SYSTEMS

The computer, especially in the form of the microprocessor, has become the principal tool for designing intelligent systems. The minicomputer and now the microcomputer have finally illustrated that a computer can be used for purposes other than solving complex equations (number crunching) or handling a payroll. The use of computing power to replace random logic in such devices as terminals, mass storage systems, microwave ovens, and automobiles illustrates the other face of computing—real-time controlling. These computers are the product of the semiconductor revolution and are illustrated in Figure 1.1. Figure 1.1a shows a board computer

(b)

Figure 1.1. (Cont.)   computing and interface logic to support large programs (256 Kbytes) in a compact space. (b) Photomicrograph of one of the integrated circuits in the 11/23 CPU.

and Figure 1.1b is a photomicrograph of one of the integrated circuits. It is clear that these computers fit into process control systems, machine tools, and robots.

An important feature of many applications is the fact that the control computer must deal with real-time signals via its input/output (I/O) channels. A simple block diagram of a typical system is shown in Figure 1.2. Here a microprocessor is connected to a memory that is probably a mixture of read-only memory (ROM) and random access memory (RAM). The ROM contains the control program and constants, and the RAM is used to store intermediate data generated during execution of the control function. The key feature of this system differentiating it from the classic computer application is the presence of sensors and effectors as the input/output system. The sensors consist of devices that sample parameters in the environment and convert the outputs into digital form, if they are not already digital, for processing. Temperature, position, video, and velocity sensors are the kinds of sensors used. The effectors are elements that actively drive the environment in some way that can be controlled via the outputs of the computer. In some instances, the digital output from the computer must be converted to analog form with a digital-to-analog (D/A) converter. Examples of effectors are relays, stepping motors, DC motors, hydraulic valves, and lamps. The basic configuration of Figure 1.2 could be used to implement an automobile fuel injection system, an automatic

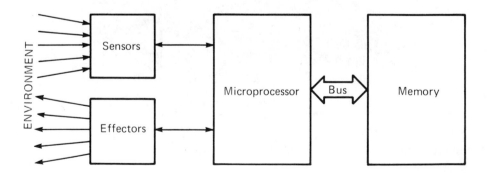

Figure 1.2. Typical microprocessor system block diagram in a real-time control application.

machine tool, or a robot. The design of such a system requires the application of several disciplines including analog design, logic design, programming, and system design.

The emphasis here is on the system and the basic concepts associated with its design. Note that the practical design of these systems requires that all the preceding skills be applied with equal emphasis. An area of importance which is often ignored in the design of systems is programming. This is in spite of the fact that several managers of programming projects have noted that each job can take up to 100 percent more time than originally scheduled [5].

Much work over the past several years has been devoted to making it easier to program computers in control as well as other applications. High level languages as tools for creating programs in the control environment are now under discussion, with languages like PASCAL and BASIC as front-runners. Special techniques have also been developed to program systems for particular applications such as robots [6]. These techniques often define high level semantics that are tailored to the application. For example, a robot command might be ROTATE ARM X DEGREES.

An important aspect of the use of microprocessors in intelligent systems is the fact that their small size and low cost make it possible to use many of them in a single system. The inter-connection of many computers is often used in applying industrial robots to an assembly line. A usual form of interconnect in these systems is loosely coupled, wherein each processor has its own local memory and the processors communicate via a special I/O channel as shown in Figure 1.3. Each of the three processors has a local bus with a local memory. Other items (such as sensors, effectors, and mass storage devices) may also be connected to the buses of each processor. The Interprocessor Communications Bus carries messages between the processors. These messages may take the form of high level commands, which in a robot may be, for instance, from a processor in the left arm to the processor in the right arm, and may mean "lift 3 mm." This form of processing, in which each processor is specialized to a particular function or set of functions, has been referred to as a distributed function multiple processor system [7].

The configuration of Figure 1.3 can be extended to implement a hierarchy in which one processor issues commands to one or more other

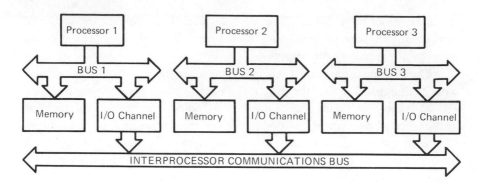

Figure 1.3.   Loosely coupled multiple microprocessor.

processors as shown in Figure 1.4. This is a three-level hierarchy wherein processor 1 provides the overall control by executing high level commands and issuing other commands to level 2. The processors in level 2 execute a portion of the commands and issue commands to level 3 to complete the specified task.

It should now be apparent that computers can deal with more interesting things than solving equations or running a payroll program on a single processor in a sterile room. The processing described here implies that computer systems used as control elements for these tasks must deal with more abstract items such as commands and symbols, while making elementary decisions.

SYMBOLS AND DECISIONS

As suggested in the previous section, symbol manipulation is a natural process for the general purpose digital computer. For example, it is possible, as anyone with some programming experience has observed, to encode natural language text into a computer. It is also possible to provide a simple symbol table for the machine that can be used to look up symbols in one language and translate them into symbols in another language. Thus, the process of elementary language translation, which certainly is not

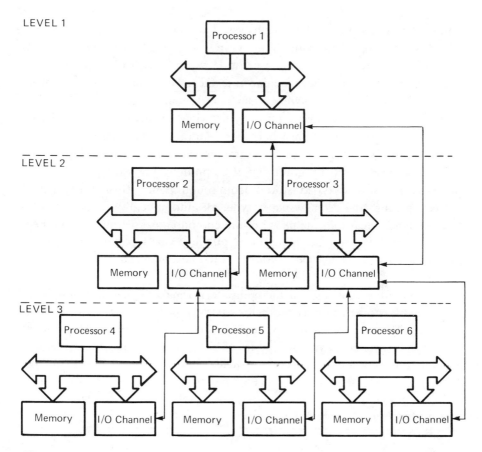

Figure 1.4. Multiple processors in a hierarchy.

number crunching, can be accomplished with these machines. The specific languages involved in the translation process are, of course, very important. The translation that occurs in the compilation of a FORTRAN or other high level language program into a machine language program is an everyday process for many computers, whereas the translation from Russian to English or from some other natural language to another natural language is not. The reason for this difference is that the artificial languages associated with computer processing are specifically designed to avoid the ambiguities and syntactical problems associated with natural languages [8].

Another interesting example of symbol manipulation is the graphical processing of information using a cathode ray tube (CRT) terminal, light pen, and push-button man-machine interface. Here the human operator works with man-oriented symbols such as schematic drawings and diagrams and operates on the computer by drawing, usually in some restricted man-oriented language, with a light pen. Automatic typesetting and machine control systems are other examples of symbol manipulation by general purpose stored program digital computers. For example, some of these machines read typed stories from bond paper, format the page, correct spelling, and set newspaper type, all automatically. It should now be abundantly clear that the image of the computer as a mammoth number cruncher that swallows and regurgitates punched cards, paper, or magnetic tape is in no way a complete picture of the system tool that the computer has become.

The unique capability of the computer to make logical decisions and then modify its behavior is the heart of the power of this device. These decisions, whether obviously simple or horrendously complex, always can and must be broken down into a series of basic decisions because they must be carried out by simple instructions such as "greater than," "less than," or "equal to." For example, the process associated with the typical decision apparently made with some frequency by members of the college population is illustrated in Figure 1.5.

WHAT IS INTELLIGENCE?

As a first step toward answering the question "What is intelligence?" we shall start with two dictionary definitions of intelligence: (1) capacity for understanding and for other forms of adaptive behavior; and (2) knowledge of an event, circumstance, etc., received or imparted; news; information. Discussions of the definition of intelligence and artificial intelligence have been in progress ever since computer operations were compared with thinking and the brain. These concepts are also part of the definition presented by Fogel et al. [9]: "the distinction between knowledge and intelligence became clear: knowledge being the ability of the individual to

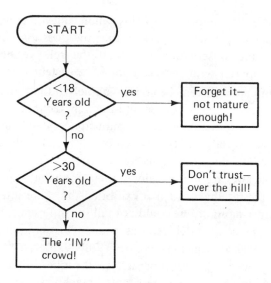

Figure 1.5. "Complex" decision process.

utilize this stored information in some worthwhile (goal-directed) manner."
Although some people may argue the point, it is generally assumed that
whatever intelligence is, it is a characteristic exhibited by man. The
question now is, "Can computers think and exhibit intelligent behavior?"
Can we create artificial intelligence? Following are some of the arguments
both pro and con concerning computers, thinking, and artificial intelligence.

First, if one considers thinking to be a uniquely human endeavor and
intelligence to be a uniquely human attribute, then, by definition, this
process and attribute cannot be associated with a computer or other
mechanical or artificial system.

On the other hand, it has been argued that if there is some fundamental physical limitation on the ability to compute, process, decide, judge, and
think that applies to the creation of machine intelligence, then this same
limitation must also apply to human intelligence. That is, any theoretical
limitation based on universal natural laws must be universally applicable to
both man and machine. This argument, of course, discounts the precept
that the essence of intelligence is mystical or mysterious.

A more scientific approach to this whole question was proposed in 1950 by Turing [10, 11], who suggested that the question can be answered by experiment and observation in which the relative behavior of the computer is compared with the behavior of a system that, by definition, thinks and exhibits intelligent behavior—namely human behavior. To this end, Turing proposed a question-and-answer technique in which the trappings of both the machine and a man are hidden and questions are asked and answered via some type of remote terminal such as a teletype. If, by asking questions, one could reliably determine whether the machine or the man were answering the questions, then one would question whether the machine were intelligent or if it exhibited the same intelligence as the man. On the other hand, if one could not tell the difference, it could be said that the machine is as intelligent as man. This imitation game is an interesting approach that has not yet been fully explored.

Perhaps a more rational approach to the question is to visualize a continuous intelligence space where men, machines, animals, plants, or what have you are positioned according to their relative intelligence. Here, perhaps, a mass of material such as rocks and plants would be at one end, and man and other higher animals would be at the other end. Thus, one could consider all things as having some degree of intelligence. This approach sidesteps or compromises the question "Are machines intelligent?" rather than truly answering it.

Another common argument against the concept of machine intelligence is that a computer is a dumb machine that does only what it is told by its human programmer. But if one critically examines the nature of human intelligence, one must admit that man's biological system along with the adaptive ability of his behavior, both endowed by nature and the totality of his experience, gives him these unique powers of thought and intelligence. Thus, the basic, built-in characteristics of man coupled with the changes in him through experience endow him with the proper "program" for successful performance in his environment. Therefore, Simon [12] has suggested that

If a computer thinks, learns, and creates, it will be by virtue of a program that endows it with these capacities. Clearly this will not be a program—any more than the human is—that calls for highly stereotyped and repetitive behavior independent of the stimuli coming from the environment and the task to be completed. It will be a program that makes the system's behavior highly conditioned on the task environment—on the task goals and on the clues extracted from the environment that indicate whether progress is being made toward these goals. It will be a *program* that analyzes, by some means, its own performance, diagnoses its failures, and makes changes that enhance its future effectiveness.

The essence of cybernetic systems and artificial intelligence is contained in this statement. The ability of a system to examine and modify its behavior accordingly is necessary if it is to have any of these attributes.

SOME TECHNIQUES OF ARTIFICIAL INTELLIGENCE

If we can now agree that it is the program stored in a computer that will be crucial if the computer is to exhibit this behavior, then let us examine the kinds of programs used to obtain results, which are called learning or intelligence.

The first technique or tool is the algorithm. An algorithm is a specific set of operations, procedures, and decisions that is guaranteed to yield the correct results. Examples of algorithms extend from the simple procedures for finding a square root and synthetic division to learning algorithms for systems that can be described by stochastic transition matrices [13].

A procedure often confused with an algorithm is a heuristic. A heuristic is a rule of thumb, a trick, strategy, simplification, or other method that aids in the solution of complex problems. The heuristic used to solve many problems in designing intelligent systems generally reduces the size of the space in which one needs to search for solutions to the problem at hand. One of the major differences between a heuristic and an algorithm is that while the heuristic generally aids in finding the solution, it does not guarantee an optimal solution or even any solution at all. With an algorithm, however, one can be sure of finding the correct result.

There are two kinds of heuristics, special and general. A special heuristic is one that applies to a particular problem, whereas a general heuristic is a process or philosophy that can be applied to a wide range of problems. For example, a game-playing program, such as chess, that identifies sequences of moves which threaten the computer's winning chances is a special heuristic for that particular game.

Anyone who has proved some theorems knows that it is generally easier to work backward from the theorem being proved to known theorems or axioms than to work forward from known theorems and axioms blindly searching for the new theorem. The process of working backward in theorem proving is a general heuristic.

Another general heuristic is the recognition of features in the present problem that are similar to problems solved previously. The critical part of this technique is the recognition of the similarity, which itself may be a special heuristic.

A final example of a general heuristic that has been developed by Newell and Simon [14] is a program called general problem solver (GPS). This process, called means-ends analysis, is related to the process of problem solving that humans employ when performing a specific task. Here the problem statement is transformed into a target or goal state that represents the solution to the problem. This state provides a means of identifying a proper solution to the problem. The program then identifies the difference between the present state and the goal state and selects sequentially the operations that reduce the difference between the new present state and the goal state. Another form of means-ends analysis is called planning, wherein a simplified statement of the problem is reduced by means-ends analysis to a plan, which is then used to operate on the full problem.

The techniques of artificial intelligence most often require that the problem be defined in some specific way, for example, the breaking down of a complex decision into a series of simpler subdecisions that lead to the final solution. The representation of a problem in a simple, easily processed form then aids in the development of a solution. Thus, the process of deciding a single move in a game in the context of the overall strategy has developed as an important exposition of some of these techniques.

The purpose of this book is to introduce the reader to the principles of engineering intelligent systems and their application. The text is divided into three major areas: background and definitions, generic applications, and system applications.

In Chapter 2 we shall explore games and some of the ways they can be played by machines in an "intelligent" way. These methodologies are not reserved for games only and have been applied to theorem proving, general problem solving, and pattern recognition [15].

Chapter 3 serves as a link from these techniques of artificial intelligence to advanced work in this area and sets the mathematical tone for Chapter 4. Chapter 4 is concerned with computing machines, their abstract representation, and their theoretical limitations. These concepts, by providing a basis for analysis, tell us just how far we can go in the application of the principles using real machines.

The definitions, descriptions, and taxonomy of intelligent systems are described in Chapter 5, and the theory of learning stochastic automata is presented in Chapter 6. These generic concepts are applied in Chapters 7, 8, 9, 10, and 13 in the areas of control, communication, computer and communication networks, reliability and repair, and pattern recognition, respectively. Chapters 11 and 12 return to background and definitions, both for support of later chapters and for historical reasons. Chapter 11, "Neurons and Neural Models," provides a historical perspective on many of the concepts extant in the early days of cybernetics. Their extension to some applications is introduced in Chapter 12, "Threshold Logic."

Chapter 14 contains an introduction to a systems application of cybernetics, which will be an important part of systems of the future. Computer vision will open several new vistas for engineers to improve productivity and quality in automatic assembly and inspection systems.

An exciting new application of these systems, robotics, is treated in Chapter 15. Robots challenge the engineer to utilize all the elements of engineering intelligent systems introduced in this book as well as a smattering of good system design, programming, and ingenuity to create cost-effective, safe, and useful tools for mankind.

SUMMARY

The application of computers in sophisticated problem-solving environments and systems has been suggested here. Technological progress has made the digital computer, especially in the form of the microprocessor, a more important tool than the operational amplifier for the engineer. The incorporation of the computer into cybernetic systems requires an understanding of the principles of artificial intelligence and adaptive, learning,

2

Game Playing and Machines

One of the first areas in which the concept of artificial intelligence through heuristics and algorithms was applied was automatic game playing by machines. Initially, there was a good deal of speculation that soon a computer would be the world chess champion because computers, by virtue of their tremendous speed and large memory, can examine all possible moves and thus always know exactly which moves lead to a win. Early investigators quickly came to the conclusion that this brute force approach leads directly down the garden path, which is a long way from a chess win.

DECISION MODELS

In the course of playing most games, one generally comes to a point where at least one decision must be made. For example, in the games of tick-tack-toe, checkers, and chess, each move requires that a decision be made by the appropriate player. The simplest decision, a binary decision, can be represented in the simple graph of Figure 2.1a. The nodes in the graph represent decision points, and the edges represent the directions in which these decisions lead. The more complex decision illustrated in Figure 2.1b has four possible moves. Here, if one reaches a point where only one of several alternatives can be successful, there is only one course of action. This is called a *forced move*.

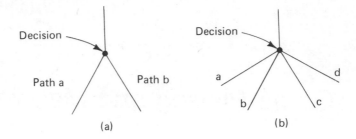

Figure 2.1a. Representation of a binary decision.
     b. Representation of a multiple-alternative decision.

The moves associated with a chess game can also be represented in a tree called a *game tree*. The initial or opening moves by the first player are given in the first level of the tree, the first moves by the second player in the second level as shown in Figure 2.2. Note that only the possible moves associated with the particular game being played are illustrated in Figure 2.2 and that all possible moves in all possible games would require branches from every node in the figure. The computer playing in a brute force manner needs only to store all possible paths in a game in its memory. It has been estimated that there are approximately 10^{120} different paths through the chess tree [1]. In contrast, it has been estimated that there are approximately 10^{11} neurons in the human nervous system [2]. Thus, the

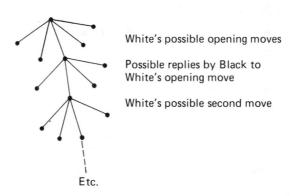

Figure 2.2. Game tree for chess.

practicality or even the desirability of storing all paths is questionable. If we could endow a chess-playing program with the ability to disregard the low-likelihood paths by some means of selective, intelligent search, perhaps it would play a reasonable game of chess. Thus, the searching and processing of trees is an important technique of heuristic programming.

GAME TREES

The techniques treated in this section can be applied in many areas. For illustration, however, we shall restrict our attention to game trees [3, 4]. Before describing game trees, some fundamental concepts behind the theory of trees will be presented.

Let us define a tree formally [5] as a finite set T of one or more nodes such that,

1. There is one specially designated node called the *root* of the tree, root (T); and
2. The remaining nodes are partitioned into $m \geq 1$ disjoint sets $T_1, \ldots, T_m$, and each set, in turn, is a tree. The trees $T_1, \ldots, T_m$ are called *subtrees* of the root.

From this definition, it follows that every node of a tree is the root of some subtree contained in the whole tree.

We now define the concepts of node degree, terminal node, and node level. The *degree* of a node corresponds to the number of associated subtrees. A *terminal node* (*leaf*) is a node with degree zero. The level of a node with respect to T is defined by saying that the root has level 0, and other nodes have a level that is one higher than they have with respect to the subtree T_j, of the root, which contains them.

These concepts are illustrated in Figure 2.3. The root of the tree is A, and it has two subtrees:

$$T_1 = \{B, D, E, H, I, J, K\}$$
$$T_2 = \{C, F, G, L, M, N, O\}$$

Tree T_1 has B as its root. Node B is at level one with respect to the whole tree; this node has subtrees $\{D, H, I\}$ and $\{E, J, K\}$. The terminal nodes in Figure 2.3 are H, I, J, K, L, M, N, O. Except for the terminal nodes, all nodes have degree 2. Having established these concepts, we can now focus on trees representing games.

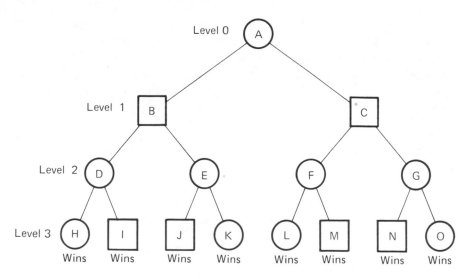

Figure 2.3. Breadth-first procedure after generation of level 3, which terminates the game.

Game trees must be generated, searched, and pruned in order to be handled economically by a computer. There are basically two types of game trees, explicit and implicit.

An *explicit* game tree is one in which the top node represents the starting position and the shape or color of the node represents the player whose turn is associated with that node. In addition, an explicit tree is one in which every move through the tree is included.

An *implicit* tree contains the starting node together with the rules necessary to generate the remainder of the tree for each particular game. These rules must include the termination criteria, which are needed to determine when the game is over, and the successor rules, which indicate the ways in which the successive positions (nodes) are generated. Naturally, a node for which the termination criteria are satisfied has no successor rule. The rules for most board game moves such as in checkers and chess are the successor rules for generating the tree for these games.

Two common procedures for generating implicit game trees are breadth-first and depth-first. *Breadth-first* generation proceeds by generating every node in level 1, every node in level 2, and so forth in a fanlike manner. After level 3 is generated, the tree may look as shown in Figure 2.3.

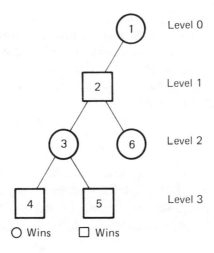

Figure 2.4. Depth-first generation after six steps.

The *depth-first* generation procedure generally works in a left-to-right manner by first generating all successive positions on the left side of the tree through the termination of the graph or to some intermediate position. It then takes the next leftmost position and generates all its successors through to termination, continuing in this manner. Clearly, for complete depth-first generation the termination criteria must be exercised at each branch end. Figure 2.4 shows the order of generation of the tree of Figure 2.3 using depth-first generation.

Two basic search procedures can be applied to game trees, namely, depth-first minimax and alpha-beta. These procedures, however, require that each move, and hence each position, be evaluated. In simple games, the tree may be sufficiently small that the terminal moves themselves can be evaluated. The intermediate moves may therefore easily be determined by examining their relationship to a final winning move. On the other hand, because of finite computer time and storage the final moves may be accessible only in the end game of larger games such as chess or checkers. For these larger games, then, the opening and middle game moves must be evaluated with respect to some intermediate nodes rather than with respect to the end or terminal nodes. It is possible, of course, to formulate an evaluation procedure that operates on the present and next lower level nodes alone. However, it is generally desirable to look as far ahead into the game tree as possible when evaluating the present move. The evaluation of either the terminal or some intermediate nodes must be projected back to the present node to determine the "best" move. It is desirable to program the computer so that it will move to the position that has been evaluated as having the highest chance of winning. Therefore, a terminal state generally has a probability of winning of one if the game is won, or zero if the game is lost.

Because the machine always moves to try to maximize the value of the present position, it is sometimes called the MAX player. The opponent, generally forced to play in a minimizing position with respect to his game, is called the MIN player. The game trees of concern here are for the MAX player only. The MIN player must generate his own tree by these or other methods.

The evaluation function is a particular relation used to evaluate the relative attributes of a particular position in a tree. The simplest and most often applied type of evaluation function is a linear weighted sum of all the characteristics associated with a particular position, j,

$$B_j = C_j \cdot Y_j = \sum_{i=1}^{N} c_{ij} y_{ij} \qquad (2.1)$$

where C_j is $1 \times N$ weight vector and Y_j is a column vector associated with the parameters in the system. Thus, we can evaluate each position in a game tree with respect to the particular position itself. This, however, does not provide us with the means for evaluating the paths through the tree that necessarily lead to a win. To do this, each position must be examined with respect to the other positions possible in that path.

Next, let us examine a method whereby these positions can be evaluated with respect to a machine win. This process assumes that we begin at the end of a tree or at some predetermined intermediate position by applying the evaluation function. We then project back up the tree by using a minimax backup procedure. Here, the value of a max position (computer move) is obtained by making it equal to the maximum of its successor moves. The value of the max position given by the square in Figure 2.5 is thus 0.6. The value of a min position is found by projecting the minimum value of the successor moves back to the min position. For instance, the value of the min position given in Figure 2.6 must be 0.1. This

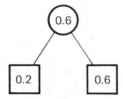

Figure 2.5.   Finding the value of a max position from its successors.

is called the *minimax* procedure, because it tends to maximize the winning chances for the machine while minimizing the winning chances of the opponent. The specific search procedures used to operate on game trees can now be examined.

The *depth-first minimax* search combines the minimax backup procedure and the depth-first generation procedure. The first step in this search is to generate the leftmost section of the tree and evaluate the last or some intermediate position; the next position is then generated and evaluated. These numbers are then backed up, and the process continues until the values of the positions associated with the next move can be determined. For example, if the final backed-up values are as shown in Figure 2.7, the computer decides to make the move associated with the highest value, in this case 0.6.

Another search procedure that can be used to operate on game trees is called the *alpha-beta* or backward pruning procedure. Compared to depth-first minimax, the pruning possible with this process can reduce the number of computations by several orders of magnitude. One advantage of the

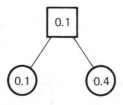

Figure 2.6.   Finding the value of a min position from its successors.

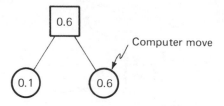

Figure 2.7.   Selection of next move after tree has been evaluated.

alpha-beta procedure accrues by combining the tree generation and position evaluation procedures. In this way, if one finds the best path in the
initial branch generation and evaluation, it is not necessary to generate and
evaluate the remainder of the tree. Consider the tree in Figure 2.8, where
the square represents the machine's moves. Three branches have been
generated, and the terminal nodes have been evaluated. Notice that the
leftmost min position has been evaluated and has a value of 0.4. Thus, we
say that the alpha cutoff is $\alpha = 0.4$. Since projections back to a max
position are the maximum value of the min position and since the value of
P_{21} is less than α, there is no need to generate P_{22}. The next branch of the
tree, say P_3, and its terminals P_{31} and P_{32} are thus generated and evaluated
with respect to the alpha cutoff.

Similarly, the game tree in Figure 2.9 can be examined using the
inverse of the alpha cutoff on max positions, that is, the beta cutoff

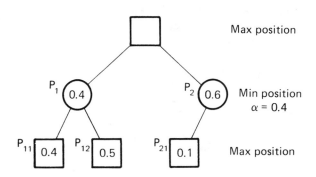

Figure 2.8.   Alpha cutoff application to a min position.

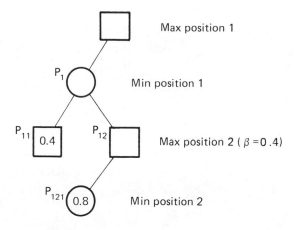

Figure 2.9. Beta cutoff application to a max position.

procedure. In this case, the projection back to min position 1 is the minimum value of max position 2, and the beta cutoff is set at 0.4. Thus, finding $P_{121} = 0.8$, which is greater than the cutoff, immediately eliminates the value of P_{12}, which will be at least 0.8. (Note that a max position picks the maximum value.) There is no need to generate P_{122}, and P_2 and its associated terminal nodes are then each generated and evaluated with respect to the beta cutoff. Thus, alpha is the maximum of a min position, and beta is the minimum of a max position. It should be obvious from these examples that the alpha-beta search procedure generally requires fewer operations than the depth-first minimax procedure.

GAMES

Having studied some general ways of representing and playing games, let us now examine some simple games, first the beloved tick-tack-toe. The process we will use to analyze tick-tack-toe, albeit not too involved, demonstrates the principles involved in formalizing a game for machine play.

The first step in formalizing board-type games is to label the positions on the board in an unambiguous way. The tick-tack-toe board can be labeled as in Figure 2.10. It is clear that the first player can make nine initial moves, the second player eight, and so on. Consequently, there are

11	12	13
21	22	23
31	32	33

Figure 2.10.   Board labeling
for tick-tack-toe.

9! = 362,880 different sequences of nine moves in the course of a game. Does this make the computerization of tick-tack-toe as difficult as the computerization of chess? The answer, of course, is no. The complete tree here is large—362,880 nodes—and brute force computing is quite lengthy, but the structure of this game is such that it can be quickly reduced to a simple game-playing algorithm. For example, it is possible to win a game in five plays where an average game may be six plays. Hence, if we consider games terminating in six moves, this reduces the number of possible sequences to

$$\frac{9!}{3!} \simeq 60,000$$

A first approach might be directed toward taking advantage of the symmetry of the board to reduce the number of tree branches to be searched. Note that the corner positions are equivalent and that the alpha-beta search generally reduces the total number of branches that must be searched. This reduces the number of branch combinations the computer must search to 1700 if it makes the second move and to 40 for the fourth move [6]. The remaining moves require only a miniscule number of searches.

Another approach to computerizing this game uses heuristic techniques to optimize each play. To do this, we must define a win matrix, **W**, which contains all the winning positions and conditional win matrices containing only two columns of the win matrix. Thus, $\mathbf{W}_{23}$ contains the second and third columns of the win matrix **W**:

$$\mathbf{W} = \begin{bmatrix} 11 & 12 & 13 \\ 21 & 22 & 23 \\ 31 & 32 & 33 \\ 11 & 21 & 31 \\ 12 & 22 & 32 \\ 13 & 23 & 33 \\ 11 & 22 & 33 \\ 13 & 22 & 31 \end{bmatrix}$$

A procedure for playing the game is defined in Figure 2.11.

At this point, let us examine tick-tack-toe in terms of the minimax search procedure presented previously. It should be clear, however, that it is not desirable to search the 9! nodes in the tick-tack-toe tree in order to find the first move. Therefore, it is necessary to evaluate moves with respect to intermediate positions in the tree as well as to take advantage of the symmetry of the game. The evaluation function that will be applied here is

"Number of winning rows remaining—if j is not a winning position."

$$E_j = \begin{cases} N - \text{if } j \text{ is a winning move for the computer} \\ 0 - \text{if } j \text{ is a winning move for the opponent or a draw} \end{cases}$$

The evaluation of the jth position, where X is the computer's mark,

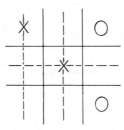

is thus $E_j = 3$, as indicated by the three dashed lines in the game above. Because of board symmetry, there are only three alternatives to consider for the first move. These alternatives are illustrated in Figure 2.12, where

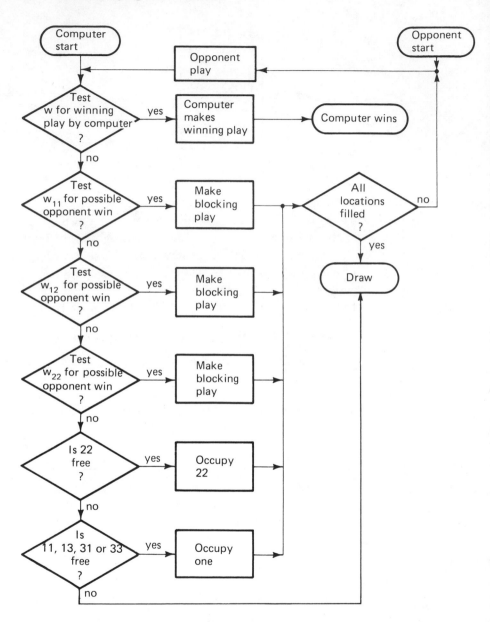

Figure 2.11.   Flowchart for computer play of tick-tack-toe.

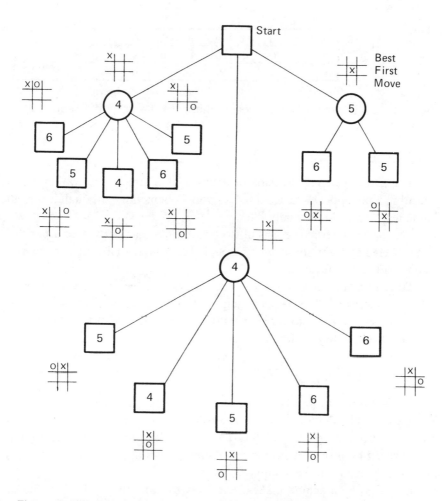

Figure 2.12.   Minimax search to a depth of two for tick-tack-toe.

generation of the tree to a depth of two is shown. The evaluation of the final positions in the tree shown have also been calculated and backed up by the minimax procedure to the other nodes. The results indicate that the move to square 22 is the best one for this evaluation procedure. The remaining moves can also be determined in this way by generating the tree from the opponent's move down two more levels, evaluating these nodes, backing up the values, and so on until the game ends.

Chips placed on board

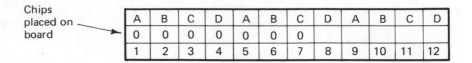

A	B	C	D	A	B	C	D	A	B	C	D
0	0	0	0	0	0	0					
1	2	3	4	5	6	7	8	9	10	11	12

Figure 2.13.   Board for last one loses where the die or card picked is 7.

LAST ONE LOSES: G-1A [7]

The game we shall describe next provides a simple illustration of an algorithm that appears to exhibit "learning" behavior, although we shall define learning more formally later.

The game material consists of twelve chips, a pair of dice, or a deck of cards labeled sequentially from 1 through 12. A board labeled as shown in Figure 2.13 is also needed.

The game proceeds as follows. The dice are thrown or a card is picked, and that number of chips is placed on the board. Each player in succession then removes from one to three chips from the board, with the player who removes the last chip losing the game.

THE G-1A CUP MACHINE

Game G-1A is simple enough, and most people can learn the winning strategy after playing a few times. The following machine using Dixie cups and cards can also learn to play G-1A. The G-1A cup machine illustrated in Figure 2.14 consists of four cups labeled A through D with three chips labeled 1 through 3 in each cup.

Initially, the machine makes its moves by randomly selecting one of the three chips in the cup associated with the present chip on the board and removing the number of chips indicated by that choice. For example, cup C is used for the position indicated in Figure 2.13. The machine then

Figure 2.14.   Cup machine for G-1A.

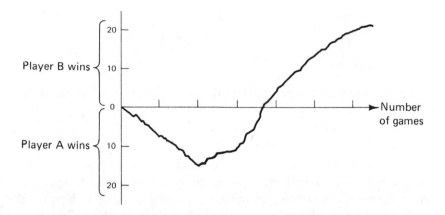

Figure 2.15. Learning curve for G-1A.

discards the last card drawn in a game that the machine loses—this includes the card drawn prior to encountering an empty cup. If the same cup is selected on two successive machine moves, the same card may be used again. A singleton card in a cup is used each time that cup is selected. An empty cup indicates a location where the machine forfeits the game.

The learning curve in Figure 2.15 indicates the rate of learning for the cup machine. It is suggested that one try this game plot and then compare learning curves for both human and machine players. It will be found that after several games, the cup machine will converge to the configuration given below:

THEORY G-1A

Consider first the case where five chips are left on the board and it is player B's turn. If player A knows the optimum strategy, player B can only lose—for, if he takes one chip, then player A will take three, leaving player B the last chip, and so forth, as tabulated:

Player A	1	2	3
Player B	3	2	1

Further examination reveals that the same situation will occur if there are 9, 13, 17, ... chips on the board. Thus, the winning strategy is clear: each player tries to leave N chips on the board, where N equals 1 MOD 4. A player facing that remainder is in a losing state.

The player who has the first move has a probability of winning, determined by the number of chips on the board, provided he makes the correct moves. For example, an initial move with 1, 5, or 9 chips on the board puts the first player in a losing state. Therefore, the probability of drawing or throwing 1, 5, or 9 on the initial play determines the probability of getting into a losing state provided the opposing player knows the winning strategy.

If cards are used to determine the number of chips for the game, there are three losing cards in the deck of twelve, and the probability of losing is

$$P(\text{first player loses}) = 3/12 = 1/4$$

$$P(\text{first player wins}) = 1 - 1/4 = 3/4$$

A converged machine will thus win three of every four games when it has the first move.

For dice, only two losing numbers can occur, 5 and 9. Since each die has six possibilities, there are $6^2 = 36$ different possible states for the dice. The losing throws are:

$$
\left.
\begin{matrix}
1, 4 \\
2, 3 \\
3, 2 \\
4, 1 \\
5, 4 \\
6, 3 \\
3, 6 \\
4, 5
\end{matrix}
\right\} \text{ eight losing throws}
$$

and the probability that the machine wins on the first move is

$$P(\text{machine loses}) = 8/36 = 2/9$$
$$P(\text{machine wins}) = 1 - 2/9 = 7/9$$

SUMMARY

Some techniques for playing games by machines have been examined in this chapter. Heuristic search procedures for searching trees and choosing moves have been explored. Although these techniques were presented in the context of games, it is important to note that these processes can also be applied in other areas, including theorem proving, pattern recognition, and learning.

EXERCISES

1. Find the backed-up values and the best initial move for square for all positions in the following trees:

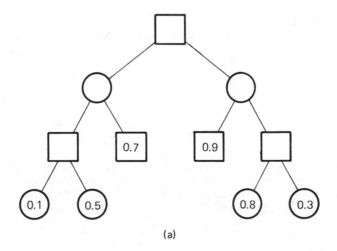

(a)

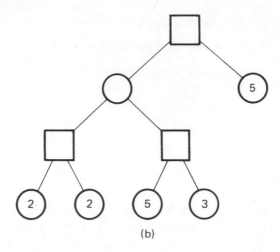

(b)

2. Are there any ways in which the computer play of tick-tack-toe given above can be improved? If so, what are they?

3. Generate the game trees for two games of tick-tack-toe with different first moves that you have played with a friend.

4. Generate three levels of a game tree for G-1A with seven chips initially on the board. What is the width of the tree at this point?

5. Using the number of winning rows remaining as the evaluation function, generate a game tree for alpha-beta search for tick-tack-toe's first move.

REFERENCES

1. FEIGENBAUM, E. A., and J. FELDMAN, eds., *Computers and Thought*, 5th ed., McGraw-Hill, New York, 1963.
2. ARBIB, Michael A., *The Metaphorical Brain: An Introduction to Cybernetics as Artificial Intelligence and Brain Theory*, Wiley, New York, 1972.
3. SLAGLE, J. R., *Artificial Intelligence—The Heuristic Programming Approach*, McGraw-Hill, New York, 1971.

4. NILSSON, Nils J., *Problem-Solving Methods in Artificial Intelligence*, McGraw-Hill, New York, 1971.
5. KNUTH, Donald E., *The Art of Computer Programming: Volume I—Fundamental Algorithms*, 2nd ed., Addison-Wesley, Reading, Mass., 1973.
6. CARNE, E. B., *Artificial Intelligence Techniques*, Macmillan, New York, 1965.
7. BLOCK, H. D., "Learning in Some Simple Non-Biological Systems," *American Scientist*, Vol. 53, No. 1, March 1965.

3

Reason, Logic, and Mathematics

In Chapter 1 the definitions of intelligence and the arguments surrounding the concept of machine intelligence were considered. In Chapter 2 we were concerned with the process of game playing by machine with algorithmic and heuristic techniques. Thus far we have been examining specific methods for obtaining desired machine behavior. It is the purpose of this chapter to present some of the more formal approaches associated with some of the processes of logic and reason that underlie the areas of artificial intelligence and computing. We shall use some specific mathematical systems to illustrate these processes.

LOGIC

Logic has been called the "grammar of reason" [1], and as such is concerned with making generalizations and, ultimately, abstractions by a system of orderly thinking. Thus, logic may be applied to the relationship between mathematics and physics or between the behavior of an electrical network and that of the nervous system. Simply, the goal of logic is progressive systemization and generalization, and the aim is the discovery of abstract forms. Logic generally takes one of two forms, deduction and induction, which then may extend to the process of abstraction. We shall first examine deduction.

DEDUCTION

Deduction is the process of reasoning from one truth value to another, and a system wherein a small number of propositions (postulates) determines all the other propositions is called a deductive system. A mathematical system is a class of propositions arranged in accordance with a sequence of logical deduction.

For example, Euclidean geometry begins with a set of basic assumptions or postulates, such as

1. A line may be extended indefinitely in both directions.
2. Through two distinct points one, and only one, straight line can be drawn.

Other original propositions that are self-evident are called axioms, such as

1. The whole is greater than any of its proper parts.
2. Things equal to the same thing are equal to one another.

Thus, based on postulates, axioms, and a collection of definitions of terms such as "A line has length but not breadth," Euclid deduced 465 propositions in a logical chain.

Another device associated with mathematical systems is the theorem, which is different from a postulate. First, a theorem must contain nothing that cannot be proved. It must be entirely implied by propositions other than itself, and it may contain no assumptions not made in the postulates.

Further, no two theorems deduced from the same postulates can be contradictory, for if this were true, then the postulates would be inconsistent. However, inconsistencies are, usually, difficult to determine. For example, DeMillo et al. [2] describes the case of two theorems independently derived, concerning a topological object called a homotopy group, each of which contradicts the other. Further, after the proofs were exchanged between the two research groups, neither could find a fault with the other group's results.

In the process of proving a theorem, it is often necessary to prove an auxiliary proposition. This auxiliary proposition is called a lemma. The logical process is used to develop the connection between a postulate and a theorem where true premises and a valid deduction always yield a true theorem.

BOOLEAN ALGEBRA OF CLASSES

To illustrate a deductive system, we shall examine the Boolean algebra of classes [3]. This vehicle has been chosen because it is a good example and is of particular value in computers and logic design. In this discussion, the concept of class refers to a group of objects such as students, faculty, computers, programs, and systems. The Boolean algebra of classes is concerned with the class of all objects to which the algebra applies. This class of all elements associated with the algebra is called the universe class, $U = 1$. On the other hand, the class that contains no elements is called the null class, $N = 0$. Any combination of elements from the universe class is itself a class. Therefore, if there are n elements in the universe class, then there are 2^n different possible classes, as that is the total number of combinations of n elements. Thus, an algebra of $n = 2$ elements x_1, x_2 has four possible classes, 0, x_1, x_2, and both elements in the class $x_1 + x_2 = 1$.

Before we formally examine the Boolean algebra of classes, it is useful, although not required in the formal development, to review the three fundamental Boolean operations. First, the union operation, designated by $A \vee B$, indicates the class that includes all elements in both class A and class B. Second, the intersection of two classes, designated by $A \wedge B$, defines the class that consists of the elements common to both class A and class B. Finally, by the complement of a class A, given by $\overline{A}$, we mean all elements of the universe class, U, that are not in the class A.

The following development of the Boolean algebra of classes proceeds from a set of primitive, undefined symbols, one basic definition, and a set of nine postulates.

The complement sign (the overbar) together with 0, 1, $\subset$ (contained in), $\wedge$ (intersection), and $\vee$ (union) are the primitive, undefined symbols. Next, we can define identity or equality:

Definition 1: $a = b$ iff (if and only if) $a \subset b$ and $b \subset a$.

The following are the postulates that will be used in this mathematical system.

- Postulate 1: $a \subset a$, which is read "a is contained in a" and means that every class includes itself.
- Postulate 2: If $a \subset b$ and $b \subset c$, then $a \subset c$: Every class includes the subclass of its subclasses. This is also referred to as transitivity.

- Postulate 3: $a \subset b \wedge c$ iff $a \subset b$ and $a \subset c$, which is read "*a* is contained in the intersection of *b* and *c* if and only if *a* is contained in *b* and *a* is contained in *c*." This postulate defines the product of classes.
- Postulate 4: $a \vee b \subset c$ iff $a \subset c$ and $b \subset c$, which is read "the union of *a* and *b* is contained in *c* if and only if *a* is contained in *c* and *b* is contained in *c*." This postulate defines the sum of classes.
- Postulate 5: $(a \vee b) \wedge (a \vee c) \subset a \vee (b \wedge c)$ indicates that the system is distributive.
- Postulate 6: $0 \subset a$ means that every class includes the null class (the class containing no elements).
- Postulate 7: $a \subset 1$ means that every class is included in the universe class (the class containing all the elements to which the algebra applies).
- Postulate 8: $a \wedge \bar{a} \subset 0$ indicates that every class and its complement are mutually exclusive.
- Postulate 9: $1 \subset a \vee \bar{a}$ means that the universe class is all the elements in class *a* or not in class $\bar{a}$.

As stated before, theorems concerning a mathematical system may be proved by combining postulates in a logical sequence. Thus, we can now begin to prove theorems in the Boolean algebra of classes. In actual practice, however, one often has a specific theorem in mind and proceeds from the postulates and previously proved theorems toward the theorem of interest. This process is similar to means-ends analysis, referred to in Chapter 1.

- Theorem 1: $a \subset a \wedge a$.
  Proof: From Postulate 3, $a \subset a \wedge a$ iff $a \subset a$ and $a \subset a$ by substituting *a* for *b* and *a* for *c*, and from Postulate 1, $a \subset a$. Q.E.D.
- Theorem 2: $a \vee a \subset a$.
  Proof: As in Theorem 1, but use Postulate 4.
- Theorem 3: $a \wedge a \subset a$.
  Proof: 1. $a \wedge a \subset a \wedge a$ iff $a \wedge a \subset a$ and $a \wedge a \subset a$ by substituting $a \wedge a$ for *a*, *a* for *b*, and *a* for *c* in Postulate 3.

2. But $a \wedge a \subset a \wedge a$ also is true by substituting $a \wedge a$ for a in Postulate 1.

3. $a \wedge a \subset a$.   Q.E.D.

● Theorem 4: $a \subset a \vee a$.

Proof: As in Theorem 3, but use Postulate 4, next use Postulate 1.

It should be clear that more theorems can be proved in this mathematical system. Additional theorems to be proved are given in the Exercises. This is a generalized Boolean algebra in that there is no restriction on the number of elements in the universe class. We may, however, impose a limit on the number of elements, say k, which results in 2^k classes, where the order of the Boolean algebra is the number of classes in it. For each value of k, a different Boolean algebra results, where one Boolean algebra is different from another if and only if some law valid in one is not valid in the other. The well-known binary Boolean algebra is of order 2^1. However, let us first examine some of the higher-order algebras.

The Boolean algebra of order 2^3 has three elements, which may be denoted by a, b, and c, and eight distinct classes, given by 0, a, b, c, $a + b$, $a + c$, $b + c$, and 1, where the plus sign $(+)$ indicates the inclusion of both terms on either side of the sign in that class. The algebra of order 2^2 has two elements, say a and b, and four distinct classes, 0, a, b, and 1. Also, the algebra of order 2^1 consists of the element x and two distinct classes, 0 and 1. Finally, the algebra of order 2^0 is rather trivial as there are no elements and only one class, namely the null class, 0.

When dealing with these algebras, it is often useful to use a schematic representation as an aid in visualizing these systems. The representation that will be used here is called the Venn diagram (Figure 3.1). The rectangular area in the figure represents the universe class, all the elements under consideration, and each circle represents a class in the system usually denoted by some literal, say a or b. The space in Figure 3.1 that is common to both a and b is $a \wedge b$. The spaces belonging to a and not b, and b and not a, are $a \wedge \bar{b}$ and $b \wedge \bar{a}$, respectively. The space that is not in either a or b is $\bar{a} \wedge \bar{b}$.

Now, to illustrate the difference between algebras of different orders we shall consider the following statements: $a \wedge b = 0$ or $a \wedge \bar{b} = 0$ or $\bar{a} \wedge b = 0$, where elements in the algebra are contained in a or b. We shall now represent elements in the algebra as dots on the diagram. Thus, if there

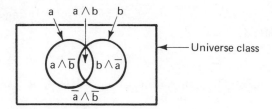

Figure 3.1.   Venn diagram for Boolean algebras.

are two elements in the system, the above statement can be satisfied as shown in Figure 3.2, where all placement combinations of two dots, elements in the classes, have been used. The above statement is not true for an algebra of order 2^3 since three dots cannot be placed in the Venn diagram such that the statement is satisfied for all possible dot placements.

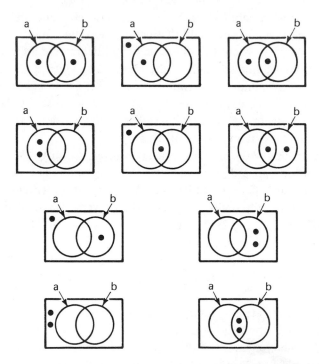

Figure 3.2.   Dot placement in Venn diagrams for Boolean algebra of classes with two elements.

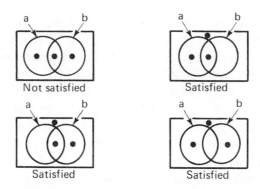

Figure 3.3. Dot placement for Boolean algebra of classes with three elements showing that the statement $a \wedge b = 0$ or $a \wedge \overline{b} = 0$ or $\overline{a} \wedge b = 0$ is not satisfied for at least one dot arrangement.

This is shown in Figure 3.3, where the statement is not satisfied for at least one dot placement, and we can conclude that it is not true in general for algebras of order 2^3.

It should now be clear that laws for specific Boolean algebras are different; however, any law in the generalized Boolean algebra of classes is a law in any other Boolean algebra. Theorems in these algebras can be deduced from previously discovered theorems in a logical chain. The incorporation of a deductive logic system in a machine is but one of the steps toward artificial intelligence.

This concludes our introduction to deductive systems as a specific method of reason and thought. The Boolean algebras of classes are an especially good example of these principles, as the title of Boole's original treatise, *An Investigation of the Laws of Thought* [4] clearly suggests.

PROPOSITIONAL CALCULUS

A system in which there is some definite class of elements and definite rules that describe the ways in which members of the class may be combined either with one another or each of the members with itself is called a logical system. The class that is of interest here is any class of propositions where there are two types, specific and general. A specific proposition is concerned with a subject that may be specified by a proper name, whereas a general proposition is concerned with members of a certain class. The propositions "A boy ran home" and "Every man is mortal" are examples of specific and general propositions, respectively. Some other examples of propositions are "Four is greater than three"; "a is contained in the universe class"; and "A triangle has three sides." The only significant aspect of any proposition, however, is its truth or falseness. The concept of a proposition is similar to an element, and the truth and falseness of a proposition are similar to the null and universe classes, respectively, of the binary Boolean algebra of classes. Thus, these two systems are isomorphic.

Thus, for the representation of propositions, p, by classes, false propositions are the null class, $p = 0$, and true propositions are the universe class, $p = 1$. It is clear then that binary Boolean algebra is appropriate here and that Venn diagrams can be used to represent propositions, as shown in Figure 3.4. Here, the areas enclosing the dot represent true propositions, and other areas represent false propositions. It can be seen from this diagram that, among other things:

1. The union of two false propositions is a false proposition, as no dot can be included in the union.
2. The intersection of a true proposition and a false proposition is a false proposition, because the region of commonality cannot include a dot or the proposition would be true.
3. A false proposition is contained in a true proposition, as the region of commonality of the true proposition is a false proposition.
4. The union of a true proposition and a false proposition is contained in a true proposition since the union of the two propositions must contain a dot; hence, it contains a true proposition.

The first two statements are obvious from common usage; however, the last two are not.

Let us now adopt symbols that are common to the propositional calculus. The notation "is contained in" is replaced by implies, $\supset$, and the

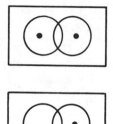

Figure 3.4.   Venn diagram for propositional calculus with two propositions p and q where, if a proposition is true, it encloses a dot.

symbol $\equiv$ is used for iff. The statement if $p \supset q$ and $q \supset r$, then $p \supset r$ is read "if p implies q and q implies r, then p implies r." Now, if $p, q, r, \ldots$ are propositions, then other propositions can be formed by means of the following operators: the overbar or negation operator, $\wedge$, $\vee$, $\supset$, and $\equiv$. The meanings of these operators are given in Table 3.1. For example, if we let $p =$ "it is raining" and $q =$ "the street is wet" and apply these propositions to the relationship

$$p \supset q \equiv \bar{q} \supset \bar{p}$$

which can be written as

> It is raining implies the street is wet is a true statement if and only if the street is not wet implies it is not raining.

Since we can apply a simple binary value to each proposition, it is useful to be able to operate on propositions that have been reduced to 0, 1 form. The mechanism for doing this is called the arithmetic of propositions and is summarized in Table 3.2.

The first identity in Table 3.2a means that a false proposition and a false proposition yield a false proposition.

Table 3.1.   Symbols and Their Meanings in Propositional Calculus

Symbol	Is Read	Meaning
$\bar{p}$	Not p	p is false
$p \wedge q$	p and q	The intersection of p and q, common to both p and q
$p \vee q$	p or q	The union of p and q, either p or q or both
$p \supset q$	p implies q	If p is true, then q is true
$p \equiv q$	p iff q	p is true if and only if q is true; p is eqiuvalent to q

The first identity in Table 3.2c means that a false proposition implies both a false proposition and a true proposition. Here the only way an implication can be false is when it is posed that a true proposition implies a false one. Also note that any false proposition can imply either a true proposition or a false proposition. Using this truth table we can now evaluate expressions in propositional calculus that do not contain variables:

Examples:

1. $1 \vee 0 \vee 0 = (1 \vee 0) \vee 0 = 1 \vee 0 = 1$

2. $\{(0 \supset 1) \vee 1 \vee 0 \supset \overline{(1 \wedge 0)}\} = \{1 \vee 1 \vee 0 \supset \bar{0}\}$
    $= 1 \supset 1 = 1$

3. $(1 \wedge 1) \supset 0 = 1 \supset 0 = 0$

In these examples, the relationships have a value of 1 or 0, which can be interpreted as valid or not valid respectively.

Table 3.2.   Arithmetic of Propositions

$\wedge$	0	1	$\vee$	0	1	$\supset$	0	1	$\equiv$	0	1	$-$		
0	0	0	0	0	1	0	1	1	0	1	0	0	1	
1	0	1	1	1	1	1	0	1	1	0	1	1	0	
(a)			(b)			(c)			(d)			(e)		

Now let us return to our first relationship between propositions concerning the weather and the condition of the street and study it with respect to the arithmetic of propositions. First, assume that the propositions p and q are true, 1, then we can say

$$1 \supset 1 \equiv 0 \supset 0$$

and from Table 3.2c we can reduce this to

$$1 \equiv 1 = 1$$

Because, from Table 3.2d, we see that 1 is equivalent to 1. Note that 1 cannot imply 0, which means the relationship "it is raining implies the street is not wet" is not valid; therefore, we let $p = 1$ and $q = 0$, which gives,

$$1 \supset 0 \equiv 1 \supset 0$$
$$0 \equiv 0 = 1$$

Now, assume p and q are false, 0, and from the arithmetic of propositions,

$$0 \supset 0 \equiv 1 \supset 1$$
$$1 \equiv 1 = 1$$

Similarly, if we let $p = 0$ and $q = 1$,

$$0 \supset 1 \equiv 0 \supset 1$$
$$1 \equiv 1 = 1$$

Thus, the relationship $p \supset q \equiv \bar{q} \supset \bar{p}$ is valid for all combinations of truth values for p and q.

Boolean algebra and propositional calculus provide a means by which we can examine the relationships between any statements in a particular mathematical system. For example, the end or goal of a problem may be to examine some aspect of a particular statement. The development of the relationship between the given information and the desired goal can be found by examining the function and applying the rules of the system, as was done in the preceding example. Thus, we have a mechanism for means-ends analysis. This process of determining the validity of a general statement by examining the fundamental relationships in the system is called the process of induction.

INDUCTION

Whereas the process of reasoning from specific truths to general truths is deduction, the process of reasoning from general observations to specific underlying truths is induction.

Russell [5] has said that there are three methods of arriving at the validity of general propositions: tautologies, complete enumeration, and induction. A tautology is a repetition that in and of itself is obvious and self-evident, such as "All men are male" or "Essential things are necessary."

Complete enumeration is a reasonable method of proof of a general observation if the number of alternatives to be examined is not too large. For example, the statement "There are four blocks on the table" can easily be verified by counting the blocks. Since this method examines all possible combinations—there are no stones left unturned—it is called the method of perfect induction. A systematic approach to this method makes use of truth tables, as illustrated in the following example.

Example: Verify the following relationship, known as DeMorgan's theorem, by perfect induction:

$$\overline{a \wedge b} \equiv \bar{a} \vee \bar{b}$$

Applying the arithmetic of propositions with a truth table that lists all possible truth values for the propositions yields

a	b	$\bar{a}$	$\bar{b}$	$a \wedge b$	$\overline{a \wedge b}$	$\bar{a} \vee \bar{b}$
0	0	1	1	0	1	1
0	1	1	0	0	1	1
1	0	0	1	0	1	1
1	1	0	0	1	0	0

We now note that the last two columns of the table, which represent both sides of the above statement, are the same, and DeMorgan's theorem is now proved.

The final method for determining the truth or falseness of a general observation is induction. Induction vis-à-vis perfect induction requires that one deal with less conclusive evidence than the complete enumeration of all possibilities. Thus, given the statement "All A is B" and a relation of intentions that exist to justify the statement, if the statement seems probable, we have an induction. For example, given the following:

$$1 + 3 = 2^2, \quad 1 + 3 + 5 = 3^2, \quad 1 + 3 + 5 + 7 = 4^2, \quad \text{etc.}$$

we induce the specific truth that the sum of the first n odd numbers is always n^2, which can now be proved.

Theorem: $1 + 3 + 5 + \cdots + r = n^2$, for all $n > 0$ with r odd, where n is the number of terms in the sum.

Proof: The first step in the proof by induction is to show that the theorem is true for $n = 1$:

$$1 = 1^2 = 1$$

Next we note that $n = (r + 1)/2$, thus, $r = 2n - 1$ and the theorem can be written in the form

$$1 + 3 + 5 + \cdots + 2n - 1 = n^2$$

Now, we assume that the theorem is true for some n,

$$1 + 3 + 5 + \cdots + r = n^2 \tag{3.1}$$

and must show that it is also true for $n + 1$, that is

$$1 + 3 + 5 + \cdots + r + r + 2 = (n + 1)^2 = n^2 + 2n + 1 \tag{3.2}$$

Now, from Equations 3.1 and 3.2 it is easily verified that

$$1 + 3 + 5 + \cdots + r + r + 2 = n^2 + r + 2 \tag{3.3}$$

but

$$r = 2n - 1$$

Hence,

$$1 + 3 + 5 + \cdots + r + r + 2 = n^2 + 2n - 1 + 2$$
$$= n^2 + 2n + 1 = (n + 1)^2 \qquad \text{Q.E.D.}$$

This process has been described most lucidly by Russell [5], where he calls the last of Peano's five propositions, the principle of mathematical induction. These propositions are

1.   Zero is a number.
2.   The successor of any number is a number.
3.   No two numbers have the same successor.
4.   Zero is not the successor of any number.
5.   Any property that belongs to zero and also to the successor of any number that has that property belongs to every number.

Let us consider briefly the way in which the theory of the natural numbers results from these three ideas ("number," "zero," and "the successor of") and five propositions. To begin with, we define 1 as "the successor of 0," 2 as "the successor of 1," and so on. We can obviously go on as long as we like with these definitions, since, by virtue of proposition 2, every number that we reach will have a successor, and, by virtue of proposition 3, this cannot be any of the numbers already defined, because, if it were, two different numbers would have the same successor; and, by virtue of proposition 4, none of the numbers we reach in the series of successors can be 0. Thus, the series of successors gives us an endless series of continually new numbers. By virtue of proposition 5, all numbers come in this series, which begins with 0 and travels through successive successors: for (a) 0 belongs to this series, and (b) if a number, n, belongs to it, so does its successor, when, by mathematical induction, every number belongs to the series.

The process of induction has been associated with what has been described as intelligent behavior. Man's continued search for new truths requires the ability to induce them from his environment. To incorporate the ability to apply induction on the part of a machine, however, is a difficult problem yet to be solved. Although computerized approaches to automatic theorem proving have been undertaken with some interesting results, these systems deal with the more structured logical methods such as the propositional calculus [6, 7, 8], and not directly with induction.

ABSTRACTION

As stated at the beginning of this chapter, the aim of logic is the discovery of abstract forms. Thus we shall now consider some definitions of abstraction and its relation to logic.

Abstraction is a process that is certainly familiar to everyone: algebra is the abstracted form of an arithmetical calculation; block and schematic diagrams are abstractions of some physical system, say a computer or a control system; and a street map is an abstraction of the streets in a particular town or city. In general, abstraction is the act of considering something as a general object apart from any special circumstances. This concept of abstraction is the one that leads to the association of mathematics with the abstract.

Abstract concepts are communicated by language and training—which may be education, indoctrination, or even brainwashing—and they are learned by observation and experience. The concept of number is learned by counting, the concept of shape by fitting objects together, the concept of quality by comparing values, the concept of rules of conduct by observing (and judging) the evidence of good or bad behavior, and an algebraic formula by seeing several examples and observing their common formal property. However, we cannot really understand these concepts without the ability to abstract the common form from the instances we have observed. This ability to recognize a common form or a common principle without the specifics has been described as scientific genius [1]. To endow a machine with the power of abstraction such that it could be called a genius is the ultimate goal of many artificial intelligence researchers. The achievement of this goal is certainly not imminent. There is much work to be done.

LOGIC REVISITED

Logical reasoning, then, is the method of following the rules as postulated in the mathematical system of interest. The Boolean algebra of classes provides one of these systems of rules.

The processes of deduction and induction provide means for generalizing and proving statements in these mathematical systems, which ultimately may lead to an abstraction. A logical system may then be visualized as an abstract form, or a relational pattern, rather than as an array of concrete things. These logical processes are basic in cybernetics, where one is interested in developing and exploiting these principles in a physical system. For example, a program that automatically proves theorems must incorporate some logical processes. A machine control of a complicated manufacturing process must, at least, be able to "deduce" the fact that something is wrong.

EXERCISES

1. Prove the following theorems in the Boolean algebra of classes:

   (a) Theorem 5: $a = a$.
   (b) Theorem 6: $a = a \wedge a$.
   (c) Theorem 7: $a = a \vee a$.
   (d) Theorem 8: $a \vee a \subset a \wedge a$.

2. Prove the following theorems in the Boolean algebra of classes:

   (a) Theorem 9: $a \wedge b \subset a$ and $a \wedge b \subset b$.
   (b) Theorem 10: $a \wedge a = a \vee a$.
   (c) Theorem 11: $a \subset a \vee b$ and $b \subset a \vee b$.

3. Let $1 =$ humans, $a =$ Americans, $b =$ Bostonians, and $c =$ criminals .

   (a) What does the class $a \wedge c$ equal?
   (b) Does $a \wedge b = b$?
   (c) What does $a \wedge \bar{c}$ equal?
   (d) What does $a \wedge \bar{b} \wedge c$ equal?
   (e) What does $b \wedge c$ equal?
   (f) Find a representation for the class of all Bostonians who are not criminals.

4. Use a Venn diagram to show whether the following statements are satisfied in the Boolean algebras of order 2^1 and 2^2:

   (a) Either $a \wedge b = 0$ or $a \wedge \bar{b} = 0$.
   (b) Either $a = 0$ or $a = 1$.

5. List all compound propositions that can be formed just from the propositions p and q under the following restrictions:

   (a) In each compound proposition p and q occur exactly once and in that order.
   (b) No operator can be used more than once.

6. Put the following argument into symbolic form: If p and q are true, then r is true. But r is false. Therefore, either p is false or q is false.

7. Evaluate the following:

   (a) $(((0 \supset 1) \supset 0) \supset 1) \supset 0$.
   (b) $(1 \supset 1 \wedge 0) \equiv \overline{(1 \vee 0)}$.

8. Prove by perfect induction:

   (a) $(A \wedge B) \vee (\overline{A} \wedge \overline{B}) = \overline{(A \wedge B) \vee (A \wedge B)}$.
   (b) $(A \wedge B) \vee (\overline{A} \wedge \overline{B}) \vee (A \wedge \overline{B}) = A \wedge \overline{B}$.

9. Prove the following theorem by induction: $1 + 2 + 3 + \cdots + n = (1/2)n(n + 1)$.

10. Show, using the arithmetic of propositions, that the statement "It is raining or I have washed my car implies the weather will be bad is equivalent to the weather will not be bad implies it is not raining and I have not washed my car" is valid.

REFERENCES

1. HILTON, Alice Mary, *Logic, Computing Machines, and Automation*, Spartan, New York, 1963.
2. DEMILLO, Richard A., Richard J. LIPTON, and Alan J. PERLIS, "Social Processes and Proofs of Theorems and Programs," Communications of the ACM, Vol. 22, No. 5, May 1979, pp. 271–280.
3. CULBERTSON, James T., *Mathematics and Logic for Digital Devices*, Van Nostrand Reinhold, New York, 1958.
4. BOOLE, George, *An Investigation of the Laws of Thought*, London, 1854, reprinted by Dover, New York, 1959.
5. RUSSELL, Bertrand, *Introduction to Mathematical Philosophy*, 2nd ed., George Allen & Unwin Ltd., London, 1920.
6. ROBINSON, J. A., "A Machine-Oriented Logic Based on the Resolution Principle," *JACM* 12, January 1965, pp. 23–41.
7. ANDERSON, R., and W. W. BLEDSOE, "A Linear Format for Resolution with Merging and a New Technique for Establishing Completeness," *JACM* 17, July 1970, pp. 525–534.
8. MELTZER, B., "Power Amplification for Automatic Theorem-Provers," *Machine Intelligence* 5, MELTZER and MICHIE, eds., American Elsevier, New York, 1970, pp. 321–336.

4

Computers and Automata

Thus far we have identified the computer as a principal element in designing intelligent systems. We have also described some of the techniques that can be used to endow the machine with some aspects of this behavior. It has also been demonstrated that, with the proper rules, a simple automaton (the cup machine) can exhibit apparent learning behavior.

It should be clear that the behavior of machines and their fundamental attributes and limitations lie at the heart of this subject. Therefore, in this chapter, we shall examine the overall descriptive behavior of automata and investigate some of its fundamental limitations.

AUTOMATA [1]

Automata usually refers to the class of systems that operate on discrete data representations in discrete time intervals, and the discipline that is concerned with the overall input-output behavior of these systems is called automata theory. Automata theory has been applied to the description of computers as well as to nerve networks, biological systems, control systems, and aspects of human behavior. Thus, it is appropriate to study automata and automata theory at this point. We shall first examine a model of a sequential machine and proceed from there to a description of general automata.

In general, a sequential machine or automaton consists of the two major elements shown in Figure 4.1, namely combinational logic and memory. The combinational logic may consist of AND, OR, NOT, NAND, NOR, or EXCLUSIVE OR operations or some combination of them all. The memory may be physically semiconductor elements, tapes or discs, or simply time delays of a so-called unit length. The input is a sequence of symbols $\{i_j\}$ that occur at finite times j. The output in the jth interval, z_j, is a function of the present input symbol i_j and the present state q_j, which is the present output of the memory. The present input to the memory is called the next-state function, which depends on the present input and the present state.

The following example will serve to illustrate the concepts contained in the preceding description. First, we shall define a unit delay element

$$q_j \rightarrow \boxed{D} \rightarrow y_i = q_{j+1}$$

where the delay between the output and input is C seconds. Next, consider the circuit shown in Figure 4.2, which is recognizable as a simple sequential circuit. The next-state equations for this machine of Figure 4.2 are

$$q_{j+1}^{(1)} = i_j \wedge q_j^{(2)} \tag{4.1}$$

$$q_{j+1}^{(2)} = i_j \oplus q_j^{(1)} \tag{4.2}$$

where $\oplus$ indicates the exclusive OR operation. The output function for this

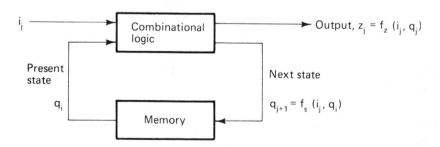

Figure 4.1.   General block diagram of sequential automaton.

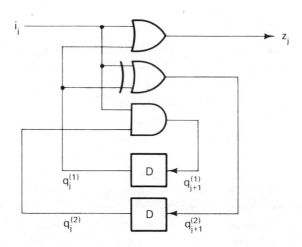

Figure 4.2.   Sequential machine using delay memory.

circuit can be written as

$$Z_j = i_j \vee q_j^{(1)} \tag{4.3}$$

These methods for describing a sequential automaton can now be generalized by means of the 5-tuple,

$$M = \langle I, Q, Z, \delta, \omega \rangle \tag{4.4}$$

where

1. I is a finite set of input symbols.
2. Q is a set of states.
3. Z is a finite set of output symbols.
4. δ is a mapping $I \times Q$ into Q called the next-state function.
5. ω is a mapping of $I \times Q$ onto Z called the output function.

Here the symbol $\times$ indicates the cartesian product. For example, if

$$I = \{0, 1, 2\} \text{ and } Q = \{a, b\}$$

then

$$I \times Q = \{(0, a), (0, b), (1, a), (1, b), (2, a), (2, b)\}$$

TURING MACHINES

Although the general description of sequential machines is of value as a tool in understanding the overall behavior of these systems, its use as a model of a digital computer is certainly limited. One reason for this is the fact that memory in even the simplest digital computer is not small and the number of expressions required to describe the machine immediately becomes prohibitive. Thus, other models are needed.

The model that is used to describe the fundamental behavior of the modern digital computer was developed by Turing in 1936 [2]. This model, called the Turing machine, which was described before the development of today's computers, was developed as a mechanism for studying the fundamental relationships involved in making computations.

A Turing machine has three basic parts, as shown in Figure 4.3: a control element, a read/write head, and an infinite-length tape. The control unit is a sequential machine and has a drive system that is capable of moving the tape in either direction. The tape, which may be thought of as any external medium in which information can be stored, read, and changed, is divided into blocks or squares that may contain either a blank

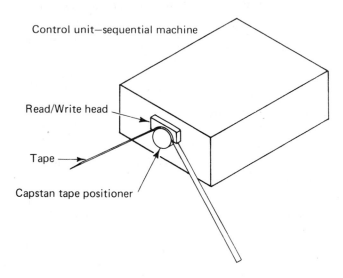

Figure 4.3.   Basic configuration of a Turing machine.

or a symbol from a finite set of symbols A. The read/write head can scan on only one square at a time, after which one of four possible events can occur:

1. Write a new symbol in the present square.
2. Position the tape such that the head is over the square to the right of the present square.
3. Position the tape such that the head is over the square to the left of the present square.
4. The machine halts.

The operation of the machine is then as follows: A tape is prepared by placing symbols in the proper squares on the tape, the sequential machine is set into its starting state, the tape is positioned on the machine with the proper square placed under the read/write head, and the machine is started.

A complete Turing machine, T, can now be defined as a 6-tuple,

$$T = \langle I, Q, Z, \delta, \omega, q_0 \rangle \qquad (4.5)$$

where

1. $I = A \vee b$ is a finite nonempty set of symbols, including b, the blank symbol, and A, any arbitrarily selected alphabet.
2. Q is a set of states.
3. Z is the output set, encompassing the alphabet, A; the blank symbol, b; and the commands: "move tape right," r; "move tape left," l; and "halt," h;

$$Z = A \vee b \vee r \vee l \vee h$$

4. δ is the next-state mapping of the sequential machine.
5. ω is the output mapping of the sequential machine.
6. q_0 is the initial state of the sequential machine at the start of a computation.

Thus, Q, δ, and ω are the same as defined for the general sequential model, and the difference between the general sequential machine and the Turing machine is the latter's ability to dynamically use the potentially infinite external tape.

It is now of interest to investigate the nature of the sequence of symbols that might appear on a tape. First, the symbols themselves are selected from the set $I = A \vee b$, where A is some alphabet, say $\{a_1, a_2, a_3, \ldots, a_n\}$ and b is the symbol used here to represent a blank square. A sequence of symbols from A (where there are no blanks in the sequence) is called a word. A sequence of symbols consisting of one or more words is called a tape expression and will be so indicated by Greek letters, α, β, $\ldots$. All tape expressions are considered to be of finite length, as we disregard the "infinite" sequence of blanks that precede and follow a tape expression. For example,

$$y = ba_1 a_3 ba_2 a_4 b$$

is a tape expression where we include blanks at the beginning and end of tape expressions.

Since the state of this system is determined by the state of the sequential machine in the control unit, it is useful to include this state information in our tape expressions as an aid in analyzing Turing machine behavior. Thus, we include a bracket within the tape expression that includes the present state of the sequential machine as well as the present tape symbol being scanned:

$$\alpha a_1 [q_j a_1] a_2 \beta$$

Here the present state of the machine is q_j, the present input symbol is a_1, which is preceded by tape expression α and symbol a_1 and followed by a_2 and tape expression β. This notation is often referred to as the instantaneous description of the Turing machine.

Let us now examine the operation of the Turing machine given in Figure 4.4 with the following tape expression positioned such that the leftmost blank is under the read/write head:

$$ba_1 a_1 a_2 b$$

The entries in the transition table are

$$q_i/s_i = \text{Next-state/Turing machine output}$$

Present input

Q	b	a_1	a_2
Present state q_1	q_2/r	q_1/b	q_2/r
q_2	q_1/r	q_1/r	q_2/h

$Q = \{q_1, q_2\}$

$A = \{a_1, a_2\}$

$Z = \{b\ a_1, a_2, h, r, e\}$

$q_1 =$ Initial state

$b =$ Initial input

Figure 4.4. Turing machine description.

The instantaneous description of the Turing machine described in Figure 4.4 with the above tape expression is

$$[q_1, b]a_1 a_1 a_2 b, \qquad b[q_2 a_1]a_1 a_2 b,$$
$$ba_1[q_1, a_1]a_2 b, \qquad ba_1[q_1, b]a_2 b,$$
$$ba_1 b[q_2, a_2]b, \qquad \text{Halt}$$

The machine with this input sequence then makes a change in the tape and halts. Consider now the operation of the machine with the following initial tape expression, $ba_1 a_2 a_2 b$:

$$[q_1 b]a_1 a_2 a_1 a_2 b, \qquad b[q_2, a_1]a_2 a_1 a_2 b, \qquad ba_1[q_1 a_2]a_1 a_2 b,$$
$$ba_1 a_2[q_2, a_1]a_2 b, \qquad ba_1 a_2 a_1[q_1, a_2]b, \qquad ba_1 a_2 a_1 a_2[q_2, b],$$
$$ba_1 a_2 a_1 a_2 b[q_1, b], \ \ldots$$

The Turing machine does not halt with this initial tape expression but continues to run ad infinitum. This kind of initial tape expression has special significance and will be discussed later.

The processes performed by a Turing machine may, of course, be concerned with specific computing functions. The definition of a function here is the common one: A function is a rule or set of rules whereby, given a number called the argument, another number can be computed called the value of the function for that argument. For example, if x and y are numbers

$$F(x) = y \tag{4.6}$$

is a function. We can also define a function as "the remainder modulo 2 of the nonnegative integers" and

$$F(0) = 0, F(1) = 1, F(2) = 0, F(3) = 1, \ldots$$

A Turing machine can be used to compute functions, as the argument can be encoded initially in some way on the tape and the result of computing the function will be left encoded on the tape.

For example, consider the smallest alphabet size $A = \{1\}$ that can be used to code on the tape. Also, let the tape expression containing $(i + 1)$ 1s represent any integer i, say

$$5 = b1111111b$$

Similarly, the sequence of integers 2, 4, 1 can be represented by

$$b111b11111b11b$$

A Turing machine control that adds two numbers in the above format is given in the accompanying table. The head is initially positioned under the leftmost blank and the initial state of the control is q_1. The machine then proceeds to replace the b between the two numbers with a 1 and replaces the last two 1s with blanks and halts. Thus, the sum of the two numbers is left on the tape in the given format.

	Q/I	Present Input	
		b	1
Present State	q_1	q_1/r	q_2/r
	q_2	$q_3/1$	q_2/r
	q_3	q_4/l	q_3/r
	q_4	—	q_5/b
	q_5	q_5/l	q_6/b
	q_6	q_6/h	q_6/h

$Q = \{q_1, q_2, q_3, q_4, q_5, q_6\}$
$A = [1]$
$Z = \{b, 1, h, r, l\}$
$q_1 = $ initial state

COMPUTABLE FUNCTIONS [3]

Before we examine the class of functions that are called computable, it is necessary to examine some specific properties of functions. Let S be the infinite set of all words that may be associated with a function to be computed by a Turing machine and let us define D as a subset of W. In this context, a function whose domain is D implies a correspondence by which we associate with each $x \subset D$ a $y \subset W$, called the value of the function where x and y are as given in Equation 4.6. The set

$$Y = \{y | f(x) = y, x \subset D\} \tag{4.7}$$

is the range of the function. Here, Equation 4.7 is read "Y is the collection of elements y such that $f(x) = y$ for x contained in D." A function such as that in Equation 4.6 may also be thought of as a mapping of elements from W into W.

Further, an r-ary function maps a set of r-tuples $(x_1, x_2, \cdots, x_r)$ of elements from W into W:

$$f(x_1, x_2, \cdots, x_r) = y \tag{4.8}$$

An r-ary function for $r \geq 1$ is called *total* if its domain corresponds to the set of all r-tuples that can be formed from W.

It is now possible to apply these definitions to the concept of functions as applied to Turing machines.

A total function of $f(x_1, x_2, \ldots, x_r)$ defined over the alphabet A will be called *computable* if there exists a Turing machine that will evaluate this function in a finite number of steps.

It is possible for a function to be computable for only a subset of all the r-tuples that can be formed from W and not for the remainder of the r-tuples in W. Such a function is called *partially computable*.

Some arithmetic operations are examples of computable functions. Thus,

$$f_1(x_1, x_2) = x_1 + x_2$$
$$f_2(x_1, x_2) = x_1 x_2$$

are computable. The function

$$f(x) = \sqrt{x}$$

is only partially computable, as the square root can be found in a finite number of steps only if x is a perfect square.

A useful device, then, for use with a Turing machine would certainly be a machine with the appropriate tape (program) that could be used to determine if any given tape will halt when run on any other Turing machine. This is often referred to as the halting problem, and the next sections are needed to develop the answer to this problem. It would also be helpful to be able to evaluate programs for general-purpose digital computers and determine whether they will halt or run on forever. Since the Turing machine is our model, the following also applies to general-purpose digital computers.

CHARACTERISTIC FUNCTIONS

A characteristic function is a device whereby given an element $x \subset G$ we can determine if $x \subset M$, where M is a subset of G. To do this, we evaluate the characteristic function $C_m(x)$, where $C_m(x) = 1$ if $x \subset M$ and we say x is accepted or $C_m(x) = 0$ if $x \not\subset M$ and we say that x is rejected. Now, if we define $C_m(x)$ to be a total function of G which is also computable, then we can use a Turing machine to evaluate the characteristic function.

In the set of words W, if a Turing machine exists that can compute $C_m(x)$ where $M \subseteq W$, then M is said to be decidable. If the converse is true (no Turing machine exists), then the set is said to be undecidable.

Given a set M and a function f whose range is M, and if unique terms in $f(x)$ can be related to the elements of M, then M is said to be an *enumerable set*. Here we let x be the nonnegative integers and define the empty set $\emptyset$ to be enumerable. For example, we can show that the set $M = \{x \mid x \text{ is an even integer}\}$ is an enumerable, albeit infinite, set given by the function

$$x = 2n \qquad \text{for } n = \text{nonnegative integers} \qquad (4.9)$$

Note that Equation 4.9 is also computable. This leads to another way of defining an enumerable set: A set M is enumerable if it is empty or if it corresponds to a set of terminal tape expressions that can be generated using a particular Turing machine.

The set of all Turing machines is also enumerable. For example, we know that the alphabet $A = \{1\}$ can be used to code any other set of symbols, as is done in conventional digital computers. Therefore, the transition diagram of the sequential machine control element has two columns corresponding to inputs of 1 and b and n rows, where each row is associated with a state of the machine. The entries in the diagram will be of the form q/z, where $q \subset Q$ and $z \subset Z$ or "don't care," in which case the number of possible Turing machines is

$$N_n = [5n + 1]^{2n}$$

from the fact that there are five elements in $\{Z\}$, n states, the "don't care" and $2n$ positions in the two columns, b and 1 [1]. Thus, there is an enumerable number of Turing machines where all the one-state machines are numbered 1 to N_1, two-state machines $N_1 + 1$ to N_2, etc. Thus we can say that the set of Turing machines is enumerable.

PREDICATES AND THE PREDICATE CALCULUS

The propositional calculus discussed in Chapter 3 provided a means whereby operations on propositions or statements by logical combinations could be accomplished. In this way, new statements can be deduced from some initial set of propositions. These propositions are declarative senten- ces that have fixed truth values, namely true or false. The predicate calculus [4] is concerned with propositions in more detail and allows the inclusion of some of the inner structure of the propositions in our analysis. For example, the statement "4 is greater than 3" has a specific truth value in propositional calculus. However, the statement "x is greater than 4" is a form that, of itself, cannot be classified as true or false and must be evaluated with the predicate calculus.

A predicate will be symbolized by $P(x)$ for a single-variable statement and, in general, an r-ary predicate will be denoted by $P(x_1, x_2, \cdots, x_r)$ for $r \geq 1$. A predicate, as with a proposition, is a device for determining the truth or falseness of a statement, except that a predicate is concerned with variables and r-tuples of variables. The predicate $P(x_1, \cdots, x_r)$ purpose is to generate a mapping of the set of all r-tuples onto the set {True, False}, and the characteristic function is a mechanism for computing this mapping:

$$C_p(x_1, \cdots, x_r) = \begin{cases} 1 & \text{for } p(x_1, \cdots, x_r) = \text{True} \\ 0 & \text{for } p(x_1, \cdots, x_r) = \text{False} \end{cases}$$

Thus, the characteristic function associated with the predicate P assigns the r-tuples to the appropriate subset of the set {True, False}.

Now, as with the Boolean algebra of classes and propositional calculus, it is necessary to define equality and the logical operations with which we operate on predicates.

Thus, two predicates are equal if and only if their characteristic functions are equal:

$$P_1(x_1, \cdots, x_r) = P_2(x_1, \cdots, x_r)$$

$$\text{iff } C_{p_1}(x_1, \cdots, x_r) = C_{p_2}(x_1, \cdots, x_r) \quad \forall \text{ } r\text{-tuples}$$

The logical operations are

1. The complement of P:

$$R(x_1, \cdots, x_r) = \bar{P}(x_1, \cdots, x_r)$$

where R is true when P is false and vice versa.

2. Predicate union:

$$R(x_1, \cdots, x_r) = P(x_1, \cdots, x_r) \vee Q(x_1, \cdots, x_r)$$

where R is true if P or Q or both are true.

3. Predicate intersection:

$$R(x_1, \cdots, x_r) = P(x_1, \cdots, x_r) \wedge Q(x_1, \cdots, x_r)$$

where R is true if and only if both P and Q are true.

4. Quantifiers: $P(y, x_1, \cdots, x_r)$ is an $(r + 1)$-ary predicate, where $y = y_0, y_1, \cdots, z$, and

$$R(z, x_1, \cdots, x_r) = \bigvee_{y=y_0}^{y=z} P(y, x_1, \cdots, x_r)$$

$$= P(y_0, x_1, \cdots, x_r) \vee \cdots \vee P(z, x_1, \cdots, x_r)$$

means that there is at least a minimum of one $(r + 1)$-tuple such that $P(y, x_1, \cdots, x_r)$ is true. Also,

$$R(z, x_1, \ldots, x_r) = \bigwedge_{y=y_0}^{y=z} P(y, x_1, \ldots, x_r)$$

$$= P(y_0, x_1, \ldots, x_r) \wedge \cdots \wedge P(z, x_1, \ldots, x_r)$$

means $P(y, x_1, \cdots, x_r)$ is true for all $(r + 1)$-tuples. The symbols

$$\bigvee_{y=y_0}^{y=z} \quad \text{and} \quad \bigwedge_{y=y_0}^{y=z}$$

are called the *bounded existential quantifier* and the *bounded universal quantifier*, respectively.

It should be clear from the preceding definitions that a predicate is computable if its characteristic function is computable. A predicate is called semicomputable if there exists a partially computable function whose domain is limited to the subset True.

A mechanism for studying semicomputable functions requires the following special predicate. One can represent every computable function performed by a Turing machine by a sequence of tape expressions $\alpha_1 \to \alpha_2 \cdots \to \alpha_k$, where α_1 is the initial tape expression and α_k is the final tape expression. These expressions are made up of symbols from the finite alphabet $I = A \lor b$, and, because the functions are computable, all computations consist of a finite number of steps. Thus, all possible tape expression sequences form an enumerable set, and a number y can be used to identify a particular sequence. Now, the special computable predicate that we associate with an arbitrary Turing machine M is $T_M(x_1, \cdots, x_r, y)$, which is assigned to the set True if and only if M with the initial tape expression $(x_1, \cdots, x_r)$ generates the sequence of tape expressions associated with the number y.

For example, if the sequence of tape expressions associated with y is $\beta_1 \to \beta_2 \to \cdots \beta_i \to \cdots \beta_k$, we merely start with β_1 in machine M and compare the tape expression so generated at the ith step β_i' with β_i. If $\beta_i' = \beta_i$ for $1 \leq i \leq k$, then $T_M(x_1, \cdots, x_r, y)$ is true; and, conversely, if $\beta_i' \neq \beta_i$, then $T_M(x_1, \cdots, x_r, y)$ is false. Since this process is always possible with a finite number of steps, we can conclude that the predicate $T_M(x_1, \cdots, x_r, y)$ is computable.

Given a semicomputable predicate $P(x_1, \cdots, x_r)$, $f_p(x_1, \cdots, x_r)$ is a partially computable function that is defined only for those r-tuples for which the predicate is true. Now there must be a Turing machine M_p that can compute $f_p(x_1, \cdots, x_r)$ in a finite number of steps for the r-tuples for which the predicate is true and it does not stop for all other r-tuples. From the previous discussion it is clear that there must be a computable predicate

$T_{M_p}(x_1, \cdots, x_r, y)$ associated with the machine M_p that will be true only when $P(x_1, \cdots, x_r)$ is true,

$$P(x_1, \cdots, x_r) = \underset{y}{\vee} T_{M_p}(x_1, \cdots, x_r, y)$$

where y ranges over all possible values. Thus, $P(x_1, \cdots, x_r)$, a semicomputable predicate, is defined in terms of the computable predicate $T_{M_p}(x_1, \cdots, x_r, y)$. The remainder of this section is concerned with the predicate associated with the enumeration of Turing machines by a Turing machine and its computability.

First, we assume that the predicate P with the associated characteristic function C_p and the complement of C_p, $1 - C_p$, are computable. But $1 - C_p$ is the characteristic function of $\bar{P}$. Thus, both P and $\bar{P}$ are computable, and any function that is computable is also semicomputable. Given the semicomputable predicates P and $\bar{P}$, there must be two computable predicates T_{M_p} and $T_{M_{\bar{p}}}$

$$P(x_1, \cdots, x_r) = \underset{y}{\vee} T_{M_p}(x_1, \cdots, x_r, y)$$

$$\bar{P}(x_1, \cdots, x_r) = \underset{y}{\vee} T_{M_{\bar{p}}}(x_1, \cdots, x_r, y)$$

It might appear thus far that all predicates are computable. It will now be shown that this is not true. Assume that the following predicate is computable,

$$P(x) = \underset{y}{\vee} T_x(x, y) \tag{4.10}$$

where $T_x(x, y)$ indicates that machine x starts out with a tape expression of machine x. This implies that $T_x(x, y)$ enumerates other Turing machines as it generates tape expressions. The fact that the set of all Turing machines is enumerable was shown earlier in this chapter. The $\bar{P}(x)$ is at least semicomputable, which implies that there is one machine z which with input x enumerates at least one tape expression which is not a description of a Turing machine.

$$\bar{P}(x) = \overline{\underset{y}{\vee} T_x(x, y)} = \underset{y}{\vee} T_z(x, y) \tag{4.11}$$

Now assume that we start with machine z; then

$$\bar{P}(z) = \overline{\underset{y}{\vee} T_z(z, y)} = \underset{y}{\vee} T_x(z, y) \tag{4.12}$$

Now, if we let machine x equal machine z, then from Equation 4.12

$$\bar{P}(x) = \underset{y}{\vee} T_x(x,y) \tag{4.13}$$

Equation 4.13 contradicts Equation 4.10 by implying $P(x) = \bar{P}(x)$, which says that the predicate determining whether machine x enumerates a Turing machine is equivalent to the predicate determining whether machine x is not a Turing machine. This contradiction does not occur if $P(x)$ is not assumed to be computable. Thus, we conclude that Equation 4.13 is a semicomputable rather than a computable predicate.

THE HALTING PROBLEM

A question that must be answered when a tape and machine are mated or if a program is run on a general-purpose digital computer is, "Will the machine stop or run on forever?" The problem that must be solved then is, "Given any machine M and an initial tape expression x, find conclusively whether the machine will or will not stop." This is called the halting problem. We shall now show that this problem in unsolvable.

Consider a machine that computes

$$g(x) = \underset{y}{\min} \, T_x(x,y) \tag{4.14}$$

which is the minimum value of Y for which the predicate $T_x(x,y)$ is true. The domain of Equation 4.14 is those values of x for which $\underset{y}{\vee} T_x(x,y)$ is true. But it has been shown that $\underset{y}{\vee} T_x(x,y)$ is a semicomputable predicate. Thus, $g(x)$ is partially computable, and the halting problem is not solvable in general. This means that there are some machine-initial tape combinations whose halting problem is not uniquely solvable.

It is interesting to note that a program written for a general-purpose digital computer merely describes a particular Turing machine-tape combination. Therefore, the problem of uniquely determining whether programs on general-purpose computers will stop or not is also not computable.

UNIVERSAL TURING MACHINES

A specific Turing machine is designed to carry out the computations associated with a given function by going through the steps indicated by the machine's control element. The universal Turing machine is designed to interpret a tape and then carry out the appropriate computational process.

Thus, the transition table for a regular Turing machine would be encoded on a tape to be interpreted by the universal Turing machine. This coding is called a program. The function to be computed is also encoded and is called the data sequence. The two sequences, program and data, are placed on the tape and form the initial tape expression for the universal Turing machine.

It should be clear from the preceding description that this process is no different from that used with a conventional stored-program digital computer, the primary difference being that the universal Turing machine has a potentially infinite memory.

STOCHASTIC AUTOMATA

The machines considered thus far are fixed and deterministic in that their responses to a particular input from a given initial state are always the same. Also, the input sequences that we have been applying to these machines have always had a particular representation associated with them. For example, a program used on a digital computer always has a specific set of symbols in a specific format associated with it. Thus, the output is determined by the program and set of data applied, where the same program and the same data always give the same output. A stochastic automaton or probabilistic machine, on the other hand, has an output that is not necessarily the same for every application of the input. Machines that behave this way in practice may have an intermittent component or be subjected to an input sequence that is generated by noise [5].

Stochastic automata have been formulated as models for systems that are made from unreliable components [6], as a representation of a discrete system disturbed by noise [7], as models for psychological learning processes [8], and as a model for adaptive and learning systems [9, 10]. It is therefore of interest here to examine some of the properties of stochastic automata, as they will be of value when we consider applications in later chapters.

There are two methods for representing stochastic automata; however, we shall restrict our attention here to the most general model as given by Booth [7]. A probabilistic machine, as with a deterministic machine, is described by a 5-tuple; however, some of the elements in the representation are different. The 5-tuple is

$$S_p = \langle x, \Psi, \alpha, \Pi, \sigma \rangle$$

where

1. x is the input set $\{0, 1, \cdots, J - 1\}$.
2. Ψ is the state set $\{\phi_1, \phi_2, \cdots, \phi_s\}$.
3. α is the output set $\{\alpha_1, \alpha_2, \cdots, \alpha_r\}$.
4. Π is the matrix of conditional probabilities $\Pi(\alpha, \Psi(j + 1)/x_1, \Psi(j))$.
5. σ is the set of all initial state probabilities associated with the state set Ψ.

The first three elements will be recognized as being identical to the terms in the description of deterministic automata given earlier. The last two elements will now be expanded.

The matrix Π is the representation of the state transition and output behavior of the stochastic automaton. For example, consider the two-state machine described in Figure 4.5 where the binary input and output formats have been specified. The rows in the matrix correspond to the set formed by the cartesian product of the input and state sets, and the columns correspond to the cartesian product of the output and state sets. Thus, all combinations of states and inputs are represented by the rows, and all combinations of states and outputs are represented by the columns of Π. The entries in the matrix represent the probability that the next state and output will occur for the present state and input given by the corresponding row. Therefore, in Figure 4.5, the probability of going from input 0 and state ϕ_2 to output 1 and state ϕ_1 is 0.4. Note that the probability of going from one input and state to any output and state for all possible outputs

$$
\Pi = x \times \Psi
\left\{
\begin{array}{c}
1, \phi_1 \\
1, \phi_2 \\
1, \phi_1 \\
1, \phi_2
\end{array}
\begin{array}{cccc}
1,\phi_1 & 1,\phi_2 & 1,\phi_1 & 1,\phi_2 \\
.3 & 0 & .4 & .3 \\
.2 & .3 & .4 & .1 \\
.3 & .2 & .1 & .4 \\
.2 & .6 & .2 & 0
\end{array}
\right\}
$$

$$\alpha \times \Psi$$

$$x = \{0, 1\} \qquad \Psi = \{\phi_1, \phi_2\} \qquad \alpha = \{0, 1\}$$

Figure 4.5. Description of a stochastic automaton.

and states must be certain and that the probability of going from some input and state to some output and state must be equal to or greater than zero. This is summarized by

$$0 \leq \Pi[\alpha, \Psi(j + 1)/x, \Psi(j)] \leq 1 \tag{4.15}$$

and

$$\sum_{\forall \phi_i(j+1)} \sum_{\alpha=\alpha_1}^{\phi_s(j+1)} \Pi[z, \Phi(j + 1)/x, \Phi(j)] \tag{4.16}$$

The matrix Π gives us the probability of going from one state to another for a corresponding input and output; however, we still do not know how to analyze the behavior of these machines until the element σ is defined.

σ is the set of all initial state probabilities associated with the state set Ψ, $\sigma = \{\sigma = [\sigma_1, \sigma_2, \cdots, \sigma_s]\}$, and a particular element in the set gives us the initial probability of being in each of the s possible states of the machine. Therefore, in this general formulation, we can know only the probability of being in a given starting state.

It is generally desirable to be able to predict in some way the response of a machine to a particular input sequence. With stochastic automata we can calculate only the conditional probability of an output sequence given a particular input sequence. To do this, we divide the matrix Π into submatrices $\Delta_x(\alpha)$, which correspond to the transition probabilities. Thus, the Π matrix in Figure 4.5 can be rewritten as

$$\Pi = \begin{bmatrix} \Delta_0(0) & \Delta_0(1) \\ \Delta_1(0) & \Delta_1(1) \end{bmatrix} \tag{4.17}$$

Now, if we define an s-row column vector of 1s as

$$h = \left. \begin{bmatrix} 1 \\ \cdot \\ \cdot \\ \cdot \\ 1 \end{bmatrix} \right\} s \text{ rows} \tag{4.18}$$

then the conditional probability of an output sequence given an input sequence $\phi_1, \phi_2, \ldots, \phi_\nu$ is, for one input and one output symbol,

$$\Pi\left(\frac{\alpha}{\Psi}\right) = \sigma\Delta_x(\alpha)h \tag{4.19}$$

and for the sequence is

$$\Pi(\alpha_1, \alpha_2, \ldots, \alpha_\nu/\phi_1, \phi_2, \ldots, \phi_\nu) = \sigma\Delta_{\phi_1}(\alpha_1)\Delta_{\phi_2}(\alpha_2)\cdots\Delta_{\phi_\nu}(\alpha_\nu)h \tag{4.20}$$

We shall now examine Equation 4.20 by means of the following example. Assume that we are given the machine described in Figure 4.5 and that we want to know the probability of the output sequence 011 given the input sequence 010. Now, by Equation 4.17 and the **II** given, we generate

$$\Delta_0(0) = \begin{bmatrix} 0.3 & 0 \\ 0.2 & 0.3 \end{bmatrix} \qquad \Delta_1(0) = \begin{bmatrix} 0.3 & 0.2 \\ 0.2 & 0.6 \end{bmatrix}$$

$$\Delta_0(1) = \begin{bmatrix} 0.4 & 0.3 \\ 0.4 & 0.1 \end{bmatrix} \qquad \Delta_1(1) = \begin{bmatrix} 0.1 & 0.4 \\ 0.2 & 0 \end{bmatrix}$$

Now applying Equation 4.20 we have

$$\Pi\left(\frac{011}{010}\right) = \sigma\Delta_0(0)\Delta_1(1)\Delta_0(1)h = \sigma\Delta h$$

where

$$\Delta = \Delta_0(0)\Delta_1(1)\Delta_0(1) = \begin{bmatrix} 0.060 & 0.021 \\ 0.064 & 0.032 \end{bmatrix}$$

and

$$\Delta h = \begin{bmatrix} 0.060 & 0.021 \\ 0.064 & 0.032 \end{bmatrix}\begin{bmatrix} 1 \\ 1 \end{bmatrix} = \begin{bmatrix} 0.081 \\ 0.096 \end{bmatrix}$$

Thus,

$$\Pi\left(\frac{011}{010}\right) = [\sigma_1 \quad \sigma_2]\begin{bmatrix} 0.081 \\ 0.096 \end{bmatrix} = 0.081\,\sigma_1 + 0.096\,\sigma_2$$

and if we say $\sigma = [0.5 \quad 0.5]$,

$$\Pi\left(\frac{011}{010}\right) = 0.045 + 0.048 = 0.0885$$

Similarly, if we have no interest in the output sequence, then it is possible to find the probability of being in the different states of the machine after a given input sequence is applied. These probabilities are referred to as the state probability vector. Here, since we are concerned only with the states, we merely lump together the appropriate matrices $\Delta_x(\alpha)$ by

$$\Delta_x = \sum_{\alpha=\alpha_1}^{\alpha_r} \Delta_x(\alpha)$$

and for the machine of Figure 4.5,

$$\Delta_0 = \Delta_0(0) + \Delta_0(1) = \begin{bmatrix} 0.7 & 0.3 \\ 0.6 & 0.4 \end{bmatrix}$$

$$\Delta_1 = \Delta_1(0) + \Delta_1(1) = \begin{bmatrix} 0.4 & 0.6 \\ 0.4 & 0.6 \end{bmatrix}$$

Now, given the initial state probability vector, we can find the state probability vector after a sequence, say 010, is applied:

$$\sigma(\phi_1 \cdots \phi_\nu) = \sigma\Delta_{\phi_1}\Delta_{\phi_2} \cdots \Delta_{\phi_\nu}$$

and

$$\sigma(010) = \sigma\Delta_0\Delta_1\Delta_0$$

$$= [\sigma_1 \quad \sigma_2]\begin{bmatrix} 0.64 & 0.36 \\ 0.64 & 0.36 \end{bmatrix}$$

$$= [0.64\,(\sigma_1 + \sigma_2) \quad 0.36\,(\sigma_1 + \sigma_2)]$$

It has now been demonstrated that we do not have to deal with deterministic systems but that we can handle systems in a probabilistic or stochastic manner.

INFORMATION THEORY [11]

The application of a specific input sequence to a stochastic machine gives us the data required to compute only the probability of obtaining some particular sequence. Hence, there is a degree of uncertainty associated with the occurrence of each output sequence. For example, if the probability of obtaining the sequence 101 is 0.4 and the probability of 110 is 0.95 for an input 111, we are more uncertain about getting the former sequence than the latter sequence. Thus, our uncertainty level is inversely proportional to the probability of occurrence of a given event. Similarly, if we know a particular sequence will occur, we learn nothing when in fact it does occur. On the other hand, if we are very uncertain that a particular sequence will occur, we learn more when it does occur. Therefore, we say that the information associated with the occurrence of a sequence or event, call it $I(E)$, is an inverse function of the probability of that event, $P(E)$:

$$I(E) = f\left(\frac{1}{P(E)}\right) \tag{4.21}$$

In the realm of information theory, the function $f(\cdot)$ has been defined as the logarithm to the base 2 of the probability of E,

$$I(E) = \log_2 \frac{1}{P(E)} = -\log_2 P(E) \text{ bits} \tag{4.22}$$

Let us now define a "black box" called a source, which emits a stream of symbols from a set of q symbols. This source has no memory; that is, the symbol emitted from the source at any time is independent of the symbol emitted at any other time. Therefore, we shall assume that there is a probability associated with the occurrence of each symbol from the source:

$$P(s_1), P(s_2), \ldots, P(s_q)$$

$$\boxed{\text{Source}} \rightarrow \{s_1, s_2, \ldots, s_q\}$$

The information associated with the occurrence of symbol s_i is

$$I(s_i) = -\log_2 P(s_i) \text{ bits} \tag{4.23}$$

and the average information from the preceding source is the sum of the information per symbol weighted by the probability of that symbol, that is, the "expected value" of the information source:

$$H(s) = \sum_{i=1}^{q} P(s_i) I(s_i) = - \sum_{i=1}^{q} P(s_i) \log_2 P(s_i) \qquad (4.24)$$

The average information $H(s)$ given by Equation 4.24 is referred to as the entropy of the source.

It can be shown that the maximum entropy occurs when all events are equally likely:

$$P(s_1) = P(s_2) = \cdots = P(s_i)$$

For example, consider the binary source $\{0, 1\}$ where the probability of zero is P_0; also

$$P_1 = 1 - P_0 = \overline{P}_0 = \frac{1}{q}$$

The entropy of this source is

$$H(s) = P_0 \log \frac{1}{P_0} + P_1 \log \frac{1}{P_1}$$

$$= P_0 \log \frac{1}{P_0} + \overline{P}_0 \log \frac{1}{\overline{P}_0}$$

Now define

$$\lim_{P_0 \to 0} P_0 \log P_0 = 0 \log 0 = 0$$

A plot of $H(s)$ as a function of P_0 is shown here where the maximum occurs when the probability of each event is equal, $P_1 = P_0 = 0.5$. Note that if the probability of an event is 1, we learn nothing by the occurrence of that event.

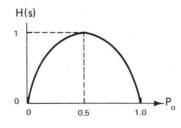

If one is given r symbols in sequence from a source of symbols $q \geq r$, then the maximum information contained in that sequence is

$$H_{max} = \log_2 r \text{ bits}$$

However, if each symbol in the sequence is repeated once, that is, each symbol is transmitted twice, then obviously the information contained in the sequence is reduced:

$$H = \log_2 \frac{r}{2}$$

The ratio of these two terms is used in the following function, which defines the redundancy in the sequence:

$$R = 1 - \frac{H}{H_{max}} \qquad (4.25)$$

This measure is most useful in coding, where one deliberately reduces the information in a sequence to overcome a noisy channel.

The concepts of information, entropy, and redundancy have been introduced here to provide the necessary background for the definitions of self-organization and the system performance measures that will be used later.

SUMMARY

In this chapter we have considered some of the models that can be applied in studying the fundamental properties of automata. The limitations of general computing machines were studied via the work of Turing. The concept of a stochastic automaton, which has certain applications in cybernetic systems, has been introduced. Finally, the fundamental definition of information and some of its ramifications have been introduced.

EXERCISES

1. Describe the following sequential machine in terms of a 5-tuple, $\langle I, Q, Z, \delta, \omega \rangle$.

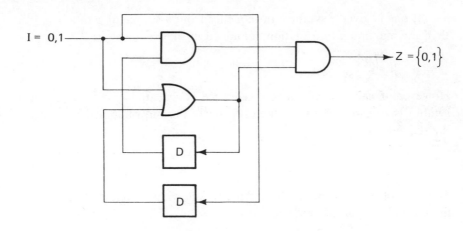

2. Describe the computations of the following machine for the following initial tape expressions:

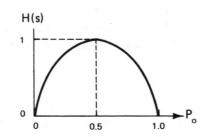

I/Q	b	a_1	a_2
q_1	q_2/r	q_1/b	q_2/l
q_2	q_2/a_1	q_3/r	q_2/h
q_3	q_2/r	q_1/r	q_3/a_1

$A = \{a_1, a_2\}$
$Q = \{q_1, q_2, q_3\}$
$Z = \{b, a_1, a_2, h, r, l\}$
$q_1 = $ initial state

1. $ba_1 a_1 a_2 a_2 a_1 b$
2. $bba_2 a_1 b$
3. $a_1 a_2 a_2$

The read/write head is placed over the leftmost symbol at the start of the computation.

3. Given the following stochastic automaton description, find the probability state vector and the probability of the output sequence 011 for the input sequence 011.

$$\alpha \times \Psi$$

$$\pi = x \times \Psi \begin{cases} & 0,\phi_1 \quad 0,\phi_2 \quad 0,\phi_3 \quad 1,\phi_1 \quad 1,\phi_2 \quad 1,\phi_3 \\ 0,\phi_1 \begin{bmatrix} 0 & 0 & 0.5 & 0 & 0 & 0.5 \\ 0,\phi_2 & 0 & 0.5 & 0 & 0 & 0.5 & 0 \\ 0,\phi_3 & 0.5 & 0 & 0 & 0.5 & 0 & 0 \\ 1,\phi_1 & 0 & 0 & 0.5 & 0 & 0 & 0.5 \\ 1,\phi_2 & 0 & 0.5 & 0 & 0 & 0.5 & 0 \\ 1,\phi_3 & 0 & 0 & 0.5 & 0 & 0 & 0.5 \end{bmatrix} \end{cases}$$

$$x = \{0,1\} \quad \Psi = \{\phi_1 \ \phi_2 \ \phi_3\} \quad \alpha = \{0,1\}$$
$$\sigma = [\sigma_1, \sigma_2, \sigma_3]$$

4. Calculate the information associated with the output sequence 010 in Exercise 3 for the input sequence 011.

5. Find the entropy associated with each row of the following matrix:

$$\begin{bmatrix} 0.1 & 0.2 & 0.1 & 0.6 \\ 0.25 & 0.25 & 0.25 & 0.25 \\ 0.9 & 0.03 & 0.04 & 0.03 \end{bmatrix}$$

6. A teletype unit is capable of encoding 64 characters for transmission down a channel. The encoded sequence uses 8 binary digits. Assuming that each character occurs with equal a priori probability, what is the entropy of the teletype source? What is the redundancy of this system?

REFERENCES

1. BOOTH, T. L., *Sequential Machines and Automata Theory*, Wiley, New York, 1967.
2. TURING, A. M., "On Computable Numbers, with an Application to the Entscheidungs Problem," in *Proceedings of the London Mathematical Society*, Vol. 42, 1936–1937, pp. 230–265.
3. MINSKY, Marvin L., *Computation: Finite and Infinite Machines*, Prentice-Hall, Englewood Cliffs, N.J., 1962.
4. KORFHAGE, Robert R., *Logic and Algorithms*, Wiley, New York, 1966.
5. BOOTH, T. L., "Random Input Automata," Proceedings, 1964 International Conference on Microwaves, Circuit Theory and Information Theory, Tokyo.
6. VON NEUMAN, J., "Probabilistic Logics and the Synthesis of Reliable Organisms from Unreliable Components," *Automata Studies Annals of Mathematical Studies*, No. 34, 1956.
7. BOOTH, T. L., "Random Processes in Sequential Networks," in *Proceedings of the IEEE Symposium on Signal Transmission and Processing*, No. 4C9, 1965, pp. 19–25.
8. BUSH, R. R., and F. MOSTELLAR, *Stochastic Models for Learning*, Wiley, New York, 1958.
9. SHAPIRO, I. J., and K. S. NARENDRA, "Use of Stochastic Automata for Parameter Self-Optimization with Multimodel Performance Criteria," *IEEE Transactions on System Science and Cybernetics*, Vol. SSC-5, No. 4, October 1969, pp. 352–360.
10. MCLAREN, R. W., "A Stochastic Automaton Model for the Synthesis of Learning Systems," *IEEE Transactions on Systems Science and Cybernetics*, Vol. SSC-2, No. 2, December 1966, pp. 109–114.
11. ABRAMSON, N., *Informational Theory*, McGraw-Hill, New York, 1963.

5

Adaptation, Learning, Self-Repair, and Self-Organization

Thus far we have been concerned with specific techniques associated with the design of intelligent systems and with characteristics of the automata that may be used to create these systems. In this chapter we shall examine the specific features—adaptation, learning, self-repair, and self-organization—these systems are often claimed to possess.

The first sections of this chapter include definition of the features and models associated with intelligent systems. The Homeostat, one of the first physical examples of an intelligent system, is then described. Finally, some techniques used in designing intelligent systems are presented.

ADAPTATION, LEARNING, AND SELF-REPAIR

The word "adaptation" has taken on several meanings in the many disciplines in which it is found. The engineer often equates learning and adaptation, whereas the psychologist makes a sharp distinction between them—and the life scientist is often found somewhere in between. The difference is a function of how broad a definition of learning one is willing to accept. Let us now consider some of the ways in which the words "learning" and "adaptation" have been used.

One definition is given by Wiener [1], who describes learning so broadly that it includes the mutation of a species with time. He defines an animal (or system) that learns as

one which is capable of being transformed by its past environment within its individual lifetime. An animal that multiplies is able to create other animals in its own likeness at least approximately, although not so completely in its own likeness that they cannot vary in the course of time. If this variation is itself inheritable, we have the raw material on which natural selection can work.

If manifested in some behavior pattern, this change will be continued through the generations if the behavior is not detrimental. Wiener calls this type of change from generation to generation racial or *phylogenetic learning*, and learning or changes in behavior that take place within a specific individual are called *ontogenetic learning*. Although both phylogenetic and ontogenetic learning (especially the former) are present in all plants and animals, the degree of the presence of one or the other types of learning is a function of the organism. For example, it is clear that in higher mammals, and especially in man, ontogenetic learning and individual adaptability are at a high level. And, as Wiener points out, "It may be said that a large part of the phylogenetic learning of man has been devoted to establishing the possibility of good ontogenetic learning." On the other hand, in birds and insects [2] the amount of ontogenetic learning that is possible is limited, and most of their behavior is based on phylogenetic learning. The gross generality of this definition is clear when one considers definitions set forth by others.

Shannon [3] gives a definition of learning that is not so encompassing as that of Wiener. Shannon's definition says: Hypothesize an organism or a machine placed in or connected to a set of environments, for which there is a measure of success or adaptation to the environment. And further, this measure is local in time, i.e., that one can measure success over short periods of time compared to the organism's life. If the measure of success tends to improve with the passing of time, for that set of environments, then the organism or machine is said to be learning to adapt to these environments in relation to the measure of success selected.

Several components of Shannon's definition are more restrictive than Wiener's; also, Shannon's use of the term "adaptation" in reference to a success measure makes for difficulty when one is trying to communicate with psychologists and some life scientists. This definition considers only the subset of all possible ontogenetic learning.

It is now of interest to consider some of the ways the word "learning" is used by the psychologist. A thorough treatment of learning is found in Osgood [4], who describes phylogenetic learning in his definition. His definition is similar to that of other psychologists and is contained in his statements, "In repeated situations of similar character, the individual organism varies and multiplies its behaviors, selection among competing responses depending upon their adaptiveness. Selective modifications of this order result from experience of the individual." This definition is similar to that of Shannon, but it points out one facet that is important to the psychologist, that is, that the organism is subjected to "repeated situations of similar character." The definitions presented thus far have been relatively consistent, and one may ask, Where do the previously mentioned difficulties in definitions arise? This can be answered when one considers some of the uses of the word "adaptation."

In engineering circles the words "learning" and "adaptive" are often used interchangeably when referring to systems that are capable of ontogenetic learning; however, the psychologists' interpretation of the word "adaptive" is likely to be colored by knowledge of the concept of adaptation level theory as used in the classical psychophysical experiments. In this context lie the phenomena of dark adaptation, pain adaptation, and sound adaptation, the ability of an observer to "tune out" one sound source (baby cry) in preference to another [4, 5]. The classic adaptation level theory has been expanded by Helson [6] into the realm of total behavior, both normal and abnormal. For purposes of this discussion three of Helson's postulates are of interest:

1. All behavior centers about the adaptation or equilibrium level of the organism.
2. Behavioral equilibrium depends on the interaction of all stimuli confronting the organism, between present and past stimulation.

3. The adaptation level is approximated as a weighted log mean of all stimuli affecting the organism. (The log relation here accounts for the nonlinear transfer characteristics of the physiological receptors in all living organisms.)

Therefore, one can conclude that the adaptation level can be likened to a behavioral threshold that is a function of the inputs to the organism. The process wherein a persistent stimulus is "tuned out" has also been observed by neurophysiologists when studying human "brain waves" or electroencephalograms (EEG) [7]. For example, when exposed to repeated auditory pulse of click stimulation, the resulting brain wave pulses continue to decrease in amplitude with each stimulus until the response disappears. This physiological equivalent to adaptation is called habituation.

The fact that confusion exists between the words "adaptation" and "learning" was recognized previously by Sklansky [8], who defines learning and self-repair as special forms of adaptation. He considers "a cell, an organ, an organism, or a species to be adaptive if its behavior in a changing environment is 'successful' in some sense." If success by some measure is a requisite, then two properties distinguish an adaptive from a nonadaptive machine: stability and reliability.

In a definition of adaptation given by Ashby [9], stability is put forth as a requirement: "A form of behavior is adaptive if it maintains its essential variables within physiological limits." An example of this property in all living systems is homeostasis. Included in this category from a physiological viewpoint are the mechanisms for maintaining the glucose level in the blood and the mechanisms for maintaining body temperature. These mechanisms are essential to physiological survival as well as to the successful performance of any desired task. This discussion suggests a distinguishing property of adaptive systems: persistence of success in a changing environment.

The second property of adaptive systems, as proposed by Ashby and Sklansky, reliability, is also based on observations of physiological systems. If a portion of a system is damaged, and the effect of the damage is gradually masked until the system's performance reaches an acceptable level, then the machine is adaptive. Thus, the second property of adaptive machines can be stated as follows: overall functional reliability in the face of unreliability of parts of the machine. In the following discussions, this property with a time constraint is associated with the concept of machine self-repair, discussed later.

A functional schema for an adaptive machine is given in Figure 5.1. The machine's input is the "stimulus" s; the machine's output is the "response" r; the measure of success is given by the critic's output or "effectiveness" measure Z. This configuration is called the MEC (machine, environment, critic) configuration. Adaptation is manifested by the presence of stability or reliability or both.

With respect to the MEC configuration,

1. The system is stable if Z remains within prescribed bounds when E changes.
2. The system is reliable if Z remains within prescribed bounds when M changes.

In this definition, note that none of the requirements for an adaptive system are functions of time.

The definition of learning and the similar effects of self-repair are closely related to time, however. Thus, the effectiveness (i.e., critic's output) is a function of time, $Z(t)$, and we say that M "learns" over a specified time interval $(0, T)$ if for an environment change at $t = 0$ then $Z(T) > Z(0+)$. In other words, a system that learns is one in which, given a change in the state of the environment at $t = 0$, the performance index at time T is greater than the performance index at time $t = 0+$.

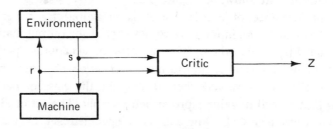

Figure 5.1. MEC configuration.

A system M undergoes self-repair over a time interval $(0, T)$ if for some machine component failure at $t = 0$, then $Z(T) > Z(0+)$. That is, self-repair occurs when a system's effectiveness at $t = 0+$ is less than that at $t = T$ when a failure in M has occurred. It is clear that the only difference between the definitions of learning and self-repair is the physical location of the change.

We shall impose one more constraint on the preceding definitions, that the performance achieve some predetermined level, $Z(t) = L > Z(0+)$, in time T.

SOME FORMALIZATION

Zadeh [10] has defined precisely an adaptive system ("An adaptive system is insensitive to changes in its environment") by characterizing its external manifestations and couching them in mathematical terms. The following is basically Zadeh's description of adaptive systems, where the input (stimulus) and output (response) sets are not necessarily functions of specific time intervals.

Consider a machine A, which may be subjected to any one of a specified set of input functions, $S_r \equiv \{u\}$, where the vector u may be a function of time. The input $\bar{u}$ may contain components that are both input or stimulus variables, that is, environmental factors and machine failures as well. It is therefore convenient to consider a family of inputs for some given criterion indexed by r. This family of inputs $S_r = \{u\}$ constitutes a source that may or may not be a stochastic process. It is now possible to define a family of sources $\{S_r\}$, in which r is a member. The representation here of the machine and its associated input and output functions is similar to the MEC configuration used by Sklansky. The model and the associated terms for this definition are shown in Figure 5.2.

The performance of a machine A is measured by a performance function P, which, for an input S_r, becomes $\mathbf{P}(r)$. If the output mapping $\mathbf{P}(r)$ is such that $\mathbf{P}(r) \subset W$, where W is a class of acceptable performance functions, then the system is said to meet a criterion of acceptability. For example, if $\mathbf{P}(r)$ is real-valued, then W may be the class of performance functions that exceed in value a prescribed number. The set of all possible input conditions is $r \subset \Gamma$, where Γ is a specified set of values of r. Associated with the family of inputs $\{S_r\}$ there exists a set of a priori probability distribution functions, M, such that for a given r a probability distribution function $\mu \subset M$ is specified.

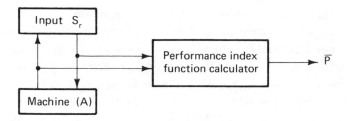

Figure 5.2. Modified MEC configuration.

It is now possible to define an adaptive system: A system A is said to be adaptive with respect to $\{S_r\}$ and W, if it performs "acceptably." In other words, $P(r) \subset W$, for every source in the family $\{S_r\}$, $r \subset \Gamma$. More succinctly, A is adaptive with respect to Γ and W if it maps Γ into W.

Next define the measure of performance for a machine as the total distance between the input and output mapping. Then we say that A is more adaptive than A', if A' is adaptive relative to Γ' and W, where Γ' is a proper subset of Γ (that is, A meets the performance criterion for a larger set of inputs than does A').

The similarity between this definition based on Zadeh and Sklansky's definitions [11, 12] lies in the fact that Zadeh includes changes that may occur as machine failures in his input vector u. This led Sklansky to "suggest that adaptivity, coined by Zadeh, be viewed as the union of stability and reliability, even though Zadeh does not associate adaptivity and reliability explicitly." Also, it is interesting to note that with this definition all systems may be thought of as being adaptive for some Γ and W.

The last statement in the preceding paragraph offers a link between definitions of adaptive systems in engineering and the concept of adaptation level found in psychology. If the adaptation levels or thresholds encountered are defined to be within an acceptable region W, then any psychological system where the concept of adaptation level is applied is adaptive in the engineering sense.

DEFINITION SUMMARY

It is now possible to summarize the definitions of adaptation, learning, and self-repair as they will be used in this book. One can say that a system is adaptive if it responds favorably with respect to a performance function

P in the face of a changing environment or internal machine structure. And one can say that a system learns if it responds acceptably with respect to a performance function *P* in time *T* after a change in its environment. A system undergoes self-repair if it responds acceptably with respect to a performance function *P* in time *T* after a change in its internal structure. Thus, the primary distinction between adaptation and learning/self-repair is that the performance in the face of changes must achieve within a specific time for learning and self-repair, and the time constraint is not imposed on an adaptive system. These definitions may appear to ignore the process of habituation; however, if one chooses one's performance function properly, the processes of habituation and adaptation will emerge identical.

SELF-ORGANIZATION

Let us now consider some approaches to the concept of a self-organizing system. Ashby [13] considers first the contradiction of organization, namely separation. Thus, a system that starts with its parts separate (i.e., each part behaves independently, and then acts so that connections are formed and the parts behave in a more coherent manner) is self-organizing in that it changes from "parts separated" to "parts joined." An example of this process is the growth of the nervous system of an embryo, where individual cells grow and then the interconnections associated with certain behaviors are formed.

A second approach given by Ashby [13] expands this definition to also include a system that changes "from a bad organization to a good one." This approach, however, leads to a definition that is similar to the one given earlier for adaptation. It is presented here to point out some of the confusion in terms associated with an emerging discipline.

It has been argued by Von Foerster [14] and Ashby [13] that there is no such thing as a self-organizing system in and of itself. The reasoning here is that for a system to become organized it must extract that organization from its environment. Hence, a system can be self-organizing only if it is defined with respect to some external source of order. Such a system, as it becomes organized, will discard behavior that is not appropriate in a sort of natural behavior selection process in the present environment. Further, if there is no order to the environment, then there is no basis for organization.

This concept was stated by Ashby [15] as the "Law of Requisite Variety: Only variety can destroy variety." This can be described in terms of a system operating in some environment where the success of the system depends on its ability to cope with the possible states of the environment. For example, as a minimum requirement, the number of possible states of the system must equal the number of possible states of the environment, although the proper states of the system must be available as well. Thus, to reduce the variety in the enviroment, the system must be capable of achieving the "requisite variety."

The fundamental principles of self-organizing systems emerge from these arguments. The first is as follows: A necessary condition for a system, A, to be self-organizing in an environment, E, is that the uncertainty in an information-theoretic sense associated with A be equal to or greater than zero:

$$I(\mathbf{A}) > 0 \tag{5.1}$$

Now, consider the contradiction to Equation 5.1: If $I(\mathbf{A}) = 0$ (which implies that the system is deterministic and rigid in its behavior), then it can be successful only in a narrower range of environments than a machine with $I(\mathbf{A}) \geq I(E)$.

The second principle is associated with the definition of a self-organizing system given by Von Foerster [14] and concerns the redundancy (as defined in information theory) that is associated with a system. For example, if a system is totally disorganized, then the uncertainty of behavior associated with the system is maximum. One does not know what the system's response to a particular input will be. However, as the system learns of its environment and organization takes place, then one is more certain about its behavior and the system is more redundant. Therefore, the requirement placed on a self-organizing system where R is redundancy is

$$\frac{dR}{dt} > 0 \tag{5.2}$$

Applying the preceding operation to the definition of redundancy, as given by Equation 4.25, we have

$$\frac{d}{dt}\left[-\frac{H}{H_{\max}}\right] > 0 \tag{5.3}$$

If both H and H_{max} are functions of time, the criterion for a system to be self-organizing is

$$H\left(\frac{dH_{max}}{dt}\right) > H_{max}\left(\frac{dH}{dt}\right) \tag{5.4}$$

The rather complex processes that are inferred in Equation 5.4 can be more easily understood by considering a few special cases. For example, assume that the maximum entropy of the system H_{max} is constant:

$$\frac{dH}{dt} < 0, \qquad H_{max} \text{ constant} \tag{5.5}$$

This means that the rate of change of entropy must be negative if the system is to be self-organizing. Also consider the case where the entropy of the system, H, is constant but the number of states in the system is growing. The criterion for self-organization now is

$$\frac{dH_{max}}{dt} > 0, \qquad H \text{ constant} \tag{5.6}$$

Here the entropy can remain constant while the system is growing only if the added states are incorporated into the system such that Equation 5.6 is satisfied.

Finally, consider the case where both H and H_{max} are functions of time and therefore the criterion is given by Equation 5.4. Here the system is said to be self-organizing if the product of the system entropy and the rate of change of the maximum entropy is greater than the product of the maximum entropy and the rate of change of system entropy. This is the situation where the system states are growing and the system organization is faster than that required to incorporate the new states.

It is now possible to summarize our definition of a self-organizing system with respect to the previous definitions. From the preceding discussion, it is clear that we must have disorganization before organization can occur. Thus, we shall assume that the initial uncertainty is at or near maximum, max,

$$H \approx \text{max}$$

and a self-organizing system is defined as an adaptive or learning system in which the initial state of the system is unknown, a random variable, or a "don't care."

SOME SYSTEM MODELS

There are two basic models of interest here. Each one contains the same basic elements, but their configurations are different. The elements are the forward transfer element, the performance evaluation element or critic, the system parameter transformation element, and the input and output functions. One of the configurations of these elements is given in Figure 5.3.

The forward transfer element (FTE) maps the input function, I, into some output function, Ω. Here, I is some function of the system input, or driving function i, the environment E (in which the system exists and must interact), and may or may not be a specific function of time: $I = f(i, E, t)$. For example, the forward transfer element may be as simple as a passive electrical network, a complex hybrid (analog-digital) system, or a network of computer systems. The output function Ω is a function of the input function I and the state Q.

The nature of the performance evaluation (PEEL) determines the character of the system, as it contains the goal orientation of the system. For example, the goal or goals contained within the PEEL may be "Reduce the error between the input and output functions" as in a simple feedback system or "Extract from the input function all sequences of symbols that make up words from Russian" or "Keep a 3G force on the system while expending no more than x pounds of fuel." The PEEL then is said to contain the goals and constraints of the system's operation and it maps the

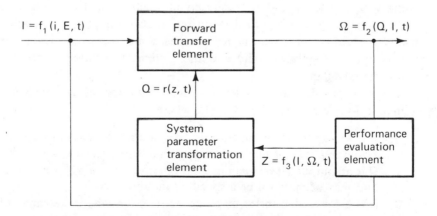

Figure 5.3.   Closed self-organizing or adaptive system.

input and output functions into a set of measures Z, which indicate the performance of the system. The PEEL or critic is often called the teacher, as its function is to provide an input to the system that tells it whether its behavior is proper or not.

In some applications the PEEL makes statistical estimates or measurements of the input signal in order to "learn" what state the system should be in. This kind of system is called "learning without a teacher." Thus, a system in which the PEEL is some external observer such as an executive computer or human critic who "teaches" the system how to behave is sometimes called "learning with a teacher," and a system in which the teacher or critic is built in is called "learning without a teacher." Tsypkin [16] has argued that there is no such thing as learning without a teacher, as the essence of teaching is contained in the goals and constraints of the PEEL that are specified by the designer, the teacher. In many systems, especially control systems, this is in fact the case. However, some systems developed lately have certain restricted abilities to independently derive subgoals within the PEEL.

The system parameter transform element (SPTE) transforms the performance measure Z into a system state such that the system behavior tends to fall into a range where the performance improves.

The second model merely places a switch between the FTE and the SPTE and isolates the SPTE and PEEL from the rest of the system. Thus, with the switch open, the state of the system cannot change, as there is no feedback or state change information supplied. This is the model for learning with a teacher and is illustrated in Figure 5.4. The method of operation for this system is such that during the learning phase, the switch is closed and, after the performance reaches some acceptable level, the switch is opened (operate mode) and the system "freewheels" until the switch is closed again.

It is now possible to consider a formal definition of an intelligent system as a 6-tuple $S = \langle I, \Omega, \alpha, Z, \gamma, Q \rangle$, where

1. I is an input set or function encompassing the environment E; however I may or may not be a specific function of time.
2. Ω is an output set or function that operates on the environment E and may or may not be a specific function of time.
3. α is a forward transfer mapping or function where the range of the mapping or function determines the domain of behavior of the system.

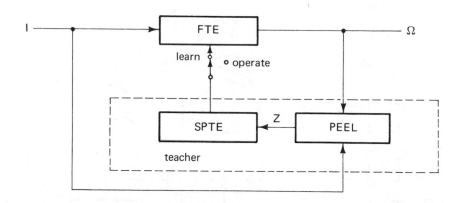

Figure 5.4.   Model of learning with a teacher.

4. Z is a performance evaluation mapping or function that operates on the input and output to indicate the behavior of the system with respect to the goals and constraints of the system.

5. γ is a system parameter mapping or function that transforms the performance measure into appropriate system parameters generally, in a manner such that the future behavior improves in some sense.

6. Q is a state set or function whose value selects a subset of the domain of behavior of the system.

HOMEOSTAT

The homeostat is one of the first physical realizations that encompassed the concepts of learning without a teacher and was developed by Ashby as an example of an ultrastable system. The word "homeostat" was derived from "homeostasis," which describes a process that is stabilizing, such as the physiological process of body temperature control.

The homeostat developed by Ashby [9] contains four identical interconnected units each with a magnetically deflected pointer or indicator on top and an appropriate sensing mechanism to determine the relative position of the pointer. The position of the pointer is controlled by several internal parameters; Ashby used the sum of three magnetic fields to provide energy to deflect the pointer. A diagram of one unit of the homeostat is given in Figure 5.5. The deflection of the pointer, M, is proportional to the

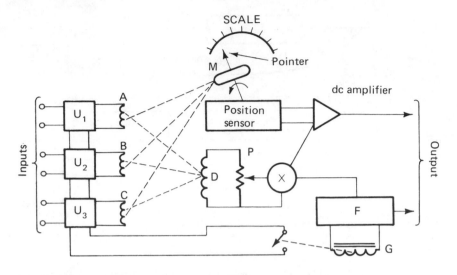

Figure 5.5.   Single unit of the homeostat.

algebraic sum of the currents in A, B, and C. D is a feedback sensor, which through potentiometer P and reversing switch X provides some feedback into the system. The magnitude and direction of the currents in coils A, B, and C are determined by the positions of the three 25-position stepping switches U_1, U_2, U_3, respectively. The magnitude and direction at each switch position is determined a priori from a table of random numbers. New positions for the three selectors U_1, U_2, and U_3 are initiated by the closure of relay G, which is governed by the value of the essential variable, F. The relay, G, is energized when the output current exceeds some preset value. Also, the position sensor is adjusted to provide an output of 0 volts of direct current when the pointer is deflected to half-scale.

Four units identical to the unit illustrated in Figure 5.5 are interconnected such that the output of each unit is connected to an input on each of the other units. Thus, when the system is turned on, the pointers are moved by the currents from the other units, which in turn change the currents, etc. The system operates as follows: The essential variable is sampled at specific intervals, say every T seconds, and if the essential variable is within acceptable limits, the stepping switch positions are not altered; conversely, if the essential variable is not within acceptable limits,

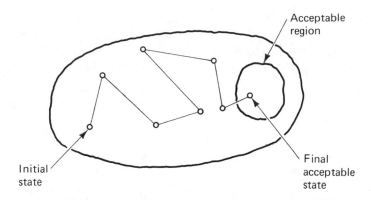

Figure 5.6. Search for a solution in two-dimensional space.

the stepping switch positions are changed.

Thus, the goal of the system is to maintain the essential variables within acceptable limits. This is accomplished by changing the system parameters when one or more of these variables are exceeded, until the value of the essential variables is within acceptable limits. This process can be thought of as a search for an acceptable set of system parameters in the n-dimensional space of all possible solutions, as illustrated in Figure 5.6 for a two-dimensional solution space. Note that the homeostat must search a four-dimensional space. Here, the initial state of the system is not in an acceptable region, and the stepping switches are moved seven times until the essential variables are within acceptable limits. Note that the nature of the homeostat forces the search of the space to be random and that it is possible for all but one state of the system to be tried before the acceptable state is found. For the complete homeostat with four sets of stepping switches (one set in each unit), there are $25^4 = 390,625$ possible states; thus, it is possible to require that 390,624 states be tried before the acceptable one is found. It is also clear that if the range of perturbation of the collection of pointers is within the range of selection by the stepping switches (a state of the system exists that will control all possible pointer conditions), the system will be ultrastable.

The homeostat can now be examined with respect to the models presented earlier. The input or environment of the system is represented by the positions of the pointers. The forward transfer element consists of the amplifiers, the present position of the stepping switches, and the coils. The output is the magnetic fields that deflect the individual pointers. The performance evaluation element includes the collection of F units, which sense the four essential variables. The output of the PEEL is the position of the relay G, which is transformed into appropriate changes in the state of the stepping switches, which are an embodiment of a system parameter transform element.

GILSTRAP'S MULTINOMIAL FORWARD TRANSFER ELEMENT

The forward transfer element realization of the homeostat is quite restrictive and certainly difficult to generalize to other systems. A unique and powerful approach to this problem has been expounded by Gilstrap [17]. The objective of his work was to create a method of generating a sufficiently large number of mappings from a set of inputs to a set of outputs such that a "requisite variety" could be realized. In many problems there is a large set of interacting variables that must be combined to create the proper output mapping. Thus, the input variables and the output mappings define nonlinear hypersurfaces. These hypersurfaces in turn are described by high degree multinomials.

Before we can examine Gilstrap's realization, it is necessary to define the three basic forms for multinomials: multilinear, homogeneous, and complete multinomials.

The first class of multinomials forms the basis for this approach and is defined as follows: A multilinear multinomial is a polynomial in m variables in which all possible product pairs, product triples, ..., and m-way products appear and no variable appears to a degree higher than the first.

A homogeneous multinomial of degree d in m variables is a polynomial where the exponents of the variables in each term sum to d and is called a multinomial of the second class.

The third class is the complete multinomial: A complete multinomial of degree n in m variables is the sum of all homogeneous multinomials from zero degree through the nth degree.

For example, the multilinear multinomial in two variables is

$$y = w_o + w_1 x_1 + w_2 x_2 + w_3 x_1 x_2$$

and the homogeneous multinomial of second degree in two variables is

$$y = w_1 x_1^2 + w_2 x_2^2 + w_3 x_1 x_2$$

where the coefficients w_i are varied to adjust the mapping achieved. Thus, since each coefficient must be adjusted, it is important to know the number of terms that must be handled. For the complete multinomial of degree n in m variables, there are

$$N_c = \frac{n+m}{n! \, m!} = \binom{n+m}{n}$$

possible coefficients. Thus, a complete multinomial of third degree in four variables has

$$N_c = \binom{7}{3} = 35$$

coefficients, which is a significant number of adjustments for a rather simple polynomial. Further, there are $N_M = 2^m$ possible coefficients for a multilinear multinomial in m variables. And for an eight-variable multinomial there are $N_M = 256$ possible coefficients, which is a rather unwieldy number of terms to accommodate.

Gilstrap's forward transfer element, which can be used for high degree multinomials, uses the simple multilinear multinomial in two variables as a building block that can be interconnected to approximate the desired hypersurface of m variables. For example, the four-input multilinear multinomial is developed with the three-building-block interconnection illustrated in Figure 5.7. Here,

$$y_1 = w_{10} + w_{11} x_1 + w_{12} x_2 + w_{13} x_1 x_2$$
$$y_2 = w_{20} + w_{31} x_3 + w_{22} x_2 + w_{23} x_3 x_4$$

and

$$
\begin{aligned}
y = {} & w_{30} + w_{31} y_1 + w_{32} y_2 + w_{33} y_1 y_2 \\
= {} & w_{30} + w_{31}(w_{10} + w_{11} x_1 + w_{12} x_2 + w_{13} x_1 x_2) \\
& + w_{32}(w_{20} + w_{21} x_3 + w_{22} x_2 + w_{23} x_3 x_4) \\
& + w_{33}(w_{10} + w_{11} x_1 + w_{12} x_2 + w_{13} x_1 x_2) \\
& \cdot (w_{20} + w_{21} x_3 + w_{22} x_4 + w_{23} x_3 x_4)
\end{aligned}
\tag{5.7a}
$$

$$y = v_0 + v_1 x_1 + v_2 x_2 + v_3 x_3 + v_4 x_4 + v_5 x_1 x_2$$
$$+ v_6 x_1 x_3 + v_7 x_1 x_4 + v_8 x_2 x_3 + v_9 x_2 x_4$$
$$+ v_{10} x_3 x_4 + v_{11} x_1 x_2 x_3 + v_{12} x_1 x_2 x_4 + v_{13} x_1 x_3 x_4$$
$$+ v_{14} x_2 x_3 x_4 + v_{15} x_2 x_3 x_4 x_1 \qquad (5.7b)$$

which is the fourth-order multilinear multinomial, where

$$v_0 = w_{30} + w_{31} w_{10} + w_{32} w_{20} + w_{33} w_{10} w_{20}$$

$$v_1 = w_3 w_{11} + w_{33} w_{11} w_{20}$$

$$v_2 = w_{31} w_{12} + w_{33} w_{12} w_{20}$$

$$v_3 = w_{32} w_{21} + w_{33} w_{10} w_{21}$$

$$v_4 = w_{32} w_{22} + w_{33} w_{10} w_{22}$$

$$v_5 = w_{31} w_{13} + w_{33} w_{13} w_{20}$$

$$v_6 = w_{33} w_{11} w_{21}$$

$$v_7 = w_{33} w_{11} w_{22}$$

$$v_8 = w_{33} w_{12} w_{21}$$

$$v_9 = w_{33} w_{12} w_{22}$$

$$v_{10} = w_{33} w_{23} + w_{33} w_{10} w_{23}$$

$$v_{11} = w_{33} w_{13} w_{21}$$

$$v_{12} = w_{33} w_{13} w_{12}$$

$$v_{13} = w_{33} w_{11} w_{23}$$

$$v_{14} = w_{33} w_{12} w_{23}$$

$$v_{15} = w_{33} w_{13} w_{23}$$

It is important to note that a four-variable multinomial requires 2^4 independent coefficients, whereas Equation 5.7 has 12 independent coefficients. Thus, there are some surfaces that cannot be generated with this interconnection of second-order blocks. The interactions of these coeffi-

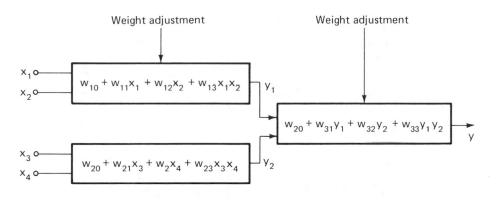

Figure 5.7. Synthesis of four-variable multilinear multinomial with two variable blocks.

cients must generally be accounted for in the system parameter transform element. The triangular configuration in Figure 5.7 is not the only way in which multinomials can be realized. For example, an $n \times m$ matrix of two-variable building blocks can be interconnected in a random manner to realize an n-variable $(m - 1)$-degree multinomial. The basic requirement to realize a large number of the possible n-variable $(m - 1)$-degree multinomials is that there be a sufficiently rich interconnection between the blocks. The network of Figure 5.8 can be used to realize a large number of functions since there are a large number of interconnections between the blocks. This network can have cross-product terms of all eight variables appearing in the output. In practice, larger networks (up to 24 variables) are often used to ensure the requisite variety for the problem at hand.

SEARCH TECHNIQUES

One of the central issues in the design of a cybernetic system is the search for the proper parameters. The character of the system often determines the method of search applied. For example, if the system is described by a discrete tree structure as in games, theorem proving, and problem solving, then it is advantageous to apply heuristic procedures such as those given in Chapter 2. On the other hand, the area of search may be

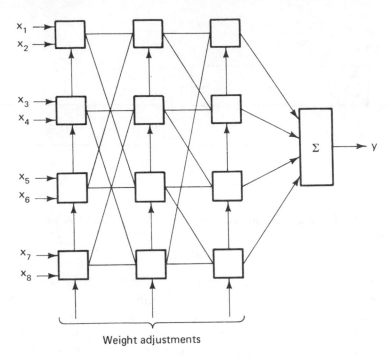

Figure 5.8.   Richly interconnected network.

the space of real numbers in a single dimension, the complex plane, or some multidimensional hyperspace. In these instances, we must resort to other techniques in order to find the appropriate parameters.

In the general formulation of search techniques that follows, it is convenient to assume that the environment is relatively constant over the period of time necessary to perform the search. Further, we shall restrict our formulations such that the goal of the search is to find either a maximum or a minimum in our function with respect to the system parameters.

First, consider functions of a single variable, $f(x)$, defined over some domain of x. The absolute or global maximum of $f(x)$ occurs at a point x_m if $f(x) \leq f(x_m)$ over the domain over which the function is defined. Conversely, the global minimum occurs at a point x_m if $f(x) \geq f(x_m)$ over the domain of definition. A maximum that is maximum for only some fraction of the domain of definition is called a relative or local maximum.

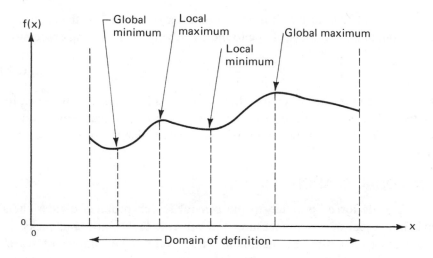

Figure 5.9. Illustration of the local global maxima and minima.

A relative or local minimum can be defined similarly. The single-dimension function in Figure 5.9 illustrates a global maximum and minimum and a local maximum and minimum. Search procedures are greatly simplified if the function of interest is unimodal—having only one maximum or minimum over the domain of definition, as shown in Figure 5.10.

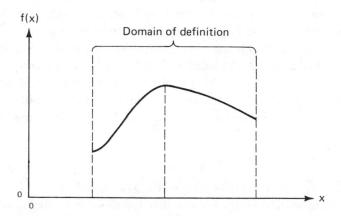

Figure 5.10. Unimodal function—only one maximum.

It should be clear that if the function is known explicitly, the maximum or minimum points can easily be found by solving the following expression:

$$\frac{df(x)}{dx} = 0 \qquad (5.8)$$

If this is the case, then of course there is no need for a search. However, for systems that must operate in an unknown or nonstationary environment, this function is not known, and one must search for the proper operating point.

UNIMODAL SEARCH

A brute force approach to the general search problem divides the x axis into equal intervals, measures the value at each point, and picks the point associated with the maximum value found. The number of search computations with respect to an exhaustive search can be reduced for unimodal functions by using the dichotomous search procedure. The first step here is to evaluate two points separated by some interval Δ in the center of the domain of definition. The half of the domain in which the maximum or minimum lies can now be determined, and two new points can be placed in the center of this interval and so forth until the value of the interval approaches ϵ. The value of ϵ clearly establishes the precision of our estimate, and procedures which modify the value of ϵ as the search progresses have also been developed [18, 19, 20].

A procedure that is similar to the dichotomous procedure but that requires even fewer searches is based on a series of numbers called the Fibonacci numbers. The Fibonacci numbers provide an approximation to the Golden section, which has some interesting implications in nature and esthetics as well as in search procedures. A discussion of the Golden section is beyond the scope of this text, but the reader will find some interesting discussions in Dantzig, Coxeter, and Gilstrap et al. [22, 23, 24].

The Fibonacci numbers are generated by the following recursive relationship

$$F_n = F_{n-1} + F_{n-2}, \qquad n > 1 \qquad (5.9)$$

where $F_0 = F_1 = 1$ and the sequence is 1, 1, 2, 3, 5, 8, 13, ... To illustrate the Fibonacci search, let us assume that the domain of definition of the function to be maximized (or minimized) is the interval $[0, 1]$, which is given by L_1. The first two points evaluated can now be found by

$$x_1 = 0 + \Delta_2 = \Delta_2$$
$$x_2 = 1 - \Delta_2$$

(5.10)

where Δ_2 is an interval given by

$$\Delta_2 = L_1 \frac{F_{n-2}}{F_n}$$

(5.11)

and the ratio $1/F_n$ is equal to or less than the precision with which we wish to estimate the maximum point. For example, if the desired precision is $\leq 5\%$, and $L_1 = 1$, $F_0 = 1$, choose $n = 7$, where $F_0/F_7 = 1/F_7 = 1/21$ $< 5\%$. After the two initial points, $f(x_1)$ and $f(x_2)$, are evaluated, one of the intervals $(0, \Delta_2)$ or $(1 - \Delta_2, 1)$ will be eliminated and a new interval $L_2 = L_1 - \Delta_2$ will be defined (note that one end of this interval will be either x_1 or x_2):

$$L_2 = L_1 - \Delta_2 = L_1 - L_1\left(\frac{F_{n-2}}{F_n}\right) = L_1\left(\frac{F_{n-1}}{F_n}\right)$$

(5.12)

A new interval Δ_3 can be defined with respect to the ends of L_2, say a_2 and b_2:

$$\Delta_3 = L_2 \frac{F_{n-3}}{F_{n-1}}$$

(5.13)

The new test points depend on the results of the first evaluations:

$$\left.\begin{array}{l} a_2 = a_1 = 0 \\ b_2 = x_2 \\ x_3 = a_2 + \Delta_3 \end{array}\right\} \quad \text{for } f(x_1) \leq f(x_2)$$

(5.14)

$$\left.\begin{array}{l} a_2 = x_1 \\ b_2 = b_1 = 1 \\ x_3 = b_2 - \Delta_3 \end{array}\right\} \quad \text{for } f(x_1) \geq f(x_2)$$

(5.15)

Evaluation of $f(x_3)$ will eliminate another interval, and the process continues until n iterations are completed where

$$L_n = L_1\left(\frac{F_0}{F_n}\right)$$

(5.16)

This procedure has been shown to be optimum in that it requires fewer evaluations of the function than any other procedure.

Thus far, we have restricted our attention to functions of a single variable. The reasons for this are clear if one considers the problems associated with multidimensional search. Consider a two-dimensional function $f(x_1 x_2)$ defined over the domain $0 \le x_1 \le 1, 0 \le x_2 \le 1$, where the maximum is to be found within 0.1 in each dimension. A one-dimensional search has 10 intervals in which the maximum can lie, whereas a two-dimensional search has 10^2. Also, note that if a one-dimensional search locates the maximum in an interval of 0.1, a two-dimensional search that is reduced to an area of one-tenth of the original area locates each dimension only to within $\sqrt{0.10} \simeq 0.316$. Additional dimensionality makes the problem increasingly difficult and costly with respect to computation time. Techniques that are analogous to the single-dimensional methods described earlier and later can also be applied to multidimensional search problems.

The final unimodal technique that is of interest here is the gradient search or method of steepest ascent or descent for maximization and minimization, respectively. Fundamentally, this method measures two points separated by some increment and estimates the slope, moves accordingly, estimates the slope again, and stops when the slope reaches some small, prespecified value. One problem with this method is immediately evident; it is possible to move in increments that cause successive points to oscillate about the maximum such that the search never converges. Despite this and other drawbacks, the straightforward formulation and simple implementation of the gradient search method makes it an important and useful tool.

Consider a specific multidimensional continuous differentiable function $f(x) = f(x_1, x_2, \cdots, x_n)$ for which we wish to find the maximum by gradient search. First, define the gradient vector:

$$\nabla f(\mathbf{x}) = \left(\frac{\partial f(\mathbf{x})}{\partial x_1}, \frac{\partial f(\mathbf{x})}{\partial x_2}, \dots, \frac{\partial f(\mathbf{x})}{\partial x_n} \right) \qquad (5.17)$$

The direction of the gradient vector indicates the way in which one may move the vector x to find the maximum. Since the direction of the maximum from some present point is known, all one needs to find the maximum is an orderly procedure—an algorithm.

1. Start at some initial point in the domain of definition that is a "guess" of where the maximum is. Note that in the case where one has a priori information, any guess is a best guess. (The remaining steps in the algorithm are iterative; that is, one repeats these steps in sequence until the last step is satisfied.)
2. Compute $\nabla f(\mathbf{x}_i)$, where i indicates the ith iteration.
3. Move in the direction of the ith gradient vector, $\alpha_i \nabla f(\mathbf{x}_i)$. α_i is the step size of the process and affects both the rapidity of convergence and the position of the search[*]:

$$\mathbf{x}_{i+1} = \mathbf{x}_i + \alpha_i \nabla f(\mathbf{x}_i) \qquad (5.18)$$

4. Terminate the computation and designate $\mathbf{x}_{i+1}$ as the maximum point if $f(\mathbf{x}_{i+1}) - f(\mathbf{x}_i) \leq \epsilon$, where ϵ is some a priori specified precision. Otherwise go to step 2.

The criterion given in step 4 is called a *stopping rule* and is just one of many that can be applied [19, 20]. The value of the step size, α_i, used in step 3 is important in gradient search. A value of α_i that is "too" large may cause the search to oscillate about the maximum, thereby inhibiting convergence, whereas a value of α_i that is "too" small may force many iterations to occur before convergence. An alternative to fixed step-size gradient search is an adaptive procedure in which α_i depends on the value of ϵ calculated in step 4 of the previous iteration. It is important to note that the feasibility of gradient search is a function of dimensionality because the gradient vector computation time increases quickly with increasing dimensionality.

Another approach to search in multidimensional space employs a randomization of the points where measurements are made. These random search techniques will be examined in four parts: true random search, creeping random search, random search with recalculation, and accelerated random search.

The true random search procedure divides the domain of definition into some finite number of multidimensional cells, say 1000, where the size of the cells and the number tested satisfy the required precision. Next, assume that one of the best 100 cells will satisfy our specifications. Then, if we choose one cell at random, the probability that it is one of the 100 best

---

[*] $\mathbf{x}_{i+1} = \mathbf{x}_i - \alpha_i \nabla f(\mathbf{x}_i)$ is used in step 3 when searching for a minimum.

is 0.1 and the probability that it is not is 0.9. Since each cell to be measured is chosen independently at random, the probability of finding at least one cell in the best 10 percent in n samples is

$$P(10\%) = 1 - (0.9)^n$$

Thus, after 44 samples, the probability of finding at least one cell that satisfies the search is 0.99. First, the chances of finding a cell that satisfies the search procedure increase rapidly with the number of samples, although there is still a finite probability 0.01 that a cell will not be found. A distinct advantage of true random search is that it is independent of the modality of the space being searched.

A modification of the random search uses a nonuniform distribution from which the sample points are selected as the search continues. The initial point is chosen by making a guess, and a nonuniform probability density function is centered on this guess. The consequent samples are then chosen from this distribution, and a cluster of measurements is created. The best of this initial set of samples is then used as the center of a new set of measurements where the same kind of distribution but with a small variance is used to generate a new cluster of points. This process is repeated until the search specifications are satisfied. Thus, the search "creeps" toward the maximum (or minimum) with increasing precision. This process is aptly named creeping random search.

A modification of the creeping random search procedure, which requires the capability of remembering and comparing the present value with the previous value, is random search with recalculation. Here, if the result of a random trial is closer to the maximum/minimum than that of the previous trial, the center of the search distribution is moved to the new point, and random trials are reinitiated. If no point closer than the present center is found in some number of trials, the search is terminated.

The final search technique of interest here is accelerated random search [24], which combines the best characteristics of the previous methods. It is faster than the other search techniques and is especially suited for multimodal as well as unimodal search. This method also requires an initial guess to start the search. However, in this case if a random trial is closer to the maximum/minimum, another step in the same direction is taken, and if this is a better point, another step in the same direction is selected, etc., until no further improvement occurs. Then the process moves back to the last point to cause improvement and commences a random search again. The normal distribution is usually used to select the random points. Also, it is possible here to use steps of increasing length while the search is successful, thereby speeding up the search even more.

SUMMARY

The general formulation of functional models of adaptive, learning, self-organizing, and self-repairing systems has been presented in this chapter. Also, some specific definitions of these terms have been considered.

The homeostat provides us with some historical perspective and a most interesting vehicle for studying the concepts of stability and reliability with respect to our general functional models.

Several techniques for searching a parameter space for a maximum or minimum have been presented. Systems in which these techniques are used are covered in later chapters.

These definitions, models, and search techniques provide us with an excellent basis for studying applications in control, communications, and pattern recognition.

EXERCISES

1. Classify the following behaviors and systems with respect to the definitions presented in this chapter:

   (a) A starfish that loses a "point" and then grows a new one.
   (b) A dual braking system in an automobile.
   (c) An antiskid braking system for a vehicle.
   (d) The AGC (automatic gain control) in radio.
   (e) A position control for a TV antenna which maintains $\pm 5°$ in winds to 100 miles per hour.
   (f) A computer that operates over a temperature range of $0 - 100°$ C.
   (g) A child who at age two can recite the alphabet.
   (h) A football player who, after a serious accident in which he loses a limb, returns as a coach of the team.

2. Find the minimum of $f(x) = 3x^2 - 4x + 1$ over the domain of definition $0 \le x \le 1$, where we want $1/32$ precision by

(a) Dichotomous search.
(b) Fibonacci search.

3. Divide the interval $0 \le x \le 1$ into 32 equal parts. Next, take five coins and lay them out to form a binary register. If all coins are tossed, we get a random sample in the above domain of definition. Perform a random search on the function $f(x) = 3x^2 - 4x + 1$ and compare this technique with the techniques in Exercise 2.

REFERENCES

1. WIENER, Norbert, *Cybernetics*, M.I.T. Press, Cambridge, Mass., 1965.
2. HUXLEY, J., *Evolution: The Modern Synthesis*, Harper & Row, New York, 1943.
3. SHANNON, C. E., "Computers and Automata," *Proceedings of the I.R.E.*, Vol. 41, 1953, pp. 1234–1241.
4. OSGOOD, Charles, *Method and Theory in Experimental Psychology*, Oxford University Press, New York, 1953.
5. KIMBLE, Gregory A., *Principles of General Psychology*, Ronald, New York, 1956.
6. HELSON, Harry, "Adaptation Level Theory," in *Psychology: A Study of a Science, Vol. I*, Sigmund KOCH, ed., McGraw-Hill, New York, 1959, pp. 565–610.
7. WOOLDRIDGE, Dean E., *The Machinery of the Brain*, McGraw-Hill, New York, 1963.
8. SKLANSKY, J., "Adaptation, Learning, Self-Repair, and Feedback," *IEEE Spectrum*, Vol. 1, No. 5, May 1964, pp. 172–174.
9. ASHBY, W. R., *Design for a Brain*, 2nd ed., Wiley, New York, 1960.
10. ZADEH, L. A., "On the Definition of Adaptivity," *Proceedings of the IEEE*, Vol. 51, March 1963, pp. 469–470.
11. SKLANSKY, J., "Adaptation Theory—A Tutorial Introduction to Current Research," *RCA Engineer*, April–May 1965, pp. 24–30.
12. SKLANSKY, J., "Threshold Training of Two-Mode Signal Detection," *IEEE Transactions on Information Theory*, Vol. IT-11, No. 3, July 1965, pp. 353–362.
13. ASHBY, W. R., "Principles of the Self-Organizing System," in *Principles of Self-Organization*, H. VON FOERSTER and G. ZOPF, eds., Pergamon, Elmsford, N.Y., 1962.
14. VON FOERSTER, H., "Environments of Self-Organizing Systems," in *Self-Organizing Systems*, M. YOVITTS and S. CAMERON, eds., Pergamon, Elmsford, N.Y., 1960.

15. ASHBY, W. R., *An Introduction to Cybernetics*, Wiley, New York, 1956.

16. TSYPKIN, Ya Z., "Self-Learning—What Is It?," *IEEE Transactions on Automatic Control*, Vol. AC-13, No. 6, December 1968, pp. 608–612.

17. GILSTRAP, L. O., Jr., "Keys to Developing Machines with High-Level Artificial Intelligence," presented at 1971 Design Engineering Conference and Show, ASME, April 1971, New York, ASME publication 71-DE21.

18. COOPER, L., and D. STEINBERG, *Introduction to Methods of Optimization*, Saunders, Philadelphia, 1970.

19. WILDE, D. J., *Optimum Seeking Methods*, Prentice-Hall, Englewood Cliffs, N.J., 1964.

20. MENDEL, J. M., and K. S. FU, *Adaptive, Learning and Pattern Recognition Systems, Theory and Applications*, Academic Press, New York, 1970.

21. GARDNER, M., *Second Scientific American Book of Mathematical Puzzles and Games*, Simon and Schuster, New York, 1961.

22. DANTZIG, T., *Numbers, the Language of Science*, Free Press, New York, 1954.

23. COXETER, H. S. M., *Introduction to Geometry*, Wiley, New York, 1969.

24. GILSTRAP, L. O., Jr., H. J. COOK, and C. W. ARMSTRONG, "Study of Large Neuromime Networks," *Final Technical Report AFAZ-TR-316, AD 824470*, Adaptronics, Inc., December 1967, McLean, Va.

6

Stochastic Automata Models

In this chapter the stochastic automata concept introduced in Chapter 4 is expanded to include the idea of "variable structure automata," also called "learning automata." Such automata provides the reader with insight into the implementation of intelligent systems as described in previous chapters. Further, in this chapter we will review and establish the foundations for the theory of "learning" stochastic automata, describe four stochastic automata models, and evaluate their performance in terms of their steady-state behavior and their average response time to changes in the environment.

Finally, a word of caution to the reader. Although most of the terminology, notation, and reference material used in this chapter comes from the stochastic automata literature, one should not ignore the parallel efforts in the area of hypothesis testing [1, 2, 3, 4, 5], which played an important role in laying the foundations of "learning" theory.

STOCHASTIC AUTOMATA IN A RANDOM ENVIRONMENT

In an earlier section a stochastic automaton, S_p (also called a probabilistic machine) was described in terms of the 5-tuple

$$S_p = \langle x, \psi, \alpha, \Pi, \sigma \rangle$$

The description of this stochastic automaton will now be slightly modified to introduce the notion of variable-structure automata [7]. That is, a stochastic automata, S, is described by the 6-tuple

$$S = \langle x, \Psi, \alpha, P, T, G \rangle$$

where

1. x is the input set that, for the purposes of this chapter, characterizes the automata models as follows:

    (a) If the input set x is binary, $\{0, 1\}$, the automata model is classified as a P-model.
    (b) If x belongs to the finite set $\{x_1, x_2, \ldots, x_k\}$ with elements in the interval $[0, 1]$, the automata is classified as a Q-model.
    (c) If x is a real number in the interval $[0, 1]$, the automata is classified as an S-model.

2. Ψ is the set of s internal states $\{\phi_1, \phi_2, \phi_3, \ldots, \phi_s\}$ where $s < \infty$ corresponds in some sense to the memory capacity of a finite automaton.

3. $\alpha = \{\alpha_1, \alpha_2, \ldots, \alpha_r\}$ is the output or action set with $r \leq s$, which implies that it is possible for states to exist that cannot be distinguished from the values of the output variable.

4. P is the state probability vector governing the choice of action in each state at time n. That is, $P(n) = [p_1(n), \ldots, p_r(n)]'$, where $p_i(n)$ is the probability of selecting action α_i at time $t = n$.*

5. T is an algorithm, also called an updating or reinforcement scheme, that generates $P(n + 1)$ from $P(n)$.

6. G is the output function that defines the value of the output variable α in each state of the automaton. G may be a stochastic function, but there is no loss of generality in assuming it to be deterministic.

This automaton operates in a random environment with random response characteristics. The environment accepts inputs from a set $\alpha = \{\alpha_1, \ldots, \alpha_r\}$ and produces outputs belonging to the set x.

---

* In our model, the time, t, is considered to be a discrete variable such that $x(t)$, $\psi(t)$, and $\alpha(t)$, respectively, represent the input, state, and output of the system at the instant t.

Corresponding to every input α_i there is an associated probability set, C, called the penalty probability set, where

$$C = \{C_1, \ldots, C_r\}$$

and

$$C_i = P_R\{x = 1 | \alpha = \alpha_i\}$$

for P-models, and

$$C = \{C_{ij}; i = 1, 2, \ldots, r; j = 1, 2, \ldots, k\}$$

where

$$C_{ij} = P_R\{x = x_j | \alpha = \alpha_i\}$$

for Q-models. If the set $C(t)$ is constant and independent of time, the environment is said to be stationary.

Figure 6.1a indicates the features of a stochastic automaton and Figure 6.1b that of a random environment, while Figure 6.1c shows a stochastic automaton and a random environment in a feedback configuration. This is very similar to the machine, environment, critic (MEC) model developed by Sklansky [6] in his study of learning systems. In this case, the actions of the automaton become the inputs to the environment. The responses of the environment, in turn, are the inputs to the automaton and, for variable-structure automata, influence the updating of the action probabilities, $P(n)$. Figure 6.2 shows the same stochastic automaton for a P-model, and Figure 6.3 for a Q-model.

Here we are particularly interested in stochastic automata models in which the action probability vector, $P(n)$, and consequently the state transition probabilities, $\pi(n)$, change with time. These automata models, also called learning automata, have the property that $P(n)$ is modified on the basis of the input sequence $x(n)$ in such a way that their performance improves in some specified sense.

Of the four classes of automata models we shall discuss, both the Linear Reward-Inaction (L_{R-I}) and Linear Reward-Penalty (L_{R-P}) automata are learning automata, whereas the Tsetlin and Cover-Hellman automata are not. This can easily be verified from Figures 6.4, 6.5, and 6.6.

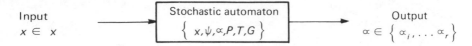

Figure 6.1a.   Stochastic automaton.

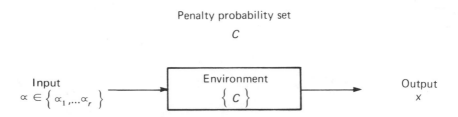

Figure 6.1b.   Random environment.

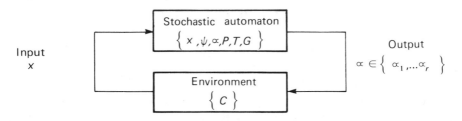

Figure 6.1c.   Feedback configuration.

Figure 6.1.   Stochastic automaton operating in a random environment.

Figures 6.4a and 6.4b present the corresponding finite state approximation (examined further in later sections) to the L_{R-I} and L_{R-P} automata. Notice from the figures that we have shown that the action probabilities, $p_i(n) = P_R\{$action α_i is selected$\}$, change with time. In contrast, it is clear from Figures 6.5 and 6.6 that the action probabilities for the Tsetlin and

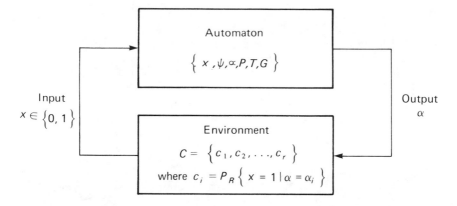

Figure 6.2.   *P*-model.

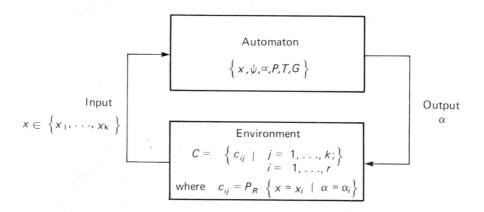

Figure 6.3.   *Q*-model.

Cover-Hellman automata are constant and independent of time. A discussion of the Tsetlin automaton is included in this chapter because of the underlying simplicity of its structure, and the Cover-Hellman automaton is presented to familiarize the reader with the desirable ϵ-optimality property of automata models.

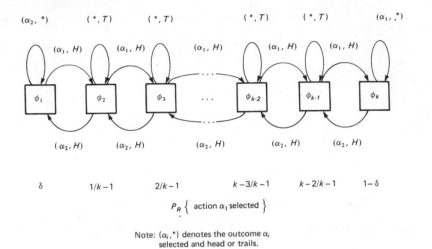

Note: $(\alpha_i, *)$ denotes the outcome α_i selected and head or trails.

Figure 6.4a. Finite state approximation of the L_{R-I} automaton.

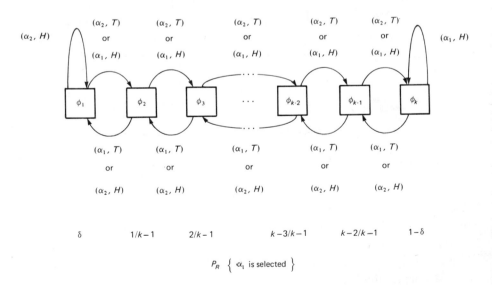

Figure 6.4b. Finite state approximation of the L_{R-P} automaton with $a = b$.

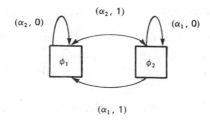

Figure 6.5a.   Tsetlin's automaton. $(\propto_i, 1)$ signifies the event "penalty received, action $\propto_1$ selected."

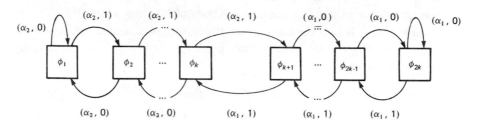

Figure 6.5b.   Tsetlin's $2k$ state automaton.

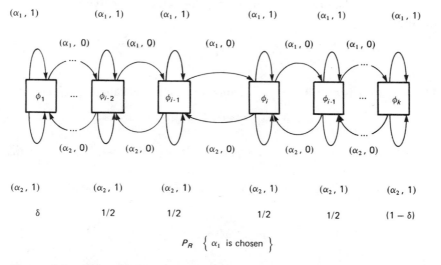

$P_R \left\{ \alpha_1 \text{ is chosen} \right\}$

Figure 6.6.   Cover-Hellman automaton.

EXPEDIENCY, OPTIMALITY, AND ϵ-OPTIMALITY

In order to present a complete description of the four classes of automata to be introduced in the next section, we first must consider some basic definitions regarding their behavior while operating in a random environment.

It is of special interest, for example, to understand the measures that have been used in the past to evaluate the performance of learning automata models. One of the most useful of these measures has been the "average penalty" received by the automaton, together with the asymptotic behavior of this average penalty. Let us now review these and other measures used in evaluating the performance of learning automata.

Expediency: If at a certain time, n, the automaton selects the action α_i with probability $p_i(n)$, then the average penalty received by the automaton conditioned on $P(n)$ is

$$M(n) = E\{x(n)|P(n)\}$$
$$= \sum_{i=1}^{r} p_i(n)c_i \tag{6.1}$$

However, if no a priori information is available and the actions are chosen with equal probability (i.e., at random), the value of the average penalty is denoted by M_0 and is given by

$$M_0 = \sum_{i=1}^{r} \frac{1}{r}c_i = \frac{c_1 + c_2 + \cdots + c_r}{r}$$

Definition 6.1 is as follows: A learning automaton is called *expedient** if,

$$\lim_{n \to \infty} E[M(n)] < M_0$$

When a learning automaton is expedient, it performs better than one that selects its actions in a purely random manner.

Optimality: Definition 6.2 is as follows: A learning automaton is called *optimal* if

$$\lim_{n \to \infty} E\{M(n)\} = c_l \tag{6.2}$$

---

* $p_i(n)$, $\lim p_i(n)$, and $M(n)$ are, in general, random variables. Hence, the expectation operator is needed in the definition to represent the average penalty.

where

$$c_l = \min\{c_1, c_2, \ldots, c_r\}$$

Therefore, optimality means that asymptotically, $M(n)$, the average penalty, achieves its minimum value as shown in Figure 6.7 for the P-model with only two actions (i.e., $r = 2$).

We now present an equivalent definition to the optimality criterion in Definition 6.2. This alternate or equivalent definition is very useful in the analysis of reinforcement algorithms and in establishing the relationships

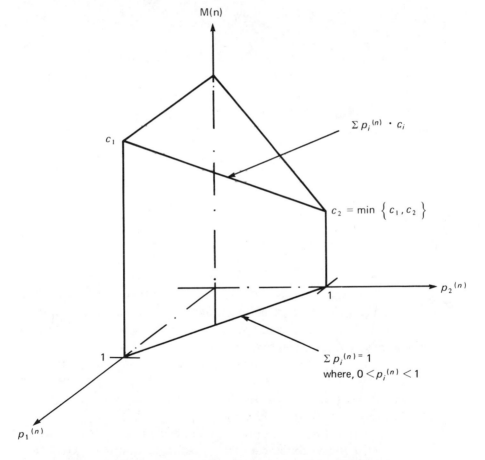

Figure 6.7. Graphic representation of the "optimality" criterion.

between expediency, optimality, and the classic measures of convergence (for example, convergence on the mean or convergence in probability). Definition 6.3: A learning automaton is called *optimal* if

$$\lim_{n \to \infty} E\{p_l(n)\} = 1 \tag{6.3}$$

where

$$p_l(n) = P_R\{\alpha(n) = \alpha_l\}$$

and where

$$c_l = \min \{c_1, c_2, \ldots, c_r\}$$

It can be shown that Definitions 6.2 and 6.3 are equivalent [15].

Furthermore, in the sense of Definition 6.3, the action probabilities $p_i(n)$, $i = 1, 2, \ldots, r$ are sequences of random variables $\{p_i(n)\}_{n=1}^{\infty}$, $i = 1$, $2, \ldots, r$ *converging in the mean* to random variables 0 or 1 depending on the value of i. That is,

$p_i(n)$, $n = 1, 2, \ldots, i \neq l$ converges in the mean

to random variable 0, or $E|p_i(n) - 0| \to 0$ as $n \to \infty$;

and

$p_l(n)$, $n = 1, 2, \ldots,$ converges in the mean

to random variable 1, or $E|p_l(n) - 1| \to 0$ as $n \to \infty$.

In the past, and due in part Definition 6.2, there has been some confusion in using the concept of an optimal automaton. For example, it has been contended that since $E\{p_l(n)\} \to 1$ as $n \to \infty$ and $E\{p_l(n)\}$ is bounded above by unity, then $p_l(n) \to 1$ as $n \to \infty$. In general, this is false. If true, it would mean that convergence in the mean implies convergence in probability, which is a false statement. Such fallacious arguments can now be avoided, given the alternate definition of optimality, Definition 6.3.

ϵ-*Optimality*: Although optimality appears to be a very desirable property, certain conditions of a given situation may preclude its achievement. In such cases, suboptimal performance is desirable. One such suboptimal behavior that has received considerable attention in the literature is ϵ-optimality as given in Definition 6.4: A learning automaton is called ϵ-*optimal* if

$$\lim_{\delta \to 0} \lim_{n \to \infty} E\{M(n)\} = c_l \tag{6.4}$$

where δ is a parameter of the reinforcement algorithm.

ϵ-optimality means that the performance of the automaton can be made as close to optimal as desired.

AUTOMATA CLASSES

Having presented the different performance measures previously used to evaluate learning automata, we now focus on the structure of each automata class and on its corresponding reinforcement algorithm as the means of achieving the desired performance.

Variable-Structure Automata

The basic idea behind any reinforcement scheme is rather simple. If a learning automaton selects an action α_i at instant n and a nonpenalty input occurs, the action probability $p_i(n)$ is increased, and all other components of $P(n)$ are decreased. For a penalty input, $p_i(n)$ is decreased and the other components are increased. These changes in $p_i(n)$ are known as reward and penalty, respectively. In some models, the action probabilities do not change; for these cases, the term "inaction" has been coined.

In general, if action α_i is selected at stage n, and

1. $x(n) = 0$ [nonpenalty], then:

$$p_j(n + 1) = p_j(n) - f_j[P(n)] \quad \forall j \neq i$$
$$p_i(n + 1) = p_i(n) + \sum_{j \neq i} f_j[P(n)]$$

or,

2. $x(n) = 1$ [penalty], then: $\qquad\qquad$ (6.5)

$$p_j(n + 1) = p_j(n) + g_j[P(n)] \quad \forall j \neq i$$
$$p_i(n + 1) = p_i(n) - \sum_{j \neq i} g_j[P(n)]$$

where f and g are nonnegative continuous functions. Further-more, the usual restrictions

$$0 < p_i(n) < 1$$

and

$$\sum_{\forall i} p_i(n) = 1$$

on the values of $P(n)$ are required. The reason for limiting the values of $P(n)$ between 0 and 1 exclusively is to avoid reaching an absorbing state prematurely.

Notice that if f_j and g_j are linear functions of $P(n)$, the reinforcement algorithm is called linear. Both linear and nonlinear reinforcement schemes have been proposed in the literature. However, earlier studies [7, 8, 9] have shown no significant difference in the performance, as far as expediency and ϵ-optimality, of nonlinear algorithms versus linear algorithms operating in stationary environments. For this reason and for simplicity, only linear algorithms are considered here.

Linear Reward-Inaction: The basic idea of the Linear Reward-Inaction (L_{R-I}) scheme is to increase the probability of selecting an action resulting in nonpenalty and inaction (no change) if a penalty results. For the L_{R-I} algorithm, we want to let $f_j[P(n)] = ap_j(n)$ and $g_j[P(n)] = 0$ for all j where $0 < a < 1$ in Equation 6.5. With these restrictions Equation 6.5 becomes

1. $x(n) = 0$ [nonpenalty]

$$p_j(n + 1) = p_j(n) - ap_j(n) \quad \forall j \neq i$$
$$p_i(n + 1) = p_i(n) + a[\sum_{j \neq i} p_j(n)]$$

2. $x(n) = 1$ [penalty] $\hspace{3cm}$ (6.6)

$$p_j(n + 1) = p_j(n) \quad \forall j$$

Linear Reward-Penalty: In the case of the Linear Reward-Penalty (L_{R-P}), a nonpenalty response from the environment increases the probability of the selected action, whereas a penalty reduces it. That is, if in Equation 6.5 we set

$$f_j[P(n)] = ap_j(n)$$

and

$$g_j[P(n)] = \frac{b}{(r-1)} - bp_j(n)$$

where

$$0 < a, b < 1,$$

then we have

1. $x(n) = 0$ [nonpenalty]

$$p_j(n + 1) = p_j(n) - ap_j(n) \quad \forall j \neq i$$

$$p_i(n + 1) = p_i(n) + a[\sum_{j \neq i}^{r} p_j(n)]$$

2. $x(n) = 1$ [penalty] $\hspace{5cm}$ (6.7)

$$p_j(n + 1) = p_j(n) + \left[\frac{b}{(r-1)} - bp_j(n)\right] \quad \forall j \neq i$$

$$p_i(n + 1) = p_i(n) - \sum_{j \neq i}^{r} \left[\frac{b}{(r-1)} - bp_j(n)\right]$$

Tsetlin Automaton: In his original work [10], Tsetlin considered a finite automaton in a random environment. In its simplest form (i.e., $r = 2$), the automaton chooses one action α_1 for as long as it results in a nonpenalty response from the environment. If the action results in a penalty response, the automaton switches over to action α_2. Figure 6.5a illustrates the structure of such an automaton by means of a state diagram.

Some well-known results for this automaton are summarized as follows:

1. The behavior of such an automaton operating in a stationary random environment is described by a Markov chain.

2. If the Markov chain is ergodic, the final probabilities of the two
    actions can be established as follows:

$$p_1(\infty) = P_R\{\alpha = \alpha_1\} = \frac{c_1}{c_1 + c_2}$$

$$p_2(\infty) = P_R\{\alpha = \alpha_2\} = \frac{c_2}{c_1 + c_2}$$

3. A Tsetlin automaton is expedient, since

$$M(\infty) = \frac{2c_1 c_2}{c_1 + c_2} \leq \frac{1}{2}(c_1 + c_2) = M_0$$

Tsetlin also considered the two-action automaton with $2k$ states,
shown in Figure 6.5b. In this case, the output function can be described as
follows:

$$\alpha(n) = G[\psi(n)] = \begin{cases} \alpha_1 \text{ if } \phi(n) \in \{\phi_{k+1}, \dots, \phi_{2k}\} \\ \alpha_2 \text{ if } \phi(n) \in \{\phi_1, \dots, \phi_k\} \end{cases}$$

Tsetlin showed that this $2k$ state automaton was ϵ-optimal. That is,

$$\lim_{k \to \infty} \lim_{n \to \infty} E\{p_l(n)\} = 1$$

for all stationary environments with $c_2 \leq 1/2$.

Cover-Hellman Automaton: Cover and Hellman [4] considered the two-
action automaton with K states, shown in Figure 6.6. This automaton was
allowed to remember only a finite k-valued statistic (each state has a
corresponding value associated with it) that summarizes past experience.
Cover and Hellman showed that:

1. Each and every k-state automata operating in an environment
    with $c_1 + c_2 < 1$ have an asymptotic average penalty bounded by
    $1 - (\gamma^{k-1}/(\gamma^{k-1} + 1))$. Or

$$\lim_{n \to \infty} E\{M(n)\} \leq 1 - \frac{\gamma^{k-1}}{\gamma^{k-1} + 1} \tag{6.8}$$

    where

$$\gamma = \text{MAX} \left\{ \frac{c_1}{c_2}, \frac{c_2}{c_1} \right\}$$

2.   The k-state automaton depicted in Figure 6.6 is ϵ-optimal, that is,

$$\lim_{\delta \to 0} \lim_{n \to \infty} M(n) = c_t$$

Note that for the k-state automaton of Figure 6.6, the output function $G(\psi(n))$ is given by Equation 6.9:

$$\alpha(n) = G(\psi(n))$$

$$= \begin{cases} \alpha_1 \text{ with prob } \delta, \text{ if } \psi(n) = \phi, \\ \alpha_2 \text{ with prob } (1 - \delta), \text{ if } \psi(n) = \phi_1 \\ \alpha_1 \text{ with prob } (1 - \delta), \text{ if } \psi(n) = \phi_k \\ \alpha_2 \text{ with prob } \delta, \text{ if } \psi(n) = \phi_k \\ \alpha_1, \alpha_2 \text{ with equal probability, if } \psi(n) \neq \{\phi_1, \phi_k\} \end{cases} \qquad (6.9)$$

RANDOM WALK MODELS

To evaluate these four classes of automata models in terms of their potential as task schedulers in a multiple-processor system and/or as link selectors in a communications network, we shall characterize their behavior in terms of random walks and Markov chains. Unless otherwise specified, the characterization and all discussions in this section are limited to P-models with $r = 2$.

Let us first consider an infinite coin-tossing experiment described as follows. Every T seconds, a coin (action) from a finite set is selected in accordance with some distribution function, and it is tossed (an action is taken). Both the outcome of the tossing and the coin selected are recorded.

Now, if $\alpha = \{\alpha_1, \alpha_2, \ldots, \alpha_r\}$ represents the finite set of coins, and if a one-to-one correspondence between the sequences $\{T, 2T, 3T, \ldots\}$ and $Z^+ = \{1, 2, 3, \ldots\}$ (the set of positive integers) is established, then the set of outcomes at every stage of the experiment is given by Equation 6.10:

$$\Omega_n = \{\omega = (\alpha, x) \mid \alpha \in \{\alpha_1, \ldots, \alpha_r\}, x \in \{\text{Heads, Tails}\} \qquad (6.10)$$

Also, the sample space for the experiment is

$$\Omega = \Omega_1 \, x\Omega_2 \, x\Omega_3 \, x \cdots.$$

If we further restrict our attention to P-models with $r = 2$, then Equation 6.10 simplifies as follows:

$$\Omega_n = \{(\alpha_1, H), (\alpha_1, T), (\alpha_2, H), (\alpha_2, T)\}$$

Furthermore, assume in this experiment that every time action α_1 is chosen, a particle lying in the interval $[0, m]$ takes one step upwards or downwards depending on the outcome of the toss. If action α_2 is chosen, the particle takes steps in the opposite direction from those for α_1. The step size in this description is not constant; it is a function of the position of the particle at stage n. Also, let $Y(n)$ be the position of the particle nT seconds after the tossing started. Clearly, $Y(n)$ depends on the experimental outcome (i.e., on the particular sequence of actions selected and on the tosses) and the stage number. $Y(n)$ can thus be described as a *discrete time stochastic process, or a random sequence.*[*] This random sequence corresponds to a random walk in the interval $[0, m]$.

Figure 6.8 illustrates one realization of this process for a unit step size. Random walks such as $Y(n)$ have been widely studied in the past [12, 13] and are best described in terms of Markov chains. Hence, by fitting the learning automata to this general model, we shall be able to make use of known results from Markov chain theory.

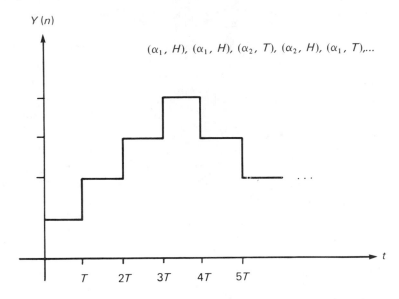

Figure 6.8. Coin-tossing experiment characterized in terms of random walks.

---

[*] Random sequences are usually denoted by subscripts, for example, Y_n. However, for the purpose of this chapter and to avoid confusion with the components of a vector in multidimensional random walks, we use the notation $Y(n)$.

First, consider Tsetlin's automaton as discussed before, and establish a one-to-one correspondence between the set, ψ, of automaton states and the finite set of points

$$\left\{0, \frac{1}{2k-1}, \frac{2}{2k-1}, \ldots, \frac{2k-2}{2k-1}, 1\right\}$$

in the interval $[0, 1]$ as follows:

$$\text{function: } \phi_i \rightarrow \frac{i-1}{2k-1}$$

Furthermore, let $x(n)$ denote a random variable whose range is in the finite set $\{+1, -1\}$, and depends on the result of the experiment at stage number n, as follows:

$$x(n) = \begin{cases} +1 \text{ if } \omega \,\epsilon\{(\alpha_1, H), (\alpha_2, T)\} \\ -1 \text{ if } \omega \,\epsilon\{(\alpha_2, H), (\alpha_1, T)\} \end{cases}$$

Also, let $\gamma = Y(0)$ denote the initial position of the particle. Then, the position of the particle nT seconds after the tossing started is given by Equation 6.11:

$$Y(n) = \gamma + \frac{x(1) + x(2) + \cdots + x(n)}{2K - 1} \tag{6.11}$$

The automaton then performs a random walk in the interval $[0, 1]$ with step size Δ equal to $1/(2k - 1)$. A particular realization of this process is given in Figure 6.9. In addition, associated with each random variable $Y(n)$ in the sequence $\{Y(n)\}_1^\infty$ is a distribution function $\sigma(n)$, which corresponds to the state probability distribution function, i.e.,

$$\sigma(n) = [\sigma_1(n)\sigma_2(n) \cdots \sigma_{2k}(n)] \tag{6.12}$$

where

$$\sigma_i(n) = P_R\left[Y(n) = \frac{i-1}{2k-1}\right] = P_R[\psi(n) = \phi_i]$$

This discrete distribution function plays an important role in the ensuing analysis of automata models. Specifically, the limiting behavior of Equation 6.12 will serve as a performance measure among these models.

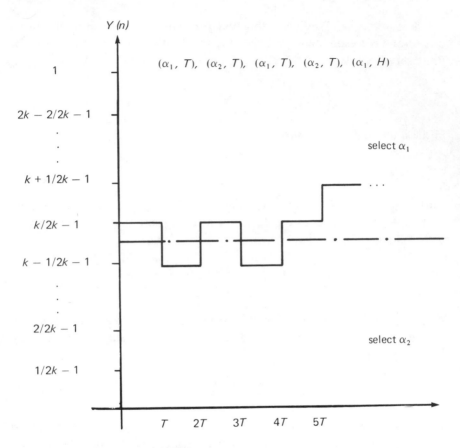

Figure 6.9.   Tsetlin's 2k automaton—one random walk realization.

Note that for Tsetlin's automaton, the output function governing the choice of actions is a deterministic function of the particle's position at stage n as given below:

$$\alpha(n) = G[\psi(n)] = G[X(n)] = \begin{cases} \alpha_1 \text{ if } Y(n) \in (1/2, 1] \\ \alpha_2 \text{ if } Y(n) \in [0, 1/2] \end{cases}$$

For stationary environments—that is, the set $\mathbf{C} = \{C_i | i = 1, 2\}$, where $C_i = P_R\{T | \mathbf{a}(n) = \alpha_i\}$ is constant and independent of n—the one-dimensional random walk is described by a homogeneous Markov chain with one-step transition probabilities given by Equation 6.13.

$$
\Pi =
\begin{array}{c}
\\
1\\
2\\
\vdots\\
k\\
k+1\\
\vdots\\
2k-1\\
2k
\end{array}
\begin{array}{c}
\begin{array}{ccccccccccc}
1 & 2 & 3 & & (k-1) & k & (k+1) & (k+2) & \cdots & (2k-2) & (2k-1) & 2k
\end{array}\\
\left[
\begin{array}{ccccccccccc}
(1-C_2) & C_2 & 0 & \cdots & 0 & 0 & 0 & 0 & & 0 & 0 & 0\\
(1-C_2) & 0 & C_2 & & 0 & 0 & 0 & 0 & & 0 & 0 & 0\\
0 & 0 & 0 & & 0 & 0 & 0 & 0 & & 0 & 0 & 0\\
0 & 0 & 0 & & (1-C_2) & 0 & C_2 & 0 & \cdots & 0 & 0 & 0\\
0 & 0 & 0 & & 0 & C_1 & 0 & (1-C_1) & & 0 & 0 & 0\\
0 & 0 & 0 & & 0 & 0 & 0 & 0 & & 0 & 0 & 0\\
0 & 0 & 0 & & 0 & 0 & 0 & 0 & & C_1 & 0 & (1-C_1)\\
0 & 0 & 0 & & 0 & 0 & 0 & 0 & & 0 & C_1 & (1-C_1)
\end{array}
\right]
\end{array}
\tag{6.13}
$$

In general [11], if the initial state probability distribution functions $\sigma(0)$ and the one-step transition probabilities of a homogeneous Markov chain are known, then the state probability distribution function $\sigma(n)$ can be uniquely determined by Equation 6.14*:

$$\sigma(n) = \sigma(0)\Pi^n \tag{6.14}$$

In a manner similar to the discussion for the Tsetlin automaton, the behavior of the Cover-Hellman automaton can be described by a particle taking a random walk in the interval $[0, 1]$ with step size Δ equal to $1/(k - 1)$, as shown in Figure 6.10 for a specific realization of the process. In this case, and for stationary environments, the random walk for the Cover-Hellman automaton is described by a homogeneous Markov chain with one-step transition probabilities given by Equation 6.15.

Next, consider the behavior of the L_{R-I} automaton for a P-model with $r = 2$. The reinforcement scheme of Equation 6.6 becomes

1. $\alpha(n) = \alpha_1$ and 0 [nonpenalty]

$$p_1(n + 1) = p_1(n) + ap_2(n)$$
$$= (1 - a)p_1(n) + a$$
$$p_2(n + 1) = (1 - a)p_2(n)$$

2. $\alpha(n) = \alpha_1$ and 1 [penalty] $\tag{6.16}$

$$p_1(n + 1) = p_1(n)$$

However, $p_2(n) = [1 - p_1(n)]$. Hence, let $p_1(n) = p(n)$, and from Equation 6.16 we have

---

* The state probability distribution function is not to be confused with the probability of selecting action at stage n, i.e.,

$$P(n) = [p_1(n)p_2(n)]$$

where,

$$p_i(n) = P_R\{\alpha(n) = \alpha_i\} \quad i = 1, 2$$

$$\Pi = \begin{array}{c} \\ 1 \\ 2 \\ \vdots \\ k-1 \\ k \end{array}
\begin{array}{c}
\begin{array}{cccccccc} \;\;1 & \;\;\;\;2 & \;\;3 & \cdots & (k-2) & (k-1) & \;\;k \end{array} \\
\left[\begin{array}{cccccc}
\delta C_1 + (1-\delta) & \delta(1-C_1) & 0 & & 0 & 0 & 0 \\[2mm]
\dfrac{(1-C_2)}{2} & \dfrac{C_1+C_2}{2} & \dfrac{(1-C_1)}{2} & & 0 & 0 & 0 \\[3mm]
0 & 0 & 0 & & \dfrac{(1-C_2)}{2} & \dfrac{C_1+C_2}{2} & \dfrac{1-C_1}{2} \\[3mm]
0 & 0 & 0 & & 0 & \delta(1-C_2) & \delta C_2 + (1-\delta)
\end{array} \right]
\end{array}$$

$$(6.15)$$

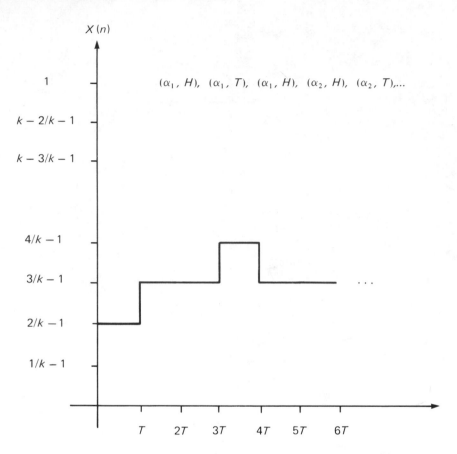

Figure 6.10.   Cover-Hellman automaton—one random walk realization.

$$p(n + 1) = \begin{cases} (1 - a)p(n) + a & \text{if } \omega \in \{(\alpha_1, H)\} \\ (1 - a)p(n) & \text{if } \omega \in \{(\alpha_2, H)\} \\ p(n) & \text{if } \omega \in \{(\alpha_1, T), (\alpha_2, T)\} \end{cases} \quad (6.17)$$

The updating of the action probabilities as given in Equation 6.15 can be thought of as describing the one-step transition probabilities in the position of a particle that undergoes a random walk in the interval $[0, 1]$. In this case, the random walk has two absorbing barriers at positions 0 and 1. In other words, $p(n) = 1(0)$; from Equations 6.17 and 6.18 it is easily verified that the automaton selects action $\alpha_1(\alpha_2)$ continuously.

Along these lines, there is a one-to-one correspondence between the position of the particle nT seconds after the tossing started, $Y(n)$, and $P(n)$.* Intuitively, this corresponds to the fact that for variable-structure automata (L_{R-I} and L_{R-P} models), the action probability vector, $P(n)$, carries all the information about past responses.

The selection of actions at each stage n is given by Equation 6.18. This means that the output function G is random in terms of the position of the particle at stage n.

$$\boldsymbol{\alpha}(n) = G(Y(n)) = G(P(n)) = \begin{cases} \alpha_1 \text{ with prob } p(n) \\ \alpha_2 \text{ with prob } 1 - p(n) \end{cases} \quad (6.18)$$

Figure 6.11a depicts the behavior of such an automaton for a specific realization of the process $[Y(n)]_1^\infty$ or $[P(n)]_1^\infty$. Note that in this random walk, the step size, $\Delta p(n)$, is proportional to the maximum possible gain or maximum possible loss as shown in Figure 6.11b. That is, $1 - p(n)$ represents the maximum possible increase and $-p(n)$ the maximum possible decrease in the position of the particle at stage number n. This follows since 1 and 0 are the largest and smallest values for $p(n + 1)$.

The fact that the step size $\Delta p(n)$ is not constant and is proportional to either $1 - p(n)$ or $p(n)$ implies that the number of states visited is infinite. This is equivalent to saying that $p(n)$ can be stored to infinite precision. Discussion of the functionality of such an approach follows.

Finite State Approximation to L_{R-I}

Although the L_{R-I} automaton performance is theoretically ϵ-optimal [13] in practice the value $p(n)$ can be stored only to finite precision, which destroys this ϵ-optimal characteristic. Moreover, to present valid comparisons, all automata must operate under the same constraints. For this reason, we now present a finite state approximation to the L_{R-I} and L_{R-P} models.

Assume that $p(n)$ is stored as a k-valued quantity belonging to the set $\{0, 1/k - 1, \ldots, k - 2/k - 1, 1\}$.

As before, $p(n)$ corresponds to the position of the particle nT seconds after the tossing started and can be thought of as the state, $\psi(n)$, of the automaton at stage n. Then, L_{R-I} takes a random walk in the interval $[0, 1]$

---

* Note that $P(n)$ and $p(n)$ are used interchangeably throughout this section. For models with $r = 2$, no confusion should arise.

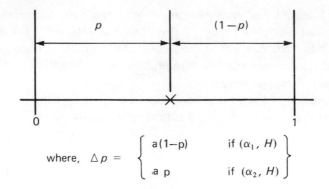

$$\text{where,} \quad \triangle p = \left\{ \begin{array}{ll} a(1-p) & \text{if } (\alpha_1, H) \\ a\,p & \text{if } (\alpha_2, H) \end{array} \right\}$$

Figure 6.11a.   One realization of an L_{R-I} random walk.

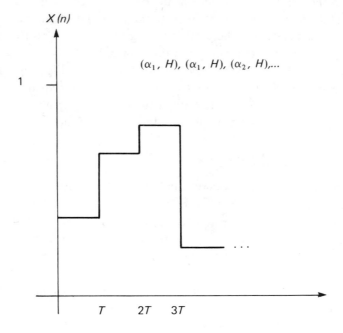

Figure 6.11b.   Step size for L_{R-I}.

Figure 6.11.   Characterization of L_{R-I} in terms of random walks.

in accordance with Equation 6.17. This leads to successive values of $p(n)$ and which, in general, are not restricted to the finite set $\{0, 1/k - 1, \ldots, k - 2/k - 1, 1\}$ creating, for stationary environments, a denumerably infinite Markov chain.

Nevertheless, it has been shown [14] that the L_{R-I} automaton achieves the ϵ-optimal behavior as $a \to 0$. That is, asymptotically, as $n \to \infty$, the probability of converging to the "inferior" action can be made arbitrarily small. Fortunately, for small values of a, the transitions described by Equation 6.17 are to neighboring values in the finite set $\{0, 1/k - 1, \ldots, k - 2/k - 1, 1\}$. Hence, the L_{R-I} automaton can be described in terms of a finite state approximation as follows. Consider an urn that contains l black balls and $k - l - 1$ red balls. A ball is drawn from the urn at random. If the ball is black, choose action α_1; otherwise, choose α_2. The ball is then replaced, and the coin corresponding to the action is tossed. If heads, then A balls of the same color as the one picked and B balls of the opposite color are added. If tails, C balls of the same color as the one picked and D balls of the opposite color are added. The experiment is then repeated. A, B, C, D are arbitrary integers.

For the L_{R-I} model, the values of A, B, C, and D are $+1$, -1, 0, and 0. Stated simply, this finite state approximation restricts the values of $p(n)(Y(n))$ to the set $\{0, 1/k - 1, \ldots, k - 2/k - 1, 1\}$ and forces the step size to a constant value independent of stage number $\Delta p(n) = \Delta = 1/(k - 1)$. Under this restriction, the structure of the L_{R-I} automaton is best described by Figure 6.4a and by the following equations:

$$\psi(n) = \{0, 1/k - 1, \ldots, k - 2/k - 1, 1\} \text{ or}$$

$$\text{function: } \phi_i \to \frac{i - 1}{k - 1}$$

$$p(n) = y(n) = \gamma(0) + \frac{x(1) + x(2) + \cdots + x(n)}{k - 1}$$

where

$$x(n) = \begin{cases} +1 & \text{if } \omega \in [(\alpha_1, H)] \\ 0 & \text{if } \omega \in [(\alpha_1, T), (\alpha_2, T)] \\ -1 & \text{if } \omega \in [(\alpha_2, H)] \end{cases}$$

$$\sigma(n) = [\sigma_1(n)\sigma_2(n) \cdots \sigma_k(n)]$$

where

$$\sigma_i(n) = P_R\left[p(n) = Y(n) = \frac{i-1}{k-1}\right] = P_R[\psi(n) = \phi_i]$$

For stationary environments, the one-step transition probabilities are given by Equation 6.19.

The random walk characterization of the L_{R-P} model follows that for the L_{R-I} model. Hence, we shall note only differences between the two models. First, the L_{R-P} automaton is described by Equation 6.20:

$$p(n+1) = \begin{cases} (1-a)p(n) + a & \text{if } \omega \in [(\alpha_1, H)] \\ (1-b)p(n) & \text{if } \omega \in [(\alpha_1, T)] \\ (1-a)p(n) & \text{if } \omega \in [(\alpha_2, H)] \\ (1-b)p(n) + b & \text{if } \omega \in [(\alpha_2, T)] \end{cases} \tag{6.20}$$

As in L_{R-I} the selection of actions is governed by Equation 6.18. However, Equation 6.20 describes a random walk in the interval $[0, 1]$ with reflecting barriers at 0 and 1. In addition, the step size, $\Delta p(n)$, is different from L_{R-I} and it is given by Equation 6.21.

$$\Delta p(n) = \begin{cases} a(1-p) & \text{if } \omega \in [(\alpha_1, H)] \\ bp & \text{if } \omega \in [(\alpha_1, T)] \\ ap & \text{if } \omega \in [(\alpha_2, H)] \\ b(1-p) & \text{if } \omega \in [(\alpha_2, T)] \end{cases} \tag{6.21}$$

For stationary environments, the L_{R-P} automaton is described by a denumerably infinite Markov chain. For the same reasons as before, a finite state approximation to this process is needed.

However, for the L_{R-P} automaton, a finite state approximation is possible only in the simplest of cases, that is, if the "learning" constants a and b are equal. For this case, the behavior of the automaton is described by Equation 6.22:

$$p(n+1) = \begin{cases} (1-a)p(n) + a & \text{if } \omega \in [(\alpha_1, H), (\alpha_2, T)] \\ (1-a)p(n) & \text{if } \omega \in [(\alpha_1, T), (\alpha_2, H)] \end{cases} \tag{6.22}$$

Furthermore, if $(1 - a)$ is taken to be as large as possible, then transitions

$$
\Pi =
\begin{array}{c|cccccccc}
 & 1 & 2 & 3 & 4 & \cdots & (k-2) & (k-1) & k \\
\hline
1 & \delta C_1+(1-\delta) & \dfrac{\delta(1-C_1)}{k-1} & 0 & 0 & \cdots & 0 & 0 & 0 \\[2ex]
2 & \dfrac{(k-2)(1-C_2)}{k-1} & \dfrac{C_1+(k-2)C_2}{k-1} & \dfrac{(1-C_1)}{k-1} & 0 & \cdots & 0 & 0 & 0 \\[2ex]
3 & 0 & \dfrac{(k-3)(1-C_2)}{k-1} & \dfrac{2C_1+(k-3)C_2}{k-1} & \dfrac{2(1-C_1)}{k-1} & \cdots & 0 & 0 & 0 \\[2ex]
\vdots & & & & & \cdots & & & \\[1ex]
k-1 & 0 & 0 & 0 & 0 & \cdots & \dfrac{(1-C_2)}{k-1} & \dfrac{C_2+(k-2)C_1}{k-1} & \dfrac{(1-C_1)}{k-1} \\[2ex]
k & 0 & 0 & 0 & 0 & \cdots & 0 & \delta(1-C_2) & \delta C_2+(1-\delta)
\end{array}
\tag{6.19}
$$

in Equation 6.22 are restricted to neighboring values in the set

$$\{0, 1/k - 1, \ldots, k - 2/k - 1, 1\}.$$

In this case, the L_{R-P} is described in terms of a finite state approximation as before, with values of A, B, C, and D equal to $+1$, -1, -1, and $+1$, respectively. Hence, the L_{R-P} finite state approximation structure is described by Figure 6.4b and by the following equation:

$$x(n) = \begin{cases} +1 & \text{if } \omega \epsilon [(\alpha_1, H), (\alpha_2, T)] \\ -1 & \text{if } \omega \epsilon [(\alpha_1, T), (\alpha_2, H)] \end{cases}$$

For stationary environments, the one-step transition probabilities are given by Equation 6.23.

ANALYSIS OF LEARNING AUTOMATA MODELS

The behavior of the automata models presented earlier has been widely studied in stationary environments [11]. It is precisely in nonstationary environments, however, that adaptive and learning models such as those presented earlier will prove most attractive. Few physical systems are strictly time-invariant. This is particularly true for the application environments to be discussed in Chapter 9. For example, in multiple-processor systems both arrival rates and processing speeds change with time, while in communication networks links and/or trunks fail, and the load (that is, total number of calls) is a time-varying function. For this reason, if learning automata are to be used as task schedulers or link selectors for outgoing calls in such systems, their behavior in time-varying environments must be studied.

To this end, we shall study all four classes of automata models in the special case of a switching environment. Such an environment is described as one in which the penalty probabilities change in relative order every t_0 seconds, as shown in Figure 6.12 for $r = 2$.

The reasons for restricting our discussion to such environments are quite simple. For $t_0 \gg 1$ (sufficiently large), the problem reduces to the analysis of a set of learning automata operating in stationary environments staggered in time, i.e, as described in Figure 6.12 for time intervals

$$\Pi =
\begin{array}{c|ccccccc}
 & 1 & 2 & 3 & \cdots & (k-2) & (k-1) & k \\
\hline
1 & C_1 + \dfrac{(k-2)(1-C_2)}{k-1} & C_2 & 0 & \cdots & 0 & 0 & 0 \\[2ex]
2 & \dfrac{(1-C_2)}{k-1} & \dfrac{(1-C_1)+(k-2)C_2}{k-1} & 0 & \cdots & 0 & 0 & 0 \\[1ex]
\vdots & \cdots & \cdots & \cdots & \cdots & \cdots & \cdots & \cdots \\[1ex]
k-1 & 0 & 0 & 0 & \cdots & \dfrac{(k-2)C_1+(1-C_2)}{k-1} & 0 & \dfrac{(k-2)(1-C_1+C_2)}{k-1} \\[2ex]
k & 0 & 0 & 0 & \cdots & 0 & C_1 & (1-C_1)
\end{array}
\qquad (6.23)$$

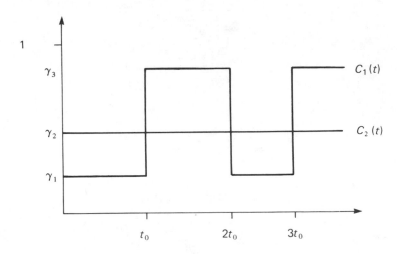

Figure 6.12 Nonstationary switching environment where $c_i(t)$, $i = 1, 2$ are time-dependent penalty probabilities.

$[0, t_0)$, $[2t_0, 3t_0)$, etc. Moreover, such environments accurately describe the type of changes we are chiefly interested in, namely, those present in multiple-processor systems (and/or communication networks). These changes include the failure of processors (or links), and the instantaneous increase or decrease in the processing loads (or calls in the network). In this system, $C_i(t)$ can be thought of as a measure of processing (or link) load.

We shall carry out our study as a comparative analysis of the automata models discussed in terms of the amount of learning associated with the learned state and the rate of learning (i.e., the convergence behavior of the learning curve). Optimally, such comparison would be greatly simplified if a closed form expression for $\sigma(n)$, the state probability distribution, were available for each model discussed. In fact, were that the case, α_1 could be selected a priori as the preferred action (i.e., assume $C_1 < C_2$) , and a comparison of the learning curves of $p_1(n)$ among the automata models could be carried out.

For example, in the case of Tsetlin's automaton with $k = 2$ (Figure 6.5a), it is easily verified that for stationary environments the homogeneous Markov chain that characterizes the process is given by Equation 6.24:

$$\Pi = \begin{array}{c} 1 \\ 2 \end{array} \begin{bmatrix} \overset{1}{(1 - C_2)} & \overset{2}{C_2} \\ C_1 & (1 - C_1) \end{bmatrix} \tag{6.24}$$

for $0 \le C_1, C_2 \le 1$, and $C_1 + C_1 \ne 0$.

Furthermore, it is well known [12, 13] that this two-state homogeneous Markov process is completely characterized by Matrix $\Pi(n)$, whose closed form solution is obtained by the use of transform methods, that is, by finding a solution to the equation

$$\Pi^g(z)[I - \Pi z] = I$$

where

$$\Pi^g(z) = \sum_{n=0}^{\infty} \Pi^n z^n$$

The closed form solution to this equation is given in Equation 6.25:

$$\Pi^{(n)} = \frac{1}{C_1 + C_2} \begin{bmatrix} C_1 & C_2 \\ C_1 & C_2 \end{bmatrix} + \frac{[1 - (C_1 + C_2)]^n}{C_1 + C_2} \begin{bmatrix} C_2 & -C_2 \\ -C_1 & C_1 \end{bmatrix} \tag{6.25}$$

Note that Equation 6.25 provides a complete description of the state probabilities at each stage n or time nT. Furthermore, it completely characterizes the statistics, or distribution function, of the random sequence $\{P(n)\}_1^{\infty}$. For example, it is easily verified that the limiting distribution function of $\sigma(n)$, given by Equation 6.26, exists:

$$\sigma(\infty) = \lim_{n \to \infty} \sigma(n) = \begin{bmatrix} \dfrac{C_1}{C_1 + C_2} & \dfrac{C_2}{C_1 + C_2} \end{bmatrix} \tag{6.26}$$

This, in turn, implies that the random sequence $\{P(n)\}_1^{\infty}$ converges *weakly*, or in distribution, to a random variable $P(\infty)$, or

$$P(n) \xrightarrow{(w)} P(\infty) \text{ as } n \to \infty$$

Hence, this knowledge allows computation of the expected value and variance of $P(\infty)$.

From Equation 6.26, it is also obvious that the rate of convergence of the process is a function of $(C_1 + C_2)$. For example, for $(C_1 + C_2) = 1$, the limiting behavior occurs after only one stage. A complete analysis of this rate of convergence can be found in Howard [15].

Unfortunately, in the majority of cases, closed form solutions for $\sigma(n)$ such as Equation 6.25 are not available. Consequently, alternate methods to compute separately the limiting distribution $\sigma(\infty)$, and the rate of learning will be used next.

Limiting Probabilities, Expediency

First, we shall compare the models in terms of their limiting behavior. That is, we are interested in the convergence of the random sequence $\{P(n)\}_1^\infty$. Specifically, if α_1 is chosen as the "preferred" action, we are interested in the values that $p_1(n)$ takes when the process is allowed to make a very large number of transitions, or

$$E[p_1(n)] \text{ as } n \to \infty \tag{6.27}$$

Therefore, Equation 6.27 poses two questions. First, we must determine whether the random sequence $\{P(n)\}_1^\infty$ or $\{p_1(n)\}_1^\infty$ converges at all and, if so, what is the type of convergence. Second, if $\{p(n)\}_1^\infty$ converges to a random variable $p(\infty)$, what is the value associated with $E[p(\infty)]$?[*] In this section, both questions are answered with the aid of Markov chain theory. The reader is referred to the works of Feller [12], Howard [15], and Kleinrock [16] for a complete discussion of Markov chains. Specifically, consider the following Lemma (presented by Feller [12]).

Lemma 6.1: If a homogeneous Markov chain is finite, irreducible, and aperiodic, then

1. It is ergodic.
2. The limiting probabilities always exist and are independent of the initial state probability distribution, $\sigma(0)$, in which case

$$\lim_{n \to \infty} \sigma_j(n) \to \sigma_j$$

---

[*] Although the action probability vector, $P(n)$, has two elements, it is actually described by either one because of the requirement that $p_1(n) + p_2(n) = 1$. Hence, for P-models, the random sequence $\{P(n)\}_1^\infty$ is replaced by $\{p(n)\}_1^\infty$ and all subscripts are dropped.

3. The *stationary probability distribution* is uniquely determined by Equation 6.28:

$$\sum_{\forall i} \sigma_i = 1$$

$$\sigma_j = \sum_{\forall i} \sigma_i \pi_{ij} \tag{6.28}$$

From Equations 6.13, 6.15, 6.19, and 6.23, we can now easily verify that for all four classes of automata models—the Tsetlin, Cover-Hellman, L_{R-I}, and L_{R-P} finite state approximation with δ not identical to 0 — their Markov chains are finite, irreducible, and aperiodic. Hence, the limiting probability distribution exists and can be found by solving Equation 6.28.

This, in turn, implies that the random sequence $\{p(n)\}_1^{\infty}$ *converges in distribution* to a discrete random variable $p(\infty)$, or

$$\lim_{n \to \infty} p(n) \xrightarrow{D} p(\infty)$$

for each of the automata models. Furthermore, the statistics of the limiting random variable $p(\infty)$ are known and given by $\sigma(\infty)$, the limiting probability distribution function. Hence, knowledge of $\sigma(\infty)$ will allow the computation of $E[p(\infty)]$, which, in turn, serves as a measure of the amount of learning of the asymptotic learned state.

Witten [5] considered this problem for the finite state approximation model of the L_{R-I} automaton, while Colón Osorio [17] considered all automata models in terms of random walks and provided the solution to Equation 6.28 for each model. The results of these and other researchers are presented here in Table 6.1, which compares all four classes of automata models in terms of their limiting behavior, or the amount of learning associated with the learned state. From this table, we see that the Linear Reward-Penalty automaton is expedient, whereas the Cover-Hellman and the Linear Reward-Inaction automata are ϵ-optimal in stationary environments. Furthermore, the limiting behavior of the Cover-Hellman and Linear Reward-Inaction automata are shown to be identical. Also notice that optimality is achieved only for a memory of infinite size, i.e., $k = \infty$. The Tsetlin automaton tends to optimality as the memory size increases to infinity in stationary environments with $C_{\min} \leq 1/2$.

Table 6.1. Comparison of Automata Models in Terms of Asymptotic Learned State

Automaton	Expediency $E[p_1(\infty)]$	Performance	Step Size
1. Tsetlin	$\dfrac{1}{1 + \left(\dfrac{C_1}{C_2}\right)^k \left(\dfrac{C_1 - d_1}{C_2 - d_2}\right)\left(\dfrac{C_2^k - d_2^k}{C_1^k - d_1^k}\right)}$	Optimal for $C_{\text{MIN}} \leqslant 1/2$	$\Delta = 1/(2k - 1)$
2. Cover-Hellman	$\dfrac{\left(\dfrac{1 - C_1}{1 - C_2}\right)^{2k-1}}{1 + \left(\dfrac{1 - C_1}{1 - C_2}\right)^{2k-1}}$	ϵ-optimal for infinite memory size, and $\delta \to 0$	$\Delta = 1/(2k - 1)$
3. L_{R-I} Finite State Approximation	$\dfrac{\left(\dfrac{1 - C_1}{1 - C_2}\right)^{2k-1}}{1 + \left(\dfrac{1 - C_1}{1 - C_2}\right)^{2k-1}}$	ϵ-optimal for infinite memory size, and $\delta \to 0$	$\Delta = 1/(2k - 1)$
4. L_{R-P} Finite State Approximation	$\displaystyle\sum_{l=1}^{2k} \binom{l-1}{k-1} \underbrace{\prod_{j=1}^{l-1} \frac{[(j-1)(1 - C_1) + (2k - j)C_2]}{[jC_1 + (2k - j - 1)(1 - C_2)]}}_{\theta}$	Expedient	$\Delta = 1/(2k - 1)$

Furthermore, Colón Osorio showed that for relatively large memory size ($s > 20$) and stationary environments, all four classes of automata perform relatively well. That is, $E[p(\infty)] \to 1$. Recall that $E[p(\infty)]$ was defined as the amount of learning associated with the learned state.

Rate of Learning, Mean First Passage Time

As mentioned earlier, if learning automata are to be considered as task schedulers in multiple-processor systems or as link selectors in communication networks, their performance and behavior in time-varying environments must be studied. To this end, we shall now define a suitable measure of the rate of learning, that is, the ability of a learning automaton to respond to changes in the penalty probability set, C. We shall also compare all automata models in terms of this measure when operating in the switching environment of Figure 6.12.

Let us consider the switching environment of Figure 6.12 during the time interval $t\epsilon[0, t_0)$. In this interval, and for sufficiently large values of t_0, the environment is stationary, with a constant penalty probability set as follows:

$$C_1(t) = \gamma_1 < \gamma_2 = C_2(t) \text{ for } t\epsilon[0, t_0)$$

In such an environment, the automata models under consideration will converge to their limiting distribution functions, $\sigma(\infty)$, as given by the solution to Equation 6.28.

Next, consider the change in the penalty probability set that occurs at time t_0. Notice that at time t_0, the relative order of the penalty probabilities is changed:

$$C_1(t) = \gamma_3 > \gamma_2 = C_2(t) \text{ for } t\epsilon[t_0, 2t_0]$$

In the aftermath of such change, it is interesting to measure how rapidly the automaton adjusts to the new environment. We are interested in determining the number of transitions, or steps, required for the automaton to reach the new preferred state, ϕ^*, for the first time.[*] Fortunately, the automata models have been characterized in terms of

---

[*] Definition: If there is a state, call it ϕ^*, the preferred state such that $P_R\{\alpha_1 \text{ is selected}/\phi^*\} > P_R\{\alpha_1 \text{ is selected}/\phi_j\}\forall j$ and $C_1 < C_2$. In the case of the L_{R-I} automaton of Figure 6.4a, ϕ_k is the preferred state.

random walks and Markov chains. In this context, the problem of determining the number of steps to reach a given state has been widely studied under the category of mean first passage time [12]. Thus, several techniques to aid in the computation of mean first passage time are available. Before proceeding with this computation, however, we shall define more formally the rate-of-learning measure under consideration.

Define the random variable Z_{ij} as the number of transitions required for the automaton to reach state ϕ_j for the first time if it started at time $t = 0$ in state ϕ_i. We call Z_{ij} the first passage time of the automaton from state ϕ_i to ϕ_j. We use $f_{ij}(n)$ to denote the probability that Z_{ij} takes a value of n, or

$$f_{ij}(n) = P_R\{Z_{ij} = n\} \quad n = 1, 2, \ldots \qquad (6.29)$$

In this equation, notice that n takes on the integral values 1, 2, 3, ... Since, by definition, no first passage time Z_{ij} can assume the value of zero, we have

$$f_{ij}(0) = 0$$

Also note that for $n = 1$, Equation 6.29 reduces to the one-step transition probabilities, or

$$f_{ij}(1) = \pi\sigma_{ij}$$

Before proceeding, we must resolve the question of whether the probability distribution of Equation 6.29 is a probability measure, that is, whether it sums to one. Clearly, $f_{ij}(.)$ is a probability measure if the automaton sooner or later enters state ϕ_j with certainty. If ϕ_j is a recurrent state, this condition is met. Recall from our previous discussion that the Markov chains of all four classes of automata models were finite and irreducible. This implies that all states are recurrent, in which case $f_{ij}(.)$ is a probability measure. Now, the mean first passage time from state ϕ_i to ϕ_j can be defined with the aid of Equation 6.29 as follows:

$$m_{ij} = E[Z_{ij}] = \sum_{n=1}^{\infty} nf_{ij}(n) \qquad (6.30)$$

The unconditional mean first passage time of state ϕ_j is given by Equation 6.31 on the next page.

$$m_j = E[Z_j] = \sum_{i=1}^{k} m_{ij}\sigma_i \qquad (6.31)$$

where σ_i is the limiting state probabilities at time t_0 in the environment of Figure 6.12.

It is precisely Equation 6.31 that represents the measure of the rate of learning for the automata models under consideration. Intuitively, m^*, represents the number of transitions, or steps, that it will take the automaton (once it has reached the steady state in environment C_a for $t\epsilon[0, t_0]$ to adjust to the new environment after t_0.[*] Now, let us turn our attention to the computation of m^* for all four classes of automata models.

Computation of Mean First Passage Time

There are basically two equivalent methods for computing the mean first passage time to the preferred state. The first method uses renewal theory, recurrent events, and generating functions to find the first passage time probabilities, $f_{ij}(n)$. Feller [12, Chapter XIV.4] describes this as follows:

Define $u_{i,n}$ as the probability that the first passage of the automaton through the preferred state occurs at transition n, given that its initial state, or position, was ϕ_i. Next, compute the generating function of $u_{i,n}$ as follows:

$$U_i(S) = \sum_{n=0}^{\infty} u_{i,n} S^n \qquad (6.32)$$

If $U_i(S)$ is known, it is easily verified that the mean first passage time from state ϕ_i to state ϕ_j is given by Equation 6.33:

$$m_{ij} = \frac{d}{ds} U_i(S)|S = 1$$

$$= \sum_{n=0}^{\infty} nu_{i,n} S^{n-1}|S = 1 \qquad (6.33)$$

$$= \sum_{n=0}^{\infty} nu_{i,n}$$

---

[*] In Figure 6.12, two possible environments can be defined:

$$C_a = \{\gamma_1, \gamma_2\} \text{ where } C_1 = \gamma_1 < \gamma_2 = C_2$$

and

$$C_b = \{\gamma_3, \gamma_2\} \text{ where } C_1 = \gamma_3 > \gamma_2 = C_2$$

However, for the automata models considered in this chapter, computation of the generating function, $U_i(S)$, involves the solution of a second-order difference equation, which in some instances is unattainable. In Colón Osorio [17] the use of this method in the computation of m_{ij} for the Cover-Hellman automaton is illustrated.

The second method available to compute the mean first passage time to the preferred state makes use of the Z-transform, the transient sum matrix,* and matrix inverses [15]. Basically, it can be shown [15] that the mean first passage time from state ϕ_i to state ϕ_j is given by Equation 6.34:

$$m_{ij} = [\delta_{ij} + t_{jj}^g(1) - t_{ij}^g(1)]\frac{1}{\sigma_j} \qquad (6.34)$$

where ϕ_j is a recurrent state; $t_{ij}^g(1)$ is the ith, jth element of the transient sum matrix; and σ_j is the limiting state probabilities. In matrix notation, Equation 6.34 is given by Equation 6.35:

$$M = [I + U(T^g(1)I) - T^g(1)][\Phi I]^{-1} \qquad (6.35)$$

where U is the square unity matrix composed entirely of ones.

This equation shows how the mean first passage time for the recurrent states of an irreducible Markov chain can be expressed in terms of the limiting state probabilities of the process and the transient sum matrix $T^g(1)$. Further, Howard [15] has shown that if the limiting state probabilities exist, then the transient sum matrix can be computed as follows:

$$T^g(Z) = [I - \Pi + \Phi]^{-1} - \Phi \qquad (6.36)$$

The computation of inverses in Equations 6.35 and 6.36 imposes practical limitations when the order of the matrix is greater than four. Consequently, a closed form solution to the mean first passage times is not always possible. However, in Colón Osorio [17] the solution to Equation 6.36 in several special cases of the switching environment of Figure 6.12 was

---

* If we express Π^n, the multistep transition matrix, in terms of its limiting state matrix and a transient matrix as follows

$$\Pi^n = \phi + T(n) \quad n = 0, 1, 2, \ldots$$

then

$$T^g(1) = T^g(z)|_{z=1} = \sum_{n=0}^{\infty} T(n)z^n|_{z=1}$$

This is called the transient sum matrix.

presented. As expected, experimental results showed that increased memory size results in better steady-state or limiting behavior. This, however, results in an increase of the mean first passage time through the preferred state, m^*. Furthermore, the L_{R-P} and Tsetlin automata, at least in the restrictive set of environments considered, behave qualitatively in a similar fashion. Their response to nonstationary environments is considerably faster than the L_{R-I} or Cover-Hellman automata. The Cover-Hellman automaton shows the slowest response to changes in the penalty probability set due to its totally random nature.

Taking into consideration the restrictions imposed on Tsetlin's automaton (i.e., $E[p(\infty)]$ deteriorates for values of $C_{\min} > 1/2$) when operating in stationary environments, and the rapid convergence of the L_{R-P} automaton in nonstationary environments, it is no surprise that, when applications of stochastic automata models to multiple-processor systems and communication networks are considered in Chapter 9, the presentation will be restricted to the L_{R-P} automaton.

CURRENT RESEARCH IN LEARNING AUTOMATA

In recent years most of the research in learning automata has been restricted to two major areas: models of learning automata operating in nonstationary environments, and application of learning automata to telephone traffic routing and multiple-processor systems. Since Chapter 9 is devoted entirely to the discussion of learning automata applications to telephone traffic routing and multiple-processor systems, we will restrict this discussion to a review of recent developments in the theory of learning automata operating in a nonstationary environment.

Basically, Narenda and his co-workers [18, 19] have proposed two mathematical models to describe the behavior of learning automata in nonstationary environments. In the first model, the environment's response characteristics are affected by the action of the automaton. The second model, which is a slight modification of the first, assumes that the penalty probabilities characterizing the environment C are a function of the probabilities with which such actions are selected, P. This research demonstrated:

1. If the penalty probabilities C are a function of the action probabilities P, then it can be shown that the vector sequence $\{p(n)\}_{n>0}$ is a homogeneous Markov process.

2. Further, if an L_{R-P} scheme is used, then the process is ergodic and converges as $n \to \infty$ to a stationary probability, which is independent of the initial distribution $p(0)$.
3. Since, for nonstationary environments, an ergodic behavior is desirable, then L_{R-P} and $L_{R-EP}{}^{*}$ are attractive reinforcement algorithms.

SUMMARY

In this chapter, the stochastic automaton model of Chapter 4 was further explored to include the concept of variable-structure automata, also known as learning automata. Furthermore, four automata models were presented as possible task schedulers in a multiple-processor system and/or link selectors for calls in a communications network. All four models were treated uniformly by characterizing them in terms of random walks and Markov chain theory. This characterization allowed us to evaluate their performance in terms of their steady-state behavior and their average response times to changes in the environment. It was shown that the L_{R-P} automata perform "better" than the others for a special class of switching environments. On this basis, the L_{R-P} automaton will be applied to both multiple-processor systems and communications networks as task scheduler and link selector, respectively, in Chapter 9.

EXERCISES

1. Discuss the relative advantages and disadvantages of expedient and optimum systems. Describe environments for which each of these systems is particularly suited.

2. (This is a research problem adequate for graduate students at the Master's level.)

    Consider a stochastic automaton that continuously updates the estimates of the penalty probability set C as follows. Let $g_i(n)$ be the current estimate of the penalty probability associated with action α_i. Then, if α_i elicits a response from the environment,

---

* L_{R-EP} is a reinforcement scheme where the penalty for a bad response is small compared to the reward for a good response.

$x(n + 1)$, the estimate of the penalty probability $g_i(n)$ is updated as follows:

$$g_i(n + 1) = g_i(n) + w[x(n + 1) - g_i(n)]$$

where w is a constant.

Furthermore, the probability of choosing action α_i at stage n for this automaton is given by

$$p_i(n) = \beta/2 + (1 - \beta)d_i(n)$$

where

$$d_i(n) = \begin{cases} 1 \text{ if } g_i(n) < g_j(n) \\ 0 \text{ otherwise .} \end{cases}$$

For this automaton called Sample Mean Automaton,

(a) Show that this Sample Mean Automaton when $w = 1/n + 1$ is asymptotically optimal.

(b) Show that, for finite values of w, that is, $w = 1/k$ where $0 < k < \infty$, the Sample Mean Automaton is equivalent to an automaton that is allowed to remember the rk previous responses of the environment; and

(c) Again for w finite and equal to $w = 1/k$, $0 < k < \infty$ with $\beta = 0$ and $r = 2$, show that the Sample Mean Automaton reduces to Tsetlin's automaton.

3. Consider Tsetlin's automata, whose homogeneous Markov chain is best described by the one-step transition probability matrix given by Equation 6.13. For this matrix,

(a) Find the stationary probability distribution function.

(b) Show that the behavior of the Tsetlin automata is optimal for $C_{min} \leq 1/2$ only.

REFERENCES

1. WALD, A., *Sequential Analysis*, Wiley, New York, 1947.
2. ROBBINS, Herbert, "Some Aspects of the Sequential Design of Experiments,"

Bulletin of the American Mathematical Society, Vol. 58, September 1952, pp. 527–535.

3. ROBBINS, Herbert, "A Sequential Decision Problem with a Finite Memory," *Proceedings of the National Academy of Science*, Vol. 42, 1956, pp. 920–923.

4. COVER, Thomas M., and Martin E. HELLMAN, "The Two-Armed Bandid Problem with Time-Invariant Finite Memory," *IEEE Transactions on Information Theory*, Vol. IT-16, No. 2, March 1970, pp. 185–195.

5. WITTEN, Ian H., "Finite Performance of Some Two-Armed Bandid Controllers," *IEEE Transactions on Systems, Man, and Cybernetics*, Vol. SMC-3, No. 2, March 1973, pp. 194–197.

6. SKLANSKY, J., "Adaptation, Learning, Self Repair, and Feedback," *IEEE Spectrum*, May 1964, pp. 172–174.

7. VARSHAVSKII, V. K., and I. P. VORONTSOVA, "On the Behavior of Stochastic Automata with Variable Structure," *Avtomatika i Telemekhanika*, Vol. 24, No. 3, March 1963, pp. 353–360.

8. CHANDRASEKARAN, B., and D. W. C. SHEN, "On Expediency and Convergence in Variable Structure Automata," *IEEE Transactions on Systems, Science, and Cybernetics*, Vol. SSC-4, No. 1, March 1968, pp. 52–60.

9. LAKSHMIVARAHAN, S., and M. A. L. THATHACHAR, "Absolutely Expedient Learning Algorithms for Stochastic Automata," *IEEE Transactions on Systems, Man, and Cybernetics*, Vol. SMC-3, May 1973, pp. 281–286.

10. TSETLIN, M. L., "On the Behavior of Finite Automata in Random Media," tr. from *Avtomatiki i Telemekhanika*, Vol. 22, No. 10, October 1961, pp. 1345–1354.

11. NARENDRA, Kumpati S., M. A. L. THATHACHAR, "Learning Automata— A Survey," *IEEE Transactions on Systems, Man, and Cybernetics*, Vol. SMC-4, July 1974, pp. 323-334.

12. FELLER, W., *An Introduction to Probability Theory and Its Applications*, Vol. 1, 3rd ed., Wiley, New York, 1968.

13. KARLIN, S., and H. TAYLOR, *A First Course in Stochastic Processes*, 2nd ed., Academic Press, New York, 1975.

14. VISWANATHAN, R., and K. S. NARENDRA, "A Note on the Linear Reinforcement Scheme for Variable-Structure Automata," *IEEE Transactions on Systems, Man, and Cybernetics,*, Vol. SMC-2, April 1972, pp. 292–294.

15. HOWARD, R., *Dynamic Probabilistic Systems: Volume 1—Markov Processes*, Wiley, New York, 1971.

16. KLEINROCK, L., *Queueing Systems, Volume I: Theory*, Wiley, Interscience, New York, 1975.

17. COLÓN OSORIO, F. C., "Scheduling in Multiple-Processor Systems with the Aid of Stochastic Automata," Ph.D. Dissertation, Electrical and Computer Engineering Department, University of Massachusetts, Amherst, Mass., 1977.

18. NARENDRA, Kumpati S., and M. A. L. THATHACHAR, "On the Behavior of a Learning Automaton in a Changing Environment with Application to Telephone Traffic Routines," *S & IS Report*, No. 7803, Yale University, October 1978.

19. KUMAR, P. R. Srikanta, and K. S. NARENDRA, "Learning Algorithm Models for Routing in Telephone Networks," *S & IS Report*, No. 7903, Yale University, May 1979.

7

Adaptive, Learning, and Self-Organizing Controllers

We shall now examine the concepts presented in Chapter 5 as applied to the area of automatic control. Automatic control systems usually incorporate feedback as a means of modifying the present input as some function of the present output. Thus, from the discussion in Chapter 5, the simplest of these systems is adaptive, and all automatic feedback control systems are sometimes called cybernetic systems. In this chapter we shall be concerned with control systems that must operate in a class of environments which precludes the use of a simple feedback control system. Some of the systems we shall study have been used extensively in the control of high performance aircraft where the dynamics of the aircraft control problem change with altitude, speed, etc. The basic control systems for rockets used in the space program also use adaptive principles in their implementation.

Much work in this area makes use of time domain analysis; therefore, we shall first review briefly the basic state variable formulation. Next, the basic types of adaptive control systems will be examined, and their operation will be compared. The class of self-organizing controllers that have been used in both aircraft and industrial control will then be introduced. A new approach to large systems that uses a hierarchy of control will then be studied.

STATE VARIABLE APPROACH

The systems we wish to control can generally be described by n-th order, constant coefficient, linear differential equations of the form

$$\frac{d^n y}{dt^n} + a_{n-1}\frac{d^{n-1}y}{dt^{n-1}} + \cdots + a_1\frac{dy}{dt} + a_0 y = u(t) \tag{7.1}$$

where $y(t)$ is the system output and $u(t)$ is the system input. The n variables in Equation 7.1,

$$y, \frac{dy}{dt}, \frac{d^2 y}{dt^2}, \ldots, \frac{d^{n-1}y}{dt^{n-1}}$$

are called the *state variables* of the system. The *state* of the system is a set of numbers such that given these numbers for some time, the input or forcing functions, and the equations describing the dynamics of the system, one can determine the future state and output of the system. A set of state variables $x_1(t), \ldots, x_n(t)$ can be defined further for the system given by Equation 7.1 as follows:

$$x_1(t) = y(t)$$

$$x_2(t)(=)\dot{x}_1(t)$$

$$\vdots$$

$$x_n(t) = \dot{x}_{n-1}(t)$$

This set of state variables can easily be used to write the high order differential equation as a set of *first*-order differential equations:

$$\dot{x}_1(t) = x_2(t)$$

$$\dot{x}_2(t) = x_3(t)$$

$$\vdots \tag{7.2}$$

$$\dot{x}_n(t) = -a_0 x_1(t) - a_1 x_2(t) - \cdots - a_{n-1}x_n(t) + u(t)$$

These equations can also be written in matrix form as follows:

$$\begin{bmatrix} \dot{x}_1 \\ \dot{x}_2 \\ \vdots \\ \dot{x}_{n-1} \\ \dot{x}_n \end{bmatrix} = \begin{bmatrix} 0 & 1 & 0 & \cdots & 0 & 0 \\ 0 & 0 & 1 & \cdots & 0 & 0 \\ \vdots & \vdots & \vdots & & \vdots & \vdots \\ 0 & 0 & 0 & \cdots & 0 & 1 \\ -a_0 & -a_1 & -a_2 & \cdots & -a_{n-2} & -a_{n-1} \end{bmatrix} \begin{bmatrix} x_1 \\ x_2 \\ \vdots \\ x_{n-1} \\ x_n \end{bmatrix} + \begin{bmatrix} 0 \\ 0 \\ \vdots \\ 0 \\ u \end{bmatrix} \quad (7.3)$$

For example, consider the following second-order differential equation describing the behavior of the simple RLC circuit in Figure 7.1:

$$u(t) = Ri(t) + L\frac{di(t)}{dt} + \frac{1}{C}\int_0^\tau i(t)\,dt \quad (7.4)$$

We can, of course, consider Equation 7.4 in terms of charge, q, where

$$i(t) = \frac{dq(t)}{dt} = \frac{dq}{dt} \quad (7.5)$$

and Equation 7.4 becomes

$$u(t) = L\frac{d^2q}{dt^2} + R\frac{dq}{dt} + \frac{1}{C}q \quad (7.6)$$

which is a second-order differential equation. Further, we can let $q = x_1$ and

$$\frac{dq}{dt} = x_2 \quad (7.7)$$

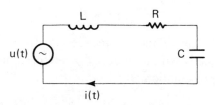

Figure 7.1.   RLC circuit with forcing function $u(t)$ and no initial energy storage.

and we can rewrite Equation 7.6 as

$$u(t) = \frac{dx_2}{dt}L + Rx_2 + \frac{1}{C}x_1 \tag{7.8}$$

But from Equation 7.8, and after some algebraic manipulation, we can obtain Equation 7.9:

$$\frac{dx_2}{dt} = \frac{u(t)}{L} - \frac{Rx_2}{L} - \frac{1}{LC}x_1 \tag{7.9}$$

Therefore, Equations 7.7 and 7.9 describe the second-order system given by Equation 7.6 with two first-order equations. Now, as in Equation 7.3, we can write a matrix representation for this system where $\dot{x}_i = dx_i/dt$:

$$\begin{bmatrix} \dot{x}_1 \\ \dot{x}_2 \end{bmatrix} = \begin{bmatrix} 0 & 1 \\ \dfrac{-1}{LC} & -\dfrac{R}{L} \end{bmatrix} \begin{bmatrix} x_1 \\ x_2 \end{bmatrix} + \begin{bmatrix} 0 \\ \dfrac{1}{L} \end{bmatrix} u(t) \tag{7.10}$$

In general, however, one or more forcing functions may be associated with each of the state variables, and the matrix form is

$$\begin{bmatrix} \dot{x}_1 \\ \dot{x}_2 \\ \vdots \\ \dot{x}_n \end{bmatrix} = \begin{bmatrix} a_{11} & a_{12} & \cdots & a_{1n} \\ a_{21} & a_{22} & \cdots & a_{22} \\ \vdots & \vdots & & \vdots \\ a_{n1} & a_{n2} & \cdots & a_{nn} \end{bmatrix} \begin{bmatrix} x_1 \\ x_2 \\ \vdots \\ x_n \end{bmatrix} + \begin{bmatrix} b_{11} & \cdots & b_{1m} \\ \vdots & & \vdots \\ b_{n1} & \cdots & b_{nm} \end{bmatrix} \begin{bmatrix} u_t \\ \vdots \\ u_m \end{bmatrix} \tag{7.11}$$

The column vector x, called the *state vector*, is similar to the state probability vector σ used in stochastic automata. We can now define a matrix notation for the *system vector differential equation* by

$$\dot{x} = Ax + Bu \tag{7.12}$$

We shall now examine the desired results from our example. The current $i(t)$ is the objective of our analysis. Therefore, the final equation for the state variable representation is

$$i(t) = x_2 \tag{7.13}$$

In general, however, the output may be a multivariable response given by the vector C, which is a function of both the state variables and the input signals:

$$C = Dx + Hu \qquad (7.14)$$

It is now interesting to examine the solution to the vector differential equation (7.12). First, take its Laplace transform

$$sx(s) - x(0) = Ax(s) + Bu(s)$$

and

$$x(s) = [sI - A]^{-1}x(0) + [sI - A]^{-1}Bu(s) \qquad (7.15)$$

where I is the identity matrix showing [1] that $[sI - A]^{-1} = \phi(s)$ is the Laplace transform of $\phi(t) = e^{At}$, where $e^{At} \equiv I + (At/1!) + ((At)^2/2!) + \cdots$ and

$$x(t) = \phi(t)x(0) + \int_0^t \phi(t - \tau)Bu(\tau)\,d\tau \qquad (7.16)$$

The matrix $\phi(t)$, called the fundamental or transition matrix, describes the natural or unforced response of the system; that is, when $u = 0$:

$$x(t) = \phi(t)x(0) \qquad (7.17)$$

If we now consider the unforced or natural response expression from Equation 7.15 with $x(0) = 0$, i.e., zero initial conditions,

$$sx(s) = Ax(s)$$

and

$$[sI - A]x(s) = 0 \qquad (7.18)$$

It can be shown [2] that Equation 7.18 has a nontrivial solution if and only if

$$p(s) = \text{determinant } [sI - A] = 0 \qquad (7.19)$$

Further, the matrix

$$K = sI - A \qquad (7.20)$$

is called the *characteristic matrix* of the matrix A, and the determinant of

Equation 7.19 is called the *characteristic function* of A. The function $p(s)$ is, in general, a polynomial of degree n, where A is an $n \times n$ matrix. The n roots of Equation 7.19 are called the *eigenvalues* of the matrix A, and the substitution of each of these values into Equation 7.18 yields the eigenvectors of the matrix A.

For example, to find the eigenvalues and eigenvectors of the following matrix

$$A = \begin{bmatrix} 1 & -1 \\ 3 & 1 \end{bmatrix} \tag{7.21}$$

we first form the characteristic function of A,

$$p(s) = \det \begin{bmatrix} s-1 & +1 \\ -3 & s-1 \end{bmatrix} = s^2 - 2s + 4 = 0$$

whose roots (eigenvalues) are

$$s_1, s_2 = 1 \pm j\sqrt{3}$$

The eigenvectors corresponding to these eigenvalues can now be found by first substituting s_1 into Equation 7.18,

$$\begin{bmatrix} +j\sqrt{3} & +1 \\ -3 & +j\sqrt{3} \end{bmatrix} \begin{bmatrix} x_1 \\ x_2 \end{bmatrix} = 0 \tag{7.22}$$

Notice that any set of values that satisfies the condition $x_2 = -j\sqrt{3}x_1$ is a solution to Equation 7.22. Hence, the eigenvector corresponding to the s_1 eigenvector is of the general form

$$x(s_1) = c \begin{bmatrix} 1 \\ -j\sqrt{3} \end{bmatrix}$$

Similarly, the eigenvector for $s_2 = 1 - j\sqrt{3}$ corresponds to the solution of the following equation:

$$\begin{bmatrix} -j\sqrt{3} & 1 \\ -3 & -j\sqrt{3} \end{bmatrix} \begin{bmatrix} x_1 \\ x_2 \end{bmatrix} = 0 \tag{7.23}$$

or, as before,

$$x(s_2) = c \begin{bmatrix} 1 \\ j\sqrt{3} \end{bmatrix}$$

The factor c in the preceding eigenvectors defines a set of infinite solutions to Equations 7.22 and 7.23, all of which are constant multiples of each other. Consideration of Equation 7.23 gives

$$-j\sqrt{3}\,cx_1 + cx_2 = 0 \qquad (7.24)$$

Substituting the terms in the eigenvector into Equation 7.24 gives

$$-j\sqrt{3}\,c \times 1 + c(j\sqrt{3}) = 0$$

which is satisfied for all c.

ADAPTIVE CONTROL SYSTEMS

An adaptive control system has two principal functional elements: (1) a plant to be controlled and a controller whose design is based on a nominal but inexact mathematical model of the plant and/or its environment, and (2) a method for dynamically altering the controller structure. A functional block diagram of an adaptive controller is given in Figure 7.2, where the fundamental system variables may be state vectors as defined in the previous section. The goal of the adaptive system is to achieve satisfactory response of the plant state $x(t)$ to an input $v(t)$, where the input is not normally known a priori. A set of inputs is applied to the controller, which generates an input to the plant. The measuring devices then make either direct or indirect measurements of the plant state. These measurements are compared with the input $v(t)$ to determine the present performance vector $p(t)$, which is mapped by the adaptive algorithm into a weighting input $w(t)$. The inputs to the variable structure controller, $m(t)$ and $w(t)$, provide the driving functions for modifying the relation between the command and plant inputs. As a result, the nominal design is dynamically changed to improve system behavior.

This functional model of an adaptive control system is, of course, similar to the general models given in Chapter 5. The variable-structure controller and plant make up the forward transfer element; the measuring

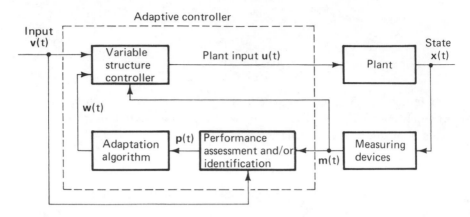

Figure 7.2. Functional block diagram of an adaptive control system.

devices and the performance assessment/identification functions correspond to the performance evaluation element; and the adaptaton algorithm corresponds to the system parameter transfer element. Different forms of the model in Figure 7.2 will be considered in the remainder of this chapter.

PARAMETER ADAPTIVE CONTROL SYSTEMS

Consider the feedback control system shown in Figure 7.3, where the gain of the amplifier, A, can be varied by some external control from an adaption algorithm, for example. Control theory provides techniques for studying the behavior of these systems with respect to gain, plant dynamics, and the feedback network. Another configuration places the adaptive gain element in the feedback loop and will be considered later in an example. In many cases, the total system behavior can be varied over a wide range by changing the gain element. Many systems can thus be adapted to perform properly over a range of environmental conditions by changing only the gain parameter. This type of control is called a parameter adaptive control system [3]. In a *parameter adaptive control system* the adaptive elements in the controller structure are adjusted according to a specified adaptation algorithm.

These systems, which have been used extensively for controller realization [4], form an important class of adaptive controllers. Their operation

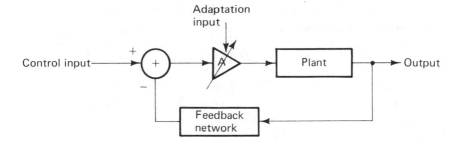

Figure 7.3.   Feedback control system with adaptive gain.

generally assumes that the environment is stationary for some fixed interval in time, and the plant and its environment are usually described by linear differential equations. The starting point in the design also requires that some a priori information exists about the plant structure and the range of the change in coefficients that might be expected. Thus, the initial plant structure is tested and evaluated by the performance assessment system for the first time interval of operation, and appropriate changes in the system gains are made by the adaptation algorithm. These gains are used over the next interval, and the process is repeated during each interval. Notice that in such systems the parameters remain unchanged for the duration of the interval, T. Hence, the system's timely response to the environment is dependent on T. Adaptive algorithms exhibiting this property are called *discrete time* algorithms.

The performance assessment/identification element is given the task of identifying the state of the plant and the environment in order to initiate changes in the system parameters. The process of identification is thus crucial in adaptive controller designs. Two methods of plant identification have been identified: explicit and implicit [3].

The explicit identification schemes are directed toward determining the state equations directly from observations of the system's behavior. Continuous determination of the system's state equations allows the controller to update the gains of its adaptive elements to the proper values within one iteration of the gain computation algorithm. Thus, explicit plant identification techniques have the advantage of being able to adapt rapidly to changes in the plant environment.

Next, let us examine the explicit identification problem for a system described by the following first-order equation,

$$\dot{x}(t) = a(t)x(t) + u(t) \tag{7.25}$$

where $a(t)$ is assumed to be slowly varying with respect to the response time of the system. Hence, without loss of generality, we can assume that the coefficients of Equation 7.25 are constant. Also, let $u(t)$ be the plant input, which is given by

$$u(t) = v(t) - k(t)x(t) \tag{7.26}$$

where $k(t)$ is the adaptive gain in the feedback loop and $v(t)$ is the system input function. Some mechanism must now be provided for determining the exact value, $a(t)$, or an estimate of the coefficient $\hat{a}(t)$.

This value is used to adjust the feedback gain, in this case according to the criterion

$$\hat{a}(t) - k(t) = b \tag{7.27}$$

where b is the fixed gain value that produces some a priori designated desirable behavior. Solving Equation 7.27 for $k(t)$ and substituting the result into Equation 7.26, we obtain the plant input as a function of the system input, $v(t)$; the system parameter estimate, $\hat{a}(t)$; and the plant state, $x(t)$:

$$u(t) = v(t) - [\hat{a}(t) - b]x(t) \tag{7.28}$$

The final system equation for the closed loop control system is

$$\dot{x}(t) = [a(t) - \hat{a}(t) + b]x(t) + v(t) \tag{7.29}$$

If the estimate is correct, then $\hat{a}(t) = a(t)$ and Equation 7.29 reduces to

$$\dot{x}(t) = bx(t) + v(t) \tag{7.30}$$

which is the desired system response. The resulting adaptive control system with explicit identification is shown in Figure 7.4.

One of the important considerations when analyzing an adaptive control system is its convergence to the desired behavior. In this context, two questions must be answered: (1) Does the system converge at all?

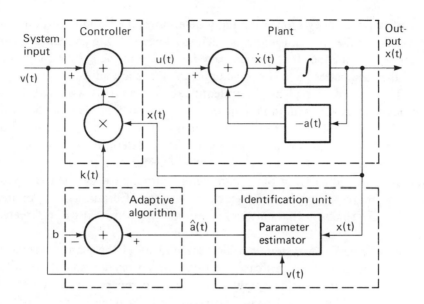

Figure 7.4.   Adaptive control system using explicit identification.

(2) Does the system converge rapidly enough to ensure stability through the convergence interval? The answer to the first question is that, in general, one can ensure so-called asymptotic stability, namely, for $v(t) = 0$,

$$x(t) \to 0 \text{ as } t \to \infty \tag{7.31}$$

For example, the system described by Equation 7.3 has a solution for $v(t) = 0$

$$x(t) = ce^{bt} \tag{7.32}$$

One can guarantee asymptotic stability by specifying $b < 0$ in the system design. This design specification can easily be extended to general n-input systems [1].

The answer to the second question is not quite as straightforward as the first, and there are several generally unknown factors that must be considered. First, the parameter estimation process may not be error-free, thereby causing incorrect adaptation. In addition, the rate at which identification errors go to zero initially determines the stability or potential instability of the system. Finally, the delays associated with gain adjustment contribute to the fact that a temporary instability in the system may exist until the parameters have converged and the gains are adjusted.

The process of explicit plant identification has tacitly assumed that a parameter estimator can, in fact, be designed. In general, identification can be accomplished if enough output variables of the system are measured to allow the status of the unknown parameters to be determined. If this occurs, the parameters are said to be *observable*. Several techniques have been developed for identifying plant parameters, although a detailed study of these techniques is beyond the scope of this text. Certain aspects of this problem are similar to the pattern recognition problem that will be treated later.

Now, consider a system in which some or all of the plant parameters cannot be identified. In this case, we must use an *implicit identification* [3] technique in which specific output variables are compared with the desired performance. This comparison is easily made by driving both the system and a model of the system with unknown parameters. The model produces the proper output for the given input function, and an error can be generated by comparing the two outputs. The error function is then used to modify the parameters of the controller, that is, to adapt the system. This kind of adaptive control system is often called a *model reference control system*.

An example of a model reference control system is given in Figure 7.5, where the error function is given by

$$e(t) = y(t) - y_m(t) \tag{7.33}$$

The objective of the adaptation algorithm is to form a variable feedback gain $k(t)$ that will cause the plant behavior to approach the model behavior.

The function of the adaptation algorithm is to produce a function $k(t)$ that will tend to reduce the error. To do this, we define a cost functional of the form

$$J[e(t)] = J = \int_t^{t+T} L(e(\lambda)) \, d\lambda \tag{7.34}$$

A functional depends on the time history of its argument rather than, like

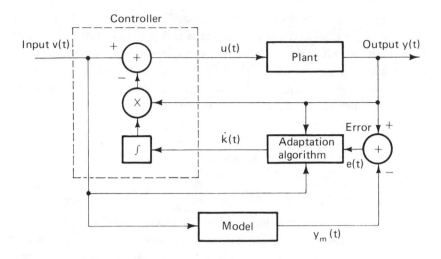

Figure 7.5. Model reference adaptive control system.

a function, on a single value of the argument. The term $L(e(\lambda))$ is a known scalar positive differentiable function with the following properties:

$$L(0) = 0$$
$$L(e) > 0 \text{ for } e \neq 0 \tag{7.35}$$

The function usually chosen is

$$L(e) = \frac{1}{2}e^2 \tag{7.36}$$

where the error signal is generally a scalar rather than a vector. The interval $t \leq \lambda \leq t + T$ is a crucial parameter in determining system adaptation. For example, if the interval is too short, there is insufficient information concerning the error to make appropriate changes in the controller parameters. One generally tries to make T large enough to include the influence of all the plant parameters on the error functional. As a lower limit, one can use the settling time of the model

$$T > \tau_M$$

The objective of the changes we make in the gain parameter is to minimize the value of the functional given by Equation 7.34. However, the relationship between the gain and the functional is not generally known a priori. Consequently, we must rely on search techniques to find the value of gain that minimizes the functional, J. To do this, a small change is made in the gain and the error change is observed. If the value of the functional increases, we reverse the direction of the gain change; if the value of the functional decreases, we continue to change the gain in the same direction. This process, a realization of the *gradient search* or *steepest descent technique*, considers a gain change, Δk, which is given by

$$\Delta k = -\alpha \frac{\partial J}{\partial k} \tag{7.37}$$

where α is a positive constant that specifies the step size of the gain change. The value of α is chosen such that several integration intervals T are needed before the final value of gain k is achieved, thereby causing the system adaptation time, T_A, to be much greater than τ_M:

$$T_A \gg \tau_M$$

There are several specific algorithms for performing gradient search in adaptive control systems [1, 5]; however, further pursuit of them is beyond the scope of this text.

It should now be clear that with implicit identification control systems, one may not know what the ideal values of the gains are. Only the direction of change is indicated within these systems. Unlike the explicit schemes, it usually takes several iterations for the gains to converge and thus for the system to adapt to plant changes. Furthermore, since adaptation is usually slow, it is often difficult to assume that the plant parameters are constant over the adaptation interval, T_A. This, compounded by the fact that the adaptation algorithm is nonlinear, makes analysis of implicit identification adaptive controllers a difficult task indeed and often makes the prediction of stability much more difficult than for explicit systems.

LEARNING CONTROLS

The control systems considered thus far have been limited to making controller changes based on the instantaneous present performance measure or the performance averaged over some interval just before the present time. They do not make extensive use of the results of previous measurements in the computation of the new parameters. It then seems reasonable that, for example, if the gradient in an implicit system is in the same direction and improves performance for some n measurements, an increase in the value of α may speed up the convergence process. On the other hand, as one approaches a minimum, a large α would cause the system to overshoot the minimum, and a decrease in α would seem appropriate. The addition of these features to an adaptive control system requires the following changes:

1. The performance resulting from a controller change must be classified as "good" or "bad," and the system must be "rewarded" or "punished," respectively.
2. The system must be capable of using the results of past behavior in determining present behavior; i.e., it must have memory.

Therefore, a *learning control system* has been defined as an adaptive controller with the additional properties given earlier [3, 6, 7]. This definition of a learning control system is not consistent with the definitions given in Chapter 5. Change 1 merely adds another constraint to the PEEL, and change 2 gives the PEEL memory. No specific time constraint on performance, a necessary condition for a learning system as defined in Chapter 5, is applied explicitly. On the other hand, most control systems in a real environment have an implicit time constraint in that performance must be acceptable within some "reasonable" period of time for the system to be useful. Learning control systems generally exhibit performance that gradually improves with time (expediency), and learning usually refers to the fact that either an improvement in the estimate of some information has occurred or some system parameters have been properly identified (learned). The amount of memory in a learning controller determines how much past experience that can be used in learning is a function of memory length. For the remainder of this chapter, we shall use the term "learning controller" to refer to an adaptive controller with the changes we have noted.

The relative behavior of a learning controller with respect to an adaptive controller can easily be seen by examining the optimization of the cost functional given in Figure 7.6 with respect to the gain k. The figure indicates that the point of *optimum* behavior for this system corresponds to

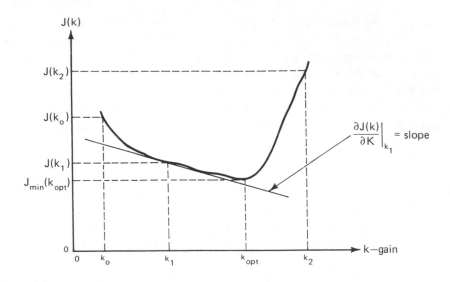

Figure 7.6.   Gradient optimization of cost functional.

the gain k_{opt}, where the cost functional is minimum. Here, *expedient* behavior occurs if the system gain becomes arbitrarily close to k_{opt} and gets closer asymptotically as the system operation progresses. The optimum gain is k_{opt}, where the cost is minimized. If we are at gain k_i initially, it is desirable to choose a gain k_j such that

$$J(k_j) < J(k_i) \qquad (7.38)$$

This ensures at least expedient system behavior. Now, if the value of α is large, then, starting with gain k_1, it is possible for the new value of gain to be

$$k_2 = k_1 - \alpha \frac{\partial J}{\partial k}\Big|_{k_1} \qquad (7.39)$$

where $J(k_2) < J(k_1)$. This behavior is typical of implicit adaptive systems. On the other hand, a learning system might remember $J(k_1)$, compare it to $J(k_2)$, *punish* the system by reducing α, go back to gain k_1, and try again. Similarly, given an initial gain of k_0 and a new gain of k_1 that satisfies Equation 7.38, the system would be rewarded and the value increased.

Because the additions to an adaptive control system in order to make a learning control system certainly increase the complexity and cost of the system, we may well ask why one would use a learning rather than an adaptive controller. The learning controller constructs a "model" of the plant by building a set of input/output relationships in its memory and by using this set of data to compute each new set of gains. Consequently, less a priori information concerning the behavior of the plant is needed to design a learning controller than to design an adaptive controller, and cost and complexity must be balanced against the available a priori information concerning the plant dynamics. The concept of a self-organizing controller includes many of these features; therefore, we shall reserve study of examples of these processes for the next section.

SELF-ORGANIZING CONTROLLERS

A self-organizing system is defined as an adaptive or learning system in which the initial state is either unknown, a random variable, or a "don't care." Thus, it is of interest to look at the simple system given in Figure 7.7, which makes use of probability state variable (PSV) encoding [8, 9]. PSV encoding associates a probability distribution function with the system parameters that are to respond to the performance evaluation. This is in contrast to the deterministic values of the system parameters used in adaptive and learning controllers. PSV encoding is accomplished by a PSV module located in the self-organizing controller. The function of the PSV is to identify one of the plant parameters, and multiple-parameter identification can be accomplished with a combination of PSV units. The identification that takes place in the PSV, however, results in a signal related to the parameter being identified only in a statistical sense. In general, these PSV identifications may be described as implicit stochastic identification without the use of a model. An interesting aspect of the configuration given in Figure 7.7 is that the performance assessment takes place within the self-organizing controller, which is in the forward loop. The input x and the sensor feedback s are compared to form an error vector e, which is applied to the self-organizing controller. The output of the controller u drives the plant, which, in turn, acts on the environment. This causes the reaction v, which is measured by various sensors in the system to form the feedback vector s. The sensors in these systems must be chosen so that the

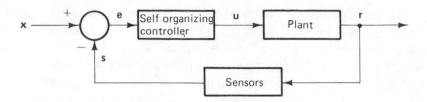

Figure 7.7.   Self-organizing controller configuration.

performance measured is appropriate to the system goals and constraints. In other words, we must ensure that the sensors measure the "essential" variables.

Assuming that the sensors can be defined correctly, it is interesting to examine the structure of a self-organizing controller in greater detail. A self-organizing controller for a single-variable error vector is shown in Figure 7.8. The predictor, which has the transfer function

$$\frac{e_p}{e}(s) = 1 + Ts \tag{7.40}$$

provides lead compensation, which can also be described as an augmented

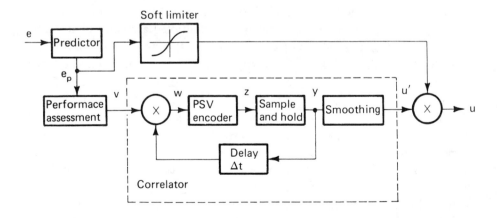

Figure 7.8.   Self-organizing controller.

derivative of the error signal. Note that here we consider the system variables as scalars rather than vectors. This simple first-order linear predictor has been used successfully in several controllers with both low and high order plants. The error function e_p is then processed by the performance assessment module to produce an output corresponding to a "reward" or "punishment" of the system's behavior. Before we describe the remainder of the controller, let us examine the performance assessment module in some detail.

Since the performance assessment must be based on the predicted error, e_p, let us define the requirements placed on this function. The augmented derivative representation of Equation 7.40

$$e_p = e + T\dot{e} \qquad (7.41)$$

provides clues to these requirements. First, the objective of the system is to reduce the predicted error to zero, which corresponds to the condition

$$e = -T\dot{e} \qquad (7.42)$$

where the error equals minus the error rate times the prediction time constant T. Equation 7.42 defines a switching line in the phase plane given in Figure 7.9. If we assume that the system error e_p corresponds to the point A, then the perpendicular distance from A to the switching line is a measure of the predicted error e_p. Thus, from A the error is driven toward the switching line, and when e_p changes sign by crossing the switching line at B, the control actions must be reversed and likewise at C and D, as shown in Figure 7.9. Once the switching line is acquired, the error behavior is given by the solution to the homogeneous differential Equation 7.43, which is

$$e(t) = e^{-t/T} \qquad (7.43)$$

and the error exponentially decreases to zero. Thus, the primary task of the self-organizing controller is to ensure acquisition of the switching line and minimization of the integral of predicted error over each assessment interval, Δt. In this context, a reasonable performance criterion is

$$P(t) = \int_{t_i}^{t_i + \Delta t} |e_p| \, dt \qquad (7.44)$$

It can be shown [8] that a simple performance value function for second-

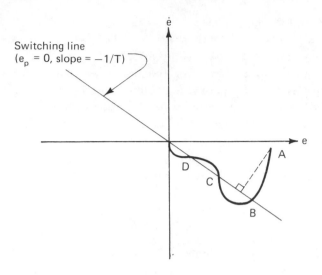

Figure 7.9.   Phase plane and switching line for $e_p = 0$.

order systems that produces a reward, $+1$, and punishment -1, and that satisfies the essential requirements of Equation 7.44 is

$$V = -\text{sgn } e_p \text{ sgn } \ddot{e}_p \qquad (7.45)$$

Thus, when the error and error acceleration have opposite signs, indicating that the predicted error is moving toward the switching line, the system is rewarded. Conversely, if e_p and $\ddot{e}_p$ have the same sign, indicating a trajectory away from the switching line, the system is punished. A block diagram of a performance assessment module that implements the function given in Equation 7.45 is shown in Figure 7.10.

The location of the differentiator breakpoints in the performance assessment module must be related to the delay interval in the correlator in order to minimize the effects of noise common to differentiator circuits [10]. Although the performance assessment module shown in Figure 7.10 was designed for second-order systems, it has been used effectively in higher order systems by decreasing the time interval of the correlator. The increased number of correlations per unit time allows the second-order assessment to follow the higher order responses of the plant.

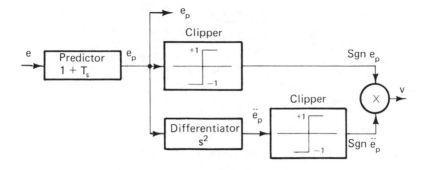

Figure 7.10. Performance assessment module.

The correlator compares the previously coded output with the reward or punishment associated with the system. The duration of the correlator delay, Δt, is from 10^{-4} to 10^{-2} times the closed loop system response time depending on the order of the plant and the band pass of the performance assessment module.

The actual correlation process occurs in the following manner. The output, $y(t - \Delta t)$, is multiplied by +1 or −1, the performance assessment, and the average of several of these individual correlations is derived in the smoothing filter in the first stage of the PSV encoder, as shown in Figure 7.11.

The main purpose of the PSV encoder is to provide a drive signal for the plant, which is decoupled from the high frequency system components and noise in the sensors. The PSV signal also provides a drive that allows "experimentation" and hence the opportunity to find better system parameters by a guided random search. The smoothed, correlated signal is thus passed through a soft limiter that merely constrains its dynamic range to correspond to the magnitude of the noise signal to produce the probability control voltage (PCV). This limiting action does not allow the probability of any one value of the PCV to become unity or zero, thus ensuring expedient behavior. The PSV is then corrupted by additive noise, thereby creating a signal in which the sign of the output is a stochastic process. The noise signal is carefully tailored by a high pass filter to eliminate low frequency energy within the plant passband from the plant actuating signal, u, which may excite low frequency oscillations in the system. The high

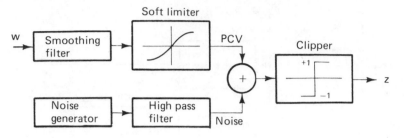

Figure 7.11.   Probability state variable (PSV) encoder.

frequency noise added to the PCV also tends to decrease the statistical correlation between the controller output signals and the sensor noise. This permits the use of high gain controllers without the usual concomitant instabilities. Finally, the hard limiter in the PSV encoder is used as a decision device, which has an output of $+1$ if the PSV plus noise signal is greater than zero and -1 if this summed signal is less than zero. The relative probability of a $+1$ or -1 PSV output is a direct function of the PCV and hence of w.

In terms of Figure 7.8, the output of the PSV encoder, z, is sampled periodically and held constant by the sample and hold element at $+1$ or -1 for a time interval Δt. Consequently, plant responses to random experiments generated by the PSV encoder can be evaluated over the finite interval Δt. This allows the plant sufficient time to respond to the experimental control signal. Since the sample rate is greater than the response rate of the plant, it is necessary to smooth the correlator output with a low pass filter or digital register to produce a final correlator output u', which will not excite instabilities in a quick reaction plant.

The plant-driving signal, u, is derived by multiplying the correlator output by a nonlinear function of the predicted error e_p. This is sometimes referred to as actuation logic. The nonlinear function preserves sign e_p while giving a gradual change in sign as e_p approaches zero, the switching line. This feed-forward sign information causes the control signal to reverse polarity quickly as the switching line is crossed. This path is necessary because the delay in the assessment-correlation process is generally too long to provide the tight control needed in this region of the phase space. Thus, if the predicted error and the correlator are in agreement, the plant signal is positive; conversely, the plant signal is negative if these two signals do not agree.

The overall behavior of a self-organizing controller is as follows. Initially, there is no information concerning which polarity of control output produces the proper plant response. The noise signal then generates an experimental control signal that is evaluated by the controller. If there is some correlation between the trial direction and system performance, this direction of control is continued. If there is no correlation, the system continues to search at random in each direction with equal probability until some correlation is found.

A particularly interesting application of self-organizing controllers is in multiple-input/multiple-output control systems where the inputs and outputs are correlated in some unknown and/or time-varying manner. Control of these complex interactive systems is accomplished by searching each response assessment for correlations to each output element. This is shown in Figure 7.12, where the correlator and actuation logic are combined because the actuation correlation logic and the sign e_p feed-forward loops are not shown. Thus, all correlations that drive the system toward a multidimensional switching hyperplane are tested, and the system converges to the proper behavior.

HIERARCHAL SYSTEMS

The interaction of several actuators in a single-goal control problem was considered in the previous section. Now, let us examine some interconnection schemes for several adaptive, learning, or self-organizing controllers when one or more controllers may influence the behavior of some other controller or controllers in a multiple-goal or -subgoal system.

Examples of the concept of hierarchal systems in both natural and man-made systems are easily found [11]. A most obvious example is the military command control hierarchy from the President through the commanding generals to the individual private. The structure of management in most corporations is another case of a hierarchal multilevel system.

An example of a hierarchal system in nature is the common alley cat. The highest level is the animal's head, containing the major overall sensors, ears, eyes, and whiskers; the effectors, eyes, head motion, mouth, and jaw; and the highest level central control and decision device, the brain.

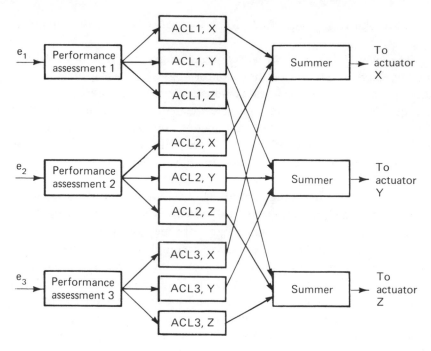

Figure 7.12. Multiple-input/multiple-output self-organizing controller (sensors have been deleted for clarity).

The next level in this system is the body, which serves as an "interface processor" between the highest level—the head—and the lowest level—the extremities. There is, of course, the effector action of body motion at this level as well as the various touch, temperature, and kinesthetic sensors. However, the spinal cord, which relays and processes information flowing through the system, accounts for this part of the system's being called an interface processor.

The extremities, legs and tail, are the lowest level of this system. The major function performed here is that of an effector. The main sensory action at this level is also associated with touch, temperature, and kinesthetics, and the amount of information processing at this level is minimal.

The overall goal of the system is to perform the needed actions coordinating and controlling each level in some way. A model of a

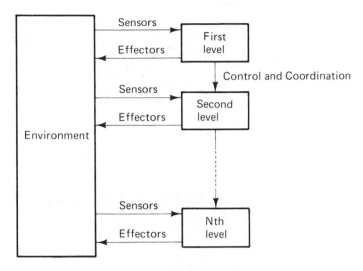

Figure 7.13.   Model of hierarchal multilevel system.

multilevel system that may be associated with the cat hierarchy is given in Figure 7.13. In this model, one can consider the first level to be a supremal unit that directs the actions of the lower levels.

Another type of hierarchal system is one in which control is distributed throughout the system. Such a system might operate in the following manner. By either internal or external means, the highest level of the system is provided with the overall objective. This level determines which portions of the task it can perform and how much will be relayed to lower levels. It then sends the remaining tasks to the next lower level, which, in turn, computes a strategy and so forth until all levels of the system needed are oriented to this task.

The model given in Figure 7.14 illustrates these concepts, where an adaptive, learning, or self-organizing unit is located at each level of the system.

The input to the whole system is presented to the first level, which does what it can, farming out the remaining work to the next lower level, etc. The performance at each level is evaluated with respect to the work it "intends" to do—thus, the "summer" at the input to the performance evaluation element.

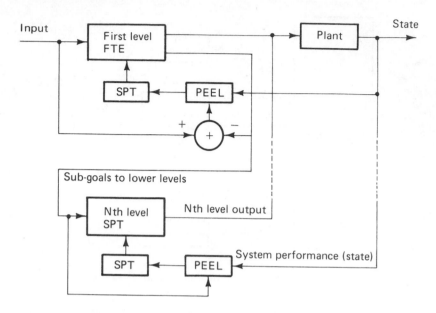

Figure 7.14. Hierarchal multilevel system of adaptive, learning, or self-organizing controllers.

SUMMARY

Applications of the concepts of adaptation, learning, and self-organization developed previously in the area of control have been explored in this chapter.

The parameter adaptive control system, one of the simplest systems, has been defined, and the problems of performance assessment/identification have been described. The concepts of implicit and explicit identification and examples of these systems were presented.

The gradient search technique and its advantages and disadvantages in implicit identification systems were used as an example. The variation in gradient step size in response to a reward or punishment was used to introduce the concept of a learning control system.

A specific example of a self-organizing controller that has been applied to the control of high performance aircraft was presented.

In the last section we introduced the problems associated with large systems in which a hierarchy is implied.

EXERCISES

1. Given the accompanying RC circuit,

    (a) Find the state-variable representation, using the voltages across the capacitors as the state variables.
    (b) Find the eigenvalues of system matrix A.

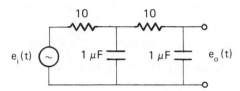

2. Describe the behavior of the parameter adaptive system shown here using frequency domain techniques for $A = -5$ and $B = 6$, and find the range of B for stable operation for $A = -5$, $+5$, and $+10$. Note: The system is stable if poles of its transfer function lie in the left half of the s-plane.

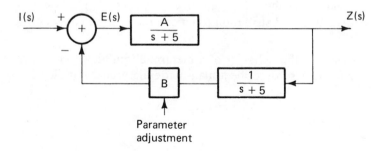

3. Describe the behavior of the gradient search technique for the maximum of the cost functional shown here for $\alpha = 10$, 5, and 2, where the system initially is at A.

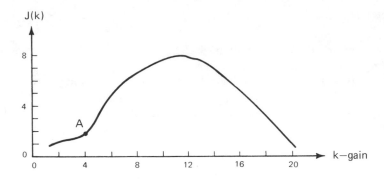

4. Using the cost functional in Exercise 3, describe the behavior of a learning control system where α can take on any one of the following values: 1, 2, 5, or 10.

5. The noise injected within the PSV encoder is one of the interesting features of the self-organizing controllers described in this chapter. Assuming that the soft limiter in the PSV encoder has a range of ±10 volts, sketch the output of the summer and the PSV encoder for normally distributed noise of 1, 5, and 10 volts RMS (root mean squared) and inputs of 1, 3, and 7 volts. Describe qualitatively the effects of these values of noise on the search behavior of the self-organizing controller. (Hint: Use probability density and distribution functions to describe your results.)

6. Describe the behavior of a hierarchal multilevel system found in nature. Also describe a man-made hierarchal multilevel system.

REFERENCES

1. DORF, Richard C., *Time Domain Analysis and Design of Control Systems*, Addison-Wesley, Reading, Mass., 1965.
2. PIPES, L. A., *Matrix Methods for Engineering*, Prentice-Hall, Englewood Cliffs, N.J., 1963.
3. PRICE, C. F., and W. B. KOENIGSBERG, "Adaptive Control and Guidance for Tactical Missiles" *ONR, Code 461*, Vols. I and II, report under Contract No. N00014-69-C-0391, Analytic Sciences Corporation, Reading, Mass., June 1970.

4. EHLERS, H. L., and R. K. SMYTH, "Survey of Adaptive Control Applications to Aerospace Vehicles," *Paper No. 68-970*, AIAA Guidance Control and Flight Dynamics Conference, Pasadena, Calif., August 1968.
5. MENDEL, J. M., and K. S. FU, *Adaptive, Learning and Pattern Recognition Systems, Theory and Applications*, Academic Press, New York, 1970.
6. FU, K. S., "Learning Control Systems—Review and Outlook," *IEEE Transactions on Automatic Control*, Vol. AC-15, No. 2, April 1970, pp. 210–221.
7. FU, K. S., "Learning System Theory," in *System Theory*, L. A. ZADEH and E. POLAK, eds., McGraw-Hill, New York, 1969.
8. BARRON, Roger, "Self-Organizing Controllers—Part I," *Control Engineering*, February 1968, pp. 70–74.
9. BARRON, Roger, "Self-Organizing Controllers—Part II," *Control Engineering*, March 1968, pp. 69–74.
10. *Analysis and Synthesis of Advanced Self-Organizing Control Systems*, Wright Patterson AFB, Ohio, final technical report, Contract AF 33(615)-3673, AFAL-TR-67-93, AF Avionics Laboratory, Adaptronics, Inc., April 1967.
11 MESAROVIC, M. D., D. MACKO, and Y. TAKAHARA, *Theory of Hierarchal Multilevel Systems*, Academic Press, New York, 1970.

8

Cybernetic Techniques in Communication Systems

Cybernetic techniques as applied to communications are the subject of this chapter. These techniques have been particularly useful in systems such as radio transmission of data, where fading, noise, and multipath distortion interfere with the communications. Similar problems also occur in wire/telephone-type communications systems, where the paths and channels for communications between any two points are generally different each time communications are established. Thus, it is often necessary to learn the status of a channel in order to optimize the receiving system before information can be transmitted, and later to adapt the receiver to changes in the channel characteristics.

COMMUNICATIONS SYSTEMS

In this chapter we shall be concerned exclusively with pulse transmission systems. This restriction is based on two important considerations: (1) most modern communication systems use these techniques exclusively, and (2) pulse systems are more amenable to the application of the adaptive and learning techniques presented in this book.

The representation of a general pulse transmission system is given in Figure 8.1. Here, the information at the input to the system is encoded in

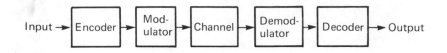

Figure 8.1.   General pulse transmission system.

some sense. For example, the coding may be simple analog-to-digital conversion, or, if the signal is already in digital form, a parity bit or error correction and/or detection coding may be imposed. This encoded signal drives the modulator, which maps the pulse sequence into an analog wave suitable for transmission over the channel. The channel is, of course, the source of all the problems of communications systems, as they have been known to introduce noise, nonlinearities, and phase and amplitude distortion and to drop out altogether. At the receiving end, the demodulator maps the received analog waveform into a pulse sequence that is a "best guess" of the sequence transmitted. The decoder operates on the binary sequence to extract the information originally impressed on the encoder. The overall objective is to transfer the information from the input to the output within some a priori specified low error rate, where the error rate is the average number of disagreements per unit of time between the inputs and the outputs. The encoding and decoding processes require special techniques that are beyond the scope of this text. However, the modulator and especially the channel and demodulator are important here.

For simplicity, the modulation processes that we shall consider represent two kinds of pulse transmission techniques: pulse amplitude modulation (PAM) and pulse code modulation (PCM). These processes are illustrated for a sinusoidal information signal in Figure 8.2. In PAM, the pulse amplitude is a function of the amplitude of the input signal at some instant of time and, in PCM, the sequence of pulses (which may be present or not, 1 or 0) in some interval of time is a function of the amplitude of the input signal at some instant of time. A fundamental requirement in these systems is that the modulating signal be sampled in accordance with the Nyquist criterion. The Nyquist criterion or sampling theorem states that a band-limited signal that is sampled at a rate equal to or greater than twice the upper band-limited frequency can be reconstructed exactly from these samples. Most information signals of consequence are band-limited— namely, they are restricted to within some finite range of frequencies. For

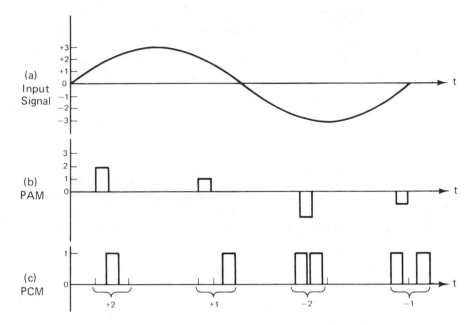

Figure 8.2.   Pulse amplitude modulation and pulse code modulation.

example, voice, video, and data signals are band-limited signals, albeit to different bands: 300 – 4000 hertz, 0 – 5 megahertz, and approximately 0 – 10 megahertz, respectively.

Also, these modulation techniques require that the range of amplitudes of the input signal be quantized into a finite number of intervals. The range of the input signal in Figure 8.2a has been quantized into seven intervals. A PAM system transmits a pulse at each sample time whose amplitude is the quantized value at that time, as illustrated in Figure 8.2b.

In general, in a PAM communication system the transmitted signal, $x(t)$, can be represented by a time series of the form

$$x(t) = \sum_{k=-\infty}^{\infty} a_k s(t - KT) \tag{8.1}$$

where a_k is the quantized amplitude of $x(t)$; where $s(t - kT)$, $k = \cdots - 1$, 0, 1, ..., represents the set of time-translated versions of a single pulse-like signal, shown in Figure 8.3 called an interpolating pulse; and where T is the sample period.

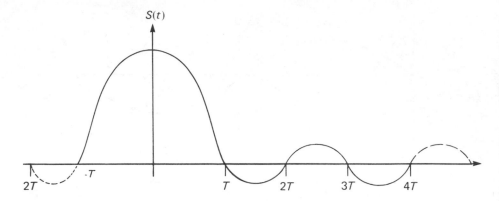

Figure 8.3.   Interpolating pulse, which has the property that $S(0) = 1$ and $S(kT) = 0 \; \forall k \neq 0$.

PCM systems, on the other hand, transmit only binary pulses over the channel. The process of PCM carries the PAM technique one step further by coding each sampled quantized element into a sequence of binary digits where each group of N bits represents the quantized amplitude of the signal at that sample time. Thus, in Figure 8.2c each group of three bits carries the amplitude information for that sample. A representation of the PCM signal is

$$x(t) = \sum_{k=-\infty}^{\infty} \sum_{n=0}^{N-1} a_{kn} s\left[t - \left(k + \frac{n}{N}\right)T\right] \qquad (8.2)$$

where $a_{kn} = \{0,1\}$ is the binary alphabet, and $s(t)$ is as in Equation 8.1. Equation 8.2 represents a series of sequences of N pulse intervals per sample period T, where the pulse shape, $s(t)$, is sent in a pulse interval to represent a 1 and nothing is sent in a pulse interval to represent a 0.

THE CHANNEL

There are two distinct characteristics of the communications channel with which one must deal when using PAM and PCM. The first is random noise, which is generally modeled as guassian and accounted for by an additive term in a hypothetical noiseless channel. There are several sources of gaussian noise in a communications system, including thermal and shot noise in the transmitting and receiving equipment.

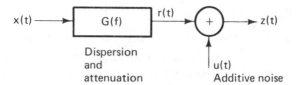

Figure 8.4.   Model of the communications channel.

The second characteristic is often associated with multipath distortion wherein there exists more than one path from the transmitter to the receiver in a radio communications system. The effects of multipath distortion are dramatically illustrated when one listens to FM stereo or watches color TV as an airplane passes between the transmitter and the receiver. Here either noise or distortion is heard from the FM receiver and the colors wash out on the TV set. A similar effect, called linear distortion, is observed on wire communications systems.

Linear distortion is generally specified as amplitude attenuation and envelope delay as a function of frequency [1]. The envelope delay, which is the derivative of the phase characteristic, is a measure of the relative time of arrival at the channel output of the various frequency components of the input signal. Now, it is a rare channel indeed whose attenuation and/or envelope delay is constant with frequency. Thus, the input signal is distorted as it passes through the channel. This distortion in pulse transmission systems causes an overlap in the arrival of the energy associated with successive symbols; the overlap is called intersymbol interference. If the channel characteristics are known, it is generally possible to compensate at the receiver to remove the intersymbol interference. However, as suggested previously, the channel is not usually known exactly and has a tendency to vary with time. The range of possible channel configurations, even in a switched telephone network, is so large that it is impractical to try to compensate in each one. Thus, the problem of compensation (or equalization) of communications channels is one in which adaptive techniques are necessary.

Finally, we can model the channel by a dispersion function $G(f)$ and additive noise, as shown in Figure 8.4. $G(f)$ is a transfer function that represents the characteristics of the channel without noise. The noise added to the output of $G(f)$ represents that added to the signal as it passes through the channel.

CHANNEL EQUALIZATION

Now that the problems introduced by the channel have been defined, let us investigate a method for equalizing these adverse effects. The signal transmitted is a series of pulses sent at discrete intervals of time. Therefore, the receiver filter $H(f)$ must be designed so that it can be sampled synchronously to produce an output sequence $\{b_k\}$ that is a best estimate of the input sequence $\{a_k\}$. To understand this problem in detail, it is useful to compare a typical waveform at the input to the receiver with an ideal waveform, as shown in Figure 8.5. The ideal waveform is maximum at the decision time for that interval and is zero for all other decision times, whereas the typical received waveform may have its maximum before or after the decision point and is not usually zero at the other decision points. The nonzero values of the received signal at other decision times thus interfere with the values of the other pulses at their decision times, causing intersymbol interference as shown in Figure 8.6. Analytically, intersymbol interference can be expressed as follows. Let the received signal $x(t)$ be expressed as in Equation 8.3:

$$x(t) = \sum_k a_k s(t - \tau_k) \qquad (8.3)$$

By sampling the received signal at the decision times kT, a collection of sample values b_k which are estimates of the corresponding a_k is obtained. The sample value b_k can be represented as in Equation 8.4.

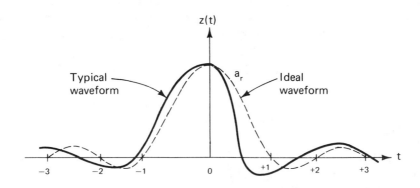

Figure 8.5. Typical received waveform and ideal waveform.

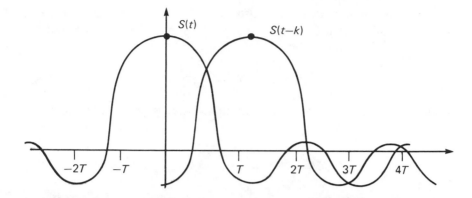

Figure 8.6. Pictorial representation of intersymbol interference.

$$b_k = x(\tau_k) = a_k s(0) + \sum_{\forall j, j \neq k} a_j s(\tau_k - \tau_j) \qquad (8.4)$$

The last term in Equation 8.4 is the intersymbol interference error generated by overlapping nonzero values of adjacent pulses at the decision times. Equalization of the intersymbol interference then requires that the effects of a pulse at times other than its sample time be zero [2].

In the design of the receiver for a communications system, more than one design criterion can be utilized. For example, let us designate the receiver response, $H(f)$, and sample its output periodically at period T, as shown in Figure 8.7. Then, the output of the receiver can be compared to the transmitted symbol, and we can use a minimum mean-squared error criterion in our design. On the other hand, a design criterion that minimizes

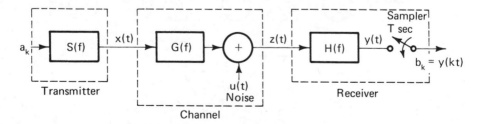

Figure 8.7. Transmitter, receiver, and channel.

intersymbol interference [1] can also be used. Let us consider the mean-squared error given in Equation 8.5 and design based on the minimization of this error:

$$I = E[(b_k - a_k)^2] \tag{8.5}$$

Equation 8.5 can be minimized using techniques from the calculus of variations [3], to give

$$H(f) = S^*(f)G^*(f) \sum_{n=-\infty}^{\infty} d_n e^{-j2\pi nTf} \tag{8.6}$$

where $S^*(f)G^*(f)$ defines a conjugate or matched filter that is optimum for additive white gaussian noise in the channel. The remainder of Equation 8.6 defines a most interesting structure consisting of a series of delays, since the term $e^{-j2\pi nTf}$ in the frequency domain defines an nT-second delay and a weighted summing net. The last element, called a transversal equalizer, is illustrated in Figure 8.8. The purpose of the matched filter is to reduce the effects of noise while the equalizer reduces the intersymbol interference.

The impulse response of the transversal filter-equalizer is given by

$$e(t) = \sum_{n=-N}^{N} d_n \delta(t - nT) \tag{8.7}$$

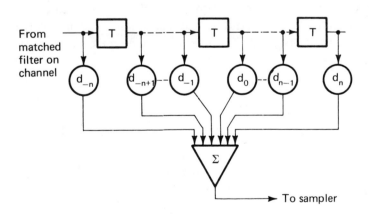

Figure 8.8.   Transversal equalizer.

and, as before, the frequency domain response is

$$E(f) = \sum_{n=-N}^{N} d_n e^{-j2\pi nTf} \tag{8.8}$$

Consider an input $x(t)$ to the filter of Figure 8.6; then the output response, $x(t)*e(t)$ is

$$h(t) = \sum_{n=-N}^{N} d_n x(t - nT) \tag{8.9}$$

At the output of the sampler, however, we are concerned only with the value of Equation 8.7 at the sampling times (kT):

$$h(kT) = \sum_{n=-N}^{N} d_n x[(k - n)T] \tag{8.10}$$

Thus, the output at each time kT is a function of the tap gains d_n and the equalizer input at times $(k - n)T$. Now, given a transmitted signal and a channel corrupted by white noise, we can compute the appropriate matched filter as well as the proper tap gains for the transversal filter. However, this information is not generally available, and we must incorporate techniques that do not require as much a priori knowledge for effective operation.

First, since we do not usually know $G(f)$ and cannot assume that the noise $u(t)$ is white and normally distributed, we are forced to sacrifice the matched-filter portion of the receiver and rely on the transversal equalizer to improve the detection process. Second, the intersymbol interference can generally be made arbitrarily small as the length of the transversal filter becomes large.

However, the number of delay elements $(2N + 1)$ is restricted, usually by cost, and must be chosen to accommodate the range of channels expected. Therefore, given a finite filter with $2N + 1$ "tap" gains d_n, the problem is reduced to determining these gains, and the method, of course, is adaptive.

Several performance criteria can be applied to derive the adaptation procedure; however, we shall restrict our attention to gradient techniques in this discussion. Thus, we form the function

$$d_n^{(k+1)} = d_n^{(k)} - \alpha \frac{\partial I}{\partial d_n} \qquad \forall k \tag{8.11}$$

which moves the values of the gains in a direction such that the mean-squared error I is reduced. The term α is the step size factor and determines the relative magnitude of the incremental gain changes. The mean-squared error can be written by combining Equations 8.5 and 8.10 as

$$I = E\left[\left\{\sum_{n=-N}^{N} d_n x(k-n)T - a_k\right\}^2\right] \tag{8.12}$$

and

$$\frac{\partial I}{\partial d_n} = 2E[\{\phi(k)\}\{x(k-n)T\}] \tag{8.13}$$

which is the correlation of the sample with the error before the nth gain element, d_n, where

$$\phi(k) = \sum_{n=-N}^{N} d_n x(k-n)T - a_k \tag{8.14}$$

A block diagram of this adaptation algorithm for one of the $2N + 1$ gain elements is illustrated in Figure 8.9. Note that the decision element in Figure 8.9 maps the transversal filter output into a specific element from the set of input symbols. The reference signal a_r is the primary difficulty in implementing this system.

There are several techniques for supplying the reference signal to the adaptation mechanism [1]. In one approach a known sequence of signals is stored in the receiver, and, after a particular coded sequence is sent, these signals are transmitted through the channel. The received signals are then compared with the stored sequence to form the error signal. This condition is often referred to as the training mode. Since the known sequence is triggered by an external command, this system may be considered "learning with a teacher" as defined in Chapter 5.

Another approach spreads the adaptation process over the operating time of the adaptive equalizer by sending pulses in a quasi-random pattern along with the data sequence. Another quasi-random generator located in the receiver that is synchronized with the transmitter is used to form the error signal.

Before the next adaptive approach is described, it is necessary to examine the output of the equalizer described thus far. The output, at the sample instants, is a signal that, if the intersymbol interference has been

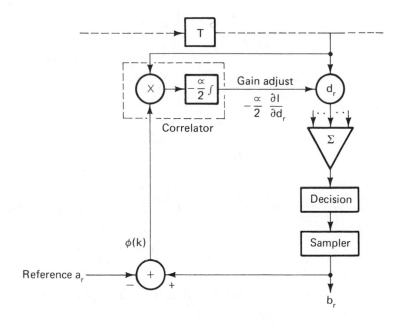

Figure 8.9. Adaptation of single gain element using gradient technique.

removed, is a noisy version of the transmitted signal. Therefore, it is necessary to apply a decision mechanism in order to determine the "best guess" of the transmitted signal. This decision mechanism takes the form of a single threshold (clipper) for binary signals, two thresholds for three-level PAM, and $N - 1$ thresholds for N-level PAM. The determination of these thresholds is the topic of the next section. Now, since specific output symbols are generated from the receiver output, it is possible to use these decisions as estimates for the reference input, as shown in Figure 8.10. Thus, if the error rate is relatively low, a good estimate of the transmitted signal is obtained from the output, and adaptation to relatively small changes in the channel can occur. However, if the channel changes rapidly or if the initial error rate is high, the adaptation becomes difficult, if indeed possible at all. This final adaptation technique, decision-directed adaptation, can be very effective when used in conjunction with one of the other techniques, the training mode process, for example. The training mode may be used upon establishing communications to initialize the tap gains, and

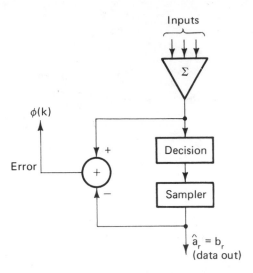

Figure 8.10.   Decision-directed equalizer.

the decision-directed process may be used to track changes in the channel characteristics while the communications are in process.

THE DECISION PROCESS

The final step before decoding in any pulse transmission system is the decision process, which classifies the signal at the sample times into one of the N levels being transmitted through the system. Thus, the signal at the output of the sampler $y(nT)$, for each time n, in a PCM system must be classified as 1 or 0. The problem is that the value of the samples at the output of the sampler is corrupted by noise, which complicates the decision process. If we assume that the noise is gaussian (i.e., normally distributed), we can represent the statistical properties of the sample $y(nT) = y_n$ for PCM as follows:

$$p(y_n/0) = \frac{1}{\sqrt{2}\,\pi\sigma} \exp\left(\frac{-y_n^2}{2\sigma^2}\right) \tag{8.15}$$

$$p(y_n/1) = \frac{1}{\sqrt{2}\,\pi\sigma} \exp\left(\frac{-(y_n - \mu)^2}{2\sigma^2}\right) \tag{8.16}$$

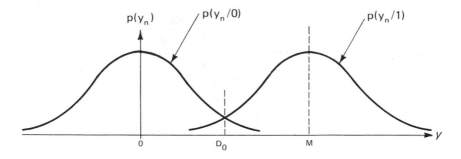

Figure 8.11. Conditional probability densities.

where σ is the standard deviation of the noise and μ is the average received value when a 1 is transmitted. Thus, Equation 8.15 is the conditional probability density of the received signal when a 0, no signal, is transmitted, and Equation 8.16 is the conditional probability density of the received signal when a 1, signal present, is transmitted. The measure of performance used to specify the received signal $y(nT)$ is the signal-to-noise ratio, which is μ/σ. The problem of determining whether a 0 or 1 is transmitted is illustrated in Figure 8.11, where one must specify a value in the signal voltage continuum above which we say a 1 was transmitted and below which we say a 0 was transmitted. An optimum decision strategy can be found using the likelihood ratio

$$L(y_n) = \frac{p(y_n/1)}{p(y_n/0)} \qquad (8.17)$$

where we compute the ratio for each y_n and compare its value with a threshold, D, and for

$$L(y_n) \geq D \qquad \text{we say 1 was transmitted}$$

$$L(y_n) < D \qquad \text{we say 0 was transmitted}$$

The value of D is given by

$$D = \frac{P_0 C_0}{P_1 C_1} \qquad (8.18)$$

where P_0 and P_1 are the a priori probabilities that a 0 and a 1 are transmitted, respectively, and C_0 and C_1 are the "costs" associated with these decisions.

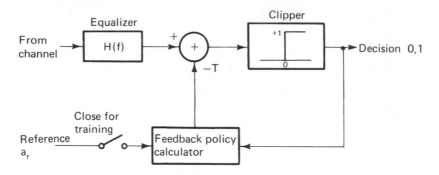

Figure 8.12.   Threshold learning process for signal detection.

The costs are generally assigned by the system designer and are based on the design constraints. Here we shall assume that the above costs are equal; then the decision problem reduces to a comparison with respect to unity:

$$\frac{P_1 p(y_n/1)}{P_0 p(y_n/0)} = 1 \tag{8.19}$$

Thus, if the transmitted signal is such that the probabilities of 1 and of 0 are equal, Equation 8.19 reduces to

$$p(y_n/1) = p(y_n/0) \tag{8.20}$$

which means that the decision threshold is placed at the point where the two probability densities are equal; their intersection, shown as point D_0 in Figure 8.11.

Consider now the case where the a priori probabilities of the symbols being transmitted change with the data at the input or where the noise or signal plus noise probability densities change each time communications are established. Here we must resort to adaptive techniques for adjusting the decision thresholds. An embodiment of an adaptive decision system for binary signals is the threshold learning process (TLP), illustrated in Figure 8.12 [4]. The noisy-equalized samples are the input to the TLP in which the threshold T is subtracted from the input sample and then to an infinite clipper that forms the binary output.

The feedback policy calculator in the TLP performs the functions of the performance evaluation element and system parameter transform of Chapter 5. The switch is used to place the system in either the operate or training mode. The operation of the system under training conditions is as follows. If the output is 1 when a 0 is transmitted, we say that a "false alarm" has occurred and it is desirable to raise the threshold. Conversely, if the system responds 0 when a 1 is transmitted, we say that a "false dismissal" has occurred and it is desirable to lower the threshold. The training process for a discrete increment TLP is described completely in Figure 8.13. The discrete increment TLP allows D to vary over a range of values from, say, 0 to k in a finite number of discrete steps, say one unit each. Thus, if $y = 1$ and $u = 0$ and the threshold is at the upper limit, k, or if $y = 0$ and $u = 1$ and the threshold is at the lower limit, 0, then we cannot change the threshold, and it remains unchanged.

The TLP is generally trained initially, and then the switch is opened and the system operates for some period of time, after which it may be retrained. The main problem with training a TLP is the same as that of the transversal equalizer, namely, the reference a_r. However, the same techniques as used previously can also be applied here.

Although the TLP has been described here as applied to signal detection, applications of it in the area of control [5] as well as in models of human visual signal detection [6] have also been described.

Channel input—u

		0	1
Decision y	0	Threshold unchanged	Move threshold down 1 step
	1	Move threshold up 1 step	Threshold unchanged

Figure 8.13.   Feedback policy for discrete increment TLP.

ERROR DETECTION/CORRECTION CODES USED IN COMMUNICATIONS SYSTEMS

In previous sections, the fundamental characteristics of the communication channel, together with techniques to mask or correct errors introduced in the channel due to noise and/or channel dispersion, were discussed. Further, a set of adaptive techniques in the design of the communication receiver, such as the transversal equalizer and the decision directed equalizer, were presented. In this section, we shall discuss another technique used quite successfully to guarantee reliable communications over a noisy channel. Fundamentally, the techniques are based on the principle of redundant encoding of data so that errors in the transmission can be detected. That is, this principle calls for the addition of redundant information so that the data being transferred becomes insensitive to noise in the channel. As an example of this technique consider a system in which every n-bit word being transmitted has appended to it a single parity bit. This parity bit is a one if an odd number of the n data bits are 1s, and a zero otherwise. In such a system any single bit error is detectable, because it produces an odd number of 1s in the word. This encoding technique is the well-known 1 bit parity check code and belongs to the general class of *error detecting/correcting codes*.

First, let us define an error detecting code to be a subset S of the universe U of vectors, chosen so that likely errors affecting a vector X in S produce vectors X' that are not in S. In this context, a code word is defined as a vector in X; while a noncode word is a vector in the set $U - S$. Now, if X is a code word and X' is a different vector produced by a failure, then X' is a detectable error if it is a noncode word; and X' is an undetectable error if it is a code word. For example, in Figure 8.14 the transformation of code word X_1 into code word X_3 due to an error introduced in the communications channel is an undetectable error, while that of code word X_2 into code word X_4 is a detectable error.

Now, in order to evaluate the robustness of a particular coding scheme, the concepts of weight of an error and the distance between code words must be introduced. The weight of an error is defined as the number of distinct simultaneous failures needed to produce that error. The distance between code words is the number of failures needed to change one code word into another code word producing an undetectable error. In this sense, the distance between code words can be considered to be a measure of the robustness of the code.

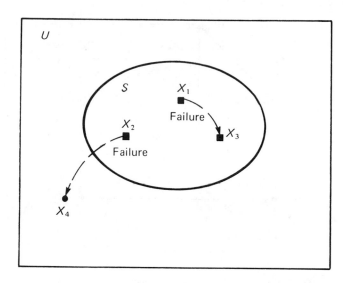

code words: X_1, X_2, X_3 detectable error: $X_2 \rightarrow X_4$
noncode word: X_4 undetectable error: $X_1 \rightarrow X_3$

Figure 8.14.   Detectable and undetectable errors.

Also, we can now define the Hamming weight of a vector X, denoted by $w(X)$, as the number of nonzero components of X. Similarly, the Hamming distance between two vectors X and Y in the code S, denoted by $d(X, Y)$, is defined as the number of components in which the vectors differ. For example, consider the five-component binary vectors, $X = \langle 1, 0, 1, 1, 1 \rangle$ and $Y = \langle 0, 1, 1, 1, 0 \rangle$. It is clear that $w(X) = 4$, $w(Y) = 3$, and $d(X, Y) = 3$. From this definition, and for binary vectors, it is easily verified that $d(X, Y) = X \oplus Y$, where $\oplus$ denotes the EXCLUSIVE OR function.

Note that, when an error occurs, a code word X changes into a code word $X' = X \oplus E$, where E is a nonzero error vector. For example, an error that changes $X = \langle 1, 0, 0, 1, 0 \rangle$ into $X' = \langle 1, 1, 0, 1, 0 \rangle$ has the error vector $E = \langle 0, 1, 0, 0, 0 \rangle$; and the weight of the error is one. An error with weight one is referred to as a single error; likewise an error with weight two is called a double error, and so forth.

The fundamental measure of the robustness of a given code S is its capability to detect errors. In this context, one considers the minimum

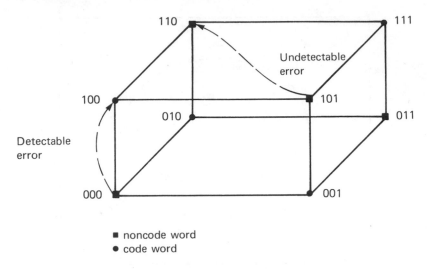

■ noncode word
● code word

Figure 8.15.   A distance-2 single-error-detecting code.

distance of a code S to be the minimum distance between all possible pairwise combinations of code words in S. One can easily verify from this definition that a code with a minimum distance of $d + 1$ can at best detect errors with weight less than or equal to d. This is illustrated in Figure 8.15 for a minimum distance-2 code with single-error-detecting capability. In this figure the code $S = \{\langle 0, 0, 0 \rangle, \langle 0, 1, 1 \rangle, \langle 1, 1, 0 \rangle, \langle 1, 0, 1 \rangle\}$ is represented by a subset of the vertices of a three-dimensional cube. Here code word $X_1 = \langle 0, 0, 0 \rangle$ is transformed by an error $E_1 = \langle 1, 0, 0 \rangle$ to noncode word $X_1' = \langle 1, 0, 0 \rangle$, a detectable error; while code word $X_3 = \langle 1, 0, 1 \rangle$ is transformed to codeword $X_4 = \langle 1, 1, 0 \rangle$ by the double error $E_2 = \langle 0, 1, 1 \rangle$, hence an undetectable error is introduced.

Furthermore, codes can also be used to correct errors as the following discussion will demonstrate. Consider a code that has a minimum distance of $2c + 1$. Then any error with weight c or less in a code word X produces an erroneous vector X' that can be correctly associated with code word X. Why? Simply note that the distance between code word X and vector X' is $d(X, X') \leq c$, while the distance between any other code word Y and X', $d(Y, X')$, is at least $c + 1$. This is illustrated by Figure 8.16.

In this figure, the code S has two code words, $\langle 0, 0, 0, 0, 0, 0, 0 \rangle$ and $\langle 0, 1, 1, 0, 1, 1, 1 \rangle$, therefore the minimum distance of the code is easily

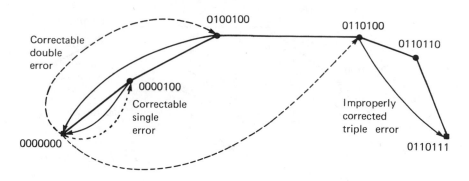

Figure 8.16.   Fragment of a distance-5 double-error-correcting code.

computed; it corresponds to the number of positions where the code words are different, 5. Furthermore, such a code can be used in a double error correction scheme as $c = 2$, ergo, the name distance-5 double-error correcting-code. Now consider two possible errors $E_1 = \langle 0,1,0,0,1,0,0, \rangle$ and $E_2 = \langle 0,1,1,0,1,0,0 \rangle$ in the transmission of code word $X_1 = \langle 0,0,0,0,0, 0,0 \rangle$. Here, E_1 represents a double detectable and correctable error, while E_2 is a triple detectable, but non correctable error. Why? First, E_1 is detectable because it transforms code word X_1 into a noncode word. Secondly, it is correctable as $d(X_1, X_1 \oplus E_1) = 2 < d(X_2, X_1 \oplus E_2) = 3$, that is, the noncode word error vector received is closer to code word X_1 than to code word X_2. A similar argument explains how error E_2 forces an improper correction of this triple error.

Finally, it is possible to use a code to correct a certain number of errors and to detect a number of additional errors. Such a case is demonstrated here in Figure 8.17 where a fragment of a distance-5 single-error-correcting, triple-error-detecting code is shown. For a code with any minimum distance, the choice of using the code to detect errors, correct errors, or both depends only on the policy of the decoder used to interpret the code.

Three generic classes of error correcting codes will be discussed in this section: parity-check codes, arithmetic codes, and checksum codes. Parity-check codes are heavily used in transmission of information in communication systems. Arithmetic codes are used in the design of reliable computing elements. Checksum codes are used in the communication between peripheral equipment and the central processing unit in a computer system.

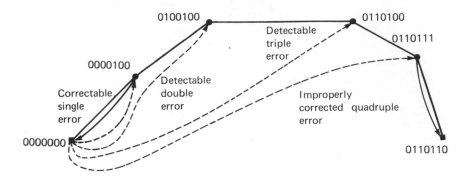

Figure 8.17.   Fragment of a distance-5 single-error-correcting, triple-error-detecting code.

Parity-Check Codes

In parity-check codes the information is encoded into vectors (or *n*-tuples or blocks) of symbols from a finite Galois field $GF(q)$ with q elements.* Although codes exist for any value of q that is a power of a prime, we shall be concerned in this section only with codes for which $q = 2$ (binary codes). More formally,

Definition. A parity-check code is a subspace of the vector space of *n*-tuples over $GF(q)$.

Parity-check codes are also called linear block codes and are used where a single component failure is assumed to affect only a single information symbol. Although a parity-check code can be specified by listing all the vectors of the code, a matrix description can also be used and is preferable, because of its compactness. Let us now state a key definition to be used in our description.

Definition. Let *H* be an $r \times n$ matrix of symbols from $GF(q)$. Then the set of *q*-ary *n*-component vectors that satisfy the matrix equation $X \cdot H^t = 0$ is called the null space of *H*.

Several important properties of parity-check codes can now be stated without proof. For a complete discussion and proofs of these properties the reader is referred to [7], [8], or [9].

---

* A finite field is an algebraic structure with a finite set of elements, an addition operator, and a multiplication operation.

Property 1. Let H be an $r \times n$ matrix over $GF(q)$ with rank $r = n - k$ (i.e., the rows of H are linearly independent). Then the null space of H is a vector subspace containing q^k vectors.

Hence, we can now define the null space of a matrix H to be the parity-check code S. For example, consider the matrix H_1 over the field $GF(2)$,

$$H_1 = \begin{bmatrix} 1 & 1 & 0 & 1 & 1 \\ 1 & 1 & 1 & 0 & 0 \end{bmatrix}$$

The null space of H_1 is the set of all 5 element binary vectors satisfying the set of simultaneous linear equations below.

$$X \cdot H' = 0 = \begin{array}{l} x_1 \oplus x_2 \oplus \quad\quad x_4 \oplus x_5 = 0 \\ x_1 \oplus x_2 \oplus x_3 \quad\quad\quad = 0 \end{array}$$

The parity-check code is $S_1 = \{\langle 0,0,0,0,0 \rangle, \langle 0,0,0,1,1 \rangle, \langle 0,1,1,1,0 \rangle, \langle 0,1,1,0,1 \rangle, \langle 1,0,1,1,0 \rangle, \langle 1,0,1,0,1 \rangle, \langle 1,1,0,0,0 \rangle, \langle 1,1,0,1,1 \rangle\}$.

Other important properties of parity-check codes have been discussed in the literature; see Wakerly [12]. However, for the purposes of this book the following property is sufficient for our present discussion.

Property 2. The null space of a parity-check matrix H has a code word of weight d if and only if there is a set of d columns of H that are linearly dependent. Further, the minimum distance of a parity-check code is equal to the minimum weight of its nonzero code words.

Basically, Property 2 allows the computation of the minimum distance of a parity-check code by just computing the smallest number of linearly dependent columns in its corresponding matrix H.

Let us consider now some binary parity-check codes, that is, codes in which information is encoded into vectors from $GF(2)$, and where addition is addition modulo 2 (EXCLUSIVE OR) and the multiplication operation is the logical AND. The most simple of such codes is the single-bit even-parity check, corresponding to the null space of the $1 \times n$ binary matrix $H = [1 \ 1 \ \cdots \ 1]$. Note that the null space of H in this case is the set of all n-bit vectors with even parity, ergo the name. This code has $n - 1$ information symbols and one check symbol. Note also that no column in H is zero, but any two columns are linearly dependent. Therefore, this code has a minimum distance of 2. This implies that such a code can at most detect a single error.

Another parity-check code widely used is the so called Hamming codes, so named after their inventor [13]. These codes are generated from the set of $r \times n$ binary matrices whose columns are the r-bit binary representations of the integers 1 through $2^r - 1$. These Hamming codes have $2^r - r - 1$ information symbols and r check symbols. For a complete description of Hamming codes see Peterson and Weldon [7].

Let us briefly describe now how parity-check codes, such as the Hamming codes, can be used to correct, not just detect single errors. Let X be the transmitted word over a communication channel, and $X' = X \oplus E$ be the received word, where E is the error vector. If there were no error in the transmission, then E is zero; if there is a single error, then E is a vector with exactly one 1 and the rest 0s. To check the received vector for errors we multiply the parity-check matrix by $X' = X \oplus E$.

$$C = (X \oplus E) \cdot H^t$$
$$= X \cdot H^t \oplus E \cdot H^t$$

The vector C is called the syndrome. Now, since X is a code word, then $X \cdot H^t$ is 0 and

$$C = E \cdot H^t$$

Thus the syndrome is a function of the error vector only. If the syndrome is zero, then either no error or an undetectable error has occurred.

If we assume a single error to have occurred (E has exactly one 1), the effect of the $E \cdot H^t$ operation is to pick off exactly one row of H^t. Further, for the purpose of this example, consider a distance-3 code in which the rows of H^t (the columns of H) are all distinct. Once the syndrome is known, the position of the single bit error that produces the syndrome can be easily deduced. It is just the position in H^t of a row equal to the syndrome. If H^t does not have a row corresponding to a nonzero syndrome, then a detectable, but uncorrectable, multiple error has occurred. Consider, for example, the seven-bit Hamming codes shown in Table 8.1 whose corresponding null space matrix H_2 is given below.

$$H_2 = \begin{bmatrix} 0 & 1 & 1 & 1 & 1 & 0 & 0 \\ 1 & 0 & 1 & 1 & 0 & 1 & 0 \\ 1 & 1 & 0 & 1 & 0 & 0 & 1 \end{bmatrix}$$

Next, assume that in the transmission of the code word $X = \langle 0, 0, 0, 0, 0, 0, 0 \rangle$ belonging to the above 7-bit Hamming code an error, in the third

Table 8.1.   Code Words of a 7-bit Hamming Code

Information Bits				Check Bits		
0	0	0	0	0	0	0
0	0	0	1	1	1	1
0	0	1	0	1	1	0
0	0	1	1	0	0	1
0	1	0	0	1	0	1
0	1	0	1	0	1	0
0	1	1	0	0	1	1
0	1	1	1	1	0	0
1	0	0	0	0	1	1
1	0	0	1	1	0	0
1	0	1	0	1	0	1
1	0	1	1	0	1	0
1	1	0	0	1	1	0
1	1	0	1	0	0	1
1	1	1	0	0	0	0
1	1	1	1	1	1	1

most position, is generated. The received word is $X' = \langle 0,0,1,0,0,0,0 \rangle$ whose syndrome, C, is given below.

$$C = X' \cdot H' = \begin{bmatrix} 1 & 1 & 0 \end{bmatrix}$$

Hence, the syndrome for word X' is identical to the third column of the parity-check matrix which in turn implies that there was a single error in the third bit position.

Arithmetic Codes

Arithmetic codes are codes that are preserved by arithmetic operations, so that the sum of two code words is a code word. Formally, let S be a code and define $\cdot$ to be a binary operation, then if $A, B \in S$ implies that $A \cdot B \in S$, we call the code S a binary arithmetic code. These codes are used primarily in the design of fault tolerant computing elements such as arithmetic and logic units (ALU) and their importance has grown significantly in recent years. However, a complete description of the properties of these codes is beyond the scope of this book. Readers are referred to the book by Wakerly [12].

Checksum Codes

To close this section we will discuss a type of code that has been used successfully and extensively in software systems to detect errors in data transmission and mass storage. In such systems, data are transmitted in packets of b-bit bytes and appended to the end of each packet is a check byte or checksum which is the sum modulo 2^b of the bytes in the packet. Systems using this scheme include the TYMNET computer communication network [10] and the PDP-11 disk operating system file storage system [11]. A complete description of this code can be found elsewhere [12].

SUMMARY

Three aspects of communications systems, in which self-organizing, adaptive, and learning techniques have been applied, were presented in this chapter. Some of these techniques are presently in use in communications systems, whereas others are relatively new and may influence the design of new systems. In particular, the equalization and detection of binary signals sent over the telephone network have required extensive use of adaptive and learning techniques to increase the rate of reliable transmission of data to and from remote computers. The ever-increasing demand for digital data transmission capability will certainly spur development of new communications systems, which will undoubtedly incorporate adaptive, learning, and self-organizing techniques in their implementation. Finally, error detecting and correcting codes were introduced.

EXERCISES

1. Find a 16-level PAM and PCM (4 bits) representation for the accompanying signal sampled once every 0.5 seconds. Does this give an accurate representation of the signal?

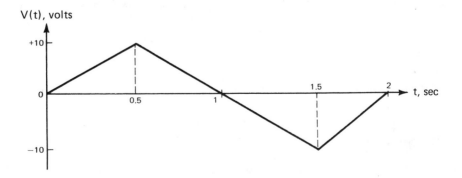

2. Given the accompanying transversal equalizer,

   (a) Write the time and frequency domain expressions for the filter for $T = 0.5$ seconds and $d_{-1} = 0.25$, $d_0 = 1.0$, and $d_{+1} = -0.50$.
   (b) Find the time domain response of the filter for the triangular input pulse.
   (c) Find values of the tap gains that will produce an output pulse as close as possible to the ideal response.

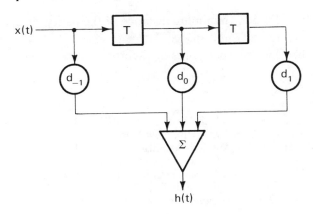

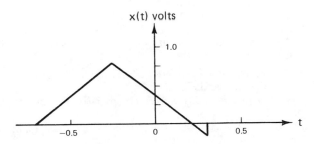

3. Consider the likelihood ratio for unequal costs $C_0 \neq C_1$ and unequal a priori probabilities $P_0 \neq P_1$ and describe their effect on the decision threshold.

4. Develop a block diagram model of the transmitter, channel, and adaptive equalizer and relate it to the general models given in Chapter 5.

5. For the following set of matrices defined over $GF(2)$

$$H_1 = \begin{bmatrix} 0 & 1 \\ 1 & 0 \end{bmatrix} \qquad H_3 = \begin{bmatrix} 0 & 0 & 1 & 0 & 0 \\ 0 & 1 & 1 & 1 & 1 \\ 1 & 0 & 0 & 1 & 0 \end{bmatrix}$$

$$H_2 = \begin{bmatrix} 1 & 1 & 0 & 0 \\ 1 & 0 & 1 & 0 \\ 1 & 0 & 0 & 1 \end{bmatrix} \qquad H_4 = \begin{bmatrix} 1 & 1 & 1 & 0 & 0 \\ 1 & 0 & 0 & 1 & 0 \\ 1 & 1 & 0 & 0 & 1 \end{bmatrix}$$

(a) Find the minimum distance of the parity check code defined by their null space.

(b) List the codewords of each one of the codes so defined.

REFERENCES

1. LUCKY, R. W., J. SALZ, and E. J. WELDON, Jr., *Principles of Data Communications*, McGraw-Hill, New York, 1968.
2. RUDIN, H., Jr., "Automatic Equalization Using Transversal Filters," *IEEE Spectrum*, Vol. 4, No. 1, January 1967, pp. 53–59.
3. FRANKS, L. E., *Signal Theory*, Prentice-Hall, Englewood Cliffs, N.J., 1969.
4. SKLANSKY, Jack, "Threshold Training of Two-Mode Signal Detection," *IEEE Transactions on Information Theory*, Vol. IT-11, No. 3, July 1965, pp. 353–362.
5. SKLANSKY, Jack, "Learning Systems for Automatic Control," *IEEE Transactions on Automatic Control*, Vol. AC-11, No. 1, January 1966, pp. 6–19.
6. GLORIOSO, R. M., "A Stochastic Model of the Human Observer as a Detector of Signals Embedded in Noise," Ph.D Dissertation, University of Connecticut, Storrs, Conn., 1967.
7. PETERSON, W. W., and E. J. WELDON, *Error-Correcting Codes*, 2nd ed., MIT, Cambridge, Mass., 1972.
8. LIN, S., *An Introduction to Error Correcting Codes*, Prentice-Hall, Englewood Cliffs, N.J., 1970.
9. STONE, H. S., *Discrete Mathematical Structures and Their Applications*, Science Research Associates, Chicago, 1973.
10. TYMES, L. R., "TYMNET—A Terminal Oriented Communications Network," *AFIPS Conf. Proc. 1971 SJCC*, Vol. 38, AFIPS Press, Montvale, N.J., pp. 211–216.
11. *Disk Operating System Monitor Programmer's Handbook*, Digital Equipment Corporation, Maynard, Mass., 1971.
12. WAKERLY, John F., *Error Detecting Codes, Self-Checking Circuits and Applications*, Elsevier North-Holland, Inc., New York, 1978.
13. HAMMING, R. W., "Error Detecting and Error Correcting Codes," *Bell Sys. Tech. Journal*, Vol. 29, No. 1, January 1950, pp. 147–160.

9

Stochastic Automata Models in Computer and Communication Networks

Stochastic automata models and a brief discussion of their properties were first presented in Chapter 4 and expanded in Chapter 6. In this chapter we apply the theory of stochastic automata to two important, closely related problems: scheduling tasks on processors in computer networks and routing calls in communications networks. As applied to computer networks, the problem is to schedule or allocate tasks to processors in such a way that a performance measure is optimized. In communications networks, the problem is to establish a communications path between a pair of nodes in the network upon receiving a request that originates in one of the nodes.

In spite of the vast body of theoretical material published in the area of stochastic automata during the last 15 years [1], few meaningful applications have been reported. An exception to this trend has been in the application of methods related to the problem of telephone traffic routing by Boehm and Mobley [2] with their decentralized routing scheme, and by Glorioso et al. [3], who first applied the concept of learning stochastic automata in traffic routing for communications networks. Similarly, in the design of multiple processor systems, Glorioso and Colón [4] first suggested the idea of using stochastic automata as models for resource allocators (task schedulers) in a distributed computer system.

LEARNING AUTOMATA AS TASK SCHEDULERS IN COMPUTER NETWORKS

An important problem in the design of multiple processor systems is scheduling and allocating tasks to processors such that a performance measure is optimized. Usually the performance measure is the total execution time (i.e., the time spent in transferring the task to the processor [communications costs], plus the time spent waiting in a queue for the processor to become available [queueing costs], plus the execution time). In this context we shall now consider the L_{R-P} automaton presented in Chapter 6 as a task scheduler in a multiple processor system. This task scheduler will assign tasks to processors such that the mean turnaround time is optimized. What makes such a scheduler different from others proposed earlier is that it functions in the presence of changes in the environment (e.g., load changes) and/or incomplete information about the state of the system. The performance of this L_{R-P} scheduler is measured in terms of the mean turnaround time and will be evaluated in this chapter via computer simulations and queueing theory.

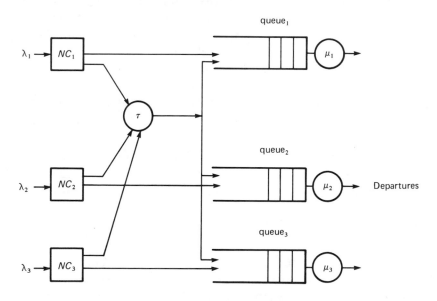

Figure 9.1a.   Three-processor queueing model.

First, a description of the L_{R-P} automaton as a model for a task scheduler will be presented. Computer simulation of a three-node, three-processor system will also be used to compare the performance of the L_{R-P} automaton (as measured by the mean turnaround time) to a fixed scheduling discipline in which arriving tasks are assigned to processors in a fixed order.

Second, queueing theory will be used to establish upper and lower bounds on the performance of the L_{R-P} automaton. To illustrate, we will consider a simple two-processor distributed system.

Consider the model of a simple distributed computer system consisting of three processors, as shown in Figure 9.1a. This model, which represents the queueing theory counterpart of the system in Figure 9.1b, is described in the next few sentences. The processors are homogeneous, each with an average processing rate of μ_1, μ_2, and μ_3. They are connected by a communications link for higher performance and reliability through load sharing.

The channel is characterized by its mean transfer rate, τ (i.e., the average number of transfers per unit of time), which is a measure of the cost to transfer tasks between processors at submittal times. Assume that the

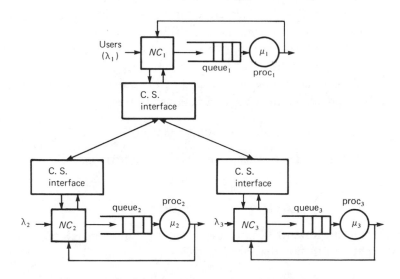

Figure 9.1b.   Three-node network.

service-time distributions of the processors are exponential. Also, the task arrival streams are Poisson, with mean arrival rates of λ_1, λ_2, and λ_3, respectively. Associated with each processor there is a queue, $queue_i$, and the queue discipline is first-come, first-served (FCFS) in the order of submittal times.

Further, in this model the network controllers (NC_i), shown in Figure 9.1, determine what fraction of the jobs arriving at $node_i$, $i = 1, 2, 3$, are scheduled locally (i.e., to $proc_i$). This scheduling is assumed to occur instantaneously. In other words, zero costs are associated with the transfer of jobs between processors. We now turn our attention to the two scheduling disciplines to be considered as task schedulers for the distributed computer system.

SCHEDULING DISCIPLINES FOR A THREE-PROCESSOR DISTRIBUTED SYSTEM

Scheduling Discipline I: L_{R-P} Automaton

In the L_{R-P} scheduling discipline, each network controller is described in terms of an L_{R-P} automaton operating in a P-environment. The automaton $\{x, \Psi, \alpha, P, T, G\}$ is described in the following manner: x is the input set from the environment and is considered to be binary, $\{0, 1\}$, where 0 is nonpenalty and 1 is penalty. Ψ is the set of s internal states. α is the set of outputs that corresponds to the selection of a processor for executing the arriving task (i.e., select $proc_i$, $i = 1, 2, 3$). $P(n)$ is the probability distribution function governing the choice of actions. That is,

$$P(n) = [p_1(n), p_2(n), p_3(n)]$$

where $p_i(n) = P_R$ {$proc_i$ is selected to execute the arriving task at time n}. Note that

$$p_1(0) = p_2(0) = p_3(0) = 1/3$$

T is the Linear Reward-Penalty described by Equation 6.8, and G is a random output function described as follows:

$$\alpha(n) = G(\Phi(n)) = proc_i \text{ with probability } p_i(n), i = 1, 2, 3$$

Hence, G corresponds to a random function selection based on a discrete probability density function $P(n)$.

To complete the description of the L_{R-P} automaton as a task scheduler in a distributed computer system, a viable definition of the penalty ($x = 1$) and nonpenalty ($x = 0$) response from the environment is needed. This definition should also include a description of the penalty probability set, C, and account for the relative speed of processors. In queueing theory [5, 6], one such measure used to evaluate the performance of systems has been the probability that a processor, or "server," is idle. This measure can be defined for the three-processor system of Figure 9.1 as follows. Let $R(t)$, $X(t)$, and $Y(t)$ be random variables corresponding to the number of tasks waiting for service in queue$_i$, $i = 1, 2, 3$, respectively at some instant of time t. Then, the joint probability distribution function is given by Equation 9.1, and it completely characterizes the state of the system at time t.

$$Q_{lmn}(t) = P_R\{R(t) = l, X(t) = m, Y(t) = n\} \qquad (9.1)$$

Furthermore, the probability that a processor is free can be easily expressed, for example if $i = 3$ this probability is given by Equation 9.2 below:

$$P_R\{\text{proc}_3 \text{ is free at time } t\} = \sum_{\forall l} \sum_{\forall m} Q_{lm0}(t)$$

$$= \sum_{\forall l} \sum_{\forall m} P_R\{R(t) = l, X(t) = m, Y(t) = 0\} \qquad (9.2)$$

Such measures seem appealing as the penalty probability set for two reasons. First, it is well known from queueing theory that if $\rho = \lambda/\Sigma\mu_i < 1$, then $Q_{lmn}(t)$ converges to a stationary distribution function given in Equation 9.3:

$$Q_{lmn} = \lim_{t\to\infty} Q_{lmn}(t) \qquad (9.3)$$

Hence, the probabilities Q_{lmn} can be considered as descriptors of the steady-state or stationary behavior of the system. Second, they allow a definition of the input set, x, in terms of P-models.

We shall now define the environment in terms of the penalty probability set as follows:

1. $x = \{0, 1\}$, where 0 (nonpenalty) corresponds to the case in which the selected processor is free, and 1 (penalty) corresponds to a busy processor.
2. The penalty probability set $C = \{C_i\}$, $i = 1, 2, 3$ is given by Equation 9.4:

$$C_1 = P_R\{proc_1 \text{ is busy}\} = 1 - \sum_{\forall m} \sum_{\forall n} Q_{0mn}$$

$$C_2 = P_R\{proc_2 \text{ is busy}\} = 1 - \sum_{\forall l} \sum_{\forall n} Q_{l0n} \qquad (9.4)$$

$$C_3 = P_R\{proc_3 \text{ is busy}\} = 1 - \sum_{\forall l} \sum_{\forall m} Q_{lm0}$$

As before, these probabilities are unknown.

Finally, the scheduling discipline for the L_{R-P} automaton can be described as the following process. When a task enters the system at the ith node (the origin node), the network controller for that node, NC_i, selects a processor to run the task based on the probability distribution function, $P(n)$. After this selection, the network controller updates $P(n)$ in accordance with Equation 6.8 (with the learning constant $a = b$) and based on the success (selected processor is free) or failure (selected processor is busy) of scheduling the arriving task. If the selected processor is busy, the tasks join the queue and wait for service. Should the queue be full, another random trial is conducted to select a processor from those remaining.

Scheduling Discipline II: Deterministic Scheduling

The other scheduling discipline we shall consider was first proposed by Krishnamoorthi [7] for queueing systems in which arriving tasks ("customers") have complete knowledge of the processors' ("servers' ") relative speed. In such systems, the network controllers allocate tasks to processors in a fixed order.

Assume, without loss of generality, that there exists a linear ordering on the processor speeds, i.e., $\mu_1 > \mu_2 > \mu_3$. The network controller assigns an arriving task to $proc_1$ if it is free. Otherwise, the controller assigns the task to the processor with the minimum expected delay through the queue, as computed by Equation 9.5:

$$\text{Expected Delay at } proc_i = \begin{cases} (queue_i + 2)\dfrac{1}{\mu_i} & \text{if } proc_i \text{ is busy}^* \\[2mm] (queue_i + 1)\dfrac{1}{\mu_i} & \text{if } proc_i \text{ is free} \end{cases} \qquad (9.5)$$

---

* $queue_i$ denotes the number of tasks waiting for service on $queue_i$. It does not include the task currently being processed by $proc_i$.

COMPARATIVE ANALYSIS OF SCHEDULING DISCIPLINES

To evaluate the performance of the L_{R-P} automaton as a task scheduler in a distributed computer system, an event time simulation model is used. The model, first used by Colón Osorio [8], was used to simulate a three-processor system under varying processing loads and under the two scheduling disciplines considered here. The results of these simulations are summarized in Figures 9.2a, b, and c. In this figure, the mean turnaround time (T) for the L_{R-P} automaton and the fixed scheduling discipline (FSD)

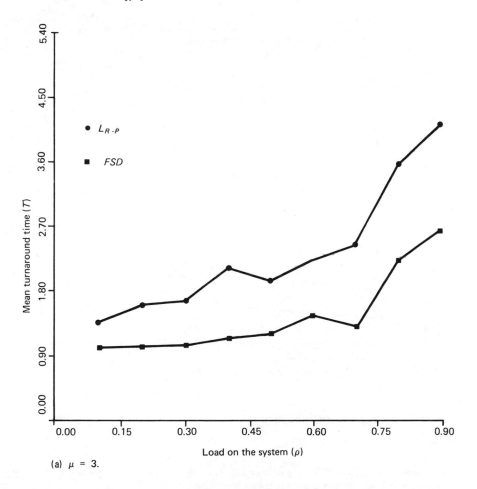

(a) $\mu = 3$.

Figure 9.2a.   Scheduling discipline simulations for $\mu = 3$.

is shown as a function of system loading (ρ).* The results show that for each value of the parameter ρ,

$$T_{L_{R-P}} > T_{FSD} \qquad (9.6)$$

These results were to be expected since the *FSD* has complete information on system parameters, namely, processor speeds (μ_i) and instantaneous queue lengths (queue$_i$), and the L_{R-P} automaton is allowed to gain

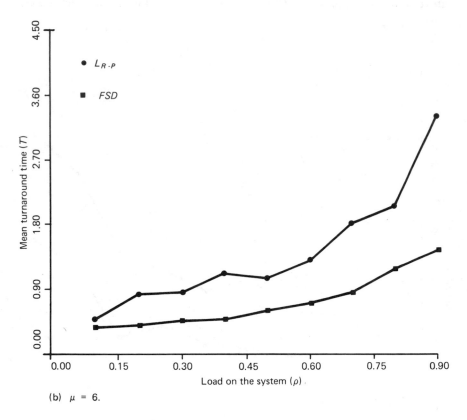

(b) μ = 6.

Figure 9.2b.   Scheduling discipline simulations for μ = 6.

---

* In queueing theory, $\rho = \sum \lambda_i / \sum \mu_i$ is used as a measure for system loading. It is well known that for $\rho \geq 1$, the queues in the system grow without bound.

information on the likelihood that a processor is either busy or free, exclusively. Hence, even when the L_{R-P} automaton operates in a stationary environment and is allowed to reach its limiting state distribution (i.e., $t \to \infty$), Equation 9.6 should hold. This is confirmed, empirically, through computer simulations, as shown in Figures 9.3a and b. In this figure, the mean turnaround times of both the L_{R-P} and *FSD* scheduling disciplines are plotted as a function of the number of iterations (completions and arrivals) the system has handled. As the figures show, for a sufficiently large number of iterations (i.e., > 6000), both the L_{R-P} and *FSD* arrive at their corresponding steady state, and

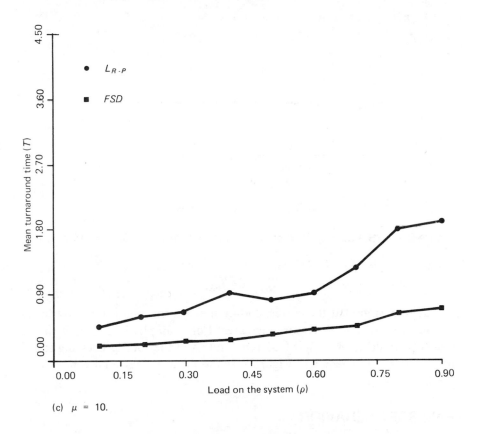

(c) $\mu = 10$.

Figure 9.2c.   Scheduling discipline simulations for $\mu = 10$.

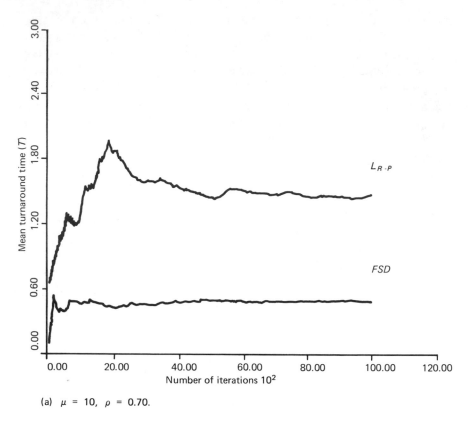

(a) $\mu = 10$, $\rho = 0.70$.

Figure 9.3a. Scheduling discipline simulations for $\mu = 10$, $\rho = 0.70$.

$$T_{L_{R-P}} > T_{FSD}$$

In addition, note that the corresponding mean turnaround time is reduced as the speed of the processors increases. For example, in Figure 9.3b the steady-state value of T_{FSD} is 0.33 time units and the total processing speed is $\Sigma_{i=1}^{3} \mu_i = 15$, whereas in Figure 9.3a the mean turnaround time is 0.46 for $\Sigma_{i=1}^{3} \mu_i = 10$.

FAIL SOFT BEHAVIOR

One compelling reason for studying learning automata as models for

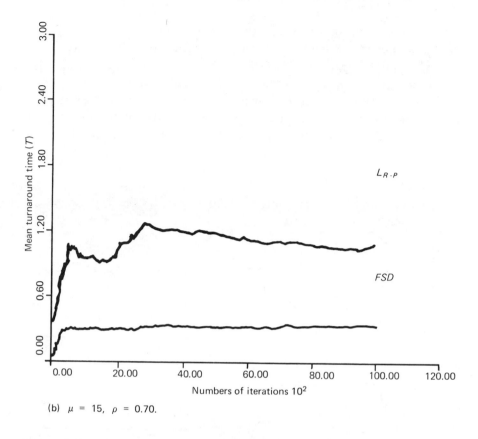

(b) $\mu = 15$, $\rho = 0.70$.

Figure 9.3b.   Scheduling discipline simulations for $\mu = 15$, $\rho = 0.70$.

task schedulers in a distributed computer system is the desire to obtain fail soft, or graceful degradation in the face of component failures. Here we are particularly interested in the performance of the task schedulers when faced with the failure of processors, i.e., $\mu_i \to 0$. This can be accomplished through simulations in which the most crucial processor, $proc_1$, is allowed to fail.

Let us consider a set of simulations of a three-processor system where the average processing rate of each processor is $\mu_1 = 6$, $\mu_2 = 3$, $\mu_3 = 1$, respectively. In such a system, the failure of $proc_1$ under several system loads (ρ) is considered, and a typical run ($\rho = 0.70$) is shown in Figure 9.4.

In the figure, the mean turnaround times for both the fixed scheduling and the L_{R-P} automaton disciplines are shown as a function of system iteration, that is, arrival or departure of tasks from the system. At iteration 3000, the mean service time for $proc_1$ is reduced 83 percent from $\mu_1 = 6$ to $\mu_1 = 1$. However, to compensate for the increased processing load, the speed of $proc_3$ is increased to $\mu_3 = 6$, and the processing load is thus maintained at a constant value of $\rho = 0.70$. This reversal of processing speeds corre-

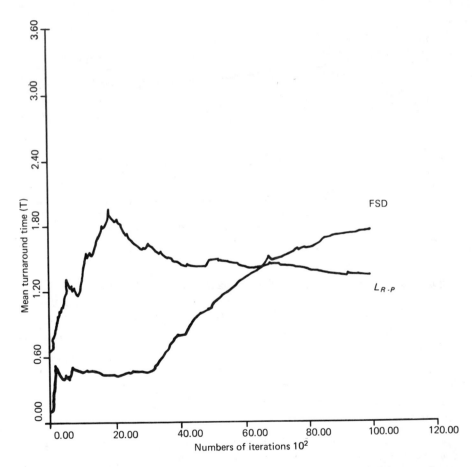

Figure 9.4. Performance of scheduling disciplines in a switching environment where $\mu = 10$ and $\rho = 0.70$.

sponds to a nonstationary switching environment such as the one in Figure 6.12, reproduced here for convenience as Figure 9.5. The results of these simulations, as exemplified in Figure 9.4, can be described as follows:

1. The fixed scheduling discipline arrives at its steady state by iteration 2000 with a mean turnaround time of 0.46 time units. After $proc_1$ fails at iteration 3000, the mean turnaround time for the *FSD* increases in time to a new steady-state value given by 1.7713 time units—a threefold degradation.

2. On the other hand, the mean turnaround time of the L_{R-P} automaton increases during the "learning period," as expected, up to iteration 2000 to a maximum value of 1.9311 time units. Changes in the environment at iteration 3000 produce temporary dislocations, but the mean turnaround time steadily decreases to a new steady-state value of 1.3425 time units.

3. It is very significant in this simulation that the L_{R-P} automaton is able to adapt to changes in the environment, whereas the *FSD* discipline is severely affected by them. This is illustrated by the fact that in Figure 9.4, the mean turnaround time of the L_{R-P}

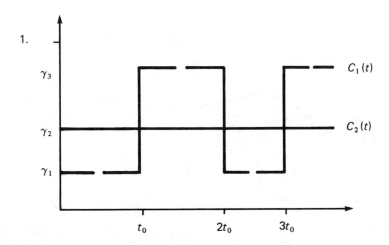

Figure 9.5.   Nonstationary switching environment where $C_i(t)$, $i = 1, 2$ are time-dependent penalty probabilities.

after iteration 6400 is less than that of the *FSD*. That is,

$$T_{L_{R-P}} < T_{FSD}$$

when the number of iterations is greater than 6400.

Next, consider the set of simulations shown in Figure 9.6, in which $\rho = 0.70$ and which confirms the results previously described by Figure 9.4. In this case, however, the average processing rates are $\mu_1 = 12$, $\mu_2 = 2$, and $\mu_3 = 1$, respectively; and the average processing rate of proc_1 is decreased

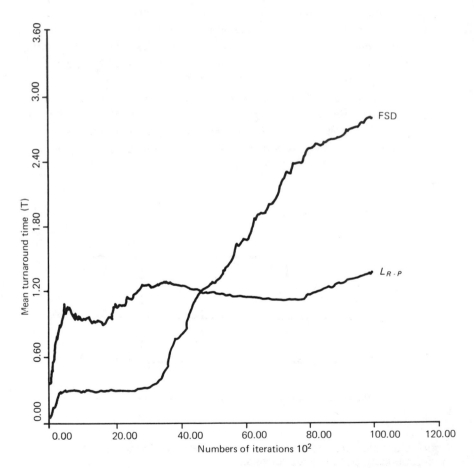

Figure 9.6. Performance of scheduling disciplines in a switching environment where $\mu = 15$ and $\rho = 0.70$.

from $\mu_1 = 12$ to $\mu_1 = 1$. This degradation severely affects the mean turnaround time of the *FSD* discipline, which changes from a steady-state value of 0.33 time units before $proc_1$ fails to a new value of 3.07 time units. Note also that, as before, the L_{R-P} performance is relatively insensitive to changes in the environment, and that

$$T_{L_{R-P}} < T_{FSD}$$

when the number of iterations is greater than 4000.

By comparing Figures 9.4 and 9.6, we can conclude that in the *FSD* scheduling discipline, an increase in the mean service time of $proc_1$ is proportionately related to an increase in the mean turnaround time of the system. It is inversely related to the number of iterations that are needed for the mean turnaround time of the L_{R-P} automaton to be exceeded by that of the *FSD*. We can also conclude that the L_{R-P} automaton is fairly insensitive to changes in system statistics. These changes provide temporary dislocations, but the L_{R-P} continues to improve in performance.

On the basis of this empirical evidence, it can be concluded that the performance of the L_{R-P} automaton, as measured by the mean turnaround time,* is significantly better than that of the fixed scheduling discipline in systems where the network statistics change with time. Of course, if the *FSD* scheduler was allowed to periodically collect information about the state of the system, its long-term performance would improve considerably. However, the decisions as to when to collect the information, and the problems associated with stale data, and increased traffic due to control message traffic (i.e., information about changes in the state of the system) will have to be addressed before such a scheme can be implemented.

EVALUATION OF STOCHASTIC AUTOMATA AS TASK SCHEDULERS WITH THE AID OF QUEUEING THEORY

We have already established the feasibility of using learning automata as task schedulers in a distributed computer system with the aid of computer simulations. We will now complete the evaluation of learning

---

* Several other performance measures, such as processor utilization (U), average queue length (L), and so forth, have been used in analyzing queueing models. However, the mean turnaround time represents the most meaningful quantity of overall performance. Nevertheless, the simulation model used in the set of experiments described was designed to accumulate *all* system statistics.

automata as task schedulers by providing bounds on their performance with the aid of queueing theory.

Consider the model of a simple distributed computer system consisting of two processors, as shown in Figure 9.7. As previously, the processors are considered to be homogeneous with different average processing rates, μ_1 and μ_2; the channel is characterized by its mean transfer rate (τ); the service time distributions of the processors are exponential; and the task arrival streams are Poisson with mean rates λ_1, λ_2. Here, p_{ij} represents the probability that the L_{R-P} automaton associated with the ith node will schedule an arriving task to $proc_j$.

We are interested in establishing bounds for the mean turnaround time of the L_{R-P} when it is used as a task scheduler in the preceding system. This can be accomplished by considering special cases of the general model shown in Figure 9.7 under different task arrival and transfer policies. First, consider the model in Figure 9.8, which represents a system with $\tau = 0$, or a system where the time to transfer information $(1/\tau)$ is infinite. In this system, there is no load balancing between processors, and arriving tasks at node i join queue i for processing. This system clearly represents an upper bound on the mean turnaround time for the L_{R-P} automaton since $1/\tau = \infty$. The model corresponds to the classic, two independent single-

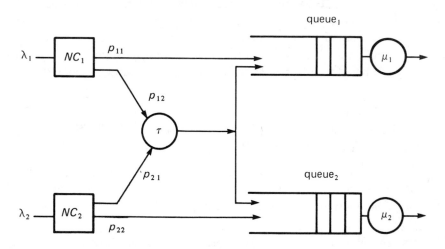

Figure 9.7.   Two-processor distributed computer system.

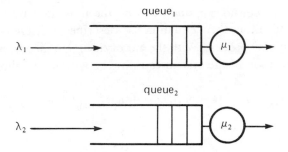

Figure 9.8.   Two processors in parallel, $\tau = 0$, no load balancing.

server single queues $(M/M/1)$ [5]. Next, consider the model in Figure 9.9. In this model, $\tau = \infty$, and tasks are transferred instantaneously among processors. The result of this assumption is the merging of the arrivals streams into a single Poisson stream with mean arrival rate $\lambda = \lambda_1 + \lambda_2$.

This system can be analyzed with the aid of queueing theory as follows. Define $X(t)$ and $Y(t)$ as random variables representing the number of tasks, including the task being served, in queue 1 and queue 2, respectively. The random variables $X(t)$ and $Y(t)$ completely characterize the state of the system, and their joint distribution function is given by Equation 9.7:

$$Q_{ij}(t) = P_R[X(t) = i, Y(t) = j] \tag{9.7}$$

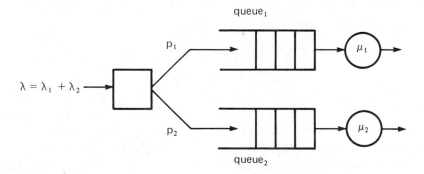

Figure 9.9.   Two-processor distributed system, $\tau = \infty$.

Next, if we consider p_1 and p_2 to be the limiting state distribution of the L_{R-P} automaton, then Equation 9.7 describes a discrete-state, continuous-time Markov process. With the aid of queueing theory, the differential difference equation of the system can now be written as follows:

$$\frac{d}{dt}Q_{ij}(t) = -(\lambda + \mu_{ij})Q_{ij}(t) + \mu_1 Q_{i+1,j}(t) + \mu_2 Q_{i,j+1}(t)$$

$$+\lambda p_1 Q_{i-1,j} + \lambda p_2 Q_{i,j-1} \tag{9.8}$$

where

$$\mu_{ij} \triangleq \begin{cases} 0 & i, j = 0 \\ \mu_1 & i \geq 1, j = 0 \\ \mu_2 & i = 0, j \geq 1 \\ \mu_1 + \mu_2 & i \geq 1, j \geq 1 \end{cases}$$

and

$$Q_{ij}(t) \triangleq 0 \text{ whenever } i, j < 0$$

and

$$p_i = \lim_{t \to \infty} p_i(t)$$

which corresponds to the balance flow equations [5] state transitions shown in Figure 9.10.

If we restrict our interest to the steady state, the state equilibrium equations are obtained from Equation 9.8 by setting $d/dt\, Q_{ij}(t) = 0$ and defining $Q_{ij} \triangleq \lim_{t \to \infty} Q_{ij}(t)$ as follows:

$$0 = -(\lambda + \mu_{ij})Q_{ij} + \mu_1 Q_{i+1,j} + \mu_2 Q_{i,j+1} + \lambda p_1 Q_{i-1,j} + \lambda p_2 Q_{i,j-1} \tag{9.9}$$

where μ_{ij}, and p_i are defined as before.

Clearly, the solution to Equation 9.9 represents a tight, lower bound on the mean turnaround time for the L_{R-P} scheduling discipline because $\tau = 0$. Unfortunately, attempts to find a solution to Equation 9.9 by generating functions or using local balance equations [9, 10], have failed. It is well known, however, that if the system of Figure 9.9 is replaced by a single-processor system with a processing rate $\mu = \mu_1 + \mu_2$, as in Figure 9.11, the mean turnaround time is minimized. Hence, the mean turnaround

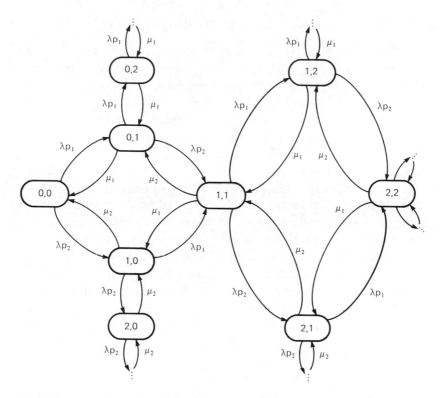

Figure 9.10. State transition diagram for the two-processor distributed system of Figure 9.9.

time of the fast processor as given by Equation 9.10

$$T = \frac{1}{(\mu - \lambda)} \tag{9.10}$$

represents a lower bound on the mean turnaround time of the L_{R-P}.

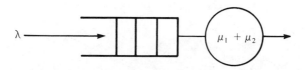

Figure 9.11.   Single fast processor.

LEARNING AUTOMATA IN COMMUNICATIONS NETWORKS

We shall now explore the application of learning automata models to the traffic routing problem in communications networks. First, let us consider the structure of a communications network as depicted in Figure 9.12. The network consists of a set of nodes and branches, or links. The nodes represent communications switching centers, which may or may not have local users. For example, node 1 may represent the main telephone switching center in New York; node 2, Boston; node 3, Los Angeles; and so forth. A branch connecting two nodes indicates that some kind of bidirectional communications path exists between respective nodes.

Further, nodes connected directly are called adjacent nodes. Any link connecting two adjacent nodes i and j will have N_{ij} channels associated with it. The number of channels for different links varies and is chosen to meet the load requirements of the system. The particular characteristics of the channels will be disregarded here and may be Teletype, telephone, video, data, etc. In general, however, the type of channel is important because it specifies the channel's bandwidth. Now, given a communications network, the problem is to establish communications paths between pairs of nodes on a request originating from one of the nodes.

Conventional routing methods operate in one of several ways. A simple method designates two or more routes from each node to every other node a priori and assigns a priority to the sequence in which the alternate routes are utilized. These paths include the routes through each intermediate node. Therefore, specification of two routes from node 1 to node 3 requires that, for instance, link sequences 1–7 and 2–8 be stored at node 1. There are, however, network conditions that can create difficulties with this

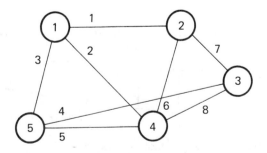

Figure 9.12.   Model of a communications network.

technique. For example, links 1 and 8 may be saturated (no channels available) or "temporarily" out of order, thus thwarting communications from node 1 to node 3 by either of these routes. Furthermore, as the size of the network increases, the storage requirements at each node multiply rapidly.

One method used to change routing, when the prespecified paths or intermediate nodes cannot be used, is to communicate network status information to all nodes in the net as the network structure changes. The problem here is that the status information occupies useful communications channels and must also be routed through the system. Moreover, network changes that result from heavy use and saturate most of the channels must be communicated at crucial heavy-load periods, thus increasing network loading even more. Other techniques have been proposed; however, a self-organizing technique appears to offer many advantages over the others [3] and is discussed in the next section.

NETWORK SPECIFICATION

In general, the network has N nodes labeled $1, 2, \ldots, N$, and M_i, $i = 1, 2, \ldots, N$ links connected to the ith node. Thus, each node may be able to communicate directly with up to $N - 1$ other nodes.

All nodes in the network are identical, and each node will be given the same a priori information, namely, the maximum number of nodes in the network, the name or code of the given node, and the name or code associated with every other node in the net. The maximum number of links that can be associated with each node will also be provided to that node.

Next, the signaling requirements for operation of the network must be defined. Each call propagated through the network will have associated with it the name of the calling node, the name of the called node, and a number called FAC, which indicates the number of facilities used for a given call. Thus, if a call has gone through four nodes not including the originating and destination nodes, FAC = 4.

The selection of an outgoing link for processing a call from node i to node j is accomplished through the use of an L_{R-P} automaton as link selector in each node. This is shown in Figure 9.13, where the link selector for the ith node is modeled as an L_{R-P} automaton operating in a random environment.

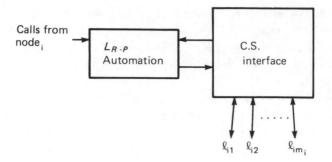

Figure 9.13a. Logical structure of link selector
at the *i* th node.

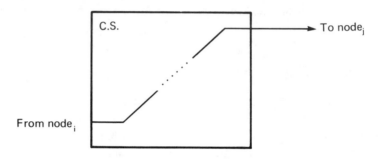

Figure 9.13b. Communications subsystem (CS).

The automaton S_i for the *i*th node can be thought of as a collection of automata,

$$S_i = \{S_{i1}, S_{i2}, \ldots, S_{iN}\}$$

where the S_{ij} automaton, $j \neq i$, serves as link selector for all calls originating in the *i*th node and destined for the *j*th node. Each automaton

$$S_{ij} = \{x, \Psi, \alpha, P_{ij}, T, G\}$$

is described as before. Ψ is the set of s internal states. α is the set of outputs corresponding to the selection of a link for routing the outgoing call (i.e., select link $l_{ij}, j = 1, 2, \ldots, M_i$). The input set from the environment is x and is considered to be binary, $\{0, 1\}$, where 0 is nonpenalty and 1 penalty. $P_{ij}(n)$ is the probability distribution function governing the choice of actions. That is,

$$P_{ij}(n) = [p_{j1}(n), p_{j2}(n), \ldots, p_{jM_i}(n)] \qquad (9.11)$$

where $p_{jk}(n) = P_R \{$link l_{ik} is selected as the outgoing link in the routing of a call from node$_i$ to node$_j\}$.

Initially there is no a priori information concerning the structure or loading of the network. As a result,

$$P_{j1}(0) = P_{j2}(0) = \cdots = P_{jM_i}(0) = \frac{1}{M_i}$$

for all S_{ij} automata.

T is the Linear Reward-Penalty described by Equation 9.12, and G is a random output function described as follows:

$$\alpha(n) = G(\Psi(n)) = \text{select link } l_{ik}, k = 1, 2, \ldots, M_i \text{ with probability } p_{jk}.$$

Intuitively, we may think of the probability distribution function $P_{ij}(n)$ for each automaton $S_{ij}(n)$ as a switching or connection matrix for the ith automaton S_i. In such a matrix, shown in Equation 9.12, the rows represent the $N - 1$ other nodes; the columns represent the M_i links associated with the ith node. The entries in the matrix, $p_{jk}(n)$, are the likelihood of reaching the jth node from the ith node via the kth link without the specification of any other link needed to complete the communication connection. Thus, the matrix associated with calls from node$_1$ in the network of Figure 9.11 is

LINKS

$$S_1(n) = \begin{bmatrix} S_{12}(n) \\ S_{13}(n) \\ S_{14}(n) \\ S_{15}(n) \end{bmatrix} = \begin{matrix} N \\ O \\ D \\ E \\ S \end{matrix} \begin{matrix} 2 \\ 3 \\ 4 \\ 5 \end{matrix} \begin{matrix} 1 & 2 & 3 \\ \end{matrix} \begin{bmatrix} p_{21}(n) & p_{22}(n) & p_{23}(n) \\ p_{31}(n) & p_{32}(n) & p_{33}(n) \\ p_{41}(n) & p_{42}(n) & p_{43}(n) \\ p_{51}(n) & p_{52}(n) & p_{53}(n) \end{bmatrix} \qquad (9.12)$$

To complete the description of the L_{R-P} automaton as a link selector in a communications network, a definition of the penalty ($X = 1$) and the nonpenalty ($X = 0$) responses from the environment, together with a description of the penalty probability set, C, is needed.

For the purpose of this discussion, we define the environment in terms of the penalty probability set as follows:

1. $x = \{0, 1\}$, where 0 (nonpenalty) corresponds to the case in which the call from node i to node j is successfully routed through the network. In this case, all links selected in the routing of the call are "rewarded" by their respective automata in accordance with Equation 6.8 (with the learning constant $a = b$). On the other hand, 1 (penalty) corresponds to an unsuccessful call, in which case all links selected in routing the call are punished by their respective automata in accordance with Equation 6.8 (with the learning constant $a = b$).

2. The penalty probability set

$$C_{ij} = \{C_{jk}, j \neq i = 1, 2, \ldots, N; k = 1, \ldots, M_i\}$$

is given by:

$$C_{jk} = P_R\{\text{link } l_{jk} \text{ is saturated or has failed}\} \qquad (9.13)$$

It is interesting to examine in some detail the method by which an alternate route is selected after the first choice has failed by being saturated or out of order:

1. The probability associated with the saturated link is reduced to a smaller value.

2. The resulting distribution is then normalized to meet the constraints of variable-structure automata:

$$0 < p_{jk}(n) < 1$$

and

$$\sum_{\forall k} p_{jk}(n) = 1$$

3. A link is then selected on the basis of the new distribution.
4. This process is continued until either a free link is found or there have been M_i unsuccessful attempts at finding a free link. If no free link is found, the call is blocked.

If the node where no free link was found is the originating node, the call is canceled and the probability distribution function governing the choice of actions $P_{jr}(i)$ is restored to its original condition. If the blocked node is not the originating node, the link or links connecting the originating node with the blocked node are punished.

A continual problem associated with any nondeterministic routing technique is the processing of a call in an endless loop of nodes called "ring around the rosey." Since this is an undesirable form of system behavior, a means for punishing it must be provided. Recall that the network signaling requires that both the source and acceptor node signals or codes be sent with each call. Therefore, all links associated with a call that loops back to the source node will be punished when this so-called path loop constraint is applied. At this point, one will notice that loops or ring-arounds that do not come back to the originating node are not specifically punished by the path loop constraint. Adjustment of this behavior is embedded in the use of the third term of the network signals, namely FAC (the number of facilities utilized, to date, for a given call). If this number is exceeded by a specified amount while processing a particular call, then that call is terminated.

Two additional constraints called MAXFAC and MINIFAC, which are related to FAC, can be applied to system operation. MAXFAC is the maximum number of facilities that can be associated with any call. This may be a physical constraint that is a function of signal losses in the network, or it may be a system constraint. If FAC $\geq$ MAXFAC, the call propagation is terminated, all associated links are punished, and the originating node processes the call again. If the MAXFAC constraint is exceeded on three successive tries with the same call, the call is canceled (blocked).

The other term, MINIFAC, is used for two reasons. The first is to place an adaptive constraint on the number of facilities used for any call, and the second is to provide a means for punishing ring-arounds that do not get back to the source node. Thus, an $N - 1$ word store is associated with each node that contains a running weighted average of the number of facilities used for the calls to every other node for the last g calls. Assume a value of $g = 3$, and the following expression is used to determine the new value of MINIFAC for a completed call:

$$\text{MINIFAC} = \frac{2}{3}\,\text{MINIFAC}' + \frac{1}{3}\,\text{FAC} \qquad (9.14)$$

where MINIFAC$'$ is the old value. Also, a multiplicative adaptive constant may be used with MINIFAC as follows. If

$$\text{FAC} \geq \gamma \times \text{MINIFAC} \qquad (9.15)$$

the call propagation is terminated, the links are punished, the call is placed again, and so on as before. The preceding two criteria limit the total number of facilities used for any calls. And, more specifically, the MINIFAC criterion, which becomes dominant as the network learns, tends to minimize the number of available paths and therefore the maximum number of facilities allowed for each communication. Note that since MINIFAC is a running weighted average, the value of γ determines the rate at which the MINIFAC criterion can increase.

These four criteria—reliable communications, path loop, MAXFAC, and MINIFAC, together with the reward and punishment procedures we have mentioned—have been shown [11] to provide all the basic means for self-organization and adaptation in a communications network.

The overall operation of even a small switching network with simultaneous and multiple demands from each node is a complex process indeed. However, the routing procedure described here can be thought of by considering that each node in the system is "doing its thing" without direct interest in any other node or links. Call requests entering a node from either a local user or another node are treated identically. That is, the present node selects an outgoing link by a strategy generally based on the probability of success from past experience in using that link to process similar requests.

Therefore, the scheduling or link selector algorithm may be considered as the forward transfer elements; the constraints reliable communications, path loop, MAXFAC, and MINIFAC represent the performance evaluation element; and the learning algorithm performs as a system parameter transform element by converting "good" or "bad" behavior into changes in the matrix entries.

EVALUATION OF STOCHASTIC AUTOMATA AS LINK SELECTORS IN A COMMUNICATIONS NETWORK

A measure that can be applied to the evaluation of network behavior, called the grade of service, is the percentage of calls completed with respect to calls attempted over some time interval:

$$G.S. = \frac{\text{calls completed}}{\text{calls attempted}} \times 100\% \qquad (9.16)$$

This measure is particularly important to the user because it is his only sample of network routing performance. The other measure of value to the designer and operator of the system is the average path length needed to process calls through the net. Generally, lower costs are associated with shorter paths. The performance of a large network (57 nodes, 88 links) with respect to these measures—grade of service and average path length— where the initial probability distribution functions governing the choice of actions are uniform (maximum entropy) is shown in Figure 9.14 [11]. As expected, the entropy decreases as the system organizes the routing. Similarly, the MINIFAC constraint causes the average path length to decrease. The final result is that the grade of service increases as the network proceeds.

Finally, this system exhibits some self-repair capability, since the performance evaluation is not a function of network status. Experiments with the large network in which facilities carrying up to 30 percent of the traffic were disabled have given the following results. Immediately, the grade of service dropped from 99.5 percent to 84.5 percent, but five minutes later it was up to 90.2 percent. The effects of damaging a portion of a smaller network (9 nodes, 25 links) are also reflected in the entropy, as shown in Figure 9.15 [3]. Here, node 5 was destroyed after 1152 calls were processed by the network, and the entropy jumped from 6 to 22 bits; but after some time, the entropy dropped to 7 bits and service was restored to normal by incorporating previously unused or lightly used links. A network in which all facilities are fully used cannot exhibit these self-repair properties; self-repair here depends on the existence of redundant network facilities. The concepts of self-repair are examined further in Chapter 10.

The pioneering work described in this section was later followed by the work of Mason [14] and Narendra et al. [15], which applied these concepts

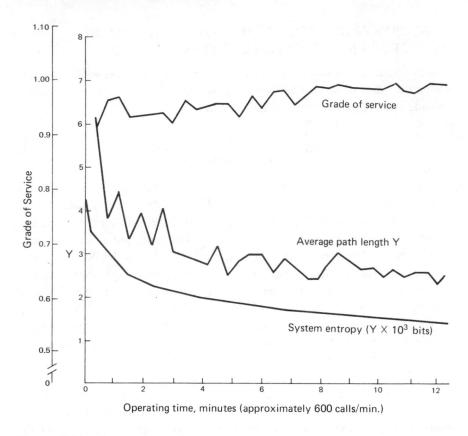

Figure 9.14. System parameters as a function of operating time for large communications network.

to the telephone traffic routing problem for a real large-scale telephone network in British Columbia. More recently, however, a group of researchers at Yale University [16, 17, 18] developed a sophisticated interactive computer program to simulate telephone traffic through a five-node network. This tool is sufficiently flexible to allow either a fixed rule or a learning scheme for routing calls in the networks. Such tools allow for an immediate testing of theoretical models (i.e., L_{R-P}, L_{R-I}, and so forth) either in an abstract environment or directly in the telephone network.

In addition, the research at Yale University has conclusively demonstrated, among other important results [18]:

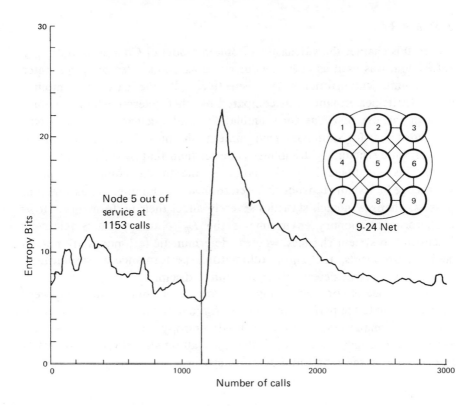

Figure 9.15.   Entropy as a function of calls processed where node 5 was out of service from call 1153.

Under abnormal network operating conditions including focussed overloads, link and node failures, the learning automata schemes consistently give superior performance over the fixed rule. In addition, learning automata techniques tend to produce a condition of equality of service to the individual call sources.

This work is being pursued actively at Yale University, Bell Laboratories, and other research centers and promises to revolutionize the circuit switching and routing techniques used in the telephone system. Further, the same techniques are being studied by computer network researchers as ways of routing packets in packet switching networks.

SUMMARY

In this chapter the stochastic automata model of Chapter 6, the L_{R-P} automaton, was used as task scheduler and as a link selector in computer and communications networks, respectively. In the case of computer networks, its performance was compared to other deterministic techniques through the use of event time simulations and queueing theory. It was concluded that for stationary environments the mean turnaround time of deterministic scheduling disciplines is better than that of the L_{R-P} automaton. This advantage in performance is due to the complete a priori knowledge of system statistics that deterministic techniques are assumed to possess; changes in such statistics severely affect their performance. However, for nonstationary environments the L_{R-P} automaton is relatively insensitive to system changes, whereas deterministic techniques are not. In such environments, the L_{R-P} automaton's performance is significantly better than those of deterministic scheduling disciplines.

In the case of communications networks, event time simulations were used to evaluate the performance of the L_{R-P} automaton as link selectors. Three performance measures were used: entropy, grade of service, and average path length. As expected, the L_{R-P} automata exhibited properties associated with self-repair and adaptive systems.

EXERCISES

1. (This problem is best solved via a computer simulation.) Given the accompanying three-node network,

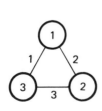

Time Called	From	To	Time Off
1	1	2	4
2	2	3	6
3	1	2	4
4	3	1	7
5	1	3	6
6	2	3	9
7	3	2	11
8	1	3	11
9	2	3	11
10	2	1	11

(a) Set up the three switching matrices needed to route communications traffic where no a priori information is available.

(b) Trace the network behavior for the following traffic schedule, with $a = b = 0.8$, using the L_{R-P} learning algorithm. Calculate the grade of service for each interval; also compute the average path length of all calls processed. Use ordered systematic search where a coin flip is used if entries are equal.

2. (This is a research problem.) Consider the two-processor distributed computer system of Figure 9.7, where the communication channel has infinite capacity, i.e., $\tau = \infty$. Further, assume that the jobs in the system are characterized by a Poisson distribution function with average arrival rates λ_1 and λ_2, respectively. Also assume that the processors in the system are described by a single-server queue model with exponential service times and known means μ_i, $i = 1, 2$ ($M/M/1$ servers). The queueing theory counterpart for the system of Figure 9.7 with $\tau = \infty$ is shown below:

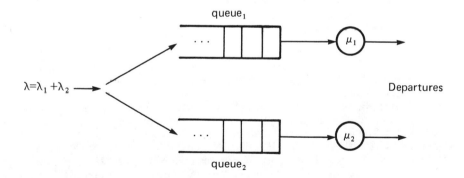

For this model, consider the following scheduling disciplines:

Scheduling Discipline I (Teller's Window [12])

A job arrives in the system to find:

(a) Both processors busy; it joins the shorter queue. If the queues are of equal length, it chooses either queue with equal opportunity.

(b)   Only one processor free; it selects the free server.
(c)   Both processors free; it selects either server with equal probability.

Scheduling Discipline II (Teller's Window with Instantaneous Jockeying [13])

This is the same as Scheduling Discipline I with one additional rule:

(d)   If, at any time, the difference in the queues exceeds 1, the last job in the longer line is transferred (jockeyed) to the end of the shorter line instantaneously.

(1)   Find the average queue lengths for Scheduling Disciplines I and II.

(2)   Show that the mean turnaround time for scheduling Discipline II is better than for Scheduling Discipline I.

(3)   Can you describe the implications of (2) in the context of task schedulers that assign jobs to processors at arrival times?

REFERENCES

1. NARENDRA, K. S., and M. A. L. THATHACHAR, "Learning Automata— A Survey," *IEEE Transactions on Systems, Man, and Cybernetics*, Vol. SMC-4, July 1974, pp. 323–334.
2. BOEHM, B. W., and R. L. MOBLEY, "Adaptive Routing Techniques for Distributed Communications Systems," Rand Corporation Memorandum RM-4781-PR, AD 630 271, February 1966.
3. GLORIOSO, R. M., G. R. GRUENEICH, and J. C. DUNN, "Self-Organization and Adaptive Routing for Communication Networks," *IEEE Electronics and Aerospace Convention Record* (EASCON), IEEE Publication 69C31-AES, Washington, D.C., October 1969, pp. 243–250.
4. GLORIOSO, R.M., and F. C. COLÓN, "Cybernetic Control of Computer Networks," Fifth Annual Modeling and Simulation Conference, Pittsburgh, Pa., April 1974.
5. KLEINROCK, L., *Queueing Systems, Volume I: Theory*, Wiley, Interscience, New York, 1975.
6. COX, D. R., and W. L. SMITH, *Queues*, Methuen, London, 1961.
7. KRISHNAMOORTHI, B., "On a Poisson Queue with Two Heterogeneous Servers," *Operations Research*, Vol. II, 1963, pp. 321–330.

8. COLÓN OSORIO, F. C., "Scheduling in Multiple-Processor Systems with the Aid of Stochastic Automata," Ph.D Dissertation, Electrical and Computer Engineering Department, University of Massachusetts, Amherst, Mass., 1977.

9. BASKETT, F., K. M. CHANDY, R. R. MUNTZ, and F. G. PALACIOS, "Open, Closed, and Mixed Network of Queues with Different Classes of Customers," *Journal of the ACM*, Vol. 22, No. 2, April 1975, pp. 248–260.

10. CHANDY, K. M., "The Analysis and Solutions for General Queueing Networks," *Proceedings of the Sixth Annual Princeton Conference on Information Sciences and Systems*, March 1972, pp. 224–228.

11. GLORIOSO, R. M., G. R. GRUENEICH, and D. McELROY, "Adaptive Routing in a Large Communications Network," *Proceedings of the 1970 IEEE Symposium on Adaptive Processes (9th), Decision and Control*, University of Texas, Austin, December 1970. IEEE Publication 70C 58-AC, pp. xv.5.1–vx.5.4.

12. GUMBEL, H., "Waiting Lines with Heterogeneous Servers," *Operations Research*, 8, 504 (1960).

13. KOENIGSBERG, Ernest, "On Jockeying in Queues," *Management Science*, Vol. 42, No. 5, January 1966, pp. 412–436.

14. MASON, L. G., "Self Optimizing Allocation Systems," Ph.D Dissertation, University of Saskatchewan, Saskatoon, SASK, Canada, 1972.

15. NARENDRA, Kumpati S., E. Allen WRIGHT, and Lorwe G. MASON, "Application of Learning Automata to Telephone Traffic Routing and Control," *IEEE Transaction Systems, Man, and Cybernetics*, Vol. SMC-7, No. 11, November 1977, pp. 785–792.

16. NARENDRA, Kumpati S., and Douglas MCKENNA, "Simulation Study of Telephone Traffic Routing Using Learning Algorithms—Part I," *S & IS Report*, No. 7806, Yale University, December 1978.

17. NARENDRA, Kumpati S, P. MARS, and M. S. CHRYSTALL, "Simulation Study of Telephone Traffic Routing Using Learning Algorithms—Part II," *S & IS Report* No. 7907, Yale University, October 1979.

18. MARS, P., and M. S. CHRYSTALL, "Real-Time Telephone Traffic Simulation Using Learning Automata Routing," *S & IS Report*, No. 7909, Yale University, November 1979.

10

Reliability and Repair

In Chapter 5 a general model and a definition of self-repair were given. The routing technique presented in Chapter 9 responded to an out-of-service facility by adapting to the new network structure such that system performance was restored. The coding of the nervous system can also operate successfully in the face of momentary nerve failure, as will be demonstrated in Chapter 11. The nervous system itself, of course, is a prime example of a reliable system. It can tolerate removal or destruction of thousands of cells and continue to operate successfully. In fact, many brain cells die each day of our lives and are not replaced or repaired—this is an amazing system indeed.

Interest in the design of reliable systems originated with the first computer systems, which used a large number of components whose individual reliability was relatively high but, when used in a large system, resulted in a system with rather poor reliability. For example, the mean time between failures (MTBF) of ENIAC, the first electronic digital computer, which was built in the early 1940s with 18,000 vacuum tubes, was approximately 5 minutes.

The reasons for the poor overall reliability of large systems and the methods for improving system reliability are the topics covered in this chapter. The orientation of this material is toward the digital computer because of the large number of components needed to create these machines. However, the principles of reliability underlying this work are applicable to other areas as well.

RELIABILITY OF SYSTEMS

The reliability of a complex system depends on the relationships among the elements of the system. The classic example is "A chain is only as strong as its weakest link." Here, the overall reliability depends on each element of the chain supporting the same load. If we denote the chain links as $L_1, L_2, \ldots, L_n$ and a probability of reliable performance for each link, $p_1, p_2, \ldots, p_n$, then the reliability of the chain is

$$R = p_1 \times p_2 \times \cdots \times p_n \tag{10.1}$$

The probability that link i will fail is

$$q_i = 1 - p_i$$

and the probability that the chain will fail is

$$Q = 1 - R = 1 - (p_1 \times p_2 \times p_3 \times \cdots \times p_n) \tag{10.2}$$

This, of course, is consistent since the probability that the chain will fail plus the reliability (the probability that it will not fail) must be unity. For our chain, then, it is clear that it will fail if any link L_1 or L_2 or L_3 ... or L_n fails,

$$Q = P(F_1 \vee F_2 \vee F_3 \vee \cdots \vee F_n) \tag{10.3}$$

where F_i is the event "link i fails." A general schematic representation of this type of system, where the failure of any one of n independent elements results in system failure, is shown in Figure 10.1. Here the system flow, which may be force in a chain, signals in a computer, or electric power distribution, is through a series of elements.

Consider the following: A controller for a computer consists of 100 levels of logic where the probability of a failure of any level is 0.01. What is the reliability of the controller?

$$R = \prod_{i=1}^{n} p(\overline{F_i}) = \prod_{i=1}^{n} p_i$$

Figure 10.1.   Series representation of a system.

but $p_i = 1 - 0.01 = 0.99$ and $R = (0.99)^{100} \simeq 0.37$. This can be interpreted by saying that on the average only one of every three controllers built will not fail. This is very poor indeed.

Again in the weak-link chain problem, it might appear reasonable to use more than one chain to hold the load. Then the system would fail only if all chains failed. The additional chains may not normally be needed, but the system would certainly be more reliable. The additional chains are called redundant elements of the system. A schematic representation of this parallel system is given in Figure 10.2.

The probability of failure of this parallel system with independent elements is

$$Q = P(F_1 \wedge F_2 \wedge \cdots \wedge F_n) \tag{10.4}$$

$$Q = q_1 \times q_2 \times \cdots \times q_n) \tag{10.5}$$

and the reliability is

$$R = 1 - (q_1 \times q_2 \times \cdots \times q_n) \tag{10.6}$$

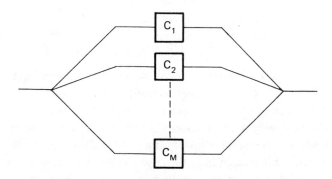

Figure 10.2.   Parallel system for improving reliability.

Note that the reliability can be stated by

$$R = P(\overline{F}_1 \vee F_2 F_1 \vee \overline{F}_3 F_1 F_2 \vee \cdots) \tag{10.7}$$

which in words is "The reliability of the system is the probability that element 1 does not fail, or that element 2 does not fail and element 1 does, or that element 3 does not fail and elements 1 and 2 do, etc." This can be written, for independent elements, as

$$R = p_1 + p_2 q_1 + p_3 q_i q_2 + \cdots \tag{10.8}$$

Suppose that a system is needed with a reliability of 0.99 and that the components available have a reliability of only 0.5. How many elements are needed to satisfy the design requirement?

First,

$$R \geq 0.99$$
$$Q \leq 1 - 0.99 = 0.01$$

Next,

$$Q = (q)^n = (0.5)^n$$

and

$$0.01 \geq (0.5)^n$$
$$\log 0.01 \geq n \log 0.5$$
$$-2 \geq -n \times 0.3$$
$$n \geq 6.6$$

It is possible to exceed the reliability requirement by using seven elements in parallel. Thus, a reliable system can be built from unreliable components[1]. Also, the construction of an ultrareliable system depends on the use of more components than would be necessary to build a less reliable system. This concept leads us to the conclusion that redundancy and reliability are directly related. This was, in fact, the case for the communications network routing described in Chapter 9. Reliability was achieved by having alternate, redundant paths through the network available to handle the traffic load.

The incorporation of redundancy in a computing system is not so simple as adding gates and flip-flops. Additional elements must be incorporated into the logical structure of the machine in a systematic way. Some of the methods for designing a reliable computing system are treated in the following sections.

It is also useful to analyze a system with respect to the expected time interval during which the system will operate reliably—the MTBF. Assume that the multiple components that make up a system fail independently of one another. Also, assume that the expected failure rate from each component is λ.

Thus, if we assume the random occurrence of a failure, the probability that all components survive to time t is

$$p(t) = e^{-\lambda t}$$

where $p(0) = 1$, which also can be stated "the first component fails after time t." Thus, if T is the random variable giving the time from 0 to the first failure, the reliability is

$$R[T > t] = e^{-\lambda t} \qquad (10.9)$$

which has a distribution function,

$$R[T \le t] = 1 - e^{-\lambda t}$$

and the probability density function is

$$f(t) = \lambda e^{-\lambda t} \qquad (10.10)$$

which is the Poisson density function. The mean survival time (MTBF) for one component of our system is

$$S_1 = \int_0^\infty t f(t) \, dt = \int_0^\infty t \lambda e^{-\lambda t} \, dt = \frac{1}{\lambda} \qquad (10.11)$$

And, if there are m independent components in the system and the system fails if any component fails, then

$$R[T > t] = e^{-m\lambda t} \qquad (10.12)$$

and the probability density function for failure is

$$f(t) = m\lambda e^{-m\lambda}$$ (10.13)

which gives a MTBF of

$$S_m = \frac{1}{\lambda m}$$ (10.14)

Now, suppose that the probability of failure of the components of a system is 0.001/hour (1 out of every 1000 of these components fails in any hour); then

$$S_1 = 1000 \text{ hours}$$

But, if there are 10,000 of these components in a system, then

$$S_{10,000} = \frac{1000}{10,000} \text{ hours} = 6 \text{ minutes}$$

Thus, a collection of components whose individual reliability appears quite good is not effective in a large system that depends on the reliable operation of each component. It should now be clear that the job of designing a sophisticated computer that will be highly reliable is no easy task. A spacecraft computer for a two-year mission must, if it is to operate continuously, have a MTBF greater than approximately 20,000 hours. There are three approaches one can take: (1) increase the reliability of the individual components, (2) reduce the number of components needed, and (3) employ components that are not necessarily needed to do the job but improve reliability by being there (incorporate redundancy). The last approach is presented in the next section.

MODULAR REDUNDANCY

A basic technique for improving the reliability of a system is to incorporate redundant elements in the design. These additional elements are usually considered in large functional blocks or modules rather than in individual components. Such modules are incorporated into a system in two basic ways: (1) they are in operation continuously and their output is considered in the total result, or (2) they exist as spares and are called on only when needed. The first method was proposed in 1956 by John von Neumann [1] as a means for incorporating the features of a parallel system into a computational unit as well as a model of the reliability of the nervous system. Let us examine this approach [2].

If one has a computational (logical) module that may fail, then it is clear that if an identical module is supplied with the same input, a comparison of the two outputs gives an indication of the logical errors that may occur. If the units operate correctly when placed in service, then a disagreement in their outputs at a later time is an indication that one of the units has failed. A system such as this would detect errors in the computation except in the very unlikely event that both units fail simultaneously. However, a system that incorporates three or more identical units with the same input can be used to correct errors by choosing the output that a majority of the modules agree on. In the simplest case, three modules are needed where two of the modules are redundant. Von Neumann also proposed that the proper output be chosen by a majority element or organ (as he called it), as discussed in an earlier chapter. This element has an output that agrees with the majority of inputs, and this system, called triple modular redundancy (TMR), is illustrated in Figure 10.3. Although it appears that TMR should improve reliability, let us now examine the gain in reliability that is actually achieved. The system pictured in Figure 10.3 is only as reliable as the majority gate that makes the output decision. This is generally a simple device and often can be made much more reliable than the computational modules, Cs. Also, other configurations that use more than one majority gate can be defined. However, as a first approximation, let us naively assume that the majority gate cannot fail. The output then will be correct as long as two or more Cs have not failed. The reliability distribution is the probability that all three modules are functioning plus the

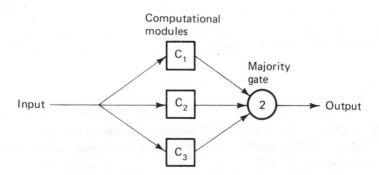

Figure 10.3. Triple modular redundancy to improve reliability.

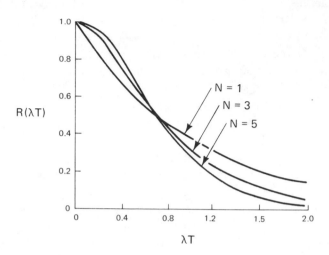

Figure 10.4.   Reliability as a function of normalized time for modular redundant systems of N elements.

probability that any two modules are functioning and the other is not,

$$R[T > t] = R^3 + 3R^2(1 - R) \qquad (10.15)$$

where R is the reliability distribution of the individual modules as given above. Substituting for R in Equation 10.15,

$$\begin{aligned} R[T > t] &= e^{-3\lambda t} + 3e^{-2\lambda t}(1 - e^{-\lambda t}) \\ &= 3e^{-2\lambda t} - 2e^{-3\lambda t} \end{aligned} \qquad (10.16)$$

The MTBF can now be computed,

$$\text{MTBF (TMR)} = \frac{5}{6\lambda}$$

and it is lower than the MTBF for a single element. However, computation of the reliability as a function of normalized time shows that for $t < 0.7$ the reliability of TMR is greater than for the single element, as illustrated in Figure 10.4 where $N = 3$.

A simple extension of the concept of TMR uses N units, where $N = 2n + 1$, feeding one majority gate; see Figure 10.5. The N module

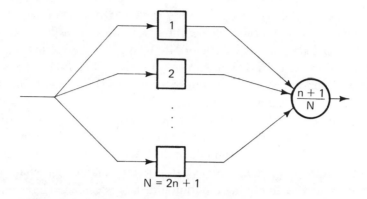

N = 2n + 1

Figure 10.5.   Modular redundancy.

system, N Module Redundancy (NMR), will work properly if all Cs work properly, if all but one C function, and so on, up to where all but n of the Cs function. If all failures are statistically independent, the distribution is

$$R[T > t] = \sum_{i=0}^{n} \binom{N}{i}(1 - R)^i R^{N-i} \qquad (10.17)$$

where

$$\binom{N}{i} = \frac{N!}{(N - i)! \, i!}$$

is the binomial coefficient. The general distribution given in Equation 10.17 can be used to compute the probability of failure as a function of normalized time. Some N module reliabilities are shown in Figure 10.4.

Now let us consider the circumstances where a majority element that does not fail simply is not available. First, the system reliability must be modified by the reliability of the majority organ, R_m:

$$R[T > t] = R_m \sum_{i=0}^{n} \binom{N}{i}(1 - R)^i R^{N-i} \qquad (10.18)$$

Here, we have assumed that the system fails if the majority organ fails. Specifically for TMR, the survival probability is

$$R[T > t] = e^{-\lambda_m t}[3e^{-2\lambda t} - 2e^{-3\lambda t}] \qquad (10.19)$$

Now, if $\lambda_m \geq \lambda$, the survival probability for a TMR system is less than that for a single computational element for all time. Thus, in a practical computational system using TMR or NMR, it is imperative that ultrareliability of the majority device be ensured. If this is done, then the majority device will tend to restore the output of a system to its proper value. Hence, it has also been called a restoring organ.

Another approach to the problem of majority organ reliability involves triplication of these units as well, as shown in Figure 10.6. Thus, a computer system that triplicates each subsection and replaces each module interconnection with three interconnections can provide reliable computation up to the point where a final single output must be decided. Here, either an external (perhaps human) observer or a very reliable restoring organ must make the decision. The responsibility placed on the restoring organs and especially this final element is great, and for this reason attempts have been made to distribute these decisions throughout a computational network. One approach to this in logical networks is described in the next section.

A simple extension of NMR has been described by Mathur and Avizienis [3]. Initially, assume that all modules are functioning normally. Later, if one or more modules fail, their outputs will differ from the outputs of the surviving modules. Thus, a simple comparator can be used to compare the outputs, and when a module fails, it can be replaced by switching in a new module. This scheme, of course, requires that some number of spares, S, be available. It is assumed that the $2n + 1$ active units

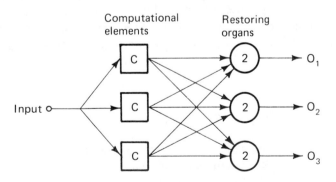

Figure 10.6. TMR as applied to both computational elements and majority (restoring) organs.

have a failure rate of λ, whereas the spares, in the dormant mode, have a failure rate $\mu \leq \lambda$. The block diagram of Figure 10.7 illustrates the major elements of this system. There are $2n + 1 + S = N + S$ computational units, a switching unit, a disagreement detector, and a restoring organ in this system. The disagreement detector monitors the relative performance of the Cs and, if a failure in one of the Cs occurs, it activates the switching unit, which in turn switches in a new C and turns off the old C. This approach has been called the hybrid (N, S) system with corresponding reliability $R(N, S)$. If we define a hybrid $(3, S)$ system, then we have a hybrid TMR system. The survival probability of this system can be defined as the probability that any two of the $S + 3$ units survive. If we now assume that $\mu = \lambda$, then the reliability is

$$R(3, S) = \sum_{i=0}^{n} \binom{S + 3}{i} (1 - R)^i R^{S+2-i}$$

$$= 1 - (1 - R)^{S+2}[1 + R(S + 2)]$$

(10.20)

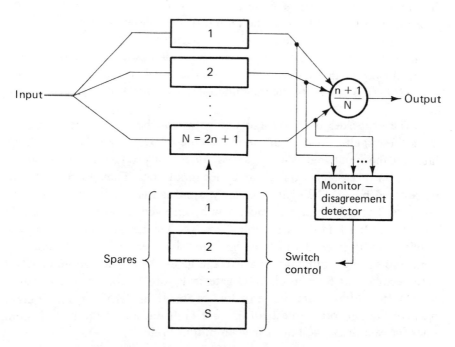

Figure 10.7. Hybrid (N, S) modular redundant system.

Equation 10.20 must be modified by the probability that the disagreement detector, the switching unit, and the restoring organ survive given by R_{DSM}:

$$R(3, S) = R_{DSM}\left[1 - (1 - R)^{S+2}[1 + R(S + 2)]\right] \qquad (10.21)$$

Equations 10.18, 10.19, and 10.21 indicate that the crucial section of any high reliability system is the final decision and correction equipment.

QUADDED LOGIC [4, 5]

Quadded logic is a method of combinational logic design that embeds the restoring organ in the network by taking advantage of the corrective properties of AND and OR logic devices. The following discussion is centered on the application of these properties. However, first it is useful to define the kind of logical error or fault that can occur.

Logical circuit elements have two output states, namely one or zero, and in modern high-gain circuits one of these outputs is achieved even if the input is not in either of these conditions. Thus, a loose connection or poor input gate will still cause the output of the following gate to be either one or zero. A failure in a logical network occurs when one or more outputs or inputs are always zero or always one under all network conditions. Thus, a logical element that fails is said to be either *stuck at zero* (*s-a-*0) or *stuck at one* (*s-a-*1). The goal of the quadded logic configuration is to mask these faults.

The properties of AND and OR gates can be used to advantage to mask these faults. For example, consider the AND gate in Figure 10.8a. A fault on the input that is *s-a-*1, say A, does not produce a faulty (stuck) output; however, an *s-a-*0 fault on either input does. Thus, *s-a-*1 faults can be restored by an AND gate. Similarly, *s-a-*0 faults can be restored by an OR gate. The only thing that must now be resolved is the way in which we ensure that *s-a-*1 faults are applied to AND gates and *s-a-*0 faults are applied to OR gates. To do this, one must be prepared to quadruple the logic and supply redundant inputs to the gates. Thus, the two-input AND gate becomes the four-input AND gate in Figure 10.8b, where the redundant A and B inputs are the same logical functions derived from different parts of the network. Note that an *s-a-*1 fault on one of the logical input lines for each literal will not cause an output fault.

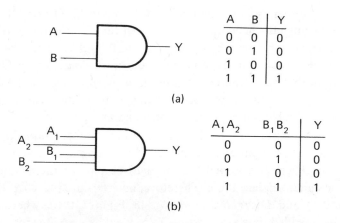

(a)

(b)

Figure 10.8. (a) AND gate. (b) Two-variable AND gate for quadded logic. The truth table is for a gate with no input faults.

Next, let us examine the interconnection scheme necessary to correct faults using quadded logic gates. Given the network shown in Figure 10.9, one of the A inputs to the first AND gate is s-a-1 and one of the E inputs to the second AND gate is s-a-0. The s-a-1 fault on A_1 is restored by gate 1, since the correct logical value still is on A_2. The s-a-0 fault on E_1, however, propagates through gate 2, and D is also s-a-0. The OR gate restores the logic since D_2 is still correct. The general configuration for

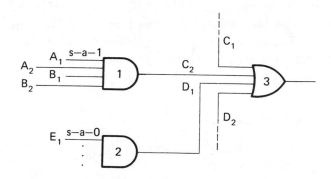

Figure 10.9. Logic configuration for quadded logic.

quadded logic then requires that redundant input AND and OR gates be staggered through the network. Thus, an s-a-1 fault on the input to an AND gate is corrected by that gate, and an s-a-0 fault is corrected by the following OR gate. Similarly, an s-a-0 fault on the input to an OR gate is corrected by that gate, whereas an s-a-1 fault is corrected by the following AND gate. It is important to note that this configuration can correct only single faults; double faults propagate through and are not corrected.

One additional logic function must be incorporated into the quadded logic configuration in order to realize any logic function, namely inversion. To be sure, inverters cannot be allowed to be part of the cascade, as no correction can take place there. Therefore, inverters are placed at the inputs to the AND and OR gates as shown in Figure 10.10, where they are eventually quadded. It is also possible to move the inversions forward to the outputs of the gates and quad the inverters there. The extension of these concepts to NAND and NOR logic should now be clear since a NAND gate is equivalent to a NOR gate with each input inverted.

Next, let us examine the specific interconnections necessary to implement a reliable logic network using quadded logic. To accomplish this, consider the simple logic network shown in Figure 10.11a, which realizes the function $Y = (A + B)(C + D)$. Let us assume that this network is embedded in a larger network that will provide the proper number of redundant logic inputs for each input literal. Recall from Figure 10.8b that each input literal for each quadded logic gate has two inputs. Thus, since there will be four gates for each gate in the net of Figure 10.9, there are eight inputs associated with each literal. The specific interconnection of the quadded gates for the network of Figure 10.11a is shown in Figure 10.11b. The complexity of the quadded logic net is clear in this figure; 4 logical inputs become 32 logical inputs, 2 two-input OR gates become 8 four-input OR gates, and 1 two-input AND gate becomes 4 four-input AND gates.

Figure 10.10.   Incorporating inversion in quadded logic.

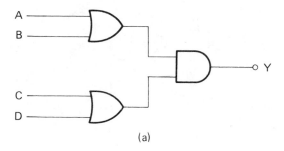

(a)

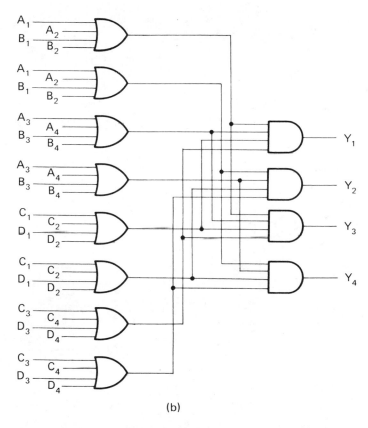

(b)

Figure 10.11. (a) Simple logic network. $Y = (A + B)(C + D)$. (b) Quadded logic configuration for $Y = (A + B)(C + D)$.

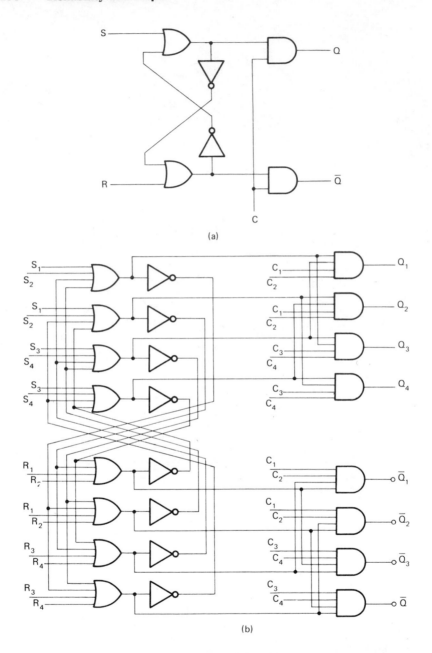

Figure 10.12.   (a) Gate realization of $R - S$ flip-flop. (b) Quadded version of $R - S$ flip-flop.

Generally, however, quadded logic networks require eight times the hardware of the irredundant realization. The problem of generating the quadded network given the logic function is clearly quite formidable. However, algorithms that achieve this can certainly be formulated, thereby allowing automatic computer design.

The final output of a quadded network must still be resolved. A majority gate as used in NMR can be placed at the output of the last level to decide on the final output. This, of course, must be highly reliable if the full advantages of the quadded configuration are to be realized.

Finally, the realization of a computer must use storage elements as well as combinational logic circuits. Since the realization of flip-flops can be obtained using gates, these connections can also be quadded. A gate realization of an R-S flip-flop is shown in Figure 10.12a. The quadded version of this device is given in Figure 10.12b. Specific rules for quadding flip-flop circuits exactly are not known, and one must rely on cut-and-try methods. For example, one type of fault can exist in the flip-flop circuit but not get out of the feedback loop (see the Exercises). Another approach to repair in networks with memory is treated in the next section.

THE SEQUENTIAL PRIME IMPLICANT FORM [6, 7]

NMR techniques apply to any modular system, and quadded logic applies to combinational logic and to a certain extent to sequential networks. The sequential prime implicant form (SPIF) is a tool for testing the behavior of sequential networks. For example, it can be used to test elements for replacement in a hybrid, modularly redundant system. The following treatment considers first the general nature of the SPIF and later its application to self-repairing systems.

First, let us consider the synchronous circuit given in Figure 10.13, where

$$Q_1 = \overline{Q}_2 C \vee Q_1 \overline{C}$$
$$Q_2 = Q_1 C \vee Q_2 \overline{C}$$

$$(10.22)$$

describes the next state condition for each flip-flop. The overall behavior of a sequential network can be described by state transition diagrams—one for each possible input condition. The fact that there is only a single input, the clock, simplifies the problem. However, extension to other input

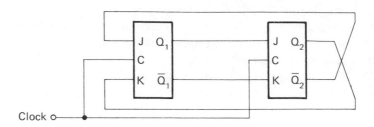

Figure 10.13.   Synchronous sequential circuit.

configurations is straightforward. The state transition tables are given in Figure 10.14, where the diagram for $C = 0$ is trivial, as no changes take place under this condition. Note that the form of the state transition table resembles that of the maps used for minimization of combinational logic functions. Thus, another way of describing these state diagrams can be drawn from combinational logic. Relabel the present state $A_1 A_2$ and the next state $B_1 B_2$ and write the Boolean equations from the maps, as we would for combinational nets. Thus, for $C = 1$,

$$f(C = 1) = \overline{A}_1 \overline{A}_2 B_1 \overline{B}_2 C \vee \overline{A}_1 A_2 \overline{B}_1 \overline{B}_2 C \vee A_1 A_2 \overline{B}_1 B_2 \overline{C}$$
$$\vee \; A_1 \overline{A}_2 B_1 B_2 C$$

$$(10.23)$$

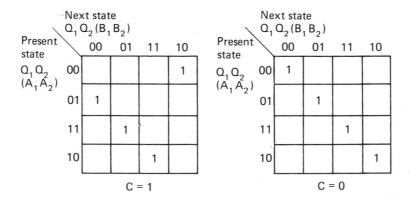

Figure 10.14.   Transition table for sequential circuit of Figure 10.13.

and for $C = 0$,

$$f(C = 0) = \overline{A}_1 \overline{A}_2 \overline{B}_1 \overline{B}_2 \overline{C} \vee \overline{A}_1 A_2 \overline{B}_1 B_2 \overline{C} \vee A_1 A_2 B_1 B_2 \overline{C}$$
$$\vee\ A_1 \overline{A}_2 B_1 \overline{B}_2 \overline{C} \tag{10.24}$$

and

$$f = f(C = 0) \vee f(C = 1) \tag{10.25}$$

and we have the Boolean expression that describes the state behavior of the network. These Boolean expressions can now be manipulated as in any Boolean algebra [6]. Since the maps given previously cannot be reduced, then Equations 10.23 and 10.24 are the minimal forms for the network. Hence, they are called the sequential prime implicant form (SPIF). The SPIF, then, is a logical function that produces a logical one when proper transitions of the sequential network occur. Thus, $\overline{\text{SPIF}}$ indicates improper transitions and can be used to monitor failures in the sequential network. The use of $\overline{\text{SPIF}}$, however, requires that both the previous and present states for all memory elements be available. Since, for anything but the simplest of systems, the number of connections would be prohibitive, another way of generating the SPIF is needed.

To accomplish this, let us consider the case where only a restricted number of memory elements are monitored. The transition tables so generated are called *projections* of a SPIF. There are two types of projection; one can be found from the SPIF of the network and is called a *complete projection*, and the other is generated from observations of some of the memory elements and may or may not be complete. An incomplete projection is called *partial*. For example, consider the network given in Figure 10.13, where the cycle of operation is

Q_1	Q_2
0	0
1	0
1	1
0	1
0	0
$\vdots$	$\vdots$

Now, if one tries to generate transition tables from observation of only Q_1, then the accompanying tables will result. This projection is partial, and

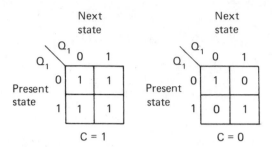

because there is more than one 1 per row, these tables are contradictory—the next state is not uniquely defined. Also a table or SPIF where there is no 1 in one or more rows is called unresolved. The complete projection from Q_1 of this SPIF can be found from the original function by replacing terms associated with the other memory elements by 1s; here terms with a subscript of 2 are replaced by 1s:

$$f_1 = \overline{A}_1 B_1 C \vee \overline{A}_1 \overline{B}_1 C \vee A_1 \overline{B}_1 C \vee A_1 B_1 C$$
$$\vee \overline{A}_1 \overline{B}_1 \overline{C} \vee \overline{A}_1 \overline{B}_1 C \vee A_1 B_1 \overline{C} \vee A_1 B_1 \overline{C} \tag{10.26}$$

Equation 10.26 can be reduced by application of the Quine-McCluskey techniques to

$$f_1 = C \vee A_1 B_1 \vee \overline{A}_1 \overline{B}_1 \tag{10.27}$$

The transition tables for this projection are given in Figure 10.15. Another projection can be combined by forming the product (AND) of the two projections to generate a new projection. This projection will also be contradictory, indicating that another element must be monitored (the present and previous states of the other memory element in this case) to form the proper SPIF. For example, consider the projection formed by examining the previous state of both Q_1 and Q_2, the present state of Q_1, and the clock.

$$f_2 = C(\overline{A}_1 \overline{A}_2 \overline{B}_2 \vee \overline{A}_1 A_2 \overline{B}_2 \vee A_1 \overline{A}_2 B_2)$$
$$\vee \overline{C}(\overline{A}_1 \overline{A}_2 \overline{B}_2 \vee \overline{A}_1 A_2 B_2 \vee A_1 A_2 B_2 \vee A_1 \overline{A}_2 \overline{B}_2) \tag{10.28}$$

The product of all projections of the SPIF will reveal the original SPIF of the net. In this example, the original SPIF, Equation 10.25, is needed to

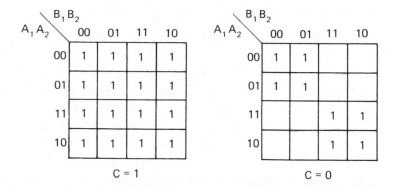

Figure 10.15.   Transition table for complete projection of the SPIF for Q_1.

describe all state transitions. However, the entire SPIF is not always needed to describe all allowable state transitions, and the problem reduces to finding a minimal set of projections with which one can differentiate proper from improper network operation. An ideal condition would be a minimal set of projections whose product forms the whole SPIF.

Once the projections are found, it is only necessary to build a logical network which will signal an improper transition, and hence will indicate a failure in the sequential network. This network can be designed from the inverse SPIF, $\overline{\text{SPIF}}$. For our example, the inverse SPIF can be found from the maps of Figure 10.16, which are the complements of the maps in Figure

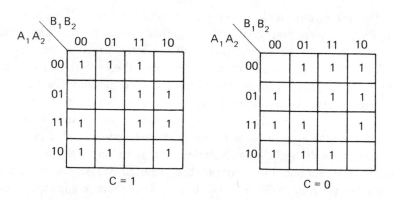

Figure 10.16.   Maps for the inverse SPIF of example.

10.14. The function that indicates a failure in the network of Figure 10.13 is

$$f = C(\overline{A}_2 \overline{B}_1 \vee A_1 \overline{B}_2 \vee A_2 B_1 \vee \overline{A}_1 B_2)$$
$$\vee \overline{C}(A_1 \overline{B}_1 \vee \overline{A}_1 B_1 \vee \overline{A}_2 B_2 \vee A_2 \overline{B}_2) \tag{10.29}$$

A $\overline{\text{SPIF}}$-monitored sequential network can be incorporated into a system in several ways. First, two identical networks can be built into a system where one network is monitored. If the monitor indicates failure of this first network, the second network is automatically switched in. Another method uses two networks, with each net monitored. If the first net fails, the second net is switched in and an external alarm sounds. If the second net fails, the new network, which should have been installed by the operator, is switched in. Another way to use this monitoring technique is in the hybrid, modularly redundant system. The output of the $\overline{\text{SPIF}}$-designed monitor is used to initiate the switching in of a new module, as shown in Figure 10.7.

The techniques treated in this and the last section are concerned with specific logical approaches to the problem of masking faults that can occur in combinational and sequential switching circuits. These and other techniques must be integrated into a complete system in order to achieve computational reliability. In the rest of this chapter we present some approaches to the architecture of reliable computers.

ARCHITECTURE OF RELIABLE COMPUTERS [8, 9, 10, 13]

The interest in reliable computers began when a large number of components were first connected together and the resulting system's reliability was unsatisfactory. Initial efforts were aimed at increasing the reliability of the individual components. Thus, the evolution from vacuum tubes to transistors, to integrated circuits, and to medium-scale and large-scale integrated circuits now enables us to design rather sophisticated computers with tolerable reliability. However, computers that do not employ redundancy still cannot achieve the reliability needed in aerospace missions, aircraft traffic control, telephone switching systems, or crucial business transactions. For example, the required MTBF for short-mission computers is from 2000 to 5000 hours, and these computers typically employ triple modular redundancy in the arithmetic and control units [9].

The requirements for long space missions such as the Jupiter Fly-by place the extreme requirement of 10^5 hours on MTBF. Thus, a great deal of effort has been directed toward the design of computers that can achieve these specifications. The application of TMR to nonredundant computers typically yields a gain of only approximately two in MTBF. Thus, incorporation of TMR throughout present spacecraft computers would not significantly increase the MTBF.

The STAR (self-testing and repairing) computer was designed and built at the California Institute of Technology, Jet Propulsion Laboratory, as a vehicle for the development of high-reliability aerospace computers. The STAR was designed to cope with four major classes of faults: transient, permanent, random, and catastrophic. *Transient* faults may exsit for only one machine cycle, whereas *permanent* faults are the *s-a-*0 or *s-a-*1 variety. *Random* faults are those which are neither permanent nor fleeting or transient but occur at random intervals. *Catastrophic* failures occur when one failure causes faults that are distributed throughout the system.

The correction of faults in a computer system cannot be allocated solely to the hardware but must include the software as well. The imposition of additional work on the programmer, however, is, as in most other computer designs, desirable to avoid. However, the backing up and restarting of a program after a fault is detected must be a software-hardware task. Certain error detection and correction tasks can be handled by either the hardware or the software, and when there was a choice most systems in STAR were implemented in hardware. For example, it is well known that noise on buses and in core or MOS memories can cause errors, typically in one bit of a parallel bit stream. Therefore, one redundant bit is often added to the system, which is 0 if there are an even number of 1s in the string and which is 1 if there are an odd number of 1s in the string. Thus, if the number of 1s is odd and this "parity" bit is 0, then one knows that an error in either the bit stream or the parity bit has occurred. If this occurs in reading a word from memory, then one may merely read the same location again, in which case the bit string and the parity bit probably agree. The rereading of a given location can be accomplished with either software or hardware. Additional redundant bits can be added to a bit string to detect and correct more than one fault [11, 12] as presented in Chapter 8. All machine words of STAR, both data and instructions, are encoded in error-detecting codes that act while a program is in execution.

The hardware of the STAR is organized around a module replacement system. Therefore, one or more spares and the associated switching hardware must be available to replace operating units when permanent faults are detected. Each of these modular units is self-contained and includes its own instruction decoder and sequence generator. This enables each unit to operate independently, thus isolating failures from other parts of the system. It is interesting to note that decentralization and distribution of control also allowed the communications network in Chapter 9 to achieve a high degree of reliability. All modules are permanently connected to the appropriate buses. Modules are designed to fail and power-down with their outputs in a floating state, thereby not disturbing the buses. This configuration also obviates the need for an input-output switching network for each module—the active module is the one that is powered. Since the remaining modules are not powered, their MTBF is generally greater than that for the powered modules.

The replacement of modules is controlled by a central processor called TARP (test and repair processor). The TARP contains the fault location logic and generates clock and control-sync signals, program recovery registers, and module power switching logic. It should be clear that the TARP must be extremely reliable since it controls the remainder of STAR. This high reliability was achieved by making the TARP a hybrid [2, 3] system. That is, it is TMR with two spares. Before we examine the details of the TARP, it is useful to examine the structure of the STAR, given in Figure 10.17. The TARP is connected via the control bus and the status lines to monitor each element of the system, and it controls the active modules via the power switch lines. The validity of every word sent on the two memory buses is checked with respect to the coding placed on the signals. Also, the status messages from the functional units are checked with respect to the predicted response. Faults or errors detected by the TARP interrupt normal operation, and the recovery mode is entered. In the recovery mode a rollback point address register points to the location where normal operation is to be resumed. Then either the TARP restarts the program at the rollback point or, if a module fails repeatedly, it is replaced and the program is restarted from the rollback point.

It is now of interest to examine the nature of the coding used in the STAR, as it is a simple but effective system. The STAR words are 32 bits wide divided into eight 4-bit "nibbles." Data are transmitted in a series-

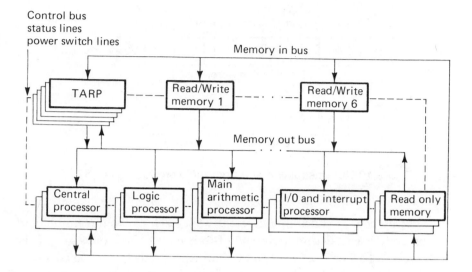

Figure 10.17.   STAR architecture.

parallel manner on a four-line data bus, where one nibble is transmitted in parallel and the eight nibbles are transmitted in serial. The formats of the instruction and operand words are shown in Figure 10.18. Note that the seven rightmost operand nibbles make up a b field and that the leftmost nibble makes up the c field. The 28-bit b field is the desired binary number, and the c field is the check nibble, which is computed from

$$c(b) = 15 - |b|_{15} \qquad (10.30)$$

where $|b|_{15}$ is the residue modulo 15 of the binary number b. If one considers $c(b)$ the lowest-order nibble, then the operand word is always a multiple of 15. The checking algorithm then merely computes a residue modulo 15 of the received word, and if it is nonzero, then an error has occurred. This same modulo 15 residue code is used on the address part of the instruction word, where

$$c(a) = 15 - |a|_{15} \qquad (10.31)$$

This code uses four redundant error-detecting bits, one for each line of the data bus.

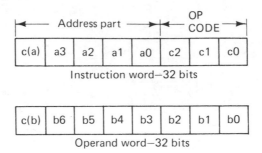

Figure 10.18. Instruction and operand word formats of STAR.

The op code is coded in a different way. Each of the three nibbles of the op code is encoded in a two-out-of-four code, where only two of the four bits can be 0 or 1 for valid codes. This leaves only 6 valid op codes per nibble and a total of 6^3 valid op code forms. The check circuit for op code errors then looks for nibbles where there are less than or more than two ones or zeroes.

The STAR computer is a very interesting design in that it employs several of the available techniques for repair and reliability in one computer, including TMR, hybrid (N, S) redundancy, module replacement, and error-detecting codes.

The STAR represents an effort to achieve extremely high reliability in a potentially hostile environment. These and other techniques have also been applied to other more earthly environments. Most of these systems have been used in special applications and are not universally available volume manufactured products. However, the evolution of computer system use is now reaching the point at which the total life-cycle costs of a system, including the cost of being down, are being more closely examined by the consumer. Thus, in the future, the design of general-purpose systems that can tolerate some or all types of faults will be increasingly important.

One down-to-earth problem in which a great deal of attention has been paid to reliability is the design of the telephone system. Although this is a somewhat specialized problem, most of the techniques for achieving reliable operation are general.

The evolution of the Electronic Switching System (ESS) is an interesting example of a reliable computing system [14]. The requirements of ESS are not as stringent as those for STAR. The principal goals of ESS(A) are to be out of service for no more than a few minutes per year and to provide a 99.99 percent grade of service (no more than 0.01 percent of the calls handled are to be processed incorrectly). The system then must have sufficient redundancy so that no single failure can bring the complete system down. Also, when an element does fail, the failure must be easily diagnosed and repaired. The other significant difference between ESS and STAR is economic. A computer for a spaceship is often tailored for a single mission or single type of mission and, because its failure can result in loss of the complete mission whose cost is higher than the cost of the computer, the cost of the computer is not a very important factor. However, ESS installations will eventually be located in every neighborhood and town in the country. Therefore, more attention to manufacturability and cost must be paid to ESS design.

The approach used in ESS is to duplicate the processor and run one and all or part of the second processor as a backup. A block diagram of the No. 2 ESS in Figure 10.19 illustrates the way in which this telephone circuit switching system operates. The program store contains the operating program and may be a read only memory (ROM), while the transient call data are stored in the central store. The central control contains the main logic and registers needed to process calls by establishing line connections via the peripherals. Both processors are run in the so-called synchronous and match mode, wherein each processor's call store input registers are compared by the matcher in the maintenance center. One of the processors is on line while the other runs in a shadow mode. If a mismatch occurs, then a failure detection program is run in the on-line processor to determine if it is at fault. If a hard fault is found, the second processor is switched on-line and diagnostic routines are run to isolate the problem in the faulty processor. More contemporary ESS units combine the program and call stores into one random access memory (RAM) and load the program from a tape unit. Also, instead of running both processors synchronously, the on-line processor duplicates the call store data in other processors' memory as shown in Figure 10.20. Fault-detection circuitry and self-checking programs are contained and operated in the on-line processor. Hard failures cause the backup processor to come on line by bootstrapping the program from the tape. Diagnostics are then run in the down machine and alarms are activated to indicate the failure. The self-diagnostics run in ESS aid the

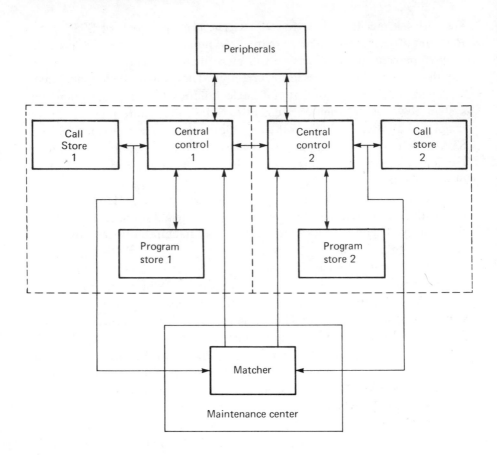

Figure 10.19.   Block diagram of Number 2 electronic switching system.

service personnel in repairing and getting the failed unit back on–line. This repair process must be rapid, because a failure in the on-line processor while the other processor is being repaired is a system failure.

Experience with ESS in its various forms shows that hardware failures account for 20 percent of the total failures, whereas software deficiencies, including incorrect implementations and design errors, account for only 15 percent. Procedural errors account for 30 percent of the failures and are primarily human errors of the operational or maintenance personnel. The remainder of the failures, 35 percent, are caused by recovery deficiencies—

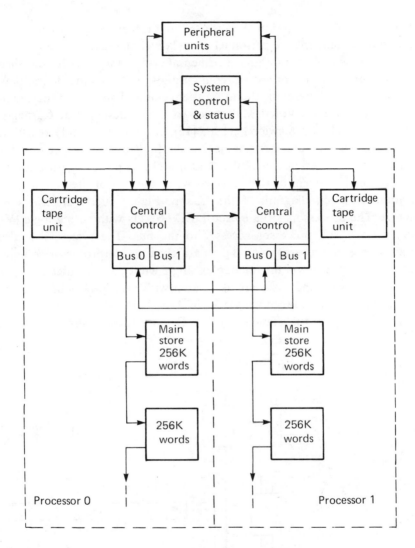

Figure 10.20. Block diagram of electronic switching system Number 3A which does not use synchronous and matching operation, but instead uses error detection circuitry and software to initiate the back-up processor.

which cover the range of problems from inadequate fault detection and isolation to problems of initializing a backup system. Note the principal differences between ESS and STAR occurred because of different economic and environmental constraints. ESS is used in a rather benign environment where trained maintenance personnel are relatively handy.

Let us now look at another experimental system that uses off-the-shelf microcomputers in a triplicated configuration with voting to achieve reliability with both permanent and transient faults. This system, designated C.vmp (Computer, Voted Multiprocessor), was designed at Carnegie-Mellon University by Siewiorek et al. [15] to provide reliable real-time computing with software transparency to the fault tolerant aspects of the system. The basic design is modular, and it includes power distribution so that parts of the system can be serviced while the rest of the system is in operation. A block diagram of the C.vmp, Figure 10.21, illustrates its structure. The processors (P) are each DEC LSI-11s with voting logic (V), which votes on all processor accesses to the bus. The system can also operate with each processor working separately and interprocessor communications taking place via the full duplex single-word parallel interfaces (L). The memories (M) and disks are associated with each processor, and the user terminals are interfaced via the Serial Line Unit (SLU).

The buses are the standard DEC Q bus, which allows standard

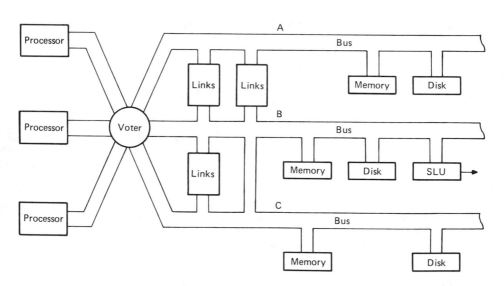

Figure 10.21.   Block diagram of C.vmp—A triplicated voting system for high reliability.

memories and peripherals to be connected to C.vmp. The bus, however, does not have access to every transaction that takes place in the processor. Hence the voter cannot directly monitor the six general-purpose registers in each of the processors. However, in the course of operation it has been discovered that all but one of the registers, the stack pointer, are loaded or stored once every 24 instructions for an "average" program. Thus, the voter gets to look at these registers often enough to test them. On the other hand, the stack pointer must be cycled on a regular basis in order for it to be tested by the voter. This allows a standard board computer to be triplicated by the addition of a voter.

The voter looks at each bus and puts the results out directly on bus A and multiplexes it to the other buses. Disagreement detectors are also within the voter, one for each bus, which can be used to monitor the failures in each of the three parts of the system. The multiplexers located in the voter are also used to reconfigure C.vmp into a loosely coupled multiprocessor for a higher performance non-fault-tolerant system.

The triplication of a standard microprocessor has two effects, improved reliability and decreased performance. The reliability of C.vmp has been measured and reported in terms of a failure record and failure recovery data, Tables 10.1 and 10.2. The failures were recorded in two categories, best and worst case. Worst-case data include crashes that may have been software or user caused, whereas the best-case data do not include these. Crash-recovery requirements are a relatively good indication of the extent of the failure. Thus, the types of recovery needed for C.vmp were recorded for a range of recovery actions including: *Continue* execution at the same location without any changes to processor registers or memory, *Restart* the program in memory, *Reload* the program into memory, *Reset* the processors and reload the program, and *Debug* the hardware to restore stable operation. The experience with the operation of C.vmp provides an indicator of the system reliability gained and the effort required to build a voting computing system from standard board computers.

An alternative to a triple-redundancy voting computer exists in a general-pupose system using a dual configuration that is, in many ways, similar to ESS. This architecture created by Tandem Computers [16, 17] avoids single points of failure in the hardware with a basic dual processor system. The architecture's basic reliability comes from this and the fact that it is intended for use in transaction, terminal-oriented applications with

Table 10.1.   Failure for C.vmp over 9 month period. Note worst case includes software or user induced crashes while the best case does not.

C.vmp Crash Data (Worst Case)					
Month	Mean	Std Dev	Median	Number	Uptime
August	64.8	91.9	28.0	5	323.8
September	108.7	139.6	35.6	4	434.9
October	35.5	51.1	19.8	16	568.3
November	49.3	33.0	52.0	10	492.9
December	204.8	191.6	113.1	3	614.5
January	95.4	104.3	70.5	7	667.7
February	258.8	78.6	258.8	2	517.6
March	298.3	276.4	298.3	2	517.6
April	352.4	114.2	352.4	2	704.7
Total	96.5	167.8	30.6	51	4921.1
C.vmp Crash Data (Best Case)					
Month	Mean	Std Dev	Median	Number	Uptime
August	81.0	96.1	34.6	4	323.8
September	217.4	132.4	217.4	2	434.9
October	142.1	44.5	125.7	4	568.3
November	246.5	167.3	246.5	2	492.9
December	614.5	0.0	614.5	1	614.5
January	–	–	–	0	667.7
February	517.6	0.0	517.6	1	517.6
March	–	–	–	0	596.7
April	704.7	0.0	704.7	1	704.7
Total	328.1	470.8	114.3	15	4921.1

All times given in Table 10 are in hours. (Std Dev is the standard deviation.)

access by multiple users. Each processor has its own memory with a six-bit error correcting code, which corrects all single-bit errors and detects all double errors. The basic architecture illustrated in Figure 10.22 shows that the fundamental structure is a dual system in which each I/O device is accessed by a dual ported controller connected to two processors. Interprocessor communication takes place on a dual bus called the Dynabus. The bus controllers are small and are not part of any processor. The system can be expanded up to 16 processors. Power supplies are associated with each processor, and the I/O controllers receive power from two power supplies, each of which can power it. This allows the I/O system to remain functional

Table 10.2. Recovery data for range of recoveries for C.vmp.

C.vmp Crash Recovery Data (Worst Case)					
Month	Continue	Restart	Reload	Reset	Debug
August	0	1	3	0	1
September	0	0	2	0	2
October	0	5	7	1	3
November	0	1	7	1	1
December	0	0	2	0	1
January	0	7	0	0	0
February	0	1	0	0	1
March	0	2	0	0	0
April	0	2	0	0	0
Total	0	19	21	2	9
C.vmp Crash Recovery Data (Best Case)					
Month	Continue	Restart	Reload	Reset	Debug
August	0	0	3	0	1
September	0	0	0	0	2
October	0	0	1	0	3
November	0	0	0	1	1
December	0	0	0	0	1
January	0	0	0	0	0
February	0	0	0	0	1
March	0	0	0	0	0
April	0	1	0	0	0
Total	0	1	4	1	9

if a power supply fails or if it is turned off to service a CPU. The key element in a transaction-oriented system is the mass storage system, typically discs, which store each transaction. The discs are dual ported and can be set up so that there is a duplicate image on a second disc should one disc or controller fail.

The glue that makes this system work is the software—both systems and applications—which must have the knowledge of the system needed to take advantage of the hardware redundancy to achieve reliable operation. The fact that the system is designed for a multiuser transaction environment makes it ideal for assigning different users to different processors.

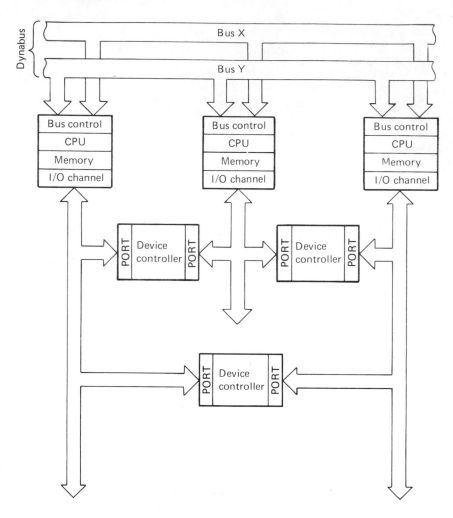

Figure 10.22. Architecture of the Tandem system which uses up to 16 processors for transaction processing.

Thus, as parts of the system fail, the users that can be are redirected to other processors by the system and those which cannot are without service. Similar action takes place with the switchover from one disc to another. The system software must perform all of these actions. The failure of a piece of hardware can also cause the user application running on the system to fail.

Therefore, the application software must be written with the "hooks" required to deal with changes in the system. These hooks include checkpoints in the program that preserve the state of the application by restarting the program should a failure occur. The general problem of software fault tolerance has only been getting specific attention for a short time and has very different problems from that of hardware.

The task of designing fault tolerant software does not have the same underlying problems as in the design of fault tolerant hardware. In hardware systems one can usually assume that the existing hardware is designed and works as expected. In software, no-bug software is virtually impossible to achieve and becomes more elusive as software systems get more complex. Therefore a first reaction might be to find a method for assuring that a program is correct.

Work in the area of verification and proofs of correctness has not been successful and offers little help to the designer of a reliable system. Thus, the philosophy used in designing fault tolerant software is that there will be residual errors in both design and implementation. The design of any system which is fault tolerant requires the use of redundant elements. In hardware one can supply spares; but in software, since one cannot guarantee the correctness of the design or its implementation, redundancy must be supplied spacially and/or temporally [19].

Spacial redundancy means that spare copies of the data are stored or different designs of the same program are part of the system. *Temporal redundancy* means that some parts of the system will require recomputation once a fault is detected, thus requiring more time.

A term used to describe the objective of fault tolerant software is *coverage* [19], which is the probability that a system can recover from a failure. Note this in contrast to the term *component reliability*, which is the probability that a component fails. This philosophy is best summarized by the goals of the Hydra operating system for C.mmp multiprocessor built using 16 PDP-11 processors at Carnegie-Mellon University [15]:

1. Be able to detect (almost) any failure
2. Limit the damage caused by a failure
3. Make failures transparent if possible
4. If an error is not transparent: a) place the system in a consistent state so recovery is possible and b) report the failure to higher

level software which can direct intelligent recovery and make the failure transparent to higher levels.

Reporting and recording are important parts of software fault tolerance for both immediate systematic recovery and subsequent software repair and evolution.

A method for using design redundancy for creating a fault tolerant software system has been discussed by Randall [15, 18]. This method requires that the software system be structured into pre-specified blocks called *recovery blocks*. Each block contains within itself the operations of error detection and recovery and any stand-by spares.

Error detection uses an *acceptance test*, which is based upon the goals of the program block. The test is not a complete proof, but is based on an analysis of key variables associated with the block. The acceptance test is defined by the designer as part of the program. The individual instances of the program are called the primary alternate, secondary alternate, and so on.

The primary alternate is the first code entered within the recovery block. If that execution passes its acceptance test, then that block is assumed to have executed correctly. If the acceptance test fails, then the system is reset and the secondary alternate is entered and executed. If the acceptance test fails, the next alternate is entered and so on until the acceptance test is passed or until there are no other alternates to try.

In the last case, the failure is reported as unrecoverable. There are significant problems in trying to store and restore all the states for resetting a complex software system. Therefore, the designer must assure that the only non local variables associated with a recovery block are recorded and reset upon the occurrence of a failure.

There are several significant differences between hardware and software fault tolerant design. The complexity of software and the variety of interfaces and interactions make it a different design process from that associated with hardware. However, the design of VLSI (Very Large Scale Integration) circuits is beginning to look much more like software and we may see some of these techniques for software fault tolerance applied to the complex hardware of the future.

SUMMARY

The elementary approaches for achieving systems that are reliable and/or can be repaired were presented in this chapter. The techniques all make use of redundancy to provide the added reliability. TMR, hybrid (N, S) modular redundancy, and quadded logic all use more components than are absolutely needed for functionality.

The architectures presented use several additional concepts, including error correcting codes, residue arithmetic, and special system software, to aid in the reliability of those systems.

The reader should not conclude that the techniques described here are the only ways to improve the reliability of a system. It is useful to remind oneself that they are not a substitute for good engineering design practice and the full testing of it.

EXERCISES

1. Calculate the reliability of the following networks:

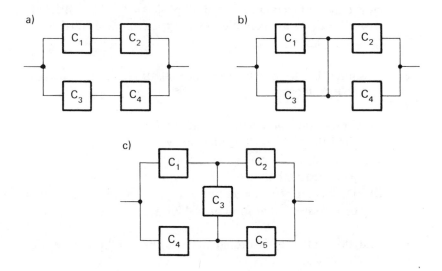

2. Given a component with an expected failure rate of 0.93/sec, find

    (a) The MTBF of the component.
    (b) The MTBF of a system with 10 of these components in a series.
    (c) The MTBF of a system with 100 of these components in a series.

3. Compute the reliability of the complete TMR system shown in Figure 10.6, where the failure rate of the restoring organs is λ and of the Cs is λ.

4. Design a quadded network that realizes the function $Y = AB + CD$ using AND or OR gates.

5. Design a quadded network that realizes the logical function $Y = A(B + C)$ using NAND and NOR gates.

6. A system using 1000 components connected in a series is to be constructed. The reliability of the system must be equal to or exceed 0.96. What is the required reliability of the individual components?

7. Show that the logical product of all projections of the SPIF of the network used as an example, reveals the complete SPIF given in Equation 10.25.

8. A counter that follows the sequence 00, 01, 11, 10 is to be part of a reliable system.

   (a) Design the counter using J-K flip-flops.
   (b) Find the SPIF of the entire network.
   (c) Is there a minimal set of projections (other than the complete SPIF) that covers the network?
   (d) Design an error-indicating network for this sequential circuit. Assume that flip-flop delays are twice the gate delays.

9. Find the fault that is propagated within the flip-flop of Figure 10.12b but does not get out.

REFERENCES

1. VON NEUMANN, J., "Probabilistic Logics and the Synthesis of Reliable Organisms from Unreliable Components," Automata Studies, in *Annals of Mathematical Studies*, No. 34, C. E. SHANNON and J. McCARTHY, eds., Princeton University Press, Princeton, N.J., 1956.
2. MOORE, E. F., and C. E. SHANNON, "Reliable Circuits Using Less Reliable Relays," *Journal of the Franklin Institute*, Vol. 262, 1956, pp. 191–208; 281–297.

3. MATHUR, F., and A. AVIZIENIS, "Reliability Analysis and Architecture of a Hybrid-Redundant Digital System: Generalized Triple Modular Redundancy with Self-Repair," *AFIPS Spring Joint Computer Conference Proceedings*, Vol. 36, 1970, pp. 375–383.

4. TRYON, J. G., "Quadded Logic," in *Redundancy Techniques for Computing Systems*, R. H. WILCOX and W. C. MANN, eds., Spartan, New York, 1962, pp. 205-228.

5. PIERCE, W. H., *Failure-Tolerant Computer Design*, Academic Press, New York, 1965.

6. BEIZER, B., "A New Theory for the Analysis, Synthesis, Cutting and Splicing of Sequential Switching Networks," Ph.D Dissertation, University of Pennsylvania, Philadelphia, Pa. 1966.

7. ROBERTS, David, C., "A Processor for Implementing SPIF Techniques for Self-Repair, Part I—Theory and Application, Part II—Design Goals and Program Operation," *Computer Design*, Vol. 8, No. 12, December 1969, pp. 59-64; and Vol. 9, No. 1, January 1970, pp. 63–69.

8. AVIZIENIS, A., G. C. GILLEY, F. P. MATHUR, D. A. RENNELS, J. A. ROHR, and D. K. RUBIN, "The STAR (Self-Testing and Repairing) Computer: An Investigation of the Theory and Practice of Fault-Tolerant Computer Design," *IEEE TRANSACTIONS ON COMPUTERS*, Vol. C-20, No. 11, November 1971, pp. 1312–1321.

9. AVIZIENIS, A., "Design of Fault-Tolerant Computers," in *1967 Fall Joint Computer Conference, AFIPS Conference Proceedings*, Vol. 31, Washington, D.C., 1967, pp. 733–743.

10. AVIZIENIS, A., "An Experimental Self-Repairing Computer," in *Information Processing '68, Proceedings of the IFIP Congress*, Vol. 2, 1968, pp. 872-977.

11. ROTH, J. P., W. G. BOURICIUS, W. C. CARTER, and P. R. SCHNEIDER, "Phase II of an Architectural Study for a Self-Repairing Computer," *SANSO-TR-67-106*, U. S. Air Force Space and Missile Systems Command, Los Angeles, Calif., November 1967, AD 825460.

12. CARTER, W. C., and W. G. BOURICIUS, "A Survey of Fault-Tolerant Computer Architecture and its Evaluation," *Computer (IEEE)*, Vol. 4, No. 1, January/February 1971, pp. 9–16.

13. *Proceedings of IEEE on Fault-Tolerant Digital Systems*, Vol. 66, No. 10, October 1978.

14. TOY, W. N., "Fault-Tolerant Design of Local ESS Processors" Proceedings of the IEEE, Vol. 16, No. 10, October 1978, pp. 1126–1145.

15. SIEWIOREK, Daniel P., Vittal KINI, Henry MASHBURN, Stephen McCONNEL, and Michale TSAO, "A Case Study of C.mvp, CM* and C.vmp: Part I—Experiences with Fault Tolerance in Multiprocessor Systems" Proceedings of the IEEE, Vol. 66, No. 10, October 1978, pp. 1178–1199.

16. KATZMAN, James A., "A Fault Tolerant Computing System," Proceedings of the Eleventh Hawaii International Conference on System Sciences, University of Hawaii, Honolulu, January 1978, pp. 78–80.

17. BARTLETT, Joel F., "A "Nonstop" Operating System," Proceedings of the Eleventh Hawaii International Conference on System Sciences, University of Hawaii, Honolulu, January 1978, pp. 87–91.

18. RANDALL, B., P. A. LEE and P. C. TRELEAVEN, "Reliability Issues in Computing System Design", ACM Computing Surveys, Vol. 10, No. 2, June 1978, pp. 123–165.

11

Neurons and Neural Models

Thus far, we have been concerned with specific physical systems in which the concepts of adaptation, learning, self-organization, and self-repair have been incorporated. As suggested in Chapter 5, however, these concepts also have significance in psychology and physiology. Certainly we can find examples of adaptation, learning, self-organization, and self-repair in nature, specifically in the human nervous system and the brain. Ashby [1] described many of these processes in his specification of a *Design for a Brain*. Attempts to understand physiological systems and processes and to use this understanding in creating new designs have continued since that time. For example, this "bionic" approach was, in part, responsible for the development of the self-organizing controller described in Chapter 7 [2, 3]. This early interest in the use of physiological phenomena also led to the study of the basic processing element of nervous systems, the neuron.

Elementary neurophysiology is presented here as an introduction to some of the processing models of the neuron. Specific models describing detailed analog neuronal behavior will not be presented, however. These models have been applied to the design of adaptive, learning, self-repairing, and pattern recognition systems as well as to the computer itself. They also provide a basis for understanding brain functioning.

PHYSIOLOGY OF THE NEURON

Most of what is known about the neuron is based on experimental observation of sciatic (motor) neurons [4, 5]. These relatively large cells lend themselves to external and internal probing. However, the behavior of all neurons is similar to that of sciatic neurons.

It would be foolish to suppose that the brain could be sufficiently characterized by studying only afferent neurons to the cortex of the brain or sciatic nerve functioning. Many phenomenologically obvious questions preclude this reasoning. Where, for instance, is the memory located within the cerebellum, and how is it organized? Where is the "screen" on which consciousness is played? These questions have yet to be answered in even the anatomical sense.

Although an attempt to model the brain in its entirety would thus prove insurmountable at this time, there is still much to be learned from the study of information processing in the nervous system. Recent work has indeed led to some very interesting models of portions of the brain—models that are both anatomically and phenomenologically sound. The main thrust of this work has been aimed at understanding portions of the brain that are highly stylized in their structure or in which it is known that certain behaviors are centered. Of note is the model of the reticular formation as developed by Kilmer et al. [6]. This part of the brain is analogous to a major state generator of a computer, as it is here that the overall state of the animal—e.g., sleep, eat, groom, and mate—is determined. This model considers both the anatomical and behavioral aspects of this portion of the brain. Another portion, the cerebellum, has received a great deal of attention because of its uniform structure and the fact that the learning of many motor tasks centers here. Marr [7, 8], Albus [9], and Mortimer [10] have developed theoretical and logical neural models of this most interesting region. A study of the behavioral and anatomical nature of perception and the eye-brain system has been undertaken by Didday [11] and Arbib [12]. They have attempted to understand the processing that occurs when an object is viewed and patterns in an animal's environment are recognized.

With these thoughts in mind, we have included a physiological description of the neuron in this chapter. The description, by no means to be considered anatomically or functionally exhaustive, is rather intended to serve as a basis for the various attempts at modeling the logical behavior of this biological structure.

The neuron, shown in general form in Figure 11.1, consists of a nucleus and associated protoplasm (cytoplasm). This organism exists at a very high metabolic rate and is interconnected with numerous adjacent cells. Abundant branches (dendrites) comprise the outer surface of the neuron; these units bring information into the cell body or soma.

A long, thin cylindrical fiber called the *axon* may be considered the output cable of the nerve cell. The axon is capable of electrochemically transmitting information concerning the state of the cell. Depending on the particular function of the neuron, the axon may vary in length from less than a millimeter up to a meter, and in width from 0.1 micron to 1 millimeter. This substructure undergoes considerable arborization as it terminates in endbulbs near the dendrites of other neurons. These near-connections, or the locus of interaction between an endbulb and the cell on which it impinges, were termed "synapses" by Sir Charles Sherrington, who laid the basis of what is now known as synaptology [13]. An impulse traveling down the axon is terminated at the endbulbs. If conditions permit, it is regenerated by the next neuron in the chain. This retransmission was experimentally postulated by Sir Henry Dale and Otto Loewi some 50 years ago, the process being sometimes electrical and sometimes chemical. The speed of impulse propagation along the axonal fiber is given approximately by the following relationship: velocity = frequency × diameter. This quantity may approach 100 meters per second in some intermuscular neurons.

A neuron produces an output only when enough impulses are presented to its dendritic area in a short period of time (the latent period of

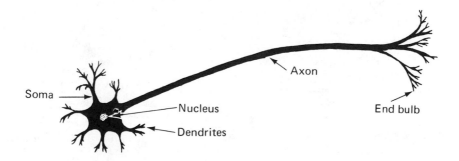

Figure 11.1. Neuron.

summation). In actual fact, some inputs hinder firing; thus, it would be correct to say that a neuron fires when the active excitatory inputs exceed the active inhibitory inputs by an amount equal to the "threshold value" of the cell. A portion of the soma called the *spike initiator loci* performs this summation and comparison, producing a pulsed output signal for the stated conditions of input.

To understand this process in greater anatomical detail, we must consider the previously mentioned work of Sir John Eccles [13]. Through the use of the electron microscope, it has been determined that the distance from the endbulbs or synaptic knobs to the synaptic membrane of the adjoining dendrite is a remarkably uniform 200 angstroms. This space, termed the *synaptic cleft*, is shown in Figure 11.2. Throughout the structure of the endbulbs are numerous tiny sacs (vesicles) containing a transmitter substance for relaying the impulse to the dendrite of the attached neuron. The transmitter substance triggers a neural reaction that is a function of the ionic composition of the cell and the axon.

The internal fluid of the cell is at a more negative potential (70 millivolts) than the surrounding solution of ions. This condition allows the concentration of chloride (Cl^-) ions to be about 14 times greater on the outside of the neuronic membrane than on the inside. What is not fully explained, however, is the 30 to 1 concentration difference of the potassium (K^+) ions. This condition would require a potential difference of 90 millivolts, a disparity of some 20 millivolts from the existing conditions.

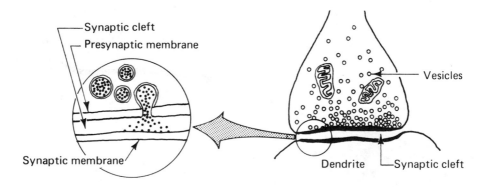

Figure 11.2.   Endbulb and synaptic cleft.

Investigation also reveals that the concentration of sodium (Na^+) ions outside the cell exceeds the internal concentration by a factor of 10. This is a truly remarkable state of affairs, because the sodium ions must be pumped against a potential of 130 millivolts—70 millivolts of internal potential plus 60 millivolts to allow for the concentration difference.

The biochemical status of the nerve cell is illustrated in Figure 11.3. Since the normal resting potential in the cell is −70 millivolts with respect to the outside of the cell, there must be a metabolic mechanism that maintains the imbalance of $−90 − (−70) + 60 = 40$ millivolts between the outside and the inside of the cell. A metabolic sodium pumping mechanism that maintains this difference has thus been hypothesized.

The work of Hodgkin [14], Huxley [15], and Katz [16] has also shown that the propagation of the nerve impulse is accompanied by an abrupt change in the permeability of the cell membrane—sodium ions are allowed to enter the cell in an avalanche type of reaction that depolarizes the cell from 0.1 to 2 millimeters along its length. The fact that the axon now becomes positive constitutes the actual nerve impulse that is propagated along the axon. After the impulse has traveled the length of the axon, the membrane becomes impermeable to sodium, and an effective potassium gate opens. Thus, the resting potential of the cell is restored in about a millisecond.

The maximum rate at which pulses can be propagated down a nerve cell is approximately 500 per second. The typical amplitude of a nerve pulse is approximately 100 millivolts; that is, the pulse reaches +30 millivolts. The delay time between excitation of the nerve and pulse generation is from 0.1 to 1 millisecond.

With these facts in hand, we are now ready to consider the action at the synapse. The function of the excitatory synapse is to allow sodium ions to enter the cell body in a depolarizing action. When the cell has been depolarized to some threshold value, the nerve impulse is initiated. Each excitatory impulse is summed by actually changing the permeability of the cell to sodium ions in unit steps. This action allows the sodium ions to flow along their electrochemical potential gradient. The transmitter substance, acetylcholine, is the agent responsible for this change in permeability. This substance is injected across the synaptic cleft and attaches itself to the synaptic membrane within a few microseconds. The effect of the acetylcholine is diminished in approximately one millisecond by the enzyme cholinesterase. In the inhibitory synapse, the transmitter substance acts to

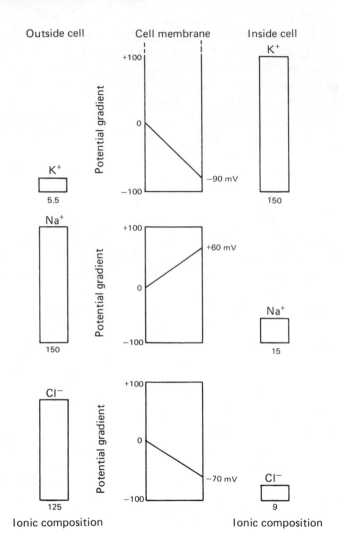

Figure 11.3. Relative densities of cellular ions and potential gradient necessary to maintain these densities.

change the permeability of the cell membrane to allow either potassium ions to flow from or chlorine atoms to flow into the cell.

In summarizing, we should note that all the ions mentioned have diameters less than 2.9 angstroms. This dimension represents the resolvability limit of the best electron microscopes. As a result, there is still much to understand about neural functioning. Several gross manifestations of nervous activity have been examined along with the concepts of inhibition, summation, threshold values, and the chemical explanation of their functioning. The response of a neuron to its input has been termed "all or nothing." This is partially true in that a spike of voltage appears on the axon only if the algebraic sum of the inputs exceeds the threshold value of the cell. Further intensification of the inputs does not alter the characteristics of the output spike itself. On the other hand, the neuron does indicate the intensity of its inputs by its frequency of response, functioning in the manner of a voltage-controlled oscillator [17].

The frequency of neural activity of neurons in a physiological sensor system has been shown to be proportional to the logarithm of the intensity of the input stimulus. Thus, most nervous information appears to be transmitted by the frequency of the nerve response. From the standpoint of reliability, this is significant. The failure of a single neuron to fire does not have the consequences it would have in an all-digital system. Here, the only effect is a blurring of the intensity function. The information train is not destroyed; the output is simply momentarily incorrect by a small value. This system, called integral pulse frequency modulation (IPFM) [18], has been overlooked in many all-digital approaches to neural modeling. Finally, the threshold value of a neural element is a function of time and is subject to various influences. For example, after once firing the unit enters a *refractory period* during which it is incapable of firing again. Repeated firings also raise the threshold value of the cell (the cell is said to fatigue).

INFORMATION CODING IN NERVE PULSES

Let us now consider the nature of the informational coding of nervous pulses in more detail. Examine the plot of pulse frequency versus excitation as given in Figure 11.4. It is clear that pulse frequency is directly proportional to excitation. The information carried through the nervous system is contained in the *time between successive pulses*. For example, a high level of excitation generates a high-frequency pulse stream whereas a low level of excitation generates a low-frequency pulse stream. Thus, for a particular amount of excitation, $s(t)$, the pulse sequence is

$$P_T = \sum_{n=1}^{\infty} \delta(\theta(t) - 2\pi n) \qquad (11.1)$$

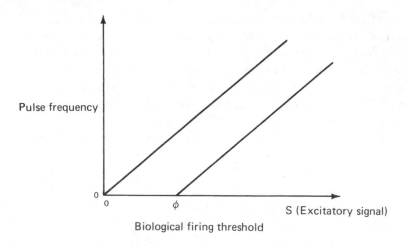

Figure 11.4.   IPFM response characteristics.

where an expression for $\theta(t)$ can be found from an analogy to frequency modulation:

$$\theta(t) = 2\pi K_0 \int_0^t s(t)\,dt + 2\pi\theta_0 + \omega_c t \qquad (11.2)$$

Equation 11.2 represents the argument of the periodic carrier function of frequency ω_c. Here, the carrier frequency ω_c and initial phase θ_0 are assumed to be zero. Therefore, the pulse generation criterion becomes

$$2\pi K_0 \int_0^t s(t)\,dt = 2\pi n \qquad (11.3)$$

from Equation 11.1. Now, consider the interval after a pulse is generated where the instantaneous frequency is

$$\gamma_i = \frac{1}{t_i - t_{i-1}}$$

$$2\pi K_0 \int_{t_{i-1}}^{t_i} s(t)\,dt = 2\pi i, \qquad \text{where } i = n \qquad (11.4)$$

The pulse generation criterion now becomes

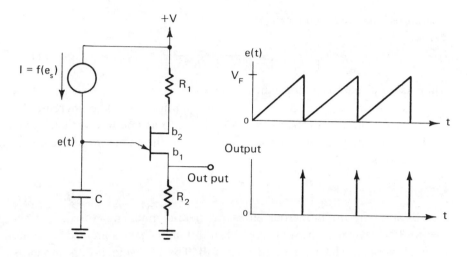

Figure 11.5.   Model of IPFM generator where Vf is the firing of the unijunction transistor.

$$\int_{t_{i-1}}^{t_i} s(t)\, dt = \frac{i}{K_0} \tag{11.5}$$

where $K_0 > 0$ and is a constant associated with characteristics of the cell. A simple model that generates IPFM pulses is illustrated in Figure 11.5. The current source charges the capacitor as a function of the stimulus e_s. When the voltage across the capacitor, $e(t)$, equals the firing threshold of the unijunction transistor, V_F, a pulse is generated at the output.

Now we can consider the case in which the input is a step function, $s(t) = S_0 u_{-1}(t)$:

$$K_0 \int_0^{t_i} S_0\, dt = i$$

and

$$K_0 S_0 t_i = i$$

Also,

$$t_{i-1} = \frac{i - 1}{K_0 S_0}$$

Therefore, the pulse frequency is

$$\gamma_i = \frac{1}{(i/K_0 S_0) - [(i-1)/K_0 S_0]} = K_0 S_0 \qquad (11.6)$$

which is a pulse train of constant frequency.

The nature of IPFM can now be summarized. The incremental amplitude of the input information is coded into a time interval such that the longer the interval between pulses, the lower the value of the excitation and vice versa.

MODELS

In studying the numerous efforts in neural modeling we can readily discern that several of the more significant attempts have stemmed from the original work of McCulloch and Pitts [19]. The McCulloch-Pitts model is not a complete physiological model of an actual nerve cell but rather a simple two-state representation of the logical processing that occurs in nerve cells. The basic McCulloch-Pitts neural cell is shown in Figure 11.6. The output fiber of the cell relays information concerning the state of the neuron—firing or not firing—and eventually becomes an input to another cell (or the same cell). Any number of inputs are allowed, and they are divided into two classes: excitatory and inhibitory inputs. The excitatory input, represented by a line terminating in an arrowhead, tends to excite the cell in a unit increment toward firing. For the present discussion, the excitatory lines carry a weight of one. The inhibitory input, represented by a line terminating in a small circle, is capable of totally inhibiting the cell

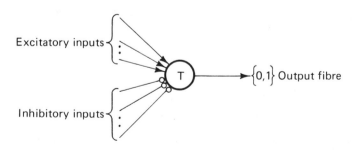

Figure 11.6. McCulloch–Pitts model.

from firing. Let T represent the numerical value of the firing threshold for the cell. The McCulloch-Pitts cell will fire when the sum of the excitatory inputs is equal to or greater than the threshold value, T, and no inhibitory input is activated, or more formally,

Input Conditions	Output
$E \geq T, I = 0$	Firing
$E \geq T, I > 0$	Not firing
$E < T, I = 0$	Not firing
$E < T, I \leq 0$	Not firing

Thus, for the single cell the output at $t + \Delta T$ *is not* a function of the output at t.

Ordinary Boolean logic functions can be readily implemented from this general configuration; examples of the logical AND and the logical OR are shown here.

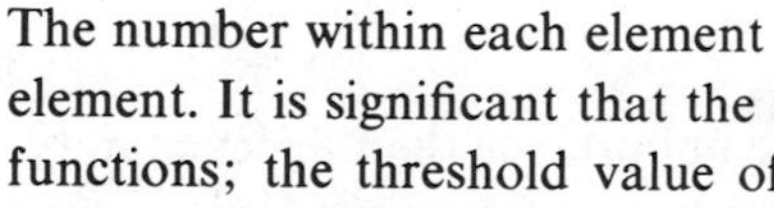

AND gate 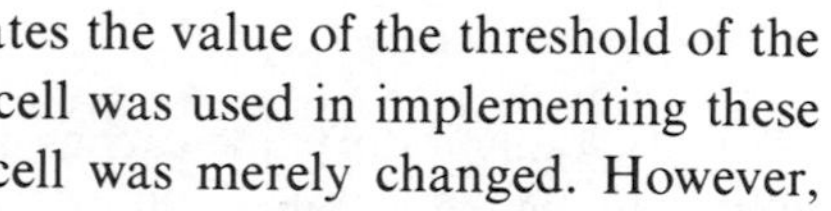   OR gate

The number within each element indicates the value of the threshold of the element. It is significant that the same cell was used in implementing these functions; the threshold value of the cell was merely changed. However, Figure 11.7 shows the basic implementation of all the minterms of three variables. Significantly, in several cases more than one cell is needed to form the minterm.

Another model of the logical behavior of the neuron is a variation on the basic McCulloch-Pitts cell. The linear weighted model, shown in Figure 11.8, is a cell with basic characteristics similar to those already mentioned. The important difference is that the inhibitory inputs now have a weight of

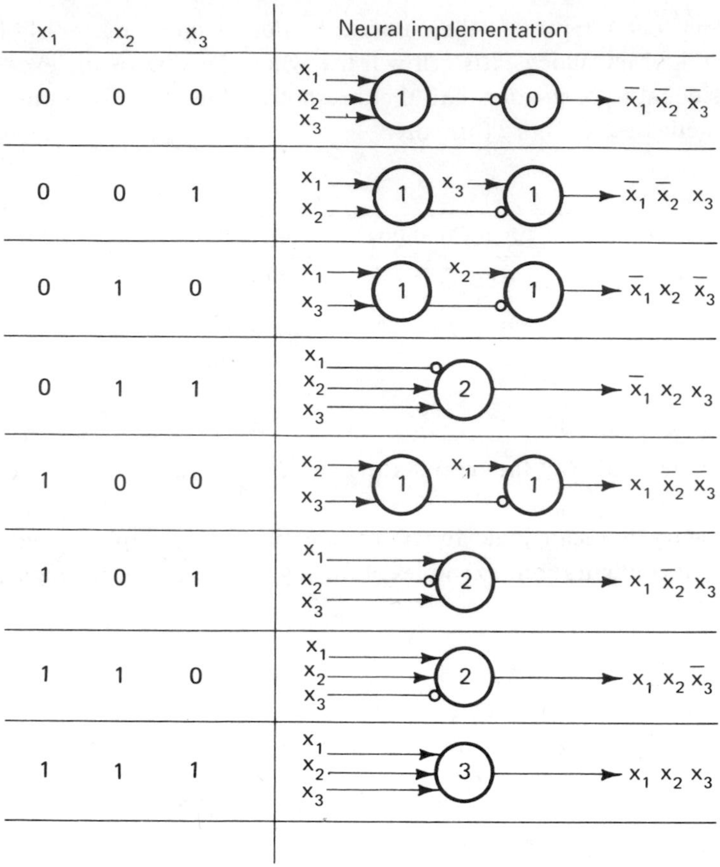

x_1	x_2	x_3	Neural implementation
0	0	0	x_1 x_2 x_3 → (1) →o (0) → $\bar{x}_1 \bar{x}_2 \bar{x}_3$
0	0	1	x_1 x_2 → (1) x_3 → (1) → $\bar{x}_1 \bar{x}_2 x_3$
0	1	0	x_1 x_3 → (1) x_2 → (1) → $\bar{x}_1 x_2 \bar{x}_3$
0	1	1	x_1 x_2 x_3 → (2) → $\bar{x}_1 x_2 x_3$
1	0	0	x_2 x_3 → (1) x_1 → (1) → $x_1 \bar{x}_2 \bar{x}_3$
1	0	1	x_1 x_2 x_3 → (2) → $x_1 \bar{x}_2 x_3$
1	1	0	x_1 x_2 x_3 → (2) → $x_1 x_2 \bar{x}_3$
1	1	1	x_1 x_2 x_3 → (3) → $x_1 x_2 x_3$

Figure 11.7.   Three-variable minterm realizations with neural elements.

-1. Thus, an inhibitory line carries no more importance than the excitatory input. The cell fires when the difference between the sum of the active excitatory inputs and the sum of the active inhibitory inputs is equal to or greater than the threshold value of the cell. An example of how logic may be performed with this element is shown in the accompanying network in Figure 11.9, which provides an output if one, two, or three, but not four of the inputs are true. We can readily see that the type of logic involved is essentially the same as for the McCulloch-Pitts neuron, the only difference being in the specific implementation.

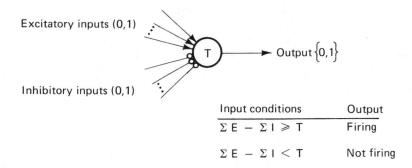

Input conditions	Output
$\Sigma E - \Sigma I \geqslant T$	Firing
$\Sigma E - \Sigma I < T$	Not firing

Figure 11.8. Linear weighted cell model.

A final model is the majority organ used in Chapter 9. Here the output fires if the majority of the inputs are excitatory.

It is also useful to hypothesize methods whereby memory may be implemented within a neural array. A simple neural memory model incorporates the fact that there is an inherent delay in the propagation of signals through a neuron. It is thus reasonable to consider the *unit delay organ* shown in Figure 11.10a. Here, an input at some time t appears at the output at time $t + \Delta T$. A memory element using the delay in the feedback arrangement is shown in Figure 11.10b. A single pulse entering the write

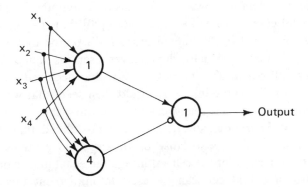

Figure 11.9. Implementation of a logic network using the McCulloch–Pitts cell.

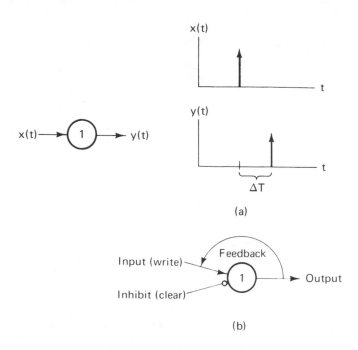

Figure 11.10.   Unit delay organ and its use as a memory element.

line when the inhibit line is zero propagates through the cell continuously until the inhibit line is activated, causing the pulse to be "forgotten."

Another model for neural memory has been hypothesized from clinical data. Medical case histories have indicated [20] that the perception of an event must be stored in the human brain for a period of time before one has recall of that event. A man who receives a serious injury affecting brain functioning will not be able to recall events that occurred during some 20 to 30 minutes prior to the injury. It would then seem that we can speak of a short-term memory that reinforces itself in time, thus becoming a long-term memory. Physiologically, it has been postulated that the endbulbs increase in size with repeated use or that specific proteins are formed, changing the threshold of the cell. Although the exact nature of this process is unknown, a neural cell can be used to implement this function by lowering the threshold of the cells involved in repeated use. Thus, consider the cell shown in Figure 11.11a, whose behavior is identical to the memory

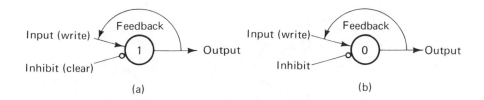

Figure 11.11.   Short-term and permanent memory configuration with neural elements.

cell shown in Figure 11.11b. After repeated firings, the cell threshold becomes lower and eventually looks like the cell in Figure 11.11b, where the threshold has been reduced to zero. Since the inhibition in this state has no effect, the cell will continue firing indefinitely, thereby implementing permanent memory.

THRESHOLD LOGIC

The logical behavior of neurons as represented by the models given in this chapter has led to the specification of a logical element that has been used to implement computer elements as well as certain types of pattern recognition systems. Thus, it is useful both practically and pedagogically to investigate this so-called threshold logic element.

A general single-level threshold logic element is shown in Figure 11.12. This device has N binary inputs and a binary output function F. Each input line X_i has a weighting factor W_i operating on the binary input. W_i is allowed to take on both positive and negative values. The transmission function (F true or equal to one) is present when the sum of each input multiplied by its respective weighting value is equal to or exceeds the threshold T. This is expressed as

$$F = 1 \text{ if,} \qquad \sum_{K=1}^{N} X_k W_k \geq T \qquad (11.7a)$$

Conversely, the negation (F false or equal to zero) is present when the weighted sum is less than the threshold. This condition is written

$$F = 0 \text{ if,} \qquad \sum_{K=1}^{N} W_k X_k < T \qquad (11.7b)$$

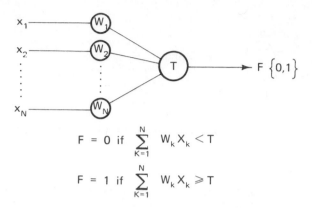

$$F = 0 \text{ if } \sum_{K=1}^{N} W_k X_k < T$$

$$F = 1 \text{ if } \sum_{K=1}^{N} W_k X_k \geq T$$

Figure 11.12.   General single-level threshold logic elements.

Basically, the threshold element renders a single yes or no decision as to whether a given set or class of inputs is present. This dichotomy may be viewed geometrically. As in logic design, any Boolean function may be written in disjunctive normal form. This form involves the OR function on the standard product terms (minterms). These minterms may be mapped into an N-dimensional cube in a Euclidean hyperspace. Functions of three variables may be mapped onto the cube as shown in Figure 11.13.

If the vertices representing the minterms of F can be separated from those of $\overline{F}$ by a single hyperplane, the function is said to be linearly separable and can be realized by a single threshold element. This follows directly from the fact that Equation 11.7a defines a hyperplane of order $N - 1$. Several examples of logic realization with threshold elements are given in Figure 11.14. It should now be apparent that both the McCulloch-Pitts and linear weighted neurons are special cases of single-level threshold elements.

Let us consider some of the basic properties of linearly separable functions [21]. Some definitions are necessary before considering the properties themselves:

1.   A *switching function* F is any Boolean function of binary variables $X_1, \ldots, X_n$. A + in a switching function indicates logical union,

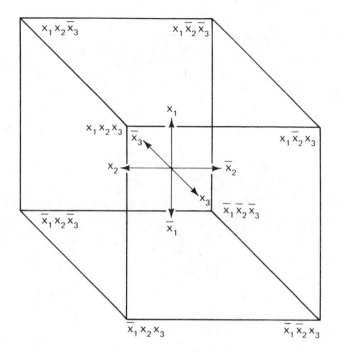

Figure 11.13. Three-variable hyperspace.

and the juxtaposition of two or more variables, such as $X_1 X_2$, indicates intersection.

2. A *plane function P* is defined as any function of the form

$$\sum_{K=1}^{N} W_k X_k$$

where the W_k are real constants.

These definitions plus the previous discussion on linearly separable functions lead to the first property of threshold logic elements.

Property 1: Any linearly separable switching function can be realized by a single threshold element.

The consequences of this property are immediately obvious. Any

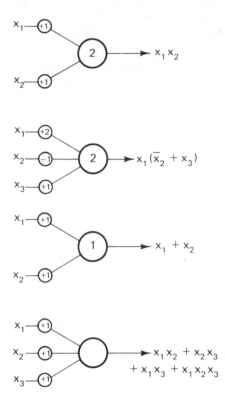

Figure 11.14.   Examples of threshold logic.

hypercube, such as the one shown in Figure 11.13, can be separated into two distinct regions by a plane function P. Additionally, the plane function, which has as its basic element $W_i X_i$, is the weighted sum of binary inputs. Any plane function can be realized with a single threshold element.

Property 2: If a linearly separable function is expressed in nonredundant disjunctive form, no variable can appear both complemented and uncomplemented.[*]

A function with this property is called a *unate* function. Note that the unateness of a function is a necessary but not sufficient condition for linear

---

[*] Here "nonredundant disjunctive form" means that the function has been reduced and is written as a sum of products.

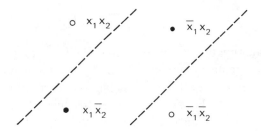

Figure 11.15.   Hyperspace representation of two binary variables.

separability. For example, consider the EXCLUSIVE OR in two variables:

$$F = \overline{X}_1 X_2 + X_1 \overline{X}_2$$

This function is easily represented as the two solid points in the hyperspace for two variables in Figure 11.15 (in this case hyperspace is merely a plane).

It is clear that no single linear hyperplane (in this case a straight line) that separates the two desired points from all the others can be drawn. As the dotted lines in Figure 11.15 illustrate, the function can be separated only by two linear hyperplanes. Thus the EXCLUSIVE OR function, which is not unate, is not linearly separable. A plane function P that separates a space is called a separating plane (SP) function.

Property 3: If a variable appears uncomplemented in the nonredundant disjunctive expression of a linearly separable function, its coefficient in the SP function is positive; conversely, if the variable appears complemented, its coefficient is negative.

This property is necessary in order to maintain the algebraic consistency of the definition of the threshold element. Thus, a complemented term tends to inhibit the generation of an output from the element when that form is true by decreasing the value of the function with respect to the threshold

$$-W_k X_k + P' = T \tag{11.8}$$

An uncomplemented term tends to facilitate the generation of an output from the element when that term is true by increasing the value of the function with respect to the threshold

$$W_k X_k + P' = T \tag{11.9}$$

Property 4: A unate function is linearly separable if and only if the function obtained from the reduced minterm form by uncomplementing all the complemented variables is itself linearly separable. In addition, the separating plane equations of the two functions are related as follows. If a complemented variable is uncomplemented, the sign of its coefficient is changed from negative to positive, and the magnitude of that coefficient is added to the threshold. And, if an uncomplemented variable is complemented, the sign of its coefficient is changed from positive to negative, and the magnitude of that coefficient is subtracted from the threshold.

This property is clear if one considers that the physical realization is independent of the sense of any of the literals, whereas the function realized is dependent on the sense of the literals. For example,

$$F(X_1, X_2, \cdots, X_M = 1, \cdots, X_N) = F(X_1, X_2, \cdots, \overline{X}_M = 1, \cdots, X_N)$$

and conversely

$$F(X_1, X_2, \cdots, X_M = 0, \cdots, X_N) = F(X_1, X_2, \cdots, \overline{X}_M = 0, \cdots, X_N)$$

$$\tag{11.10}$$

Thus, the sense of the literal does not affect the linear separability of the function, although the functions realized are different. Consider the realization of the function

$$Y = X_1 X_2$$

with the SP equation

$$X_1 + X_2 = 1$$

as shown here.

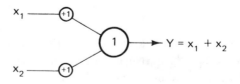

If one changes the sense of the literal X_2 to $\overline{X}_2$, the new function

$$Y = X_1 + \overline{X}_2$$

is still linearly separable. Its realization is shown here.

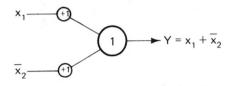

Consider the binary relationship

$$-\overline{X} = X - 1 \tag{11.11}$$

Similarly, the weighted variables satisfy the relation

$$-W_k \overline{X}_k = W_k X_k - W_k \tag{11.12}$$

It is now possible to convert a complemented literal to an uncomplemented literal and vice versa by direct substitution of Equation 11.11. For example, the SP equation for the function $Y = X_1 + \overline{X}_2$,

$$X_1 + \overline{X}_2 = 1$$

can be changed to one with uncomplemented literals by substituting

$$\overline{X}_2 = 1 - X_2$$

This gives a new SP equation,

$$X_1 + 1 - X_2 = 1$$

and

$$X_1 - X_2 = 0$$

which is the SP equation for the function

$$Y = X_1 + \overline{X}_2$$

$X_1 \; X_2 \; X_3$	$\Sigma \; W_k \; X_k$	$\bar{Y}$
0 0 0	0	1
0 0 1	−1	1
0 1 0	−1	1
0 1 1	−2	0
1 0 0	−2	0
1 0 1	−3	0
1 1 0	−3	0
1 1 1	−4	0

$T = 1.5$

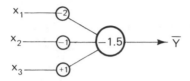

Figure 11.16.   Threshold realization of $Y = X_1 X_2 + X_1 X_3$.

Property 5: If F is linearly separable with the SP equation

$$\sum_{K=1}^{N} + W_k X_k = T \qquad (11.13)$$

then the complement of F is linearly separable with the SP equation

$$\sum_{K=1}^{N} - W_k X_k = -T \qquad (11.14)$$

For example, the realization of the function

$$Y = X_1 + X_2 X_3$$

is possible with the SP equation

$$2X_1 + X_2 + X_3 = 1.5$$

The complement of the function is

$$\bar{Y} = \overline{X_1 + X_2 X_3}$$

and

$$\overline{Y} = \overline{X}_1 \overline{X}_2 + \overline{X}_1 \overline{X}_3 \tag{11.15}$$

and the SP equation is

$$-2X_1 - X_2 - X_3 = -1.5$$

The gate that realizes $\overline{Y}$ in Equation 11.15 is illustrated in Figure 11.16. It is clear that the gate in Figure 11.16 does realize $\overline{Y}$ as given.

Property 6: If F is linearly separable with the SP equation

$$\sum_{K=1}^{N} W_k X_k = T$$

then the complement of F is realizable with the SP equation

$$\sum_{K=1}^{N} W_k \overline{X}_k = \sigma - |T|$$

where

$$\sigma = \sum_{K=1}^{N} |W_k|$$

Thus, the complement of the function used in the illustration of Property 5 can also be realized with the SP equation

$$2\overline{X}_1 + \overline{X}_2 + \overline{X}_3 = 2.5$$

$X_1 \ X_2 \ X_3$	$\overline{X}_1 \ \overline{X}_2 \ \overline{X}_3$	$\Sigma \ W_k \ \overline{X}_k$	Y	
0 0 0	1 1 1	4	1	
0 0 1	1 1 0	3	1	
0 1 0	1 0 1	3	1	$T = 2.5$
0 1 1	1 0 0	2	0	
1 0 0	0 1 1	2	0	
1 0 1	0 1 0	1	0	
1 1 0	0 0 1	1	0	
1 1 1	0 0 0	0	0	

Property 7: If F is linearly separable with the SP equation

$$\sum_{K=1}^{N} W_k X_k = T$$

then the dual of F is realizable with the SP equation

$$\sum_{K=1}^{N} W_k X_k = \sigma - T$$

where the dual of $Y = F(X_1, X_2, \ldots, X_n)$ is

$$Y^d = \overline{F}(\overline{X}_1, \overline{X}_2, \cdots, \overline{X}_n)$$

The dual of

$$Y = X_1 + X_2 X_3$$

is

$$Y^d = X_1 \cdot (X_2 + X_3)$$

This is accomplished by complementing the function and then complementing each literal in the resulting expression. The SP equation of this dual is

$$2X_1 + X_2 + X_3 = 4 - 1.5 = 2.5$$

X_1 X_2 X_3	$\Sigma X_k W_k$	Y^d	
0 0 0	0	0	
0 0 1	1	0	
0 1 0	1	0	
0 1 1	2	0	
1 0 0	2	0	$T = 2.5$
1 0 1	3	1	
1 1 0	3	1	
1 1 1	4	1	

The properties given here illustrate some of the characteristics useful in analyzing and synthesizing threshold logic networks. Although they are by no means exhaustive, these properties are fundamental and serve as the basis for understanding these devices.

SUMMARY

This brief physiological description of the neuron has introduced some of the detail associated with processing in "natural" systems. A serious student of engineering cybernetics must continually be aware of new discoveries in neurophysiology and brain functioning as a source of new design approaches. Certainly, the brain and nervous system represent a unique system that has survived, functioned, and evolved over the ages and merits the attention of engineers and computer scientists.

The processing and communication processes that take place in nervous systems were also introduced in this chapter. The all-or-nothing pulse generation associated with nerve elements was illustrated by means of IPFM. IPFM has also had certain impact in the area of automatic control because of its inherent noise rejection properties—another example of the bionic approach [22].

Some logical processing models of nervous behavior were also considered in this chapter. These models led directly to the threshold logic element as a processing device. The properties introduced here will serve as a basis for threshold logic synthesis in Chapter 12.

EXERCISES

1. Write the truth table for the neuron circuit shown here. With respect to conventional AND, OR, and NOT logic, what function does the second neuron perform?

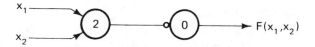

2. Consider the neuron-effector circuit shown here. The neuron is
    under steplike excitation $i(t)$ and is generating the pulse train $e(t)$.
    The effector is responding directly to the instantaneous pulse rate
    as follows:

    $$R(t) = \frac{1}{t_{i+1} - t_i} \qquad \text{for } t_{i+2} > t \ge t_{i+1}$$

    where t_i is the time of occurrence of the ith pulse.

    (a) Plot the effector response, $R(t)$.
    (b) Plot the effector response, $R(t)$, for the case where the
         neuron fails to fire at pulse time 4.

3. Draw a circuit using neural models with total inhibition that
    realizes the EXCLUSIVE OR

    $$F = A\bar{B} + \bar{A}B$$

4. Find a circuit using neural models with total inhibition that is
    equivalent to the majority organ with three inputs used in Chapter 9.

5. An element in a memory network in which the threshold varies as
    a function of the number of times the element fires is given below.
    The initial threshold is unity.

    (a) Write an expression and plot the value of the threshold as a
         function of the firings, N, if the threshold decreases by 0.1
         with each firing. How many firings are required for the
         memory to become permanent?
    (b) Write an expression and plot the value of the threshold as a
         function of firing if the threshold decreases by 0.1 with the
         first firing and decreases by twice the previous increment

thereafter. How many firings are required for the memory to become permanent?

(c) Write an expression and plot the value of the threshold as a function of firing if the threshold decreases by 0.4 with the first firing and decreases by one-half the previous increment on subsequent firing. What is the value of the threshold as N approaches infinity?

6. Write an expression for the pulse frequency output of an IPFM generator under the following excitation conditions:

   (a) Ramp input, $s(t) = ts_0$, $t \geq 0$.
   (b) Square law input, $s(t) = t^2 s_0$, $t \geq 0$.

7. Write the separating plane function and draw a schematic for a threshold logic realization for

$$Y = X_1 \overline{X}_2 + \overline{X}_2 X_3 + X_1 X_3$$

8. Which of the following functions are realizable with a single-threshold element?

   (a) $Y = X_1 X_2 + \overline{X}_1 \overline{X}_2$.

   (b) $Y = X_1 \overline{X}_2 \overline{X}_3 + X_1 X_2 \overline{X}_3 + X_1 X_2 X_3 + X_1 \overline{X}_2 X_3$.

   (c) $Y = X_1 \overline{X}_2 \overline{X}_3 + \overline{X}_1 X_2 \overline{X}_3 + X_1 X_2 X_3 + \overline{X}_1 \overline{X}_2 X_3$.

   (d) $Y = \overline{X}_1 X_2 X_3 + \overline{X}_1 X_2 \overline{X}_3$.

   (e) $Y = X_1 X_2 + \overline{X}_1 X_2 + X_1 \overline{X}_2 + \overline{X}_1 \overline{X}_2$.

   (f) $Y = \overline{X}_1 X_2 \overline{X}_3 \overline{X}_4 + X_1 \overline{X}_2 X_3 \overline{X}_4 + \overline{X}_1 X_2 \overline{X}_3 X_4 + X_1 \overline{X}_2 \overline{X}_3 X_4$
        $+ X_1 X_2 \overline{X}_3 X_4$.

REFERENCES

1. ASHBY, W. R., *Design for a Brain*, Science Paperbacks, Chapman & Hall, London, 1966.
2. LEE, R. J., "Letter to the Editor," *Astounding Science Fiction*, July 1953.
3. CENTNER, R. M., J. M. IDELSOHN, et al., "Bionics Self-Adaption Capability," *Technical Report AFAL-TR-67-35*, Bendix Research Laboratories for Air Force Avionics Laboratory, Wright Patterson Air Force Base, Dayton, Ohio, April 1967.
4. ECCLES, J. C., *The Physiology of Nerve Cells*, Johns Hopkins Press, Baltimore, 1957.
5. KATZ, B., *Nerve, Muscle, and Synapse*, McGraw-Hill, New York, 1966.
6. KILMER, W. L., W. S. MCCULLOCH, and J. BLUM, "A Model of the Vertebrate Central Command System," *International Journal of Man-Machine Studies*, Vol. 1, 1969, pp. 279–309.
7. MARR, D., "A Theory for Cerebral Neocortex," *Proceedings of the Royal Society, London, B.*, Vol. 176, 1970, pp. IGI–234.
8. MARR, D., "Simple Memory; A Theory for Archicortex," *Philosophical Transactions of the Royal Society, London, B.*, Vol. 262, No. 841, 1971, pp. 23–81.
9. ALBUS, James S., "A Theory of Cerebellar Function," *Mathematical Biosciences*, Vol. 10, No. 1, February 1971.
10. MORTIMER, J. A., "A Cellular Model for Mammalian Cerebellar Cortex," *Technical Report*, Computer and Communication Sciences Department, University of Michigan.
11. DIDDAY, Richard L., "The Simulation and Modeling of Distributed Information Processing in the Frog Visual System," Ph.D Thesis, Stanford University, Stanford, Calif., 1970.
12. ARBIB, M. A., "How We Know Universals: Retrospect and Prospect," *Mathematical Biosciences*, Vol. 11, 1971, pp. 95–107.
13. ECCLES, J. C., "The Synapse," *Scientific American*, Vol. 212, No. 1, January 1965, pp. 56–66.
14. HODGKIN, A. L., "The Ionic Basis of Nervous Conduction," *Science*, Vol. 145, September 1964, pp. 1148–1153.
15. HUXLEY, A. F., "Excitation and Conduction in Nerve: Quantitative Analysis," *Science*, Vol. 145, September 1964, pp. 1154–1159.
16. KATZ, B., "Nature of the Nerve Impulse," in *Biophysical Science, A Study Program*, J. L. ONCLEY et al., eds., Wiley, New York, 1959, Chapter 50.
17. JONES, R. W., et al., "Pulse Modulation in Physiological Systems, Phenomenological Aspects," *IRE Transactions on Bio-Medical Electronics*, Vol. BME-8, No. 1, January 1961.
18. LI, C. C., "Integral Pulse Frequency Modulated Controls Systems," Ph.D Dissertation, Northwestern University, Evanston, Ill., 1961.
19. MCCULLOCH, W. S., and W. PITTS, "A Logical Calculus of the Ideas Immanent in Nervous Activity," *Bulletin of Mathematical Biophysics*, Vol. 5, 1943.

20. WOOLDRIDGE, D. E., *Machinery of the Brain*, McGraw-Hill, New York, 1963.
21. LEWIS, P. M., and C. L. COATES, *Threshold Logic*, Wiley, New York, 1967.
22. PAVLIDIS, T., and E. I. JURY, "Analysis of a New Class of Pulse-Frequency-Modulated Feedback Systems," *IEEE Transactions on Automatic Control*, Vol. AC-10, No. 1, January 1965, pp. 35–43.

12

Threshold Logic

The use of the threshold logic elements both as logical devices and as elements in an adaptive system is considered in this chapter. At present, the apparent advantages of threshold devices as elements in computer systems have not been realized, and their eventual application appears limited. However, threshold element arrays have been used in cybernetic systems, especially for pattern recognition. The study of threshold logic includes many of the concepts that will be useful in our examination of pattern recognition in Chapter 13 as well as in placing in perspective the logical behavior of the neural models presented in Chapter 11.

NUMBER OF LINEARLY SEPARABLE FUNCTIONS

It is clear from the previous discussion that all functions of N variables cannot be realized by a single threshold element. The question then arises, "How many of the 2^{2^N} switching functions of N variables can be realized by a single threshold element?"[*] It is most difficult to enumerate all linearly separable functions of N variables. However, one may readily establish an upper bound on this number [1]. For example, consider the threshold function given in Chapter 11,

---

[*] Recall, a switching function is a binary-valued function of binary-valued variables. Hence, for each one of the possible 2^N input values of N variables, two functions can be defined; or a total of 2^{2^N} possible functions can be enumerated.

$$\sum_{K=1}^{N} W_k X_k = T \qquad (12.1)$$

where we now let $T = W_0$, and consider it to be function of W rather than X. This equation can be rewritten as

$$\sum_{K=1}^{N} W_k X_k - W_0 = 0 \qquad (12.2)$$

Now, for each of the 2^N combinations of the X_k variables, there exists an equation in the $(N + 1)$-dimensional W space such as Equation 12.2. Further, if we consider any such combination, then the locus of all values of W_k and W_0 for which Equation 12.2 is satisfied plots a hyperplane in this space. This plane goes through the origin since the equation is satisfied by

$$W_k = W_0 = 0 \qquad \forall k$$

and divides the $(N + 1)$-dimensional space into two regions. For example, if we consider a single binary variable X_1, then the $2^N = 2$ equations of the planes are

$$W_1(1) - W_0 = 0$$

$$W_1 - W_0$$

and

$$W_1(0) - W_0 = 0$$

$$W_0 = 0$$

These planes, the W_1 axis and a $45°$ line passing through the first and third quadrants, define regions in W space for which values of W_1 and W_0 will realize each of the Boolean functions indicated here:

X	F_0	F_1	F_2	F_3
0	0	1	0	1
1	0	0	1	1

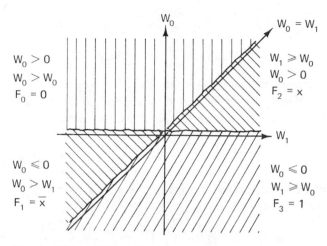

Figure 12.1.   Distinct regions in *W* space.

Figure 12.1 illustrates this in the two-dimensional W space. Any point in a given region in W space defines the values of the variables W_0 and W_1 that will realize the function associated with that region. Thus, the point $(W_1 = 2, W_0 = 1)$ will realize the function $F_2 = X$ with the plane equation, $2X - 1 = 0$. There are four regions in the two-dimensional W space of Figure 12.1 and thus there are four linearly separable functions of one variable. The number of regions into which the 2^N planes divide W space is equal to the number of linearly separable functions of N variables. It is important to note that some of the 2^N planes, for $N > 1$, do not define any different regions in the W space. Therefore, the example of one variable is unique, and in general it is difficult to calculate the exact number of distinct regions whose boundaries are defined by the plane equations. However, the maximum number of regions into which any P planes, not necessarily defined by plane equations, divide an S space can be calculated as follows. First, let $R(P, S)$ be the maximum number of regions into which P, $(S - 1)$-dimensional hyperplanes divide the S space. Clearly,

$$R(P, 1) = 2 \quad \text{for } P \geq 1$$

since a line can be divided into two regions by a point at the origin, but additional points at the origin do not increase the number of regions. Also,

$$R(1, S) = 2 \qquad \text{for } S \geq 1$$

since one plane divides any space into exactly two parts.

Hence, $R(P, S)$ can be evaluated by applying a recursion equation that reduces the resultant expression to one of the forms we have shown. If one considers only $P - 1$ hyperplanes in S space, then there are $R(P - 1, S)$ regions. The Pth hyperplane can be divided into at most $R(P - 1, S - 1)$ regions by the original $P - 1$ planes. Thus, a new region is added only if the new plane is intersected by one of the $P - 1$ planes, and the desired recursion relation is

$$R(P, S) = R(P - 1, S) + R(P - 1, S - 1) \tag{12.3}$$

Performing one recursion on the right side of Equation 12.3 gives

$$R(P, S) = R(P - 2, S) + 2R(P - 2, S - 1) + R(P - 2, S - 2)$$

Another recursion gives

$$R(P, S) = R(P - 3, S) + 3R(P - 3, S - 1) + 3R(P - 3, S - 2)$$
$$+ R(P - 3, S - 3)$$

Continuing this process $R - 1$ times,

$$R(P, S) = \binom{P - 1}{0} R(1, S) + \binom{P - 1}{1} R(1, S - 1)$$
$$+ \binom{P - 1}{2} R(1, S - 2) + \cdots + \binom{P - 1}{P - 1} R(1, S - P + 1)$$
$$\tag{12.4}$$

$$= \sum_{i=0}^{P-1} \binom{P - 1}{i} R(1, S - i) \tag{12.5}$$

But $R(1, S - i) = 2$. Therefore Equation 12.5 becomes

$$R(P, S) = 2 \sum_{i=0}^{P-1} \binom{P - 1}{i}$$

Note that in Equation 12.4 if P is greater than or equal to S, the resultant terms are degenerate, as

$$R(1, Q) = 0 \quad \text{for } Q \leq 1$$

Therefore,

$$R(P, S) = 2 \sum_{i=0}^{S-1} \binom{P-1}{i} \tag{12.6}$$

The upper limit on the number of linearly separable functions of N variables in $(N + 1)$-dimensional W space is

$$U(N) = 2 \sum_{i=0}^{N} \binom{2^N - 1}{i} \tag{12.7}$$

It is possible to obtain a solution of Equation 12.7 in closed form by noting that for N large,

$$2 \sum_{i=0}^{N-1} \binom{2^N - 1}{i} \ll 2 \binom{2^N - 1}{N} \tag{12.8}$$

Therefore,

$$U(N) \simeq \frac{2(2^N - 1)!}{N! \, (2^N - 1 - N)!} \tag{12.9}$$

Since the numerator contains N more terms in the $2^N - 1$ factorial expression than the $2^N - 1 - N$ factorial expression of the denominator, a further approximation is

$$U(N) \simeq \frac{2(2^N)^N}{N!} \tag{12.10}$$

Stirling's approximation is a closed-form approximation for $N!$, where N is large:

$$N! \simeq \sqrt{2}(\pi N) \left(\frac{N}{e}\right)^N \tag{12.11}$$

Finally, Equation 12.10 can be rewritten as

$$U(N) \simeq \frac{\sqrt{2}}{\pi N} \left(\frac{e2^N}{N} \right)^N \qquad (12.12)$$

The actual number of realizable threshold functions $E(N)$ has been calculated by others using enumeration and linear programming techniques for up to seven variables [1, 2, 3]. Table 12.1 lists the number of functions $F(N) = 2^{2^N}$; and the number of realizable threshold functions, $E(N)$, as a function of N. It is interesting to note that $F(N)$ increases at a much higher rate than does $E(N)$ or $U(N)$, indicating that single-level threshold logic becomes less powerful as N increases.

The design of a practical threshold element, however, requires some additional consideration. The concept of a *gap* describes the requirements on the region in which a decision can be made for a particular function. For example, consider the three-input AND gate shown in Figure 12.2. If the threshold is made $T = 3$, then the appropriate decision such that the three-input AND is realized can be made. Note, however, that if the threshold is made slightly greater than 2, the decision can also be made. Thus, the threshold can be such that

$$2 < T \leq 3$$

and in general the notation is

$$l < T \leq U$$

and the separating plane equation is

$$Y = (X_1 + X_2 + X_3) 3 : 2$$

Table 12.1. Number of Functions, Number of Realizable Threshold Functions on N Variables, and Maximum Number of Realizable Threshold Functions as a Function of N

N	$F(N)$	$E(N)$	$U(N)$
1	4	4	4
2	16	14	14
3	256	104	128
4	65,536	1882	3882
5	$4,295 \times 10^9$	94,572	412,736
6	$18,4480 \times 10^{16}$	15,028,134	151,223,522
7	$\simeq 3.4 \times 10^{38}$	8,378,070,864	189,581,406,208

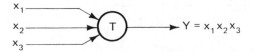

Figure 12.2.   Threshold AND gate for $T = 3$.

and in general the separating plane equation is written as

$$Y = (W_1 X_1 + W_2 X_2 + \cdots + W_n X_n) \, U : l$$

Also, the concept of a gap comes into play when one is dealing with real systems where tolerance, temperature, noise, and other parameters come into play and the ideal input-output relationship given in Figure 12.3a cannot be realized. Instead, the threshold transfer function may exhibit hysteresis, as shown in Figure 12.3b.

Thus, the wider the gap one can obtain in the theoretical realization of a particular function, the wider the tolerance on the components used in the physical realization of the device to perform the operation.

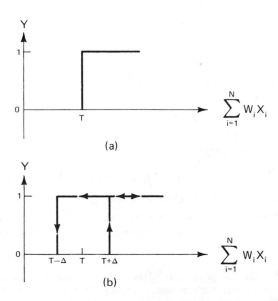

Figure 12.3.   Comparison of (a) ideal and (b) physically realizable threshold functions.

RELATIVE COEFFICIENT VALUES OF
SINGLE LOGICAL ELEMENTS

At this point, it is of interest to consider the relative magnitude of the weights of the coefficients of the variables in the SP equation. The assignment of these weights must be related to the relative influence of a particular variable on the truth or falsehood of the function being realized. For example, consider the function

$$Y = X_1 + X_2 X_3$$

The fact that the variable X_1 alone can control the value of the function Y indicates that it must have this influence in the SP equation. Also, since the combination by logical AND of the variables X_2 and X_3 can influence the value of the function Y, the total weight of these two variables must equal that of X_1. However, individually the variables X_2 and X_3 must have weights less than that of X_1. Thus, the relative weights of the three variables are

$$W_1 > W_2 = W_3$$

which is consistent with its SP equation:

$$2X_1 + X_2 + X_3 = 2$$

Another way of looking at the relative weights of the variables is to examine the relative number of minterms that are included in the expressions associated with a given variable. Thus, consider the function where a variable, X_1, appears as a single term in the irredundant disjunctive form and no other variable appears alone:[*]

$$F(X_1, X_2, \cdots, X_N) = X_1 + F'(X_1, X_2, X_3, \cdots, X_N)$$

The number of minterms associated with the variable X_1, $N(X_1) = 2^{N-1}$, is greater than the number of minterms associated with any other variable, and the weight of X_1 in the SP equation must also be greater than the weight

---

[*] In this form the function is represented as a sum of products (terms) of independent variables; it is irredundant in that no term or no variable in any term can be deleted without changing the function being represented.

of any other variable. If two or more variables appear alone in the irredundant disjunctive form, then all these variables have equal weight greater than the weights associated with any other variables.

Next, consider terms in the irredundant disjunctive form that contains two variables, say

$$F(X_1, X_2, \cdots, X_N) = X_2 X_4 + X_2 X_3 + F''(X_1, X_2, \cdots, X_N)$$

The variables associated with more two-variable terms than the other variables not already ordered (here the only time that variables are considered ordered is when a greater-than relationship has been established) must have more minterms associated with them than any of the remaining variables but less than the number of minterms associated with a variable that appears alone. Variables that appear alone can influence the value of the function, as the truth of the function can be totally affected by the value of one of these single-variable terms. Thus, minterms included by a single-variable term and also associated with a higher order term or terms cannot be considered when weighting variables associated with higher order terms.

For the preceding example, the relative weight magnitudes when the two-variable terms are considered are

$$W_1 > W_2 > W_3 = W_4$$

Thus, the set of variables associated with the largest number of minterms must have greater weight than all the remaining variables and so forth but less weight than any single-term variable.

The process of relative weight assignment is continued until either all the variables have been considered or all the terms in the irredundant disjunctive form have been examined.

This process can be seen more clearly by examining the following example. Given the function

$$Y = X_1 + X_2 X_3 + X_3 X_4$$

one can easily generate a Karnough map. However, here the map is

$X_1 X_2$

$X_3 X_4$	00	01	11	10
00			1	1
01			1	1
11	3-4	2-3-4	1-2-3-4	1-3-4
10		2-3	1-2-3	1

generated such that the minterms associated with single-variable terms are considered first and are indicated by the subscript of the associated variables, two-variable terms are considered next, and minterms not associated with the single-variable terms are indicated by the subscript of the associated variables. The entries in the map, i, indicate minterms affected by that literal, X_i. It is clear in the accompanying map that X_1 has more influence on the value of the function than any other variable, etc.; the relative coefficient order is then as follows:

$$W_1 > W_3 > W_2 = W_4$$

From the preceding, the procedure for establishing the weight-magnitude hierarchy is as follows:

1. Consider all single-variable terms in the irredundant disjunctive form with complemented variables uncomplemented; these variables have greater weight than any other variables. If there are no single-term variables, proceed to order the two-variable terms as given in step 2.

2. Examine all the next higher order terms; the variables in the lower order set, other than single-variable terms, which have not been ordered can now be ordered by weighting variables that appear in more of these terms greater than any other variables in that set. Variables that first appear in this order set can now be ordered in a similar manner. Variables associated with more of these terms have greater weight, etc. Variables in the first sets that have not been ordered may be ordered when the terms of the next order are considered.

3. Examine the terms of the next higher order and weight the variables as in 2.

4. Continue the ordering procedure until all variables have been ordered or all terms have been examined. At this point, it is possible that some variables have not been ordered and have weights equal to the weights of one or more other variables.

For example, order the relative magnitude of the weights of the variables in the function

$$Y = X_2 + \overline{X}_1 X_3 + X_3 \overline{X}_4 + X_3 X_5 X_6 + \overline{X}_1 X_5 X_6$$

First, the function is unate; hence, it may be linearly separable, and one can then uncomplement all complemented variables:

$$Y = X_2 + X_1 X_3 + X_3 X_4 + X_3 X_5 X_6 + X_1 X_5 X_6$$

Now examine all single-variable terms. Here X_2 is the only single-variable term; therefore the magnitude of W_2 is greater than the weights of any other variables. Next, examine the set of two-variable terms,

$$X_1 X_3$$

$$X_3 X_4$$

and note that X_3 appears in two terms and that X_1 and X_4 each appear once. Thus,

$$W_3 > W_4 = W_1$$

and including the single-term element, X_2, the ordering now is

$$W_2 > W_3 > W_4 = W_1$$

Next, the three-variable terms are examined:

$$X_3 X_5 X_6$$

$$X_1 X_5 X_6$$

Here, only the variables X_1, X_5, and X_6 need be considered, as X_3 has already been ordered. X_1 appears in one term; therefore, its weight is greater than that of X_4. Both X_5 and X_6 appear twice in the three-variable terms, and there they must have equal weights. The final order by weight is

$$W_2 > W_3 > W_1 > W_4 > W_5 = W_6$$

Thus, it is possible to find the order of the relative magnitudes of single-threshold realization of unate switching functions. The difficulty here is that only functions of three variables or less are necessarily linearly separable if they are unate. Therefore, one cannot be sure that the relative order is significant with respect to a realization unless the function has three or fewer variables.

SYNTHESIS OF SINGLE-LEVEL THRESHOLD LOGIC ELEMENTS

The ordering procedure given in the previous section suggests a synthesis procedure for single-element threshold functions. The procedure outlined here does not guarantee a realization for functions of more than three variables or necessarily give minimum realizations. We presented it here to give the reader an insight into threshold logic element realizations.

The following procedure is based on the fact that a relative coefficient order has been found for a unate function in an irredundant disjunctive form where all complemented variables have been uncomplemented. For example, let us assume a function where the maximum number of variables in any term in the irredundant disjunctive form is M and the minimum number of variables in any term is m. Since each term of the function must have equal influence on the value of the function, the sum of the weights of the variables in terms with the minimum number of variables must equal or exceed the threshold, and the sum of the weights of the variables in terms with the maximum number of variables also must equal or exceed the threshold and also the sum of the variables in the other terms. Consider the following function of three variables:

$$Y = X_1 X_2 + \overline{X}_3$$

Since the function is unate, we can say it is also linearly separable and uncomplement the complemented variables:

$$Y = X_1 X_2 + X_3$$

The realization can be changed to account for the complement by using Property 4 (Chapter 11). The coefficient magnitude order is

$$W_3 > W_2 = W_1$$

and

$$M = 2$$
$$m = 1$$

Also, since the weight of the two-variable and the single-variable terms must equal or exceed the threshold,

$$W_3 = 2$$
$$W_1 = W_2 = 1$$
$$T = 2$$

and the SP equation is

$$X_1 + X_2 + 2X_3 = 2$$

Further, if one considers the threshold gap, the SP equation is

$$Y = (X_1 + X_2 + 2X_3)2 : 1$$

The process of assigning weights and threshold values here is one of considering the relative weights of the variables and assigning values such that the inequality is satisfied. This procedure is easily accomplished by inspection for functions of three or fewer variables; in fact, it is possible to enumerate all realizations of functions of three or fewer variables (it is done in the next section), but it becomes increasingly difficult to obtain realizations by inspection for more than three variables. The generalization of this procedure, however, leads to another way of defining the requirements for a single-threshold realization of a given function, namely simultaneous inequalities.

A function is linearly separable, and therefore its single-threshold elements are realizable, if a set of real numbers $(W_1, W_2, \ldots, W_n, U, t)$ exists such that the following inequalities hold,

$$\begin{array}{ll} \sum_{i=1}^{N} W_i X_i^P > U & \text{for } F(P) = 1 \\ \sum_{i=1}^{N} W_i X_i^P < l & \text{for } F(P) = 0 \end{array} \bigg\} U > 1$$

where $F(P)$ is a function of the exponents P that have values of zero or one, for X_i absent or X_i present in the corresponding function. $F(P) = 1$ defines the set of exponent values such that the function Y is true, and $F(P) = 0$ defines the set of exponent values such that the function Y is false. There are $n + 2$ unknowns, and there are 2^n inequalities. These inequalities can be solved simultaneously by eliminating one variable at a time, as is done with simultaneous equalities, or the equations can be solved using the methods of linear programming in which the gap may be maximized. A simple example of the procedure used to find a threshold realization by simultaneous inequalities follows. Given the AND function

$$Y = X_1 X_2$$

the requirements for its realization can be tabulated:

X_1	X_2	Y	$\sum W_k X_k$
0	0	0	$0 < 1$
0	1	0	$W_2 < 1$
1	0	0	$W_1 < 1$
1	1	1	$W_1 + W_2 > U$

Thus, one can examine the acceptable region in the W_1-W_2 plane, where the inequalities in the table are satisfied. Note, however, that if one wished to maximize the gap, $U - l$, that $U = 2l$ will do this.

It is now possible to tabulate all single-threshold realizable functions of up to three variables, as shown in Table 12.2 [4]. Note that Table 12.2 can be used when some or all of the variables are complemented by making use of Property 4 (Chapter 11). For example, the procedure for realizing

$$Y = X_1 X_2 + X_1 \overline{X}_3 \tag{12.13}$$

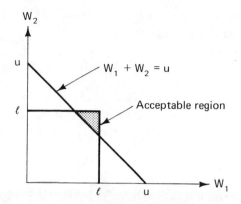

Table 12.2. All One-, Two-, and Three-Variable Threshold Functions

Switching Function	Realization	
$Y = X_1$	$Y = (X_1)$	1:0
$Y = X_1 + X_2$	$Y = (X_1 + X_2)$	1:0
$Y = X_1 X_2$	$Y = (X_1 + X_2)$	2:1
$Y = X_1 + X_2 + X_3$	$Y = (X_1 + X_2 + X_3)$	1:0
$Y = X_1 X_2 + X_2 X_3 + X_1 X_3$	$Y = (X_1 + X_2 + X_3)$	2:1
$Y = X_1 X_2 X_3$	$Y = (X_1 + X_2 + X_3)$	3:2
$Y = X_1 + X_2 X_3$	$Y = (2X_1 + X_2 + X_3)$	2:1
$Y = X_1(X_2 + X_3)$	$Y = (2X_1 + X_2 + X_3)$	3:2

is as follows:

1. Note that

$$Y = X_1(X_2 + \overline{X}_3) \qquad (12.14)$$

is realizable from Table 11.2 by

$$Y = (2X_1 + X_2 + X_3)3 : 2 \qquad (12.15)$$

2. By changing the sense of the variable X_3, Equation 11.13 can be realized by

$$Y = (2X_1 + X_2 + \overline{X}_3)3 : 2 \qquad (12.16)$$

The complemented variable, $\overline{X}_3$, in Equation 12.16 can be changed to an uncomplemented variable by using Property 4 (Chapter 11). Since $X_3 + \overline{X}_3 = 1$, Equation 12.16 becomes

$$Y = (2X_1 + X_2 - X_3)2 : 1 \qquad (12.17)$$

It should now be apparent that efficient synthesis of the threshold circuits of more than three variables is a difficult process. Although synthesis methods for these devices exist [1], they are beyond the scope of this text.

SYNTHESIS OF NONLINEARLY SEPARABLE FUNCTIONS

Thus far, we have been concerned with synthesis using single-level devices that realize linearly separable functions. The realization of nonlinearly separable functions requires more than one threshold logic device.

Since conventional logic is merely a special case of the general threshold logic, nonlinearly separable functions can easily be realized by defining an AND, OR, and NOT with threshold devices and using standard synthesis techniques. However, the remainder of this section will be devoted to a synthesis technique that was developed to describe some of the methods whereby logical functions can be synthesized using a neural model with presynaptic inhibition.

There are several other, perhaps better, methods for synthesizing nonlinearly separable functions with threshold elements. The method presented here was chosen, first, because it is interesting and effective and, second, because it has historical significance in the development of networks of neural models. Presynaptic inhibition, when activated, eliminates the effects of the excitatory input to which it is attached. This, in effect, provides a second level of logic by performing the logical equivalent of a conventional AND with an inverting input before the threshold is applied. As shown in Figure 12.4, multiple inhibit inputs can be associated with an excitatory input. The synthesis procedure that evolved from the work of McCulloch [5] and was formalized by Blum [6], which allows synthesis of all functions of N variables, will now be considered. A simple example is the Blum implementation of the exclusive OR in two variables:

$$F(X_1, X_2) = X_1 \overline{X}_2 + \overline{X}_1 X_2 \qquad (12.18)$$

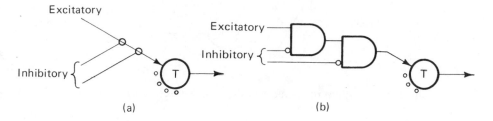

(a)   (b)

Figure 12.4.   Presynaptic inhibition and its conventional equivalent.

The synthesis of Equation 12.17 is immediately obvious from the preceding definitions and is illustrated in Figure 12.5. The initial step in the procedure is to obtain the function in disjunctive normal form and to map it into a primary Venn diagram. For example, consider the function

$$F(X_1 X_2 X_3) = X_1 X_2 X_3 \tag{12.19}$$

for which the Venn diagram is as shown.

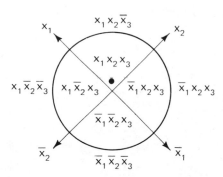

The desired term is indicated by a jot in the appropriate space, here $X_1 X_2 X_3$. It is clear that each minterm is represented by a distinct region in the Venn diagram. A weight is now assigned to each minterm region in the diagram such that the weights of the minterms of the desired function are greater than those which are not part of the function. This ensures that the function on which the threshold element operates is linearly separable. The only restriction on the weight assignment is that the weight of the null

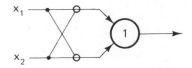

Figure 12.5.   Blum realization of the two-variable parity function.

minterm $(\overline{X}_1\overline{X}_2 \cdots \overline{X}_N)$ must always be zero. These weights are the maximum threshold values of the second-level element that will realize the corresponding minterms. Thus, by assigning different weights to the minterms, it is possible to change the function that is realized by changing only the threshold of the threshold gate. However, it is possible to realize any desired function by assigning weights of only one and zero. For functions in which the null minterm does not appear, a weight of $+1$ is assigned to the desired terms and 0 to the others. Conversely, for functions in which the null minterm does appear, a weight of 0 is assigned to the desired terms and a weight of -1 is assigned to the remaining terms. Therefore, for the function given by Equation 12.18 the weight assignment is as shown in the accompanying diagram.

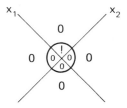

Table 12.3.   Equations Associated with Minterms

Minterms	Associated Equations
1. $X_1\overline{X}_2\overline{X}_3$	$X_1 = X_1\underline{X}_2\underline{X}_3 = 0$
2. $\overline{X}_1 X_2\overline{X}_3$	$X_2 = X_2\underline{X}_1\underline{X}_3 = 0$
3. $\overline{X}_1\overline{X}_2 X_3$	$X_3 = X_3\underline{X}_1\underline{X}_2 = 0$
4. $X_1 X_2\overline{X}_3$	$X_1 X_2 = X_1\underline{X}_2 + x_{,2}\underline{X}_1 = 0$
5. $X_1\overline{X}_2 X_3$	$X_1 X_3 = X_1\underline{X}_3 + X_3\underline{X}_1 = 0$
6. $\overline{X}_1 X_2 X_3$	$X_2 X_3 = X_2\underline{X}_3 + X_3\underline{X}_2 = 0$
7. $X_1 X_2 X_3$	$X_1 X_2 X_3 = X_1\underline{X}_2\underline{X}_3 + X_2\underline{X}_1\underline{X}_3 + X_3\underline{X}_1\underline{X}_2 = 1$

   It is now possible to write a set of equations associated with the weight assignment, as shown in Table 12.3. The underlining under "Associated Equations" is read "inhibited by." Equation 1 indicates that the algebraic sum of the excitations and inhibitions when $X_1 \overline{X}_2 \overline{X}_3$ is true equals zero. Also, equation 4 indicates that the algebraic sum of excitations and inhibitions when $X_1 X_2 \overline{X}_3$ is true or when X_1 is not inhibited by X_2, $X_1 X_2$, and X_2 is not inhibited by X_1, $X_2 X_1$ is zero. The other equations can be described in a similar manner. The order of the equations in Table 12.3 treats minterms with the most complemented terms first, etc. The remainder of the synthesis procedure is based on assigning weights to $(N-1)$-dimensional Venn diagrams that satisfy the equations in Table 12.3.

   If one assumes in order that each of the uncomplemented variables X_i is true in each minterm, then it is possible to represent the left side of each of the equations in Table 12.3 by three $(N-1)$-dimensional Venn diagrams with jots in the appropriate regions. For example, the first term on the right of equation 7 is represented by

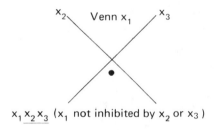

where the four spaces represent the following:

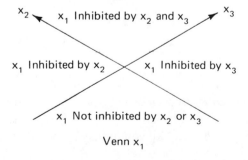

Thus, the space to the left of the line labeled X_3 represents inhibition by X_2, and the space to the right of the line labeled X_2 represents inhibition by X_3. Values can now be assigned to the spaces indicated by jots such that Equation 7 is satisfied:

$$X_1 \underline{X_2} \underline{X_3} + \underline{X_1} X_2 \underline{X_3} + \underline{X_1} \underline{X_2} X_3 = 1$$

$1 + 0 + 0 = 1$

$$x_1 x_2 x_3 + x_1 x_2 x_3 + x_1 x_2 x_3 = 1$$

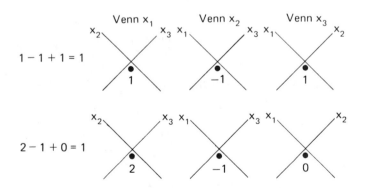

Note that this weight assignment is not the only one for which Equation 7 is satisfied. For instance, the following weight assignments and others will also satisfy Equation 7:

One can now represent each of the equations in Table 12.3 successively from Equations 7 to 1, and by carrying the assigned weights from Equation 7 to Equation 6 and so forth, all equations can be satisfied simultaneously.

The jots are inserted for each equation as it is considered, whereas the weights assigned are carried to successive equations. Each equation must be satisfied with respect to the regions where jots are entered. Thus, for the example given by Equation 12.19, the complete assignment is

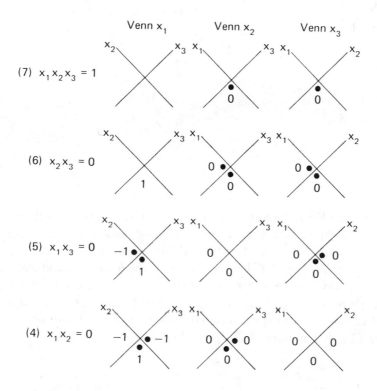

Note that up to this point the sum of the weights associated with the jots for each equation satisfy the corresponding equation. Also, note that the weights carried from the previous equations are used to satisfy the new equation only if a jot appears in that region.

The last three equations can now be satisfied by assigning weights to the remaining region in each of the Venn diagrams such that the respective equations are satisfied:

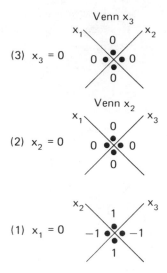

These three Venn diagrams define the structure of the network, where a positive weight indicates an excitatory input and a negative weight indicates an inhibitory input for the variable associated with that Venn. Thus, the variables X_2 and X_3 have no inputs to the final threshold element. However, X_1 has two excitatory and two inhibitory inputs to the final threshold element. The final network is shown in Figure 12.6. The interpretation of the regions and the associated weights in Venn X_1 are illustrated in Figure 12.7. A summary of this procedure follows:

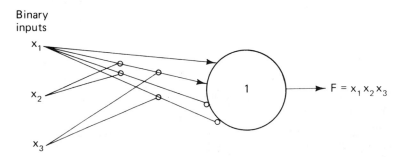

Figure 12.6   Realization of the function $F = X_1 X_2 X_3$.

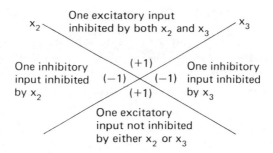

One excitatory input
inhibited by both x_2 and x_3

x_2 x_3

One inhibitory $(+1)$ One inhibitory
input inhibited (-1) (-1) input inhibited
by x_2 $(+1)$ by x_3

One excitatory
input not inhibited
by either x_2 or x_3

Figure 12.7. Interpretation of a Venn X_1.

1. Put the function to be synthesized in disjunctive normal form.
2. Map the function into the primary Venn diagram, placing jots in the regions for which the function is true.
3. Assign weights to the regions of the primary Venn diagram such that the weights assigned to the desired function's minterms are greater than those of the other minterms. The weight of the null minterm is always zero.
4. Write the equations associated with the minterms using the primary Venn diagram.
5. Fill the $(N - 1)$-dimensional Venn diagrams such that the above equations are satisfied, starting with the tautology $(X_1 X_2 \cdots X_N)$ and working to the terms with a single uncomplemented variable.
6. Synthesize the network from the final set of N Venn diagrams, where a positive number denotes excitatory inputs and a negative number denotes inhibitory inputs.
7. Choose the threshold of the second-level element such that it is no greater than the smallest weight of the minterms of the desired function.

The ability to synthesize neural networks that are functionally complete certainly satisfies one reasonable requirement for an element: to operate in a complex computational system such as the brain. This alone, however, does not explain any process of adaptation or learning in networks of these devices.

ADAPTIVE ELEMENTS AND NETWORKS

Many of the early attempts to create systems that exhibit adaptive, learning, or pattern recognition behavior started with the threshold logic unit and made parts of it variable so that the behavior could be dynamically modified. Arrays of these elements then served as forward transfer elements from which systems could be built.

One of the early and fundamental modifications of the basic neural element is the Adaline (adaptive linear element) proposed by Widrow [7]. The Adaline shown in Figure 12.8 has provisions for independent adjustment of each of the weights on the input to the threshold section. Thus, based on the assessment of the network's performance, these parameters can be adjusted. It is known, however, that this single threshold configuration is not functionally complete, and therefore we must consider multilevel configurations. A multiple adaptive linear element or Madaline for two levels is shown in Figure 12.9. The adjustments in the Madaline are only on the weights of the first-level inputs. These weights may be adjusted either continuously or incrementally over some finite range of both positive and negative values. Thus, the Madaline is a functionally complete realization of an adaptive logic system.

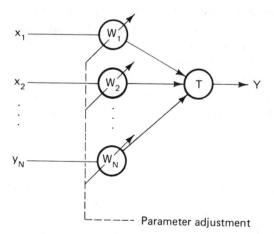

Figure 12.8. Adaline (adaptive linear element): weights are adjusted as a function of performance assessment.

Another class of networks of threshold devices is the Perceptron, which was first described by Rosenblatt [8] and later developed by Minsky and Papert [9]. The initial formulation of the Perceptron structure was based on observations of the brain and brain cell organization. The rich interneuronal connections in the brain appear to have little order, and thus one might say that initially these connections are random and, as the individual learns, that the weighting of the interconnections is varied. Thus, the simple Perceptron illustrated in Figure 12.10 consists of three basic elements: the S (sensory) units, the A (association) units, and the R (response) units,

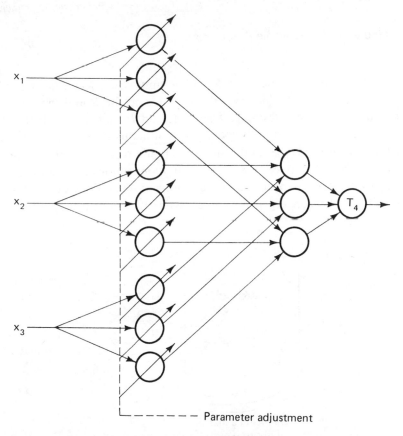

Figure 12.9.　Madaline (multiple adaptive linear element): a two-level net with adjustable input weighting.

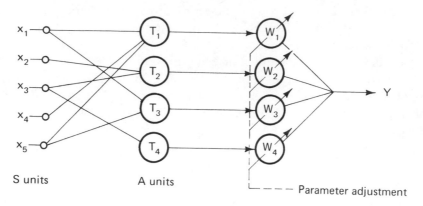

Figure 12.10.   A simple Perceptron.

where the connections between S and A units are selected in a random manner and the weights between the A units and the R units are varied as a function of network training. The S, A, and R units are each threshold devices where the S_ith unit responds to a stimulus by emitting a signal if the ith signal exceeds the ith threshold. It should be clear from our previous study of threshold devices that proper interconnections between the S and A units will allow realization of all functions of n variables. A good deal of research on the convergence characteristics of Perceptrons with various

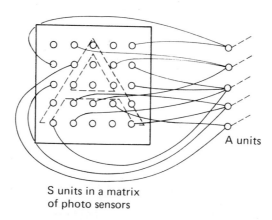

Figure 12.11.   Retina used for pattern recognition with Perceptron.

random interconnection schemes has been developed by Rosenblatt [8]. Further, the S units have been built into matrices of photo sensors, as shown in Figure 12.11, and the network has been trained to recognize certain patterns presented to this artificial retina. This type of processing will be explored more fully in Chapter 13.

SUMMARY

The limits on the number of functions realizable with a single threshold device were considered in the first part of this chapter. From this it is clear that configurations of multilevel threshold devices are required to realize all functions of n variables. The Blum procedure provides a means for the synthesis of all functions of n variables with multilevel threshold devices where the first-level gate structure is fixed. It is important to note again that conventional AND, OR, and NOT logic is merely a special case of generalized threshold logic. Finally, adaptive elements of threshold-type devices have been considered. These elements' ability to vary a set of parameters associated with the forward transfer characteristics makes them well suited for incorporation in intelligent systems.

EXERCISES

1. Order the relative weight magnitudes of the following function:

$$Y = \overline{X}_1 X_2 + \overline{X}_1 X_3 + \overline{X}_1 X_4 X_6 + \overline{X}_1 X_5 X_6 + X_2 X_3 X_4 + X_2 X_3 X_5$$
$$+ X_2 X_4 X_5 + X_3 X_4 X_5 X_6$$

2. Develop a single-element realization and write the separating plane equation for

$$Y = \overline{X}_1 X_2 X_3 + X_4 \overline{X}_1$$

3. Write the separating plane equation, draw a threshold logic realization, and design a conventional AND, OR, and NOT realization for

$$Y = X_1 (\overline{X}_2 + \overline{X}_3)$$

4. Given the coincidence function

$$Y = X_1 X_2 + \overline{X}_1 \overline{X}_2$$

(a) Synthesize Y using the Blum technique.
(b) Synthesize Y using individual threshold gates which realize AND, OR, and NOT.
(c) Compare the two realizations.

5. Given the accompanying neural network

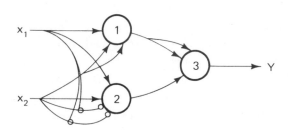

(a) Find the function realized.
(b) What functions are realized if each threshold is increased by 1? Decreased by 1?

REFERENCES

1. LEWIS, P. M., and C. L. COATES, *Threshold Logic*, Wiley, New York, 1967.
2. WINDER, R. O., "Enumeration of Seven Argument Threshold Functions," *IEEE Transactions of Electronic Computers*, Vol. EC-14, No. 1, June 1965, pp. 315–325.
3. MUROGA, S., T. TSUBOI, and C. R. BANGH, "Enumeration of Threshold Functions of Eight Variables," *IEEE Transactions on Computers, Vol. C-19, No. 9, September 1970, pp. 818–825.*
4. LEWIS, P. M., and C. L. COATES, "Realization of Logical Functions by a Network of Threshold Components with Specified Sensitivity," *IRE Trans. Electronic Computers*, Vol. EC-12, No. 5, October 1963, pp. 443–453.
5. MCCULLOCH, W. S., "Agatha Tyche: Of Nervous Nets—The Lucky Reckoners," in *Mechanization of Thought Processes*, proceedings of a symposium held at the National Physiological Laboratory, November 24–27, 1958, No. 1C, Vol. II, Her Majesty's Stationery Office, London, 1958, pp. 611–634.

6. BLUM, Manuel, "Properties of a Neuron with Many Inputs," in *Principles of Self-Organization*, H. VON FOERSTER and G. W. ZOPF, Jr., eds., Macmillian, New York, 1962.

7. WIDROW, B., "Generalization and Information Storage in Networks of Adaline Neurons," in *Self-Organizing Systems—1962*, M. C. YOVITTS, G. T. JACOBS, and G. D. GOLDSTEIN, eds., Spartan, New York, 1962.

8. ROSENBLATT, F., *Principles of Neurodynamics*, Spartan, New York, 1962.

9. MINSKY, M., and S. PAPERT, *Perceptrons*, M.I.T. Press, Cambridge, Mass., 1969.

13

Pattern Recognition

Although some facets of the pattern recognition problem have been presented in previous chapters, we shall now consider this problem in more detail in an attempt to identify its crucial aspects. Pattern recognition principles have been applied in the past to either the design of text recognition machines, which operate on data obtained by optical means, or to the processing of signals that may be associated with acoustic phenomena such as speech. The operations on these data or signals, which allow one to use a machine to perform tasks such as reading typed or handwritten text or to recognize the spoken word, can be broken down into five major areas: the input systems, feature extraction, discrimination, response selection, and the output systems. However, before we examine these areas, it is useful to consider the general pattern recognition problem.

WHAT IS PATTERN RECOGNITION?

The term "pattern recognition" and its use, "the process of," are applied to all information structures and signals. What, then, is the difference between a pattern and a signal? If one has no convenient mathematical description of the information structures or signals, then they are generally referred to as patterns. Also, patterns often take on a multidimensional nature and are expressed as n-dimensional vectors.

The elements of the n-dimensional vectors are related in some way to the pattern to be recognized. For example, the vital life signs and symptoms may make up the vector when an automatic medical diagnosis by pattern recognition techniques is to be made. These elements are sometimes called features of the pattern. A crucial aspect of pattern recognition, then, is the selection of the proper features. For example, the medical diagnosis of an infection is a difficult task if body temperature, a good indicator of the presence of infection, is not included in the pattern vector.

Once the features have been specified, it is necessary to distinguish which features make up the patterns to be recognized. Thus, for medical diagnoses, for example, it is necessary to be able to distinguish among a common cold, bronchitis, and pneumonia. This part of the pattern recognition problem—discrimination—is relatively well defined and therefore has been the object of a good deal of effort [1, 2].

A general model of a pattern recognition system is given in Figure 13.1. The input element converts the pattern from an abstract form—such as a drawing, photo, voice, or a series of medical observations and measurements—to specific physical quantities—such as a voltage waveform or an optical pattern. The second element, the preprocessor, may not exist independently; however, its function, the extraction of the proper features from the input signal, is a necessary element of a pattern recognition system. The discriminator then operates on the features such that each of the patterns to be recognized generates as unique an output as possible, which can then be categorized by the response selector. The final element is the output system, which converts the result to the form desired by the user. Examples of output systems are printers, the setting of news type, Braille feelers (for reading machines for the blind), and magnetic tape formatted properly for subsequent processing (as used in automatic bill paying and accounting systems).

The input system and feature extraction processes will be examined first, and the discriminator and response selector will be studied later.

Figure 13.1.   General model of a pattern recognition system.

INPUT SYSTEMS

As stated earlier, the purpose of the input system is to convert an abstract form into a set of physical properties that can be operated on by the remainder of the pattern recognition system. Input systems can be as simple as keyboards and push-button arrays or as complex as high-speed scanners that automatically read hundreds of documents per minute. A keyboard input is useful in systems where there is a great deal of alphanumeric information and where speed is not crucial. Another method for handling alphanumeric as well as pictorial and graphic inputs is the flying spot scanner described here.

The flying spot scanner is an uncomplicated, inexpensive, and versatile device for converting images on reflecting or transparent surfaces into electrical signals. Typically, the spot is provided by a cathode-ray tube (CRT), which is focused onto the reflecting surface by a lens, as illustrated in Figure 13.2. The position of the spot on the CRT and hence on the reflecting surface is controlled by the voltages on the horizontal and vertical plates of the CRT. In this manner a spot of light can be positioned to any place on the object surface. The amount of light reflected from the spot is indicated by the output of the light sensors, which are positioned around the object being scanned. The sensors may be photomultipliers, photo diodes, or phototransistors. Depending on the problem, the output from the

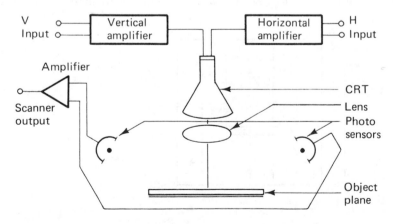

Figure 13.2. General configuration of a flying spot scanner.

sensors is quantized into from 2 to N levels. For example, two levels are generally used for reading alphanumeric symbols, whereas eight or more levels or colors may be needed for photographic recognition problems.

There are several ways in which the spot can be positioned. The simplest is the raster scan, as used for television, in which the spot is moved from left to right and from the top down, as shown in Figure 13.3. Generally, the spot is moved in increments, thereby describing blocks or resolution elements on the object space. The extraction of features from a raster scan is usually more difficult than the curve-tracing method.

Let us now examine some input systems for sound and speech recognition [3, 4]. In such systems, the electrical input is provided by a microphone, and the processing beyond that point may be either digital or analog. This processing may be considered as the feature extraction process of the system. Most acoustic systems attempt to analyze the spectral-time response (sound spectrogram) of the speech wave form, an example of which is given in Figure 13.4. The spectrograms for different words spoken by the same speaker are sufficiently different to use them as a basis for word recognition. However, the nature of speech is not understood well enough to provide high-accuracy interspeaker word recognition using the spectrogram—or any other method, for that matter.

A block diagram that is representative of many of the speech recognition systems built to date is shown in Figure 13.5. The microphone output drives a number (up to 22) of 1/3-octave filters spread over the speech

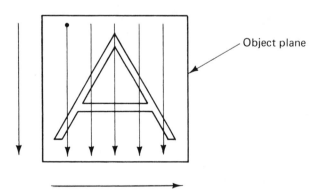

Figure 13.3.   Scan directions for conventional raster scan.

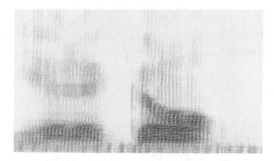

Figure 13.4.   Sound spectrogram of a two-syllable word.

spectrum. Each of the outputs of the filters is usually processed in some often nonlinear way. For example, peak detection or logarithmic amplification or both may be applied. These outputs are then multiplexed and applied to an analog-digital converter for subsequent processing by a digital computer or system. The output of this system is sampled by the processor in fixed intervals of from 10 to 100 milliseconds, depending on the specifics of the system in question.

Thus, if there are 20 filters and a sampling rate of 50 milliseconds, then for utterances of one-second duration, a vector of 400 elements is generated for processing by the remainder of the system. The object of the subsequent

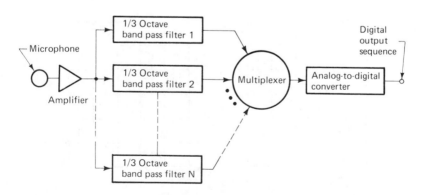

Figure 13.5.   Typical input/feature extraction system for speech recognition.

processing is to reduce these data to a single result—the word that was spoken. The methodology for making this decision is discussed later. Let us now study some feature extraction schemes for reading machines.

FEATURE EXTRACTION

The goal of the feature extraction process is to generate an n-dimensional vector from the input system, which captures the "essence" of the pattern to be recognized. It is this elusive "essence" that makes feature extraction the least understood and hence the most difficult part of designing pattern recognition systems.

Feature extraction techniques cover the gamut from ad hoc intuitive schemes through biological and behavioral analogs to sophisticated analytical techniques. In this section we shall describe examples of the first two of these approaches.

First, consider the effects of a quantized raster scan for feature extraction. Here, we shall assume that the character size is known a priori and that the character has been properly positioned in the center of the scan. These two problems, character size and position, are not insignificant in practical pattern recognition problems [5]. The quantized raster scan can be visualized as a matrix of resolution elements, also called picture elements (*pel* or *pixel*); they are illustrated in Figure 13.6. For alphanumeric characters, it is useful to quantize each into two values, 0 and 1, to represent

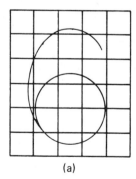

(a)

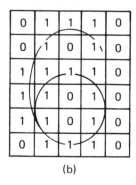

(b)

Figure 13.6. (a) Representation of raster scan by resolution elements. (b) Quantized representation of (a).

the absence or presence, respectively, of a mark in that element, as illustrated in Figure 13.6b. The input to the remainder of the system is the 30-bit word derived by taking each value as that element is scanned. For example, the word resulting from the scan of Figure 13.6b is 001110111111101001111111000000.

Notice however, that the reorientation of the character in the raster scan results in a completely different binary sequence. This can be overcome to some extent by scanning in a spiral, as shown in Figure 13.7. Here, if the number of resolution elements is sufficiently large, the binary sequence generated will be shifted only by an amount proportional to the rotation of the character. However, the spiral scan is very sensitive to translation.

As the number of symbols to be recognized and their complexity increases, the number of resolution elements needed to discriminate between patterns also increases. In some cases, up to 60×100 matrices may be needed. Thus, in the worst of cases, 6000 points must be scanned, formatted, stored, and processed in the recognition process. Contour tracing is one means of reducing the amount of data taken, handling a large number of characters and fonts (kinds of print), and providing a good feature set for the recognition of handwritten characters [5, 6]. The square trace is the simplest contour-tracing algorithm. Here, if the last point in a black-on-white field was black, the scanner then makes a 90° turn right to find the next resolution element to be tested. On the other hand, if the last point was white, it makes a 90° turn right to find the next resolution element to be tested. The square trace algorithm is illustrated in Figure 13.8.

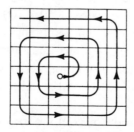

Figure 13.7.   Spiral scan to reduce the effects of rotation of the character on the scan output.

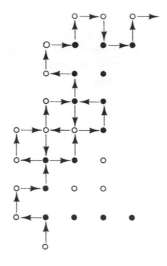

Figure 13.8.   Operation of the square trace algorithm for contour tracing.

It is possible, however, to become locked into a rectangular scan of four successive black or four successive white resolution elements, as shown in Figure 13.9a. This can be overcome in most cases by making a 45° move after three elements of the same kind have been encountered. If the edges of the character contour are not sharply defined, it is possible to trap into a six-element sequence of one-color points, shown in Figure 13.9b. This condition is a trace error, these points are ignored, and the next point to be tested is chosen at random around the trap points. The locations of the white-to-black transitions are the only points stored as features of the character being scanned. Typically, a 50×100 matrix requires approximately 600 tests and storage of 300 points for contour tracing rather than 5000 points tested and stored for raster and spiral scans of the same array.

The next class of feature extraction systems to be considered is that derived from biological and behavioral studies of both animal and human visual systems.

For example, justification of contour tracing as a feature extraction technique has been constructed from both biological and behavioral experiments. A neurophysiological study of the optic nerve complex of the frog [7] indicated that the processing of visual information includes a

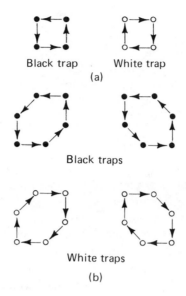

Black trap   White trap

(a)

Black traps

White traps

(b)

Figure 13.9. (a) Trace traps for square algorithm. (b) Trace traps for modified square trace algorithm.

mechanism for detecting the edge (contour) of a pattern. Other features in the frog's eye such as concavity and convexity detectors have also been used in feature extraction systems. A study by Hartline and Ratliff [8] of the eye of *Limulus* (horseshoe crab) has found that edge enhancement is an important feature for this creature as well.

Studies of the human visual system from a behavioral point of view [9, 10] indicate that edge enhancement and contours are important for human perception as well. The importance of the contrast of edges can easily be illustrated by looking at Figure 13.10, a line drawing that conveys a complete image by edges only. This fact is also used to advantage in color television processing where some edge enhancement is provided before the picture is transmitted. Here images appear sharper and the effects of noise on the TV signal are not as pronounced as they would be without edge enhancement.

These various features have been incorporated in the Minos pattern recognition machine developed at Stanford Research Institute for the U.S. Army Electronics Command [11]. Here many normalized images of the

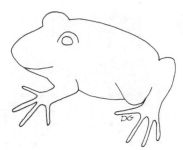

Figure 13.10.   Line drawing which illustrates the effects of edges on perception. Note that only edges are needed to convey the essence of the image.

pattern to be recognized are projected in parallel through masks with the various features etched on them. Thus, edges, concavity, and vertical, horizontal, and diagonal lines, etc., can all be detected by photosensors placed behind the mask. The outputs of the photosensors are then passed through threshold devices. The outputs from these units then make up the n-dimensional vector that is the input to the pattern discriminator. An example of the edge detection feature mask used in Minos is given in Figure 13.11a, where the white areas are opaque. Edges in several discrete orientations are detected by photocell pairs placed behind images of the object, as shown in Figure 13.11b. Thus, if an edge pair indeed is on an edge, the differential output of the quantizer will indicate the light-to-dark transition of the input symbol.

There are, of course, other features and methods for incorporating these features of biological systems into a pattern recognition system. It is important for the designer to be aware of them in developing these systems. However, the selection of the proper features for the problem at hand is indeed difficult and may even be classified as "art." There are some systematic methods for selecting features that are beyond the scope of this text [12, 13]. However, the uses of transforms in the feature extraction process are of interest.

TRANSFORMATIONS IN FEATURE EXTRACTION

Recall the input system for speech recognition discussed in an earlier section where the input signal is passed through banks of filters and analyzed as a function of time. The results of this process are similar to an

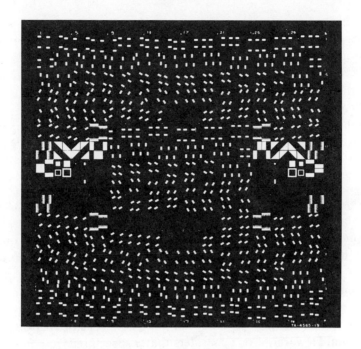

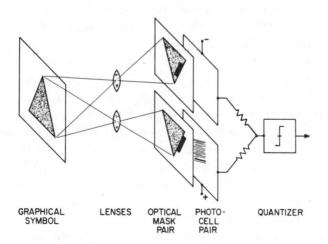

GRAPHICAL   LENSES   OPTICAL   PHOTO-   QUANTIZER
SYMBOL   MASK   CELL
                         PAIR   PAIR

Figure 13.11. (a) Mask plate for Minos for edge detection. (b) Processing system for Minos mask plates.

instantaneous Fourier analysis of the input waveform. Since there is a delay in propagation through each of the filters, one may apply the Fourier transform over each of the delay intervals to create the feature set of spectral density as a function of time. The advent of the fast Fourier transform algorithm [14] and the ability to perform Fourier analysis on a digital computer make this a useful tool of pattern recognition.

If the input waveform is denoted by $f(t)$, then the Fourier transform is given by

$$F(\omega) = \mathfrak{F}[f(t)] = \int_{-\infty}^{\infty} f(t)e^{-j\omega t}\,dt \qquad (13.1)$$

Thus, the frequency domain becomes the feature space in which the discriminator must operate. This space is generally large, and one must narrow its focus to regions in which there is a "significant" correlation between features that can be used to discriminate between input patterns. For example, it is well known that little speech information is present above 3 kilohertz or below 300 hertz. Therefore, the feature space between 300 hertz and 3 kilohertz is probably all that is needed to perform speech recognition. However, if one considers that a speech recognition apparatus must include temporal analysis of the spectral density, then it is reasonable to define the feature space as the product of the spectral density space and the utterance duration time space, typically less than one second. Thus, the feature space for speech recognition is indeed large and must be reduced further [15].

One might also incorporate the Fourier transform in image recognition by applying it, for example, to each vertical scan or part thereof, creating a spectral density for each line of the image. However, since an image exists in two dimensions, it has been found useful to apply the Fourier transform in two dimensions. The two-dimensional Fourier transform is especially important in recognizing two-dimensional images because it can easily be realized using optical techniques. Let us now examine the two-dimensional Fourier transform.

An image can be represented by an intensity function in two dimensions, that is, $f(x,y)$. The Fourier transform in two dimensions is

$$F(u,v) = \int_{-\infty}^{\infty} \int_{-\infty}^{\infty} f(x,y)e^{-j(ux+vy)}\,dx\,dy \qquad (13.2)$$

and $f(x,y)$ is given by the inverse Fourier transform

$$f(x,y) = \frac{1}{(2\pi)^2} \int_{-\infty}^{\infty} \int_{-\infty}^{\infty} F(u,v)e^{j(ux+vy)} \, du \, dv \qquad (13.3)$$

The Fourier transform can also be represented in discrete form for computer implementation, where

$$F(u,v) = \frac{1}{N} \sum_{x=0}^{N-1} \sum_{y=0}^{N-1} f(x,y)e^{(-j2\pi/N)(ux+vy)} \qquad (13.4)$$

is the forward transform and

$$f(x,y) = \frac{1}{N} \sum_{u=0}^{N-1} \sum_{v=0}^{N-1} F(u,v)e^{(j2\pi/N)(ux+vy)} \qquad (13.5)$$

is the inverse transformation. $F(u,v)$ is also a two-dimensional intensity function but in the u, v plane, where intensity transitions in the x direction of the x-y plane generate spectral components in the v direction along the u axis of the u-v plane while intensity transitions in the y direction of the x-y plane generate spectral components in the u direction along the v axis of the u-v plane. These intensity variations in the x and y directions are described in the u, v plane as spatial frequencies. Thus, it is possible to filter out specific frequencies by applying a spatial filter, $H(u,v)$ to $F(u,v)$:

$$G(u,v) = H(u,v)F(u,v) \qquad (13.6)$$

The function given in Equation 13.5 may represent the features of a particular pattern to be recognized. One distinct advantage of spatial filtering for feature extraction is that it can easily be accomplished with optical techniques [16]. Another advantage of this approach is that all elements of the two-dimensional image are processed in parallel. A square image, its two-dimensional Fourier transform image, and a three-dimensional representation of the transform are shown in Figure 13.12. A spatial filter that passes the first two harmonics of the image is a transparent circle whose radius is just greater than the distance to the second harmonic, shown in Figure 13.12d. The effects of spatial filtering on the letter E are shown in Figure 13.13, where the inverse Fourier transform of the filtered images has been applied. It is interesting to note that some of the "essence" of the letter is still present even if only the direct-current component and

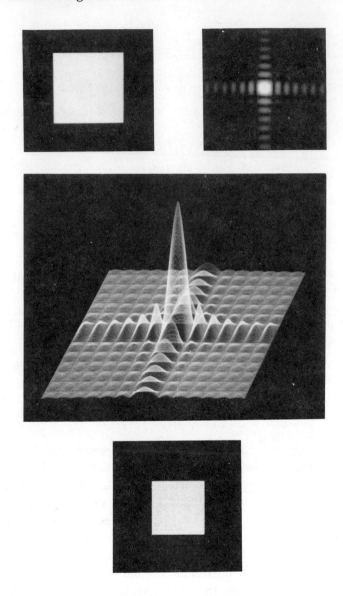

Figure 13.12.   Two-dimensional images, Fourier transforms, and spatial filtering.

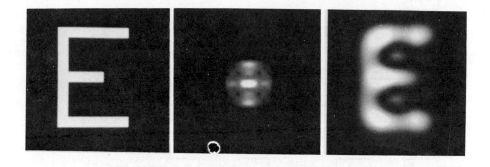

Figure 13.13.   The effects of spatial filtering on an image.

first harmonic are passed through the filter. Thus, the direct current and the first through the third harmonics might be reasonably selected as the features for the letter *E*. The perceptual aspects of spatial filtering with respect to the stimulus cues that the human visual system responds to has been treated by Ginsburg [17], and will be discussed in Chapter 14, "Computer Vision."

Another transformation that particularly lends itself to computer implementation is the Walsh-Hadamard transformation [18, 19]. This transformation is unique in that its basis is not sines and cosines but orthogonal rectangular waves called Walsh functions, whose values alternate between −1 and +1. Thus, they may be considered as sequences of binary numbers, and the number of +1 to −1 and −1 to +1 transitions per fundamental time interval is called the sequency. These orthogonal functions are illustrated in Figure 13.14. One can also represent these functions by defining the smallest interval of interest as −1 or +1. Therefore, the sequence is given by a vector whose elements are +1 or −1.

If one is concerned with a specific number of time intervals, the Walsh sequences can be represented in matrix form as follows. If there are two intervals as in a two by two array of resolution elements, then the functions in order of increasing sequence are

$$H_2 = \begin{bmatrix} 1 & 1 \\ 1 & -1 \end{bmatrix} \qquad (13.7)$$

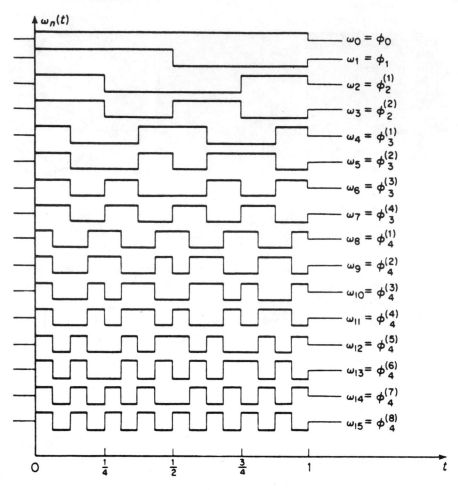

Figure 13.14. Walsh functions indexed by the number of sign changes in the interval $0 < t < 1$.

Equation 13.7 is also known as the lowest-order Hadamard matrix (a Hadamard matrix is a square matrix of $+1$s and -1s whose rows and columns are orthogonal to one another). The orthogonality property indicates that

$$[H][H]^T = N[I] \qquad (13.8)$$

where I is the identity matrix and the normalized Hadamard matrix $(1/\sqrt{N})[H]$ is an orthonormal matrix. Hadamard matrices of an order $2N$ can be constructed from matrices of order N by the following:

$$H_{2N} = \begin{bmatrix} H_N & H_N \\ H_N & -H_N \end{bmatrix} \tag{13.9}$$

Hadamard matrices of order higher than 2 must be a multiple of 4.

The discrete Walsh-Hadamard transformation for a one-dimensional function $f(x)$ is similar to the Fourier transformation except that the basis involves $+1$ and -1 and not powers of e,

$$F(\mu) = \frac{1}{\sqrt{N}} \sum_{x=0}^{N-1} f(x)(-1)^{p(x,\mu)} \tag{13.10}$$

where

$$p(x,\mu) = \sum_{i=0}^{N-1} (\mu_i x_i) = \sum_{i=0}^{N-1} (\mu_i \wedge x_i) \tag{13.11}$$

The terms μ_i and x_i are the ith bits of the binary representation of the decimal numbers μ and x, respectively. Note that the summation in Equation 13.11 is to the base 10. It is interesting to note that $(-1)^{p(x,u)}$ for successive values of x and u defines a Walsh sequence or a Hadamard matrix (see the Exercises). Similarly, the discrete two-dimensional Walsh-Hadamard transformation is given by

$$F(u,v) = \frac{1}{N} \sum_{x=0}^{N-1} \sum_{y=0}^{N-1} f(x,y)(-1)^{p(x,y,u,v)} \tag{13.12}$$

where

$$p(x,y,u,v) = \sum_{i=0}^{N-1} (u_i x_i + v_i y_i) \tag{13.13}$$

and the u_i, x_i, v_i, and y_i are as given.

The Walsh-Hadamard transformation can easily be carried out using a digital computer since it can be computed using only logical operations and adds. This transformation can easily be used on $N \times N$ arrays of resolution elements by direct application of Equations 13.12 and 13.13. The resulting intensity function of the u, v plane can then be used to generate the feature vector for the discrimination/response selection portion of the pattern recognizer.

THE DISCRIMINATION AND RESPONSE SELECTION PROBLEMS (CLASSIFICATION) [20]

Thus far we have been concerned with generating a set of measurements of some input that contain the "essence" of the patterns we wish to recognize. In general, we can represent the output of a feature extraction system as an n-tuple, $x_1, x_2, x_3, \ldots, x_n$, where this set of numbers is sometimes called the pattern and the elements are called components or features of the pattern. Thus, the discrimination problem is to classify the n measurements as being a member of one of r different responses of the output set Z, as illustrated in Figure 13.15.

The n inputs can each be associated with a single dimension of an n-dimensional Euclidean space, and each set of measurements X define a point in space. The task of the classifier is to map the points in the n-dimensional Euclidean space into the r members of the output set. A simple approach to this is to divide up the Euclidean space into r decision regions, each of which is associated with one of the possible input patterns. The surfaces in the space of X that separate one pattern from all other patterns are called decision surfaces. These surfaces are identical to the separating planes in threshold logic (treated in Chapters 11 and 12).

DECISION SURFACES AND DISCRIMINANT FUNCTIONS [1, 21, 22]

The decision surfaces in the X space are defined by the intersection of planes described by discriminant functions. Discriminant functions are chosen for all points in X associated with response i, $g_i(X) > g_j(X)$

Figure 13.15. Model of pattern classifier.

for $i, j = 1, \ldots, r, i \neq j$. Therefore, the ith discriminant function has the largest scalar magnitude when the ith pattern is present at the input. This model of a pattern classifier is given in Figure 13.16. The operation of the classifier is as follows: The input pattern X is presented, the discriminants are formed, the maximum selector determines the discriminant, l, with the largest value, and the input is then classified as the lth pattern.

One of the most important problems in pattern recognition is the selection of the discriminant functions to be used. There are several ways in which one may select discriminant functions, and each depends on the type and complexity of the pattern recognition task. For example, the dichotomization used for detection using TLPs described in Chapter 8 is completely described by the nature of the problem. Other problems may require that certain approximations be applied in the development of the discriminant functions. Finally, one may have very little information from which one can design the appropriate discriminant functions. In this case the final discriminant functions depend to some extent on adjustments made on the operation of the system. Thus, it may be necessary to apply learning techniques to the design of discriminant functions. This leads one to the concept of a trainable pattern classifier and the associated training techniques.

There are two types of methods for training pattern classifier systems: parametric and nonparametric. Parametric methods are used when each of

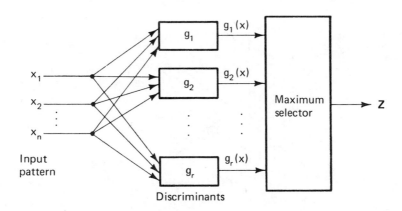

Figure 13.16. Model of pattern classifier.

the possible input categories is known a priori to be representable by a set of parameters, where some of the parameter values are unknown. The case where all the parameters are known a priori is more easily solved than the case where only one or more parameter values are unknown. In the first case, the proper discriminants would easily be designed such that the input patterns are recognized. The latter case requires certain measurements of the unknown parameter values, and a discriminant function based on these measurements can then be described.

A simple parametric method for one unknown parameter value might require that a series of measurements of that parameter be taken and the mean value of these samples be used as an estimate of the value of that parameter.

Consider the case where two parameter values are unknown. Here one may estimate the mean values of each of the parameters in the hyperspace of X as X_1 and X_2. A reasonable choice for the discriminant function is the perpendicular bisector of the points X_1 and X_2. The following discriminant function will perform as that kind of discriminant and is illustrated in Figure 13.17:

$$g(X) = (X_1 - X_2) \cdot X + \frac{1}{2}|X_2|^2 - \frac{1}{2}|X_1|^2 \qquad (13.14)$$

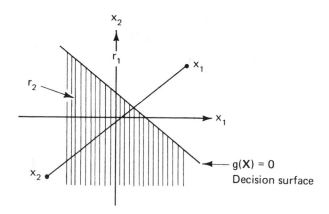

Figure 13.17.   Perpendicular bisector of means as a discriminant function.

A most difficult case of discriminant function generation is where the parameters to be used are not known a priori. In these nonparametric cases one may assume a functional form for the discriminant functions, and the coefficients of these functions may be found by training methods. Some of the forms that may be assumed are linear, quadric, piecewise linear, and Gilstrap's multinomial, for example. Other methods utilize cascaded linear and nonlinear functions or matrix representations of the input vector X and eigenvectors of the matrix as discriminants of the system.

The following linear discriminant function is often assumed:

$$g(X) = w_1 x_1 + w_2 x_2 + \cdots + w_n x_n - w_0$$

Note that this is identical to the realization of the threshold logic element described earlier. A pattern recognition learning system that uses linear discriminant functions is called a linear machine. A linear machine is illustrated in Figure 13.18. Here r linear discriminant functions are described where each function is associated with one of the r possible pattern classes. The w_{ij} represents the weights or thresholds of each of the linear functions.

Another technique for classification of patterns is called the minimum-distance classifier. Here each of the r_i possible pattern classes is associated with a point P_i in E^d (d-dimensional Euclidean space). Thus, the pattern into which a particular input X is classified is associated with the point to which the input is closest. Here the Euclidean distance is given by

$$|X - P_i| = \sqrt{(X - P_i) \cdot (X - P_i)} \tag{13.15}$$

Note that since X and P_i are vectors the $(X - P_i) \cdot (X - P_i)$ represents the dot product and $(X - P_i)(X - P_i)^T$ the matrix product. Thus, one calculates the magnitude for all i and then selects the pattern for which the magnitude is minimum. The points $P_1, P_2, \ldots, P_r$ are called prototype points, as they are generally associated with "idealized," noiseless versions of each of the input patterns.

Next, note that here $|X - P_i|^2$ is equivalent to the above; however, squaring both sides of Equation 13.15 gives

$$|X - P_i|^2 = (X - P_i) \cdot (X - P_i)$$
$$= X \cdot X + 2X \cdot P_i + P_i \cdot P_i \tag{13.16}$$

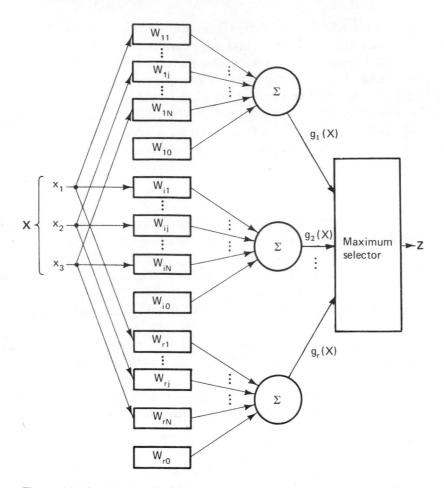

Figure 13.18.   Linear machine.

It is clear from Equation 13.16 that the comparison of X and P_i is only a function of the last two terms, and a comparison of the following terms is equivalent to Equation 13.16:

$$\max(X \cdot P_i - \frac{1}{2}P_i \cdot P_i) \quad \text{for } i = 1, \ldots, r \quad (13.17)$$

Thus, the minimum-distance classifier selects the largest of the r terms computed by Equation 13.17, and the discriminant functions are

$$g_i(x) = X \cdot P_i - \frac{1}{2} P_i \cdot P_i \qquad \text{for } i = 1, \ldots, r \qquad (13.18)$$

Equation 13.18 is linear, and therefore the weights associated with each of the x_d points in the r equations are

$$w_{ij} = p_{ij} \qquad i, j = 1, \ldots, r \qquad (13.19a)$$

and the thresholds are

$$w_{i0} = -\frac{1}{2} P_i \cdot P_i \qquad i = 1, \ldots, r \qquad (13.19b)$$

The dot product $X \cdot P_i$ is also known as template matching, correlation detection, and matched filtering.

The template-matching process can be thought of as follows. Assume that the problem at hand is to recognize the numbers 0 through 9 as printed by an electric typewriter. First, one must make templates of those characters, for example, transparencies of the characters whose densities are such that the light passing through each transparency under the same illumination is equal. The process of pattern recognition then requires that transparencies of the input patterns be compared with the templates by projecting through the two transparencies and selecting as the response the pattern associated with the template that passes the largest amount of light.

Another technique for template matching is to divide a given optical pattern into regions, which can be done with a photocell matrix, as illustrated in Figure 13.19a. To each photocell, a binary storage register is connected. This register is connected to a set of ten logical AND gates, each of which is associated with one of the input symbols. The inputs to each gate correspond to the inputs associated with each template, as is illustrated in Figure 13.19b for the number 4.

The limitations on the pattern recognition capabilities of the linear machine and the minimum-distance classifier are the same as the limitations placed on single-level threshold realizations of Boolean functions treated in Chapter 10. That is, the functions $g_i(X)$ must be linearly separable.

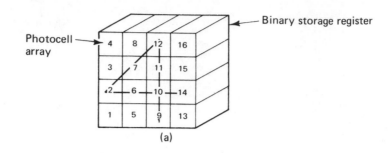

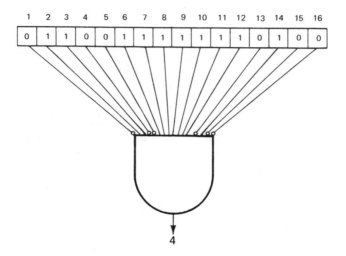

Figure 13.19.   (a) Template match with photocell matrix. (b) Shift register with 4 stored in it and template for 4 given by logical AND gate.

NONLINEAR DISCRIMINANTS

Regions in a hyperspace that are not linearly separable can often be separated with nonlinear surfaces. For example, the realization of binary parity functions cannot be accomplished with the linear hyperplanes associated with single-level threshold logic. However, it is entirely possible to realize parity functions with more than one level of logic as shown by the Blum realization in Chapter 12. The hyperplanes associated with multilevel threshold functions therefore must be nonlinear. For example, the hyper-

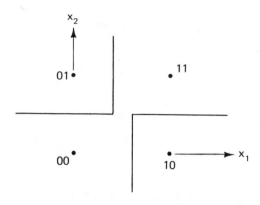

Figure 13.20. Nonlinear hyperplane realization for two-variable parity.

planes for two-variable parity appear as in Figure 13.20. It is clear from Figure 13.20 that the hyperplanes are not linear over the entire space but that they are linear over some of it. Thus, these hyperplanes are called piecewise linear, and the resulting implementation is called a piecewise linear machine.

Assume r finite point sets $\mathcal{P}_1, \mathcal{P}_2, \ldots, \mathcal{P}_r$, where each of the ith point sets consists of L_i points. Now, define the Euclidean distance $E(X, \mathcal{P}_i)$ from the arbitrary point X to the point set $\mathcal{P}_i$ by

$$E(X, \mathcal{P}_i) = \min_{j=1, \cdots, L} |X - P_i^{(j)}| \tag{13.20}$$

the minimum distance between X and each point in $\mathcal{P}_i$. Now, define a minimum-distance classifier with respect to the point sets $\mathcal{P}_1, \mathcal{P}_2, \ldots, \mathcal{P}_r$ which classifies a given pattern X into the category associated with the closest point set. Here, the $P_i^{(j)}$ are the points associated in $\mathcal{P}_i$.

Therefore, as before, define for each $i = 1, \ldots, r$ the function

$$g_i(X) = \max_{j=1, \cdots, L_i} \{P_i^{(j)} \cdot X - \frac{1}{2} P_i^{(i)} \cdot P_i^{(j)}\} \tag{13.21}$$

Thus, we have defined a minimum-distance classifier with respect to L_i different prototypes in each pattern class. This suggests a different notation for the general form for the discriminant functions,

$$g_i(X) = \max_{j=1, \ldots, L_i} \{g_i^{(j)}(X)\} \quad i = 1, \ldots, r \tag{13.22}$$

where each $g_i^{(j)}(X)$ is dependent on the subsidiary discriminant functions, as given by

$$g_i^{(j)}(X) = w_{ii}^{(j)}(x_1) + w_1 2^{(j)} x_2 + \cdots + w_{id}^{(j)} x_d + w_{i0}^{(j)} \quad (13.23)$$

The function $g_i(X)$ is dependent on the subsidiary discriminant functions, and the final discriminant functions are then piecewise linear functions. A model of this type of discrimination system is shown in Figure 13.21. The

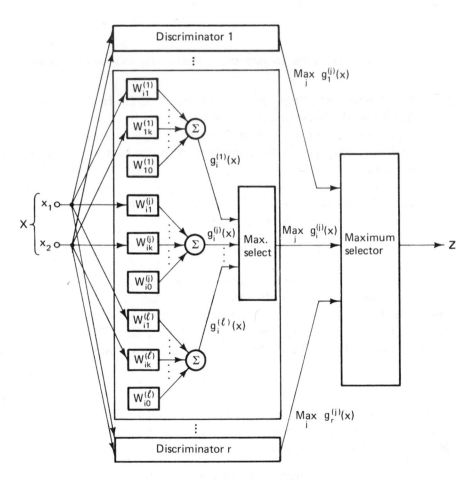

Figure 13.21.   Piecewise linear pattern recognition system.

piecewise linear machine is a general machine for dealing with nonlinearly separable functions, and the minimum-distance classifier is just a special case.

QUADRIC DISCRIMINANT FUNCTIONS

Another method for realizing nonlinearly separable functions makes use of nonlinear discriminant functions. A special kind of nonlinear discriminant is the quadric discriminant function:

$$g_i(X) = \sum_{i=1}^{N} w_{ii} x_i^2 + \sum_{j=1}^{N-1} \sum_{k=j+1}^{N} w_{jk} x_j x_k + \sum_{j=1}^{N} w_j x_j + w_0 \quad (13.24)$$

The parameters associated with quadric discriminant functions are summarized as follows:

1. N weights as coefficients of x_i^2 terms $\cdots w_{ii}$.
2. N weights as coefficients of x_j terms $\cdots w_j$.
3. $N(N-1)/2$ weights as coefficients of $x_i x_j$ terms, $k \neq j \cdots w_{ik}$.

Note that the w_{jk} terms can be described as follows:

$$\left.\begin{array}{c} w_{(N-1)N} \\ \vdots \\ w_{45} \quad \cdots \quad w_{3N} \\ w_{23} \quad \cdots \quad w_{2N} \\ w_{12} \quad \cdots \quad w_{1N} \end{array}\right\} N-1$$

$$\underbrace{\hspace{4cm}}_{N}$$

and that there are $N(N-1)/2$ terms in this representation. Since the discriminant function here is complex, it is desirable to represent $g_i(X)$ in matrix form. Let matrix A have components given by

$$a_{jj} = w_{jj} \qquad j = 1, \ldots, N$$

$$a_{jk} = \frac{1}{2} w_{jk} \qquad j, k = 1, \ldots, N, j \neq k$$

Also, let

$$B = \begin{bmatrix} b_1 \\ \vdots \\ b_N \end{bmatrix}$$

where

$$b_j = w_j, \qquad j = 1, \cdots, N$$

and let $C = w_0$.

Now,

$$g(X) = X'AX + X'B + C \qquad (13.25)$$

The term $X'AX$ is called the quadratic form.

The decision surfaces of this type of machine are sections of second-degree surfaces called quadric surfaces.

The physical implementation of quadric discriminants is not much more complicated than that for linear discriminant functions; however, it is certainly more expensive.

A model for the quadric discriminator is given in Figure 13.22. It is clear that the quadric processor requires several multipliers, which makes it considerably more expensive than a linear machine. There are N compo-

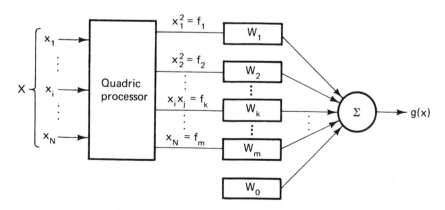

Figure 13.22.   Quadric discriminator.

nents of x_i^2 terms, $N(N-i)/2$ components of $x_i x_1$ terms, and N components of the x_i terms. Thus, there are $N/2(1+N)$ multipliers for N input dimensions.

Now, examine another form for a quadric discriminator:

$$g(X) = w_1 f_1 + w_2 f_2 + \cdots + w_m f_m + w_0 \qquad (13.26)$$

where each of the f_i is a quadric function.

This representation is a linear discriminant function on the outputs of the nonlinear processors.

SYNTACTICAL (STRUCTURAL) PATTERN RECOGNITION

In the previous sections we have introduced the well-known decision-theoretic (also known as discriminant or geometrical) approach to the pattern recognition problem. In this approach, a set of characteristic measurements or features are extracted from the patterns and interpreted as the coordinates of points in a vector (feature) space. The classification problem is reduced to partitioning the feature space into regions corresponding to patterns within the same class. Although most of the development in pattern recognition research in the last 15 years has dealt with the decision-theoretic approach and its applications, as early as 1960 a number of investigators recognized its limitations. For example, consider the class of problems generally known as scene analysis. In this class of recognition problems, the patterns are quite complex and the number of features required is often quite large, which makes the idea of using the structural information that describes each pattern to simplify its representation very attractive.

The basic idea behind this approach, which has been termed *syntactic* (or *structural*) *pattern* recognition, is to describe complex patterns in terms of a hierarchical composition of simpler patterns. For example, letters of the alphabet can be described in terms of strokes [23]. This approach draws an analogy between the hierarchical (treelike) structure of patterns and the syntax of languages; see Figure 13.23 and Figure 13.24. Patterns are specified as being built up from subpatterns in various ways of composition, just as phrases and sentences are built up by concatenating words, and words are built up by concatenating characters. Naturally, this approach is useful if and only if the fundamental subpatterns selected, called *pattern primitives*, are much easier to classify than the patterns themselves.

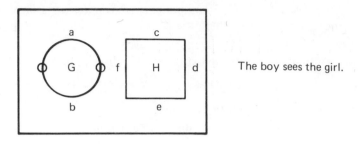

Figure 13.23.   (a) Picture of geometric figures (b) sentence.

Two important elements in the syntactical approach to pattern recognition are the pattern description language and the grammar of the pattern description language. The pattern description language provides the structural description of patterns in terms of a set of pattern primitives and their composition operation; the grammar specifies the rules governing the composition of primitives into patterns. In the syntactical approach, after each primitive within a pattern is identified, the recognition process is accomplished by performing a syntax analysis (or parsing) of the sentence describing the given pattern to determine whether or not it is syntactically correct with respect to the specified grammar. Also, the syntax analysis produces a structural description of the sentence representing the given pattern (usually in the form of a tree structure). The most attractive aspect

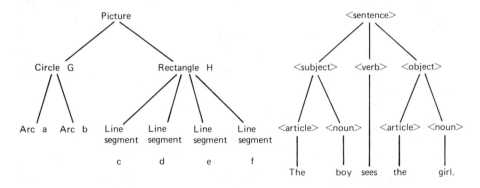

Figure 13.24.   Hierarchical structural description of (a) picture (b) sentence.

of this approach is its capability to use the recursive nature of a grammar (applying the grammatical rules any number of times) to express in a very compact way some basic structural characteristics of infinite sentences. Again, for this approach to be practical, recognition of the simple pattern primitives and their relationships, as represented by the composition operations, is essential.

The composition operations defined by the pattern description language can usually be expressed in terms of logical and/or mathematical operations. For example, if we define concatenation as the only relation (composition operation) used in describing patterns, then the rectangle of Figure 13.25a would be represented in terms of the primitive patterns of Figure 13.25b as the string "aaabbcccdd." Furthermore, if we used the symbol "+" for the "head-to-tail concatenation," then the rectangle of Figure 13.25a would be represented by "a + a + a + b + b + c + c + c + d + d," and its corresponding treelike structure would be represented by Figure 13.26. Also, the same principles can be applied to numerical patterns as shown in Figure 13.26b for the case of the structural decomposition of pattern 8.

Other alternative representations of the structural information of a pattern have been discussed in the literature, for example the "relational graph"; see Fu [24]. However, the use of tree structures as opposed to a relational graph provides a direct way of adapting the techniques of formal language theory to the problem of compactly analyzing and representing patterns containing a significant structural content. For this reason, this approach has obtained greater popularity in recent years. Because of the adoption of the technique from formal language theory, the structural

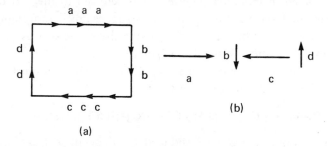

Figure 13.25.   A rectangle and its pattern primitives.

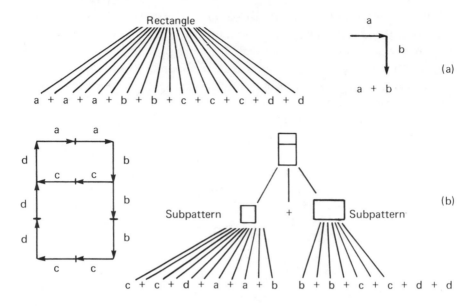

Figure 13.26. (a) Structural description of the rectangle of Figure 13.25. (b) Pattern 8 and its structural description.

approach is also sometimes called linguistic pattern recognition. In this area, Narasimhan [25] and Ledley [26] were the first to develop grammatical parsers for pattern recognition, while later Shaw [27] developed a picture description language and applied it to the analysis of bubble chamber photographs. In recent years, a significant number of research projects have been conducted in this area. The reader is referred to the text by Fu [24] for a complete description of the recent advances and a thorough presentation of this subject, which is clearly outside the scope of this book. Let us now turn our attention to the Theory of Fuzzy Sets, and its application to the pattern classification problem, which became an important area of research in the 1970s and into the 1980s.

FUZZY SET THEORY IN PATTERN RECOGNITION

In 1965 Lotfi A. Zadeh introduced the concept of Fuzzy Sets, laying the foundations for what is now called Fuzzy Set Theory. His original work was quickly followed by an intense interest in the subject with the resulting publication of numerous works both theoretical and practical in nature.

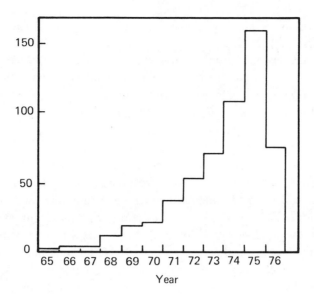

Figure 13.27. Histogram of papers on fuzzy systems against year of publication.

Figure 13.27 demonstrates the almost epidemic growth of research in this area, and the application of this theory, to areas such as: pattern recognition [41], clustering [28], political geography [32], decision making [29], robot planning [33, 34, 37], chromosome classification [36], medical diagnosis [30], engineering design [31], systems modeling [35], process control [38, 39], social interaction systems [42], and structural semantics [40], demonstrates the practical relevance of this subject. In this section, however, we will restrict our attention to the pattern recognition problem. Specifically, the fundamental definition of fuzzy sets and the associated set of valid operations will be given. Also, its application to the pattern classification problem will be presented.

Fuzzy Sets

In our natural language and description of the universe that surrounds us we often come in contact with classes of objects which do not have a precisely defined criteria of membership. For example, if we consider "the class of tall people," "the class of beautiful women," or "the class of numbers which are much greater than one," ambiguity arises with respect to membership. That is, how would a number such as 10 be classified with respect to the class of numbers much greater than 1. Clearly, the above classes do not constitute sets in the usual mathematical sense, but nevertheless play an important role in human thinking.

The concept to be explored here is that of a fuzzy set, a class or set with a continuum of grades of membership. These fuzzy sets constitute a natural generalization of classical sets in that a continuous rather than binary membership function is applied, i.e., in the context of sets there is a mapping $f_A(.)$ which associates with every element in the universe a value in $\{0, 1\}$ depending upon whether the element being evaluated "belongs to" or "does not belong to" the set A. On the other hand the mapping in fuzzy sets is to the interval $[0, 1]$ of real numbers with the value of $f_A(.)$ representing the degree of membership in set A. These concepts will become clear once the following set of definitions is presented.

Definitions: Let Ω be a space of points (objects), with an element of Ω denoted by x. Hence, $\Omega = \{x\}$.

A fuzzy set A in Ω is characterized by a membership (also called characteristic) function $f_A(.)$ which associates with each point in Ω a real number in the interval $[0, 1]$, with the value of $f_A(x)$ representing the degree of membership of x in A. Thus, the nearer the value of $f_A(x)$ to unity, the higher the degree of membership of x in A. Clearly, when A is a set in the ordinary sense, its membership function takes only two values 0 and 1, with $f_A(x) = 1$ or 0 depending on whether x "belongs" or "does not belong" to A.

For example, consider Ω to be the real line R and let A be the fuzzy set of numbers greater than 1. Then, one can give a precise, although subjective, characterization of A by specifying $f_A(.)$ on R. Some of the values such a function may take are: $f_A(0) = 0$, $f_A(1) = 0$, $f_A(5) = 0.01$, $f_A(10) = 0.2$, $f_A(100) = 0.95$, and $f_A(500) = 1$.

In some cases, as will be seen later in our discussion of fuzzy sets as applied to the pattern classification problem, it may be convenient to concretize the concept of an element or point "belonging to" a fuzzy set A by selecting two values ϵ_1 and ϵ_2 in the interval $[0, 1]$ and agreeing that

(a) x belongs to A if $f_A(x) \geq 1 - \epsilon_1$,
(b) x does not belong to A if $f_A(x) \leq \epsilon_2$, and
(c) x is indeterminate relative to A if $\epsilon_2 < f_A(x) < 1 - \epsilon_1$.

In effect, this amounts to using a three-valued characteristic function, with $f_A(x) = 1$ if $x \in A$; $f_A(x) = 1/2$, say if x is indeterminate relative to A; and $f_A(x) = 0$ if $x \notin A$. For the purpose of our discussion and whenever no confusion is possible we will use the symbol $f(.)$ instead of $f_A(.)$ for the characteristic function.

Although this concept of a characteristic function allowing the degree of membership of an element to a set to range continuously through the interval $[0, 1]$ is in itself appealing, it requires further extension if a fuzzy set thus defined is to assume a role similar to that of classical sets in mathematics. What do we mean by the complement of a fuzzy set, or by the union, or intersection of two fuzzy sets? If a car, x, belongs 0.7 to the fuzzy set of sleek cars and 0.9 to the set of fast cars, then what degree of membership to the sets of "not-sleek," "sleek-or-fast," or "sleek-and-fast" cars does it have? To answer this question one may use the consistency argument, i.e., the theory of fuzzy set operations must reduce to classical set theory when the degrees of membership are restricted to the binary values, $\{0, 1\}$. This consistency argument forces at least the following constraints upon the operations on fuzzy sets:

$$f(x) = 0 \rightarrow \overline{f(x)} = 1; \tag{13.27}$$

$$f(x) = 1 \rightarrow \overline{f(x)} = 0; \tag{13.28}$$

$$f_A(x) = 0, f_B(x) = 0 \rightarrow f_{A \cup B}(x) = 0, f_{A \cap B}(x) = 0; \tag{13.29}$$

$$f_A(x) = 0, f_B(x) = 1 \rightarrow f_{A \cup B}(x) = 1, f_{A \cap B}(x) = 0; \tag{13.30}$$

$$f_A(x) = 1, f_B(x) = 1 \rightarrow f_{A \cup B}(x) = 1, f_{A \cap B}(x) = 1 \tag{13.31}$$

There are further constraints if the natural numerical order relation of degrees of membership is to be consistent with the set theoretical concepts of union and intersection. We must have that degree of membership in the union of A and B (member of either) is not less than membership in either or,

$f_{A \cup B}(x) \geq f_A(x)$ and $f_{A \cup B}(x) \geq f_B(x)$, which may be expressed:

$$f_{A \cup B}(x) \geq \max\{f_A(x), f_B(x)\} \tag{13.32}$$

A similar consistency argument for the intersection of fuzzy sets A and B will require that:

$$f_{A \cap B}(x) \leq f_A(x) \text{ and } f_{A \cap B}(x) \leq f_B(x), \text{ or}$$

$$f_{A \cap B}(x) \leq \min\{f_A(x), f_B(x)\}$$

$$(13.33)$$

However, we may need not carry this argument any further as Gaines [44] has shown that the consistency argument results in a set of equations defining operations on fuzzy sets identical to those proposed by Zadeh in his original work. Given the clarity of Zadeh's presentation, we now define operations on fuzzy sets based on this orginal set of definitions.

1. A fuzzy set is empty if and only if its membership function is identically zero on Ω.
2. Two fuzzy sets A and B are equal, written $A = B$, if and only if $f_A(x) = f_B(x)$ for all x in Ω (also written as $f_A = f_B$).
3. The complement of a fuzzy set (A) is denoted by A' and is defined by Equation 13.34:

$$f_{A'} = 1 - f_A$$

$$(13.34)$$

As in the case of ordinary sets the notion of containment plays a central role in the case of fuzzy sets. This notion and the related notions of union and intersection are formally defined as follows:

1. Containment. A is contained in B (or A is a subset of B) if and only if $f_A \leq f_B$.

2. Union. The union of two fuzzy sets A and B with respective characteristic functions $f_A(.)$ and $f_B(.)$ is a fuzzy set C, written as $C = A \cup B$, whose characteristic function is related to those of A and B by

$$f_C(x) = \max\{f_A(x), f_B(x)\}, \forall x \in \Omega$$

$$(13.35)$$

Note that the $\cup$ operation on fuzzy sets has the associative property, that is, $A \cup (B \cup C) = (A \cup B) \cup C$.

3. Intersection. The intersection of two fuzzy sets A and B with respective characteristic functions $f_A(.)$ and $f_B(.)$ is a fuzzy set C, written as $C = A \cap B$, whose characteristic function is related to those of A and B by

$$f_C(x) = \min\{f_A(x), f_B(x)\}, \forall x \in \Omega \qquad (13.36)$$

Several other properties of fuzzy sets could be described such as the distributive law and the fuzzy set theory counterpart to De Morgan's Law. However, this material is well covered in the literature; see the classical work by Zadeh [43] or the excellent survey paper by Gaines [44]. Instead, we will now briefly describe how fuzzy set theory can be applied to the pattern classification problem. Other applications of fuzzy set theory will not be discussed here as they are beyond the scope of this book.

Fuzzy Sets and Pattern Classification

Let $x^1, \ldots, x^n$ be given members of a class of patterns or set A in the universe, Ω. In pattern classification we are interested in identifying those properties of $x^1, \ldots, x^n$ which they have in common and which, in aggregate, define the pattern class or set A. The notion of a fuzzy set provides a natural as well as convenient way of giving a more concrete meaning to this problem. Specifically, let f^i denote the value of the characteristic function, f, of a fuzzy set A at a point x^i in Ω. A collection of pairs $\{(x^1, f^1), \ldots, (x^n, f^n)\}$ or for short $\{(x^i, f^i)\}^n$ will be called a collection of samples or observations from A, i.e., the training set. The problem is then to estimate the characteristic function of the set A from the samples $(x^1, f^1), \ldots, (x^n, f^n)$. Once an estimate of the characteristic function, f, has been constructed it can be used to compute the values of f at points other than $x^1, \ldots, x^n$.

An estimate of f employing the given finite set of samples $(x^1, f^1), \ldots, (x^n, f^n)$ will be denoted by $\tilde{f}$ or, more explicitly, by $\tilde{f}(x; \{(x^i, f^i)\}^n)$. To make this problem meaningful, one must have some a priori information about the class of functions to which f belongs. As in interpolation theory, this approach involves choosing—usually on purely heuristic grounds—a class of estimates of

$$f : F = \{f(x;\lambda) | \lambda \in R'\}$$

and finding that member of this family which fits, or fits "best" the given samples $(x^1, f^1), \ldots, (x^n, f^n)$.

A special case of this procedure which applies to ordinary rather than fuzzy sets is the discriminant function technique used in previous sections for distinguishing between two sets of patterns via a separating hyperplane. Stated in terms of a single set of patterns, the problem in question is essentially that of finding, if it exists, a hyperplane L passing through the origin of $R'(\Omega = R'$, by assumption) such that given the points $x^1, \ldots, x^n$ belonging to the set A, they are all on the same side of the hyperplane. In this case since A is a set, $f^1 = f^2 = \cdots = f^n = 1$. In effect, $f(x;\lambda)$ is of the form

$$f(x;\lambda) = 1 \text{ for } \langle x, \lambda \rangle \geq 0,$$
$$f(x;\lambda) = 0 \text{ for } \langle x, \lambda \rangle < 0, \tag{13.37}$$

where $\langle x, \lambda \rangle$ denotes the scalar product of x and λ, and the problem is to find a λ in R' such that

$$\langle x^i, \lambda \rangle \geq 0 \text{ for } i = 1, \ldots, n$$

Hence, f is the discriminant function in pattern classification problems. Note that from our previous discussion the pattern classification problem has been stated in terms of finding the characteristic function corresponding to a fuzzy set A.

Finally, it is noted that in most practical situations the a priori information about the characteristic function of a fuzzy set is not sufficient to construct an estimate of $f(x)$ which is "optimal" in a meaningful sense. Thus on many occasions one is forced to use heuristic rules for estimating $f(x)$. [43]

SUMMARY

We have examined several aspects of pattern recognition from input system through discrimination. The output system has not been discussed because its form depends more critically on the application than does that of the other parts of the system. Generally, the output from the discriminator is in a form that can easily be interfaced to digital or analog hardware such as printers, displays, loudspeakers, and computers.

The sophisticated reader may lament the fact that his "pet" technique of pattern recognition has been left out of this chapter. However, we hope that this introduction will give you a relatively broad brush of this fascinating area and that you will use the references as additional reading.

EXERCISES

1. Discuss the relative differences in scanning with horizontal versus vertical lines, especially with respect to image size and position.

2. Explain why it is difficult to use a spiral scan with systems that have a small number of resolution elements. Use examples in your answer.

3. Devise an algorithm for contour tracing that eliminates as many "traps" as possible.

4. Find the Fourier transform of the letters O, A, and T centered in a 5×8 array. Note features that are different between characters. (It is recommended that a digital computer be used to solve this problem.)

5. Find the Walsh-Hadamard transform of the letters O, A, and T centered in an 8×8 array. Note features that are different between characters. (It is recommended that a digital computer be used to solve this problem.)

6. Show that $g(X)$ in Equation 13.14 is the perpendicular bisector of the line between X_1 and X_2.

7. Show that $(-1)^{p(x,\mu)}$, where $p(x, \mu) = \sum_{i=1}^{N-1} \mu_i x_i$, generates Walsh sequences for x and μ integers, and for increasing integer values of x and μ, generates Hadamard matrices. Note that N must be odd for Walsh sequences and a multiple of 4 for Hadamard matrices of order higher than 2.

8. Draw a block diagram for the quadric machine described by Equation 13.26.

REFERENCES

1. PATRICK, E. A., *Fundamentals of Pattern Recognition*, Prentice-Hall, Englewood Cliffs, N.J., 1972.
2. SEBEYSTIAN, G. S., *Decision Making Process in Pattern Recognition*, Macmillan, New York, 1962.
3. POLS, Lewis C. W., "Real-Time Recognition of Spoken Words," *IEEE Transactions on Computers*, Vol. C-20, No. 9, September 1971, pp. 972–978.
4. GLENN, James W., and Myron H. HITCHCOCK, "With a Speech Pattern Classifier, Computer Listens to Its Master's Voice," *Electronics*, Vol. 44, No. 10, May 10, 1971.
5. TROXEL, D. E., F. F. LEE, and S. J. MASON, "A Reading Machine for the Blind," *Digest of the 7th International Conference on Medical and Biological Engineering*, 1967.
6. KOLERS, Paul A., and Murray EDEN, eds., *Recognizing Patterns: Studies in Living and Automatic Systems*, M.I.T. Press, Cambridge, Mass., 1968.
7. LETTVIN, J. Y., H. R. MATURANA, W. S. MCCULLOCH, and W. H. PITTS, "What the Frog's Eye Tells the Frog's Brain," *Proceedings of the IRE*, Vol. 47, 1959, pp. 1940–1951.
8. HARTLINE, H. K., and F. RATLIFF, "Inhibitory Interaction of Receptor Units in the Eye of Limulus," *Journal of General Physiology*, Vol. 39, 1957, pp. 357–376.
9. HALL, E. L., R. P. KRUGER, S. J. DWYER, III, D. L. HALL, R. W. MCLOREN, and G. S. LODWICK, "A Survey of Preprocessing and Feature Extraction Techniques for Radiographic Images," *IEEE Transactions on Computers*, Vol. C-20, No. 9, September 1971, pp. 1032–1044.
10. UHR, Leonard, ed., *Pattern Recognition*, Wiley, New York, 1966.
11. HUBER, William A., "MINOS III—Adaptive Learning/Digital Computer Data Classifier," *U.S. Army Electronics Command R&D Technical Report ECOM-3135*, Fort Monmouth, W. Va., June 1969.
12. NELSON, G. D., and D. M. LEVY, "A Dynamic Programming Approach to Selection of Pattern Features," *IEEE Transactions on Systems Science and Cybernetics*, Vol. SSC-4, July 1968, pp. 145–150.
13. MUCCIARDI, A.N., and E. E. GOSE, "A Comparison of Seven Techniques for Choosing Subsets of Pattern Recognition Properties," *IEEE Transactions on Computers*, Vol. C-20, No. 9, September 1971, pp. 1023–1031.
14. COOLEY, J. W., and J. W. TUKEY, "An Algorithm for the Machine Calculation of Complex Fourier Series," *Math. Comput.*, Vol. 19, No. 90, 1965, pp. 297–301.
15. NIEDERJOHN, Russell J., and Ian B. THOMAS, "Computer Recognition of Phonemic Segments in Connected Speech," *Proceedings of the National Electronics Conference*, Vol. 26, 1970.
16. GOODMAN, Joseph W., *Introduction to Fourier Optics*, McGraw-Hill, New York, 1968.
17. GINSBURG, Arthur P., "Psychological Correlates of a Model of the Human Visual System," M.S. Thesis, School of Engineering, Air Force Institute of Technology, June 1971.
18. GOLOMB, S. W., et al., *Digital Communications*, Prentice-Hall, Englewood Cliffs, N.J., 1964.

19. ANDREWS, H. C., "Multidimensional Rotations in Feature Selection," *IEEE Transactions on Computers*, Vol. C-20, No. 9, September 1971, pp. 1045–1051.

20. NILSON, N. J., *Learning Machines—Foundations of Trainable Pattern Classifying Systems*, McGraw-Hill, New York, 1965.

21. NAGY, G., "State of the Art in Pattern Recognition," *Proceedings of the IEEE*, Vol. 56, No. 5, May 1968, pp. 836–862.

22. FU, K. S., *Sequential Methods in Pattern Recognition and Machine Learning*, Academic Press, New York, 1968.

23. LINDSAY, P. H. and D. A. NORMAN, *Human Information Processing*, Academic Press, New York, 1972.

24. FU, K. S., *Syntactic Methods in Pattern Recognition*, Academic Press, New York, 1974.

25. NARASHIMHAM, R., Information and Control 7, 1964, p. 151.

26. LEDLEY, R. S., *Science* 146, 1964, pp. 216–223.

27. SHAW, A. C., Information and Control 14, 1969, pp. 9–52.

28. BEZDEK, J. C., "Cluster validity with fuzzy sets", *Journal of Cybernetics*, 3, 1974, pp. 58–73.

29. BAAS, S. M. and KWAKERNAAK, H., "Rating and ranking of multiple-aspect alternatives using fuzzy sets," Memorandum #73, Department of Applied Mathematics, Twente University of Technology, Enschede, The Netherlands, April 1975

30. ALBIN, M., "Fuzzy sets and their application to medical diagnosis," Ph.D dissertation, Department of Mathematics, University of California, Berkeley, Ca., 1975

31. BECKER, J. M., "A structural design process," Ph.D Thesis, Department of Civil Engineering, University of California, Berkeley, Ca., 1973.

32. GALE, S., "Conjectures on many-valued logic, regions, and criteria for conflict resolution," Proc. 1975 Int. Synp. Multiple-Valued Logic, IEEE 75CH0959-7C, pp. 212–225.

33. GOGUEN, J. A., "On fuzzy robot planning," In ZADEH, L. A., FU, K. S., TANAKA, K. and SHIMURA, M., Eds., *Fuzzy Sets and Their Applications to Cognitive Decision Processes*, Academic Press, New York, pp. 429–447.

34. KLING, R., "Fuzzy-PLANNER: Reasoning with inexact concepts in a procedural problem-solving language," *Journal of Cybernetics*, 4 1974, pp. 105–122.

35. FELLINGER, W. L., "Specifications for fuzzy systems modeling language," Ph.D Thesis, Oregon State University, Corvallis, 1974.

36. LEE, E. T., "Shape-Oriented chromosome classification," *IEEE Trans. Syst. Man Cybern.*, SMC-5, 1975, pp. 629–632.

37. LEFAIVRE, R. A., "The representation of fuzzy knowledge," *Journal Cybernetics*, 4, 1974, pp. 57–66.

38. MAMDANI, E. H., and ASSILIAN, S., "Prescriptive Method for deriving control policy in a fuzzy logic controller," *Int. Journal Man-Machine Studies*, 7, 1975, pp. 1–13.

39. MAMDANI, E. H., and PROCYK, T. J., "Application of fuzzy logic to controller design based on linguistic protocol," 3rd Eur. Meeting Cybern. Syst. Res., Vienna, 1976.

40. RIEGER, B., "Fuzzy Structural Semantics. On a generative model of vague natural language meaning," 3rd Eur. Meeting Cybern. Syst. Res., Vienna, 1976.

41. SIY, P., and CHEN, C. S., "Fuzzy logic for handwritten numerical character recognition," *IEEE Trans. Syst. Man Cybern.*, SMC-4, 1974, pp. 570–575.
42. WENSTOP, F., "Deductive verbal model of organizations," *Int. Journal Man-Machine Studies*, 8, 1976, pp. 293–311.
43. ZADEH, L. A., FU, K. S., TANAKA, K., and SHIMURA, M., Eds., *Fuzzy Sets and Their Applications to Cognitive and Decision Processes*, Academic Press, New York, 1975.
44. GAINES, B. R., "Foundations of fuzzy reasoning," *Int. Journal Man-Machine Studies*, 8, 1976, pp. 623–668.

14

Computer Vision

The principles and techniques used to identify patterns in usually specific visual fields such as reading documents were introduced in Chapter 13. Researchers in the area of computer vision have taken the next step of looking at the more general problem of extracting useful information from representations of complex visual scenes. Much of the original work in computer vision was aimed at solving the most general of problems in order to make a machine "see." However, the largest application space for the initial results of this work is in the restricted set of environments associated with automatic inspection and sensor-controlled manipulation, including robotics, biomedical, and satellite imaging systems. In fact, it has been said that if the pattern recognition work had earlier been diverted to inspection and robotics, the research payoff would have come sooner and more general principles of vision would now be known. Be that as it may, the research results of the last ten years have established several principles for gathering, analyzing, and interpreting visual scenes by machines.

This chapter examines the problems of machine vision in both general and restricted environments and describes various analysis techniques and methods for interpreting the data before discussing some present and potential applications of computer vision.

VISION

The ultimate goal of computer vision researchers has been to approximate as closely as possible the human vision system. Consider for a moment the principal characteristics of the human vision system.

The absolute sensitivity of the human eye depends on adaptation in response to light intensity and is accomplished by a combination of the action of the pupil and biochemical changes in the eye. However, the sensitivity of the dark-adapted eye is of the order of a single quantum. Human ability to judge colors, sizes, and shapes consistently under wide ranges of illumination color, shadows, and intensities is remarkable [1, 2]. For example, the color reproduction of photographs taken in tungsten lamp illumination and in bright sunlight with the same film and filtering is noticeably different; yet our perception of colors while in these as well as other environments remains remarkably constant. The visual process requires that the eye-brain system interpret the images projected onto the retina. These two-dimensional images contain all the information from which a person gleans the characteristics of and relationships between objects in the environment. Since there must be a mapping from the retina images to the interpretation of the environment, it is conjectured that individual perceptual learning is involved in the visual process [3]. The resulting perceptual process is described as a table look-up wherein the visual cues on the retina are compared with relevant stored data. The resulting perception is the closest stored hypothesis. This system allows behavior to proceed in the absence of the complete information needed to analytically describe the scene. Thus, a human being can deal effectively with insufficient or shadowy illumination as well as with other difficult visual situations.

This process suggests a technique that may be appropriate for computer vision systems. Here a data base containing the elemental characteristics of visual scenes is used to compare the input visual cues to determine the appropriate behavior for the present perceived environment. If this type of system is incorporated, we can anticipate that our computer vision system will respond to some of the inputs in a manner similar to the way a person responds. In fact, these comparisons suggest a methodology for testing and evaluating such systems.

Consider the images in Figure 14.1 known as the Muller-Lyer illusion, in which the vertical segments appear to be of different heights when, in fact, they are the same length. In terms of the stored model theory, an explanation of this illusion is that the leftmost image represents an outside corner of a square object, the rightmost image represents an inside corner of, for example, a room, and the perceptual system shrinks one and enlarges the other to compensate for the distortion caused by perspective [3]. The theory is that because the drawings are incomplete we are comparing and we are compensating in our perception to correspond to a built-in visual model of a real object and that the phenomenon of size constancy creates the illusion. Thus, it can be suggested that the elemental line relationships that create the Muller-Lyer illusion be incorporated into our computer vision system.

Another illusion, the impossible triangle devised by S. Lionel and R. Penrose shown in Figure 14.2, can be explained as follows: our internal table contains information on the interpretation of depth which, based on the fact that the line drawing contains incomplete information with respect to our table, is interpreted as impossible. This illusion illustrates the problem of dealing with two-dimensional projections of three-dimensional images, for if one were to look at the impossible triangle from a different angle it would look totally possible, as the figure illustrates. It is not too difficult to imagine computer vision systems in which this type of illusion could occur, especially in fixed environments such as manufacturing or inspection situations.

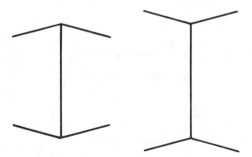

Figure 14.1. Muller–Lyer illusion. The theory suggests that stored interpretations of incomplete visual cues create the illusion.

Figure 14.2.   Impossible triangle.

Finally, the problems of dealing with incomplete information are amply illustrated in the simple drawing of Figure 14.3. This is the Ponzo or railway lines illusion, said to be caused by the depth distortion that the perceptual system applies to the angled lines. Here the model in the perceptual system may be said to be expecting the size of objects to decrease as they get "further away." Our perceptual system interprets the

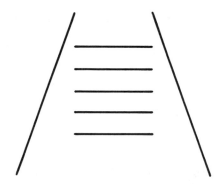

Figure 14.3.   Ponzo or railway lines illusion. The upper lines appear longer, but all horizontal lines are the same length.

"more distant" lines as longer than the "closer" lines when, in fact, the horizontal lines are of equal length.

These simple illusions and their explanations are interesting examples of the complexity and the elemental problems of endowing a machine with visual capabilities. The interested reader will find the first three references at the end of this chapter worthwhile reading.

THE GENERAL MACHINE VISION PROBLEM

The process of endowing a machine with vision requires a system of input, storage, processing, and analysis not unlike that used for general pattern recognition systems. The input for general vision systems requires that as much detail about the environment as is possible be gathered. Thus, most of these systems use high resolution raster scans with from 256×256 to 1024×1024 pixels. Each pixel often is further divided into levels of intensity called gray scale. With four levels of intensity, each scan contains from 131,072 to 2,097,152 bits (65,536 to 262,144 bytes). Some systems require color information, which triples the amount of information contained in each scan of a scene.

Real-time visual processing systems often use video systems or charge-coupled device (CCD) imaging systems (solid-state cameras). Systems used to deal with photographic types of data such as that gathered by the Earth Resources satellites are scanned by high resolution, slow speed, laser-based scanners. All these techniques create massive amounts of data.

One of the difficult and costly aspects of general computer vision systems is handling all the data effectively, especially in real time. For example, a simple 64-Kbyte scanner will completely fill the directly addressable memory of a 16-bit computer like the PDP-11. These systems can thus consume great amounts of computer time and memory space just to gather the data, much less to process it. For instance, a computer with a 500-nanosecond cycle time in a 16-bit wide memory requires 16 milliseconds just to access a single 64-Kbyte scan without doing any processing whatsoever.*

The representation of this image data, both in raw (scanned) form and subsequent to its processing, is another problem in dealing with general vision systems. The problem exists because the format determines the

---

* If done in a strictly sequential fashion; that is, with pipelining, overlap, and parallel processing excluded.

method and speed of access, and hence processing, of the data. Because of the problems associated with configuring and programming the processing system, most of the effort in vision research is in this area rather than in creating and evaluating new processing algorithms and heuristics.

A general model for a vision system is presented in Figure 14.4 to illustrate the kinds of function used. This model is based on a description given in Hanson and Riseman [4]. The image acquisition function is, as already indicated, a scene or photo scanning system that divides the image into pixels and stores them in a memory, or otherwise makes the data available to the low level vision-processing element. Low level processing refers to the manipulation and storage of the data associated with the direct representation of the image. This processing includes segmenting the scene into regions whose representation has some common characteristic such as intensity, color, or texture. Extracting these physical characteristics from a numerical representation is still an open problem for several constrained and for most general, unconstrained scenes. Thus, additional information such as stereopsis and range is added to some systems to aid in determining the segments of a scene, which introduce their own problems of complexity.

Intermediate level vision processing generally refers to the process of assigning higher level constructs to regions indicated by the low level processing of usually a two-dimensional representation of the image of interest. Items such as surfaces and volumes are identified by considering two-dimensional shape, highlights and shadows, perspective, and occlusion.

The high level vision-processing function is more dependent than the other levels of processing on the goals of the vision system because that function is responsible for assigning "meaning" to the scene by interpreting it in terms of what is desired in the real world. For example, the high level element of a manufacturing vision system which must determine that a particular desired part is behind an undesired part acts on data that may be only a partial representation of the scene. Here, all the data concerning the

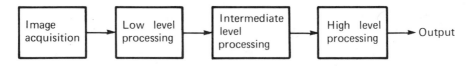

Figure 14.4.   General model of a vision processing system.

shapes, elements, and shadows in the scene are interpreted with respect to the goal of finding the desired part. This aspect of vision bears some similarity to the decision processes in pattern recognition systems, and some of the same techniques, such as pattern matching, can be applied.

The flow of processing in the general visual system is a mechanism whereby each intermediate step increases the state of knowledge of the visual scene. Each step also builds a data structure in a form that can be optimized for that stage. For example, one cannot deal with texture information from processing at the single pixel level but must build a data structure from the pixel information, from which texture can more easily be extracted. Another advantage also flows from the hierarchical approach to vision in that decisions concerning the content of the scene can be deferred until the last stage of the process. This concept has been formalized by Marr [5] as the "Principle of Least Commitment," which states that one should avoid premature interpretations in order to ensure that subsequent stages do not have to deal with biased information. In fact, Ehrich and Foith [6] state, "Distortions, misinterpretations, or loss of information due to the basic representations are likely to affect all subsequent processing modules and make the following analysis more difficult, if not impossible."

The preceding general model of vision is most appropriate for "real world" images like those we encounter in our daily lives. However, many practical vision systems are used in constrained environments, where the goals can easily be met after low or intermediate level processing. An image that we know a priori may contain cylindrical or square objects may be completely processed after the intermediate processing determines that the desired cylindrical object is present in the image.

The general goal of "duplicating" the human vision system may be impossible if we view the problem in the most general sense. However, according to Gregory's model [1] for explaining illusions, our general system, human vision, offered as the de facto existence proof, may indeed be highly sensitive to context. Thus, it may be more productive to consider constrained, goal-oriented visual environments instead.

GOAL-ORIENTED MACHINE VISION

As appealing as it may appear at first glance, the generality of a general vision environment is the quicksand in which many research projects have become mired. It has been argued [7] that generality in systems as complex as vision may not be as satisfactory as domain-specific systems for application-oriented vision systems. Some of the difficulties associated with designing a general vision system are related to the lack of context within which the system can narrow the number of choices (reduce the entropy). If the entropy can be decreased, then the computational burden of making a decision is reduced. The specialization of the system for an application domain allows one to use specific knowledge of the domain, often referred to as a knowledge-based system. Such systems have emerged recently as a means for applying artificial intelligence techniques. The following models, based on Bullock [7], are ways of using application-specific knowledge in different vision applications. Although application-specific knowledge is required, the models themselves are general.

The first class of vision problems considered is very similar to the pattern recognition task and its system model, as Figure 14.5 illustrates. The elements of processing include feature analysis, scene representation, and matching, and the model is called a matcher. The feature analysis function extracts from the scene the generic elements needed to build up an abstract representation of the scene to be presented to the matching device or comparator. The output is binary, indicating "match" or "no match." Systems such as this have applications in machine vision for automation and inspection of a single part or in other similarly simple, well-known environments.

In the next model, the goal of the system is to identify elements of a given set of objects and the locations of these elements in a scene. The

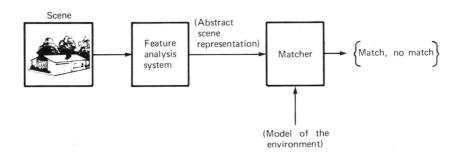

Figure 14.5. Simple matching model of a vision system for simple, well-known environments.

model, presented in Figure 14.6, has a larger "knowledge base," a set of object models, and the more complicated task of both identifying and locating objects in the scene. The matcher and evaluation system work together to test the alternatives and determine the most likely outputs. This kind of system, called a queueing system, can also deal with a wide variety of scenes such as a collection of weather patterns from several individual satellite photos. The range of applications for systems employing queueing models is itself wide, encompassing both a few object models in a single environment and larger sets of object models in several different environments.

The final model is actually more a class of models than a single model. Called interpretation, it involves feedback to the vision system in the form of questions about the features or context of an object. The questions can come either from within the vision system or from the system with which the vision system is interacting. Thus, an interpretation system that must deal with details of position, features, context, etc. is considerably more complex than a queueing or matching system, which only names or counts objects and/or identifies their positions. As a result, an interpretation system has more than one possible model. One such model, shown in Figure 14.7, has an internal goal subsystem that provides the "questions" to

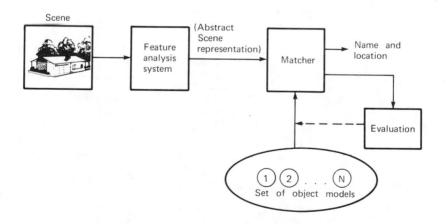

Figure 14.6. Queueing model of a vision system for dealing with a set of objects.

be answered by the vision system about a particular scene. The unique elements of the interpretation system of Figure 14.7 include two sets of object models, one preassigned by the type of task and the other built in situ according to the kinds of questions to be answered. The model builder sometimes uses new features prescribed by the model-building process. It is important to note that this model, only one of many possible using interpretation, depends on the type of vision task for both its detail and knowledge base.

These three approaches span a range of complexity from a simple model to the creation of models based on questions to be answered by the vision system. Bullock [7] has constructed a table of characteristics for these models with comparisons to the human vision system, part of which is reproduced in Table 14.1. The key properties of the models are the relatively small object set, the context set, and the low variances within them. As one examines the interpretation model for the upper range, it becomes clear that the number of models that must be tested grows quite

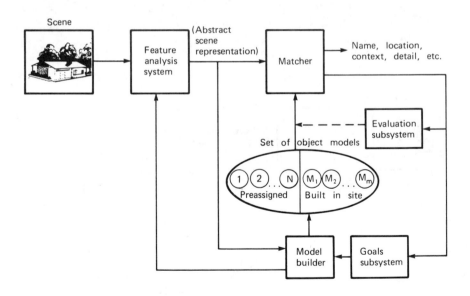

Figure 14.7. Interpretation model of a vision system with an internal goal subsystem.

Table 14.1.   Characteristics of Knowledge-Based Systems Versus Human Vision

Characteristic	Matching	Queueing	Interpretation	Human
Object set size	1	$10^2 - 10^3$	$10^2 - 10^3$	$\gg 10^6$
Object set variance	Low	Low	Low	High
Context set size	1	$< 10^3$	$< 10^3$	$\gg 10^6$
Context "understanding"	No	No	Yes	Yes
Context variation	Low	Low	Low	High
Frame size (pixels/frame)	10^4	10^4	10^{10}	10^7
Reliability (in %)	60–80	60–80	60–80	35–50

large, and the computational problem that the knowledge-based approach was supposed to alleviate is back once more. The exact point where knowledge-based systems and general systems converge depends on technology on the one hand and on our basic knowledge of vision on the other. For example, more insight into the segmentation problem may provide the techniques needed for better feature analysis in knowledge-based systems.

LOW LEVEL PROCESSING

Of all the types of processing in a vision system, low level processing must deal with the largest quantity of information. The goal of low level processing [8] is to transform the "large spatial array of pixels into a more compact description of the image in terms of visually distinct syntactic units and their characteristics, including location." The syntactic units of interest usually include regions in which one or more common attributes such as color, texture, shape, size, and location can be ascribed.

The creation and selection of attributes that one can use in vision systems has received a great deal of attention. Currently there is no consensus among researchers about which attributes form the complete generic set needed for a general vision system. In fact, most of the approaches utilize a multilevel system in which many techniques are used simultaneously.

One approach proposed by Hanson and Riseman [8, 9] is called the processing cone; it illustrates this process. The model, shown in Figure 14.8, was conceived as a parallel process that could be implemented with an array of microcomputers. Each computer accesses a window of data in a set of planes at the level below the present plane. The flow of processing is

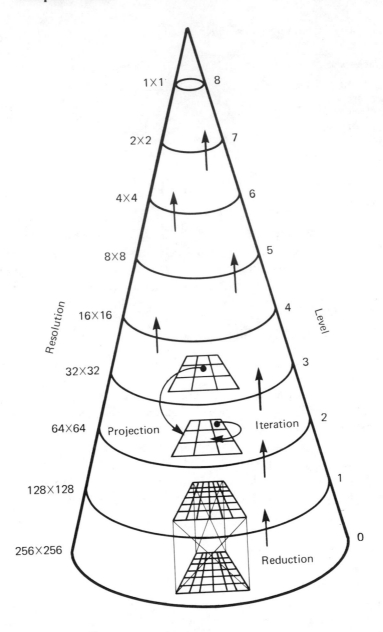

Figure 14.8. Processing cone model for low-level vision as a framework for applying segmentation, texture, edge detection, and other algorithms, heuristics, and so forth.

upward, with processing in each level working upward or across windows. At each level the goal is to decrease the resolution presented to the next higher level in the cone. Within the cone are three modes of operation— reduction, iteration and projection—each applied throughout the cone. Reduction proceeds upward through the cone as data are reduced in that direction. Because the windows in the cone do not overlap, reduction applied to the set of pixels in a window may identify it as being, for example, of a particular color or texture. Iteration is processing that occurs across windows at a single level of the cone. Since iteration works within a level, it provides a method for dealing only with interwindow interaction; iteration does not affect the resolution at that level or the data passed to the next level. Finally, the projection process reflects a feedback mechanism for information at a higher level to affect processing in lower levels.

EDGES, BOUNDARIES, AND REGIONS IN LOW LEVEL PROCESSING

Within the processing cone, specific functions are performed to accomplish the low level processing task. In most systems, edges are used as the basic discriminant by which boundaries between potential regions are determined. Boundaries are then used to test for regions, where a region is a set of pixels in which a common attribute or common attributes are present. Thus, the usual processing flow is from edges to boundaries to regions up the processing cone.

Edges in a scene represent local points of discontinuity in a measure of the scene such as intensity or color and are characterized by a location and direction. Detection of edges depends on the form of input and the goal of the vision system. For example, a system whose input creates binary pixels in a high contrast scene can make use of contour tracing, described in Chapter 13. However, in systems with multivalued pixels and/or scenes with texture, it is usually more effective to use a spatial differentiation technique to find edges [10]. Most spatial differentiation schemes examine a small number of pixels around each pixel to determine the relative intensities. The intensity gradient at each pixel is found and then tracked to find the edges. For example, the gradient of the pixel at location (x,y) is found for each of the eight directions around the location, that is, $G_1(x,y) \cdots G_8(x_1,y)$. The gradient at that pixel location can then be defined as

$$G(x,y) = \text{MAX}\,(G_i(x,y)) \quad i = 1, \ldots, 8 \qquad (14.1)$$

The gradient can then be tested against an absolute threshold, G_T, to determine if it is a candidate for further consideration. The threshold is used to limit the number of pixels for subsequent processing and is a parameter for adjustment by projection in the cone processing model. Paths of constant gradient can then be traced through the scene to define edges. This process gives edges of different gradient intensities, which can further lend insight into the subsequent levels of processing. Premature selection of the path with the highest gradient magnitude is a possibility but, in a general system, would violate the "Principle of Least Commitment."

Edges, however, are not sufficient to describe complex scenes. They must be aggregated and pruned so that edges passed to the next level are logically consistent boundaries of objects in the scene. The next step in processing must then incorporate contextual information to organize edges into boundaries and vertices. A method for accomplishing this, called relaxation [9, 11], allows a local edge to be examined in the context of surrounding edges. One defines a local neighborhood of an edge and then applies the definition to each edge. The result either supports the edge in that neighborhood or suggests that it is inconsistent and is a candidate for elimination. Relaxation can be applied in a discrete fashion, or relative probabilities that each edge is consistent can be determined. The process is propagated to each edge in the scene, and the total context is affected by each edge.

To illustrate the relaxation process, consider the following simplified example from Zucker [11] for a simple figure and neighborhood using a discrete rather than a probabilistic process. The neighborhood is defined by the label set λ with which each edge can be labeled and by the allowable junction combinations. The label set is

$$
\lambda = \begin{cases}
+ \text{ for convex edge} \\
- \text{ for concave edge} \\
\rightarrow \text{ for occluding edge with object below} \\
\leftarrow \text{ for occluding edge with object above}
\end{cases} \tag{14.2}
$$

Where possible, these labels are applied initially to the edges in the scene; relaxation is then applied to resolve inconsistencies or partial labels. Consider the lines from a scene shown in Figure 14.9a with the initial labeling as given. The fact that a_1 has all possible labels indicates that initial

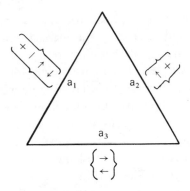

(a) Simple lines from a scene and the
initial labelling.

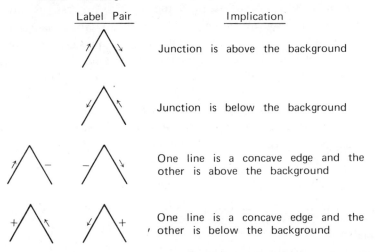

(b) Neighborhood rules, λ_{ii}, which form the constraints to be applied
to the lines in the scene of which (a) is a part.

**Figure 14.9. Simple lines from a scene and the neighborhood rules with
which discrete relaxation can be applied.**

labeling was not possible and the other two sides were only partially
labeled. The remainder of the neighborhood rules, λ_{ij}, are now applied to
each side, a_i, in Figure 14.9b. The label λ at a_i is kept if and only if there
is a label that is compatible with λ' for every neighbor a_j, $(\lambda, \lambda') \epsilon \lambda_{ij}$. Using

the neighborhood rules, the flow of the process proceeds by comparing the labels at each edge in parallel and discarding the inconsistent labels. For example, in Figure 14.9 the $-$ and $\rightarrow$ labels on a_1 are not consistent with the two labels on a_2 and are discarded. The final labeling for the drawing is given in Figure 14.10a. One can then create a labeling network or graph as in Figure 14.10b that describes all possible final label interpretations. The labeling network nodes correspond to object-label pairs, and an edge joins two nodes if and only if $(\lambda, \lambda') \epsilon \lambda_{ij}$. Now, cliques (full cycles) in the network define possible interpretations in a global sense of the scene edges and are given in Figure 14.10c for the edges in Figure 14.9.

In a complex image where the context can propagate throughout and where noise can create edges, it is more realistic to use a probabilistic relaxation labeling process instead of the discrete process just illustrated. The probabilistic process assigns probabilities to labels using the same parallel iterative process used in the discrete process to denote the probability that the label λ exists in the scene context $p_i(\lambda)$. Thus, $p_i(\lambda)$ denotes the probability that label λ exists for object a_i. The probabilistic process then applies a measure, $r_{ij}(\lambda, \lambda')$, to a label pair to determine the compatibility. The compatibility measure $r_{ij}(\lambda, \lambda')$ controls the contribution that the probability of feature label λ' on object a_j makes to the probability of feature label λ on object a_i. The compatibility function takes the following form:

$$r_{ij}(\lambda, \lambda') = \begin{cases} -1 \text{ if } \lambda \text{ at } a_i \text{ is incompatible with } \lambda' \text{ at } a_j \\ \;\;0 \text{ if } \lambda \text{ at } a_i \text{ is independent of } \lambda' \text{ at } a_j \\ +1 \text{ if } \lambda \text{ at } a_i \text{ is compatible with } \lambda' \text{ at } a_j \end{cases} \quad (14.3)$$

This function behaves much like the reward and punishment feedback in the adaptive communications network in Chapter 9 in updating the label probabilities of node matrices for one communications network. Here, the following update function is applied:

$$\Delta P_i(\lambda_k) = \sum_{j \in N} w_{ij} \sum r_{ij}(\lambda_k, \lambda_m) P_j(\lambda_m) \quad (14.4)$$

where

$$P_i^{t+1}(\lambda_k) = \frac{P_i^t(\lambda_k)[1 + \Delta P_i^t(\lambda_k)]}{\sum_{k=1}^{N} [P_i^t(\lambda_k)(1 + \Delta P_i^t(\lambda_k))]} \quad (14.5)$$

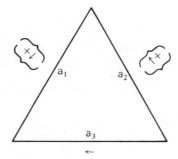

a.   Final labelling for edges of scene of Figure 14.9.

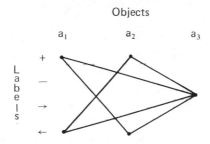

b.   Labelling network for edges in scene of Figure 14.9.

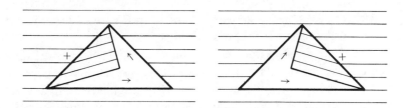

c.   Global interpretations of edges in scene of Figure 14.9 from labels and network.

Figure 14.10.   Relaxation labeling and global interpretations for edges from scene in Figure 14.9.

and

> N is the total number of objects in the neighborhood i
> w_{ij} is a weighting term of the influence of a_j on a_i
> t is the iteration number

Note that the denominator of Equation 14.4 is a normalizing term used to ensure that summation across all labels for the ith object equals one.

The labeling of boundaries from detected edges in a scene makes use of both the specific edge information and other terms that depend to some extent on the nature of the visual problem and the designer's goals. For example, the selection of the label set λ and the neighborhood rules λ_{ij} can be used to specialize the resultant boundaries toward specific features such as rectangular areas or circular sections. There is still work left for the designer!

Another approach to representing scene data that preserves the data structure through several levels of the processing cone has been proposed by Ehrich and Foith [6]. This approach uses intensity profiles of each horizontal scan of a scene as the basic information. From this a relational tree (R-tree) is constructed within which one-dimensional contextual relationships defined by the peaks and valleys of the basic information are stored. For example, the intensity profile in Figure 14.11a is labeled with respect to its peaks, and peaks are delimited by valleys on either side. Peak p_7 is thus delimited by the valleys to the left and right, and the valley to the left also delimits peak p_3. Notice that peaks p_3 and p_9 are nested within the set of peaks described by p_7, and that p_7 is concatenated with the peaks described by p_{19} and p_{21}. The whole intensity profile can be described by its largest peak or peaks, in this case as illustrated in Figure 14.11b, the R-tree. The vertex on the right has four descendants, because the valley minima at 14, 17, and 22 are all the same height. The valley at 11 defines the division between the two major sets of branches in the R-tree, whereas each of the other valleys induces a node in the tree [12]. Each vertex in the R-tree contains an attribute list containing specifics such as widths, heights, and peak and valley locations. Thus, the R-tree can be used to reconstruct the original image, and the R-tree data structure is said to be representational, whereas the direct edge detection process (since it is not invertible) is said to be interpretive.

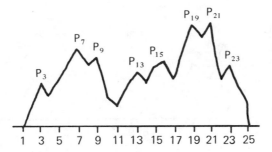

(a) Intensity profile with the peaks labeled.

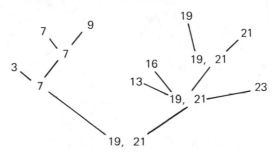

(b) R-tree for the intensity profile in (a).

Figure 14.11.   Intensity profile and its R-tree.

Still, additional levels of processing must take place in a vision process, and the "peak" method is indeed amenable to such processing. In fact, the authors claim that because this approach is region-oriented, it can improve the performance of a line finder. Edges can be found using the R-tree alone by examining the slopes between peaks and valleys and selecting points that exceed a given slope threshold. Point candidates can be found by searching the R-trees for a single direction scan-sag horizontally or by creating trees for both scan directions and merging the edges found in each direction into a single data structure. The edges found using this technique have been used directly as boundaries [6], although a relaxation process could also be used.

(a) Original intensity profile.

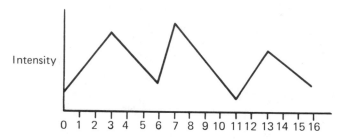

(b) Intensity profile after application of the splinter rule.

Figure 14.12. Application of the splinter rule for data-driven region formation.

Independent of the method used to determine the boundaries, the formation of regions from boundaries is a difficult process. The process makes use of a priori knowledge, is data driven, or, as in most cases, uses a combination of both knowledge-independent and knowledge-based processing. The general goal of region formation is to suppress local textural variations and reduce the scene representation to a small number of large regions, each with its associated attributes identified.

There are many different approaches to region formation including the use of histograms, clusters, relaxation or cluster labels, and the further application of R-trees. Most of these techniques, however, require some kind of constrained environment in order to describe them and are not appropriate for this discussion. One simple data-driven region formation scheme based on R-trees illustrates the general process. This scheme, called

Figure 14.13.   Illustration of the representation of a complex scene after low-level vision processing.

the splinter rule [6], eliminates local low contrast texture and forms larger regions in the following manner. All maximal sets of consecutive peaks are located in the intensity profile whose valleys strictly ascend and then strictly descend in height from left to right. The peaks in each such "peak group" are merged into a new peak whose height and location are that of the highest peak in that "peak group." The application of the splinter rule is illustrated in Figure 14.12.

The effects of the application of edge detection and boundary relaxation processes on a complex scene are shown in Figure 14.13. Note that the low contrast texture such as that on the roof and the shrub and lawn has been removed.

HIGHER LEVEL PROCESSING

Low level processing generally supplies data structures that represent regions and/or surfaces to the higher level processing system. Because region formation often uses a combination of knowlege-based and data-driven processing, higher level processing requires a stronger emphasis on knowledge-based processes. The purpose of higher level processing is interpretation of the image, with the capability of extracting more detail as it is needed. For example, the output may be "The scene is that of a house," but if the user of the vision system requires more detail, questions like "What color is it?" or "Does it have shutters?" can be asked and subsequently answered as in the interpretive model given in the last section.

The following description of the elements of higher level processing is based on the work of Hanson and Riseman [9]. The general task of higher level processing is to manipulate knowledge that occurs in two basic forms [9]. The first form is procedural, wherein the vision system invokes processes that allow the information to be consistently integrated into the other scene data. The second form is declarative, and has been likened to human long-term memory by Hanson and Riseman [9]. It is used in a matching process.

The system of scene interpetation builds a description in a "short-term memory" by making and testing various hypotheses. Hypotheses are generated with both declarative and procedural knowledge using either a bottom-up or top-down formulation.

The bottom-up formulation uses the features stored in short-term memory that were derived from both low level processing and subsequent higher level processing. These features include color and texture of regions to hypothesize objects, shapes of boundaries and regions to hypothesize surfaces, volumes, and objects.

The top-down formulation analyzes predictions from a knowledge base stored in "long-term memory." An example is the manipulation of stored three-dimensional shape representations for matching regions.

The types of features of interest in the top-down and bottom-up formulations as well as the kinds of processing applied are illustrated in Figure 14.14. All the features on the left side of the figure except the schema either are self-explanatory or were discussed earlier. The schema, which is the highest level structure in the vision process, includes the description of objects and scenes and their relationship. In particular, spatial relationships between objects and their relative importance in building a model in short-term memory for testing hypotheses made on the scene are part of the schema. The problem of interpretation cannot rely on the existence of schemata for every possible situation that a general vision system may encounter. Unexpected scenes and contexts must also be dealt with. The new situation can be handled if the higher level processing builds a model, in terms of the object parts and surfaces which it does understand, with which to process the new scene. A further improvement in the higher level

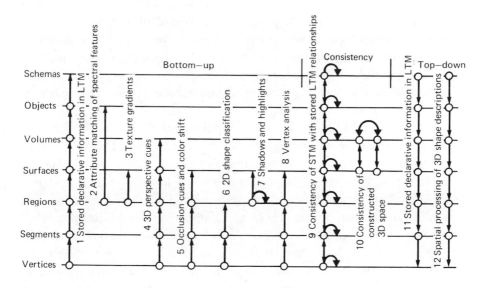

Figure 14.14. Features and their role in hypothesis generation and testing using either the bottom-up or top-down formulation.

processing can obtain if the low level processing is tuned by feedback from the higher levels [6, 13].

At this point, one could compare this general purpose approach to the specialized knowledge-based interpretive system described earlier. They do indeed look similar. It has been argued that the general purpose system without a specific schema for dealing with a given scene, such as a weather photo, should be able to handle that scene as well as a specialized weather system after developing the proper internal model. This noble goal presents an interesting challenge to our de facto model, the human vision system. How well could a naive observer interpret a weather photo? Wouldn't some knowledge of meteorology and weather photo patterns help?

MACHINE VISION APPLICATIONS

The focus of the last few sections has been on general vision systems. However, as stated earlier, it may be more productive to consider constrained, goal-oriented systems. This has indeed been the case for applications of machine vision. The state of knowledge of vision and image processing technologies has at last progressed to the point where machine vision systems can be economically applied in industrial environments. Application-oriented research on productivity, the subject of a National Science Foundation program, has produced a base of new knowledge to enhance this process.

Industrial applications of vision appear in the areas of sensor-controlled manipulation (including robots) and inspection. The subsequent discussion will present areas of potential as well as current applications.

The first area, sensor-controlled manipulation, involves interaction with and control of machines that perform a large number of the tasks in a manufacturing environment. These applications, which generally involve the selection, movement, and processing of materials with programmable automation (i.e., robots), have been summarized by Rosen [14] and are shown in Figure 14.15. A specific high payoff area for vision systems is viewing parts in a bin or on a belt and identifying their location and orientation in the presence of other, perhaps occluding parts. This allows for both the selection and orientation of parts (orientation is one of the most common tasks in manufacturing operations). Automatic equipment and vision also have application where the physical environment is uncomfortable and/or unhealthy for a human operator, such as in metal refining, foundry work, and paint spraying.

The other area where even the simplest of vision systems have had substantial payoff is inspection. The equipment now available in the form of solid-state (charge-coupled device, or CCD) linear and two-dimensional imaging arrays has made the generation of image data simple and inexpensive. Thus armed, the inspection environment—including optics, viewing angle, lighting, and background—can be carefully controlled. And, since the models of the objects to be observed are known precisely, simple measurements or matching can be used effectively. In some cases, measurements of simple image parameters such as the width of a particular scan line or set of scan lines are sufficient. These inspection applications are classified as quantitative. The other class of inspection operations, qualitative applications, includes observations such as whether the surface is unmarred, the unit works, or all parts are present. These applications have also been classified by Rosen [14] and are presented in Figure 14.16.

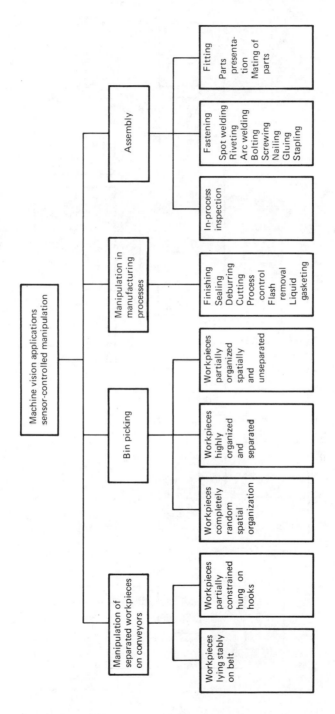

Figure 14.15. Compilation of applications—both present and potential—of machine vision in sensor-controlled manipulation.

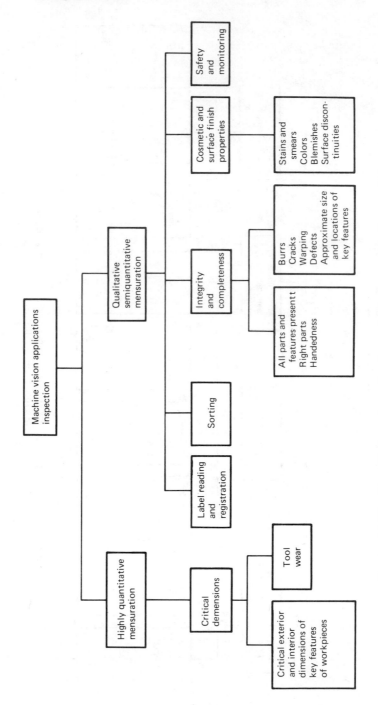

Figure 14.16. Compilation of applications—both present and potential—of machine vision in inspection tasks.

Finally, inspection, sensor control, and programmable automation can be integrated in a system wherein a vision system controls a machining operation while inspecting the machine tool for wear. The robot is brought into play to replace the worn machine tool.

SUMMARY

The concepts and application of computer or machine vision are some of the truly amazing outgrowths of progress in both our knowledge of artificial intelligence and the technology needed to create successful systems. In this chapter we have attempted to acquaint the reader with the basic concepts as well as some of the specifics of computer vision systems. This aspect of engineering cybernetics, vision, is relatively new—most of the work has been reported since 1969, and there is still much to be learned. Therefore, perhaps more important in this chapter are the topics not covered, including the details of region formation and segmentation, other approaches to higher level processing, the use of color, the problems of representing and interpreting in two dimensions what is present in three dimensions, the role of stereo vision, and the use of still motion. Still, the vision systems that will prevail, both general and specific, and their relationship to the principles presented in the previous chapters will remain.

The interested reader is referred to the books and articles listed at the end of the chapter for further information. In particular, Hanson and Riseman [4], Winston [15], Duda and Hart [16], and Rosenfeld et al. [10, 17, 18] contain most of the information on the current state of the art in computer vision.

EXERCISES

1. Compare the "model" process for human vision used to explain illusions to the models proposed for both specific and general vision systems. Where do they differ? Where are they similar?

2. Many industrial computer vision tasks use 100×100 binary CCD imaging devices for input. Determine the cycle time of a processor and the amount of memory needed to process the image if the task must look at 120 parts per minute and each image requires

100 processing steps per pixel. Assume the memory can be written and read at the cycle time of the processor. Is there a processor available at this time that can do this? A microprocessor?

3. Restate the "Principle of Least Commitment" in an abstract manner. Does it apply to any other engineering task with which you are familiar? If so, describe it and how it applies.

4. Describe the matching, queueing, and interpretation models of knowledge-based vision systems using the concepts presented in Chapter 5.

5. Using the images defined earlier, determine the number of processing steps needed to apply the matcher model. Assume that the feature analysis system reduces the data structure by a factor of 5 using 10 steps per pixel and a correlation match on 20 objects must be tested.

6. In the impossible triangle that follows, the label set is

$$\lambda = \begin{cases} I - \text{side-oriented into the plane of the paper} \\ O - \text{side-oriented out of the plane of the paper} \end{cases}$$

and the initial labeling is as given on the figure. The constraint set for adjacent sides for a real triangle is

$$\lambda_{ij}(\lambda, \lambda') = \begin{cases} O, O \\ I, I \\ O, I \\ I, O \end{cases}$$

Using the relaxation labeling process, determine the labels and the labeling network for the impossible triangle. What is the cycle length for any of the possible global interpretations? Does this seem consistent with your feelings as you view the triangle?

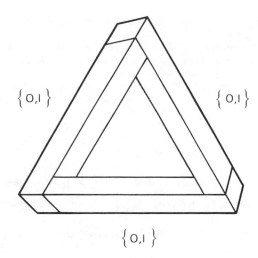

$\{0,1\}$ $\{0,1\}$

$\{0,1\}$

7. Compare formally the update process for probabilistic relaxation labeling with the update process for communications network described in Chapter 9.

REFERENCES

1. GREGORY, R. L., *The Intelligent Eye*, McGraw-Hill, New York, 1970.
2. GREGORY, R. L., *Eye and Brain*, Weidenfeld and Nicholson, London, 1966.
3. HELD, R., ed., *Image, Object, and Illusion*, Scientific American, W. H. Freeman, San Francisco, 1974.
4. HANSON, A. R., and E. M. RISEMAN, eds., *Computer Vision Systems*, Academic Press, New York, 1978.
5. MARR, D., "Early Processing of Visual Information," AI Memo 340, M.I.T. Artificial Intelligence Labortory, Cambridge, Mass., December 1975.
6. EHRICH, R. W., and J. P. FOITH, "Topology and Semantics of Intensity Arrays," in *Computer Vision Systems*, A. R. HANSON and E. M. RISEMAN, eds., Academic Press, New York, 1978.
7. BULLOCK, Bruce L., "The Necessity For A Theory of Specialized Vision," in *Computer Vision Systems*, A. R. HANSON and E. M. RISEMAN, eds., Academic Press, New York, 1978.
8. HANSON, A. R., and E. M. RISEMAN, "Preprocessing Cones: A Computational Structure for Scene Analysis," COINS technical report 74C-7, University of Massachusetts, September 1974.
9. HANSON, A. R., and E. M. RISEMAN, "Segmentation of Natural Scenes," in *Computer Vision Systems*, Academic Press, New York, 1978.

10. ROSENFELD, A., and A. C. KAK, *Digital Picture Processing*, Academic Press, New York, 1976.
11. ZUCKER, Steven W., "Relaxation, Labelling, Local Ambiguity, and Low Level Vision," in *Pattern Recognition and Artificial Intelligence*, C. H. CHEN, ed., Academic Press, New York, 1976.
12. EHRICH, R. W., and J. P. FOITH, "Representation of Random Waveforms by Relational Trees," *IEEE Transactions on Computers*, Vol. C-25, July 1976, pp. 725–736.
13. TENNENBAUM, J. M., and H. G. BARROW, "IGS: A Paradigm for Integrating Image Segmentation and Interpretation," in *Pattern Recognition and Artificial Intelligence*, C. H. CHEN, ed., Academic Press, New York, 1976.
14. ROSEN, Charles A., "Machine Vision and Robotics: Industrial Requirements," *SRI International*, Technical Note 174, SRI Project 6284, November 1978.
15. WINSTON, P., *The Psychology of Computer Vision*, McGraw-Hill, New York, 1975.
16. DUDA, R. O., and P. E. HART, *Pattern Classification and Scene Analysis*, Wiley, New York, 1973.
17. ROSENFELD, A, *Picture Processing by Computer*, Academic Press, New York, 1969.
18. ROSENFELD, A., ed., *Digital Picture Analysis*, Springer-Verlag, New York, 1976.
19. TANIMOTO, S. and KLINGER, eds., *Structural Computer Vision*, Academic Press, New York, 1980.

15

Robotics

The concept of a robot is not new. In fact, it clearly predates modern electronic technology by several years. Thus, to put the subject in perspective, this chapter begins with a brief history of robots and robotics. As we shall see, recent technological developments and the need for improved productivity have created a substantial business for industrial robots and opportunities to apply engineering cybernetic principles to the design and application of robots. Industrial robots and their applications provide a framework for much of this chapter. They are also an excellent example of the need for an interdisciplinary approach—computers, control, mechanics, and manufacturing—to problem solving.

HISTORY OF ROBOTICS

The word "robot," which is older than most of the language of technology, has been attributed to a playwright. In the 1922 play *R.U.R.* by the Czech Karel Capek [1], the title is an acronym for Rossum's Universal Robots, which became so sophisticated that they took over the world. Robot is a contraction of the Czech words "robota," or work, and "robotnik," or serf.

Capek's concept of an anthropomorphic automaton with super intelligence continues today with the beloved R2D2 and C3P0 of *Star Wars*, shown in Figure 15.1. However, anthropomorphic automata date back several hundred years. These early machines, built for entertainment purposes, often took the form of a musician or small animal. Among the better known are the full-sized musicians built in the mid-1700s by Jacques de Vaucanson. These devices, which incorporated mechanical technology 100 years ahead of its time, were eventually destroyed, and only a few documents describing their operation have survived [2, 3]. Another Vaucanson invention, the punched-card programming of Jacquard Looms, has indeed survived and is often referred to as the precursor to modern data storage and programming.

Figure 15.1. *Star Wars'* **R2D2 and C3PO—A contemporary version of our models of anthropomorphic automata.**

The latter half of the eighteenth century seems to have been a productive one for clever mechanicians in the field of automata. The writing automaton built by Henri Maillardet in 1805, which followed several others built in that period, survives today at the Franklin Institute in Philadelphia. This machine uses a series of cams as a read-only memory to program the machine to write and draw [4]. As the photograph in Figure 15.2 reveals, the arm articulation is quite sophisticated. The output, shown in Figure 15.3, is equally impressive.

The Industrial Revolution apparently diverted much of the creativity devoted to entertainment automata to more financially rewarding pursuits. However, much of the technology continued to find its way into timepieces and musical devices, including the player piano and other nonanthropomorphic musical automata. Still, the concept of robots as intelligent

Figure 15.2. Sophisticated arm of Henri Maillardet's writing automaton built in 1805.

Figure 15.3.   A drawing produced by Maillardet's automaton. This drawing was created in five minutes by decoding the information stored in cams that serve as Read Only Memory.

machines persisted, especially in the literature of science fiction. In particular, Isaac Asimov [5, 6] created some intriguing stories around his "three laws of robotics" beginning in 1950:

First Law—A robot must never harm a human being, or, through inaction, allow a human being to come to harm.

Second Law—A robot must always obey a human being, unless this is in conflict with the first law.

Third Law—A robot must protect itself from harm, unless this is in conflict with either of the first two laws.

These laws may appear outlandish at first glance. But if we consider the rapid advances in computer technology from the 1950s to the 1980s, it becomes apparent that some form of the laws of robotics may be needed before the turn of the century.

The more recent history of technology contains the seeds for the growth of robots as economically viable devices in research and manufacturing environments. Pioneers in nuclear science quickly realized the need for a method of remotely handling dangerous radioactive materials, and the discipline of telecherics was born. A *telecheric* or *teleoperator* is a device that

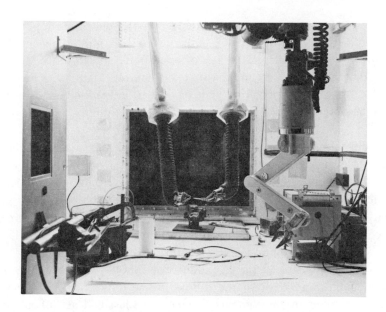

Figure 15.4.   A teleoperator (telecheric) for remotely handling or manipulating objects, which illustrates the level of mechanical sophistication needed to develop robot articulation.

translates motions by an operator into similar motions in a remote location. The operator views the remote manipulator through leaded glass or a closed circuit television system for visual feedback. Primitive teleoperators were entirely mechanical systems that transferred both the operator's force and position to the remote location. The direct mechanical coupling allowed the operator to "feel" what was taking place remotely. Later devices used servo systems to amplify the operator's force but needed additional equipment to provide feedback. The typical teleoperator in Figure 15.4 illustrates the sophisticated mechanical nature of these systems. The mechanical elements of teleoperators and their control have been one basis for modern robots.

The other development that has contributed to the evolution of robots is numerical control (NC). Numerical control describes machines whose actions are controlled by a sequence of numbers [7]. These machines are common devices such as milling machines and lathes to which digitally controlled servos have been added. The sequence of numbers is fed into the machine on punched paper tape. This technique is still in use, although many of the newer machines use direct computer-generated inputs called direct numerical control (DNC). A typical DNC milling machine uses stepping motors to control each axis of operation and can move in steps of a few thousandths of an inch with excellent repeatability. The human operator is usually responsible for loading and unloading such machines, although some modern industrial robots are beginning to perform these tasks.

From telecherics, then, came the mechanical and control knowledge needed to design an articulated appendage, while from numerical control came the technology for operatorless control of that appendage. The confluence occurred in 1954 [8] when George Devol began his patent activity on what was to become the beginning of the industrial robot. The first company formed to manufacture industrial robots based on Devol's work was called Unimation and was started in 1956. In the early 1960s, Unimation demonstrated its first industrial robots [9, 10, 11, 12]. These early machines and most of the robots in use today perform "pick and place" operations in enviroments that can be classified as difficult for or even hostile to human beings. Applications include forging, die casting, stamping, molding, loading, welding, and palletizing, shown in Figure 15.5. Since the 1960s, several thousand robots have appeared from many firms throughout the world, including Olivetti, Cincinatti Milicron, and Seiko.

Presently, a new confluence of technology is taking place that will draw on current robot technology as a key element. Computers are now being used extensively as an aid to designers by providing an interactive access to large amounts of data with commensurate processing power. Computer-aided design (CAD) systems allow the designer to test various ideas by modeling the system under design and displaying the results in animated or graphic form. The data base formed in this design process can be sent directly to a manufacturing data base and controller. The manufacturing controller then transmits commands to an assortment of DNC machines and robots that implement the design. As far-fetched as this may appear to the harried designer or manufacturing engineer, several elements of these systems are already in laboratory and operational use. The photographs in Figure 15.6 present a mechanical CAD system tied to a DNC machine.

Applications other than industry have also contributed to robotics. Explorations of the oceans and space have each led to the development of

Figure 15.5.   Typical tasks for industrial robots.

robotic systems to aid in the study of these hostile environments. For example, the articulation that dug samples from the Martian surface, shown in Figure 15.7, required many elements of intelligent systems to accomplish its feat, including communications, control, computation, reliability, and vision. Much research has also been done on alternate motive systems such as pedipulators [13, 14] and on the design and control of vehicles for remote explorations [15]. However, despite these advances and despite the fact that a "domestic" robot is periodically announced as a product (although none has been delivered to date), the principal effort and economic impact lie in industrial robots. The remainder of this chapter thus focuses on industrial robots and their application.

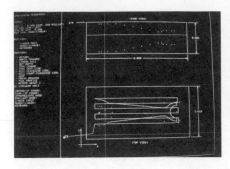

a. CAD design.

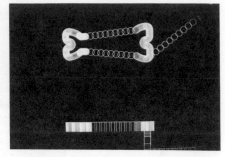

b. Simulation of dynamic characteristics.

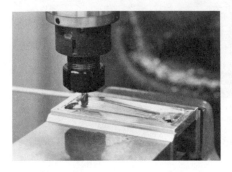

c. DNC machine making part.

d. Final part.

Figure 15.6. Designing and manufacturing mechanical parts without a machinist.

Figure 15.7. Remote gathering of samples and their analysis accomplished on Mars by a robot handler.

ROBOT CLASSES AND CHARACTERISTICS

Robots can be classified in many ways. In the previous section, we broadly used the industrial robot as a major category. There are many dimensions through which a cut will produce a classification. To establish a generic classification system, we shall use the two primary classification dimensions of degrees of freedom and type of control.

The degrees of freedom (DOF) of a mechanical system refer to the number of physical axes through which motion can occur. In robotics, DOF can often be equated with the number of joints in the robot. Figure 15.8 represents a schematic of some primitive robot configurations. The simple arms in Figure 15.8a, with one arm fixed and the other able to rotate about it, are a single-degree-of-freedom mechanical system. If we add a joint to the base of the fixed arm in Figure 15.8a, the resulting system has two DOF. By adding a rotating shaft with a forked end to the free end of the system in Figure 15.8b, we obtain a three-DOF system, shown in Figure 15.8c. This system has limited ability to pick up and move some objects.

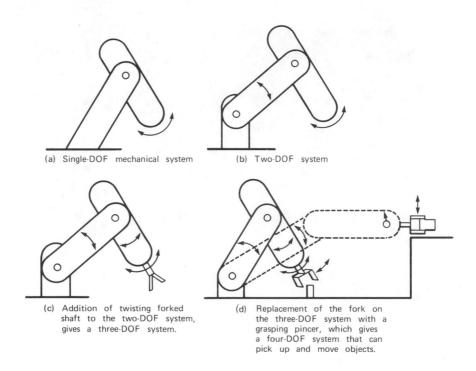

(a) Single-DOF mechanical system

(b) Two-DOF system

(c) Addition of twisting forked shaft to the two-DOF system, gives a three-DOF system.

(d) Replacement of the fork on the three-DOF system with a grasping pincer, which gives a four-DOF system that can pick up and move objects.

Figure 15.8.   Effect of increasing degrees of freedom on a simple mechanical system.

Finally, in Figure 15.8d, we can convert the fork to a simple fixed "thumb" and moveable "finger" configuration to obtain a primitive pick-and-place mechanism with four DOF. For the task illustrated, rotation of the gripper is not really needed. But if the gripper is rotated by 90° before releasing the object onto the platform, the system can probably handle a wider variety of objects. Thus, the complexity of a mechanical system is usually represented by the number of degrees of freedom it possesses.

Typical present-day industrial robots have from one to six degrees of freedom, although more are certainly possible. For example, the "wrist" in Figure 15.8d can be made more flexible by adding rotation to the twisting already in that joint. Similarly, a fourth DOF can be added to the shoulder, where the arm joins the base to allow rotation of the arm in and out of the page. In Figure 15.9, a photograph of a six-DOF arm (with the gripper

Figure 15.9.   Photograph of a six-DOF arm.

typical of industrial robots) shows the mechanical complexity added by each DOF.

Industrial robots are also classified by the mechanical configuration of the individual elements of the arm and the actuators. These classifications are illustrated schematically in Figure 15.10. This classification begins with simple movements in a rectangular coordinate system such as the $x - y$ table shown in Figure 15.11.

The $x - y$ table is not a common configuration for the anthropomorphic system; however, the cylindrical class is typical of simple pick-and-place robots illustrated in Figure 15.12a. Examples of spherical and jointed robots are given in Figures 15.8 and 15.9. The difference between these classes of robots lies in the space in which the robot can work, commonly called the work envelope, and the angles with which the robot can approach a workpiece.

Generally, a jointed machine can approach the work more flexibly than a spherical machine, which is more flexible than a cylindrical machine, which is more flexible than a rectangular machine.

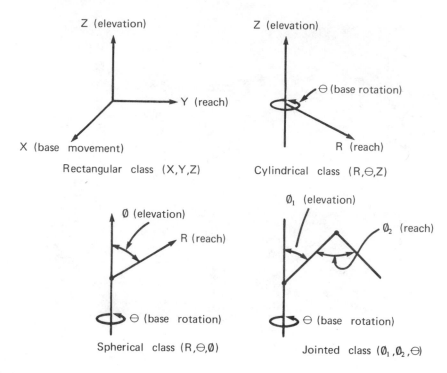

Figure 15.10. Industrial robot classification based on mechanical configuration of arm elements.

The work envelope of a cylindrical machine is illustrated in Figure 15.12b. Similarly the work envelope of a spherical machine and a jointed machine is illustrated in Figure 15.13.

The next type of robot classification is concerned with the robot control system. All robots have one functional element in common, usually called the sequencer. In the most abstract case, a sequencer contains the goals of the system and the tools needed to compute and execute the plan to achieve those goals. Much basic research has been done on the process of planning and integrating sensor data into the goals of a robot system [15, 16]. A robot planner requires three inputs:

1. The initial state or current state of a robot.
2. A set of operators which allows the robot to move from one state to another.
3. The goal or state specification.

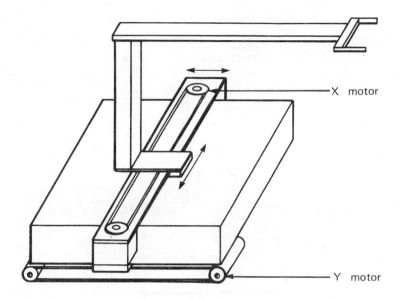

Figure 15.11. $X - Y$ table with cantilevered arm and fixed elevation Z.

The planner selects a set of operators which will take the robot from its current state to the goal state. The planning process in a real environment must be dynamic to be able to react to changes which may alter an intermediate state in the execution process. However, in most contemporary industrial robots, the sequencer contains an exact description of the movements the robot is to perform. The simplest systems use relays or electronic logic and/or memory pre-set to the desired sequence of events.

Robots at the next level of sophistication use a random access memory to store the sequence. These systems can be programmed either by manually taking the robot to the desired points or by loading the program from a computer. A mini- or microcomputer is often incorporated into such systems to handle the internal control functions as well as the interface to the "outside world." The sequencer interacts with each DOF effector and sensor to determine where the robot is at specific instants. The lowest levels of the robot control hierarchy then consist of servo mechanisms, whose complexity may run from simple limit switches to adaptive or learning control systems, described in Chapter 7.

Some simple two- and three-DOF pick-and-place robots are controlled with mechanical limit stops and switches to sense position [17]. Most

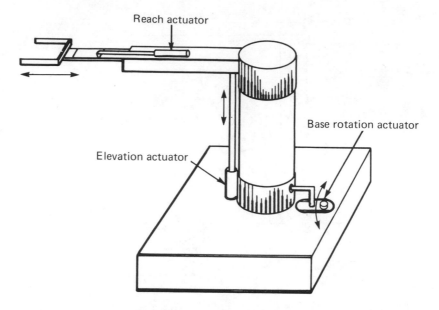

Figure 15.12a.   Cylindrical coordinate robot.

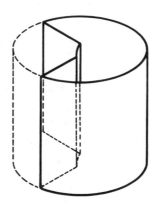

Figure 15.12b.   Work envelope of cylindrical machine is a section of a cylinder.

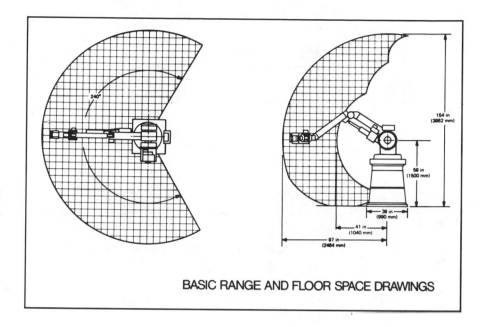

BASIC RANGE AND FLOOR SPACE DRAWINGS

Figure 15.13.   Work envelope of a jointed robot.

modern robots use more sophisticated digital controllers in which the present position is sensed through digital encoders. The actuators are controlled by comparing the present and desired positions and velocity in a mini- or microcomputer and feeding the proper digital or analog control information to them. If needed, the desired positions and velocities are stored in the local memory of the robot. The technology of the memory currently used in many robots includes plated wire and magnetic core, which offer reliability in the harsh environments where the machines are used.

A block diagram showing the relationship of the elements of control is presented in Figure 15.14a. Note that the feedback in this system is concerned only with the position velocity of the robot itself. No information about the conditions of the outside world and the robot's impact on it

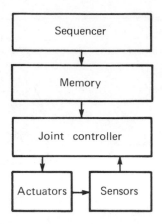

(a) Open-loop controller-sequencer, memory, and
local control relationships for a typical robot.

is provided to the local controller. This type of robot controller, typical of many of the machines in use today, is thus called an open-loop controller and is characterized by its fixed control strategy.

The second major category of robot control system makes use of other kinds of sensors, such as tactile force and vision, to affect the control strategy used to perform a given task. Here, the local control strategy can be modified in response to changes in the local environment such as "the object slipped out of the gripper and is now on the table" or "the object is upside down." This type of control, called closed-loop local control, is given in schematic form in Figure 15.14b. It is often desirable to distribute the sequencer into at least two locations, the second one a central coordination computer. This is frequently done in manufacturing environments to allow the actions and interaction of robots and other machines to be coordinated. Most current sensor-based robot control systems can be modeled as in Figure 15.14b. One of the first instances of a sensor-controlled mobile robot was SHAKEY, built in the late 1960s at SRI [18]. Because the state of the microprocessor art was not developed at the time, radio links to a computer were used to integrate the sensors with the controls. SHAKEY was able to maneuver down halls and around objects—a remarkable feat for then and now.

The final class of robot controller is necessarily more abstract since there are no instances of it yet. It is only a matter of time, however, before

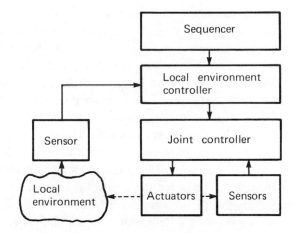

(b)   Closed-loop local controller, which uses sensors
to dynamically modify the control strategy.

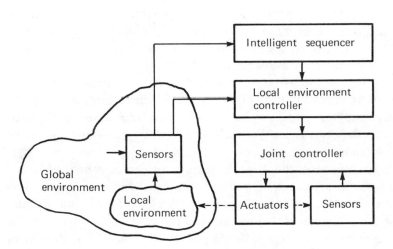

(c)   Intelligent closed-loop controller, which uses
local and global sensors to create as well as
modify the local and global strategy.

Figure 15.14.   The three classes of robot controllers.

an application is announced. This type of controller uses internal world models and has more sensors than those needed to perform any predefined types of functions. It has a very intelligent sequencer that works on goals at multiple levels—some for the task at hand, others for the next anticipated tasks, and still others related to the very existence of the controller itself. It is this last set of goals that surely demonstrates the need for Asimov's Laws of Robotics. This type of controller, for which a block diagram is shown in Figure 15.10c, must be more tenacious than the others and is called an intelligent closed-loop controller. Notice that it is hierarchically organized and, as such, should be compared with the models in Chapter 7.

It is interesting to consider the controller class and application of industrial robots. Some of the simplest, earliest robots used in pick-and-place applications have four or fewer DOF and a controller that moves the arm to a predetermined limit at full speed and then stops. This type of open-loop controller is often called a bang-bang system because the motor *drives at full speed to the stops with a "bang."*

Another type of industrial robot uses a more sophisticated open-loop controller, in which an operator "teaches" the robot by manually moving it through the desired sequence. The sequence is stored in the local robot memory and is followed repeatedly in operation. Called a copying robot, this type is exemplified by the paint-spraying robot shown in Figure 15.15. Many machines currently available are copying robots.

A third type of industrial robot with a closed-loop local controller is usually used for assembly tasks. This system, which requires more intelligence than a copying robot, may be driven from a large computer that can control more than one robot. We shall discuss this type of system further in a later section.

The experience of the last 20 years provides a sound base for establishing the technical requirements for industrial and other robots. The first requirement is reliability and the associated problem of failure mode. The reliability requirement that has evolved for most applications is 97 to 98 percent uptime, with a typical design goal of 98 percent [19]. Most users demand that service downtime be a maximum of 8 hours for robots working two shifts per day, which translates into a mean time between failures of 400 hours.

The other aspect of reliability is the behavior of the robot with a transient failure and its failure mode. Often driven by several-tens of

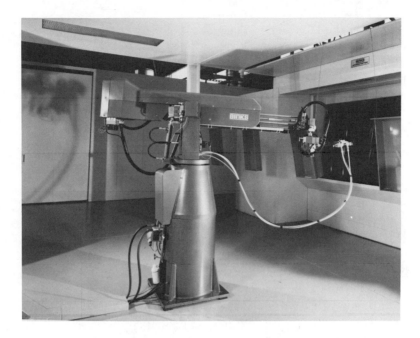

Figure 15.15. Copying robot, one of the most common types available. The Binks paint spraying robot repeats the steps taught to it by an expert paint sprayer.

horsepower hydraulic systems, industrial robots are capable of doing severe damage if they go out of control. As a result, control and exception detection mechanisms must be robust. In addition, the electrical environment for many robots can be classified as severe. A robot welding an automobile body on an assembly line can generate several volts of noise over a wide frequency range, which can easily introduce transient faults into the control system. Further, the failure or transient interruption of the power supply must not cause the robot to get into a mode of action that is catastrophic. To date, most robot control systems do not use redundant techniques but instead rely on high quality components and carefully engineered and tested designs.

The other technical requirement for industrial robots of interest here is the physical environment in which they must operate. This environment, which has been summarized by Engelberger [19], is given in Table 15.1. As is clear from the table, environmental requirements for robots are at best hostile. Consequently, these machines have design requirements that are not found in most other systems incorporating such a wide range of technology.

Several of the hazards listed in the table need amplification. The ambient temperature specification means that the usually sensitive electronic equipment must incorporate special components, and the radiant heat specification requires that this equipment must be shielded from the heat. Materials (such as the gripper) that face the radiant heat must also be able to withstand the heat blast. The implications of the sprays, fumes, and vapors, and particulate matter are that the external materials must be able to withstand direct assault and that sensitive parts of the robot must be sealed or in other ways isolated from the onslaught of these insidious hazards. The open-flame specification calls for protection of exposed parts of the robot, especially the flammable hydraulic fluids used in the actuators. A hole in the hydraulic system could feed flammable fluid directly onto a fire, destroying the environment as well as the robot. To prevent such a holocaust, the explosion specification says that no part of the robot can have an element capable of creating a spark.

Surely, the applications are rare in which all these hazards are present simultaneously. However, since the industrial robot is flexible automation (in contrast with fixed automation, which is designed for a specific task), methods for dealing with all these potential hazards must be considered in robot design.

One further specification for industrial robots that must be considered is positional accuracy. Because most contemporary robots do not have local environmental sensors to provide control feedback, the robot must be able

Table 15.1. Environmental Hazards for Industrial Robots

- Ambient temperatures up to 120° F without cooling air.
- Radiant heat source temperatures up to 2000° F.
- Shock excursions up to 1/2 inch with repetitions up to 2 per second.
- Electrical noise conditions of power line dropouts, motor-starting transients, welding radiation, and RF heating.
- Sprays of water and other coolants, some corrosive.
- Fumes and vapors from process chemicals and steam cleaning.
- Particulate matter such as sand, metallic dust, and hot slag.
- Fire and explosive risk from open flames, gases, and vapor mixtures.

to move accurately to the prespecified positions by itself. This requirement is a function of the application, varying from 0.001 inches for assembly robots to 0.01 inches for larger pick-and-place robots. The use of vision and more sophisticated sensors will allow closed-loop accuracy equal to the assembly task without requiring such extreme open-loop accuracy.

SENSORS AND CONTROL SYSTEM CONSIDERATIONS

We have thus far been concerned with the basic articulation of a robot arm that primarily has open-loop controllers. To move to the next level of control—closed-loop local control—sensors must be included in the robot system.

One of the most important sensors, vision, was discussed in some detail in Chapter 14. Historically, vision was one of the first sensors used, for two reasons. First, the other sensors that were tried initially, such as contact and force, proved too slow for the task. Second, our heavy reliance on vision makes it relatively easy to project that need onto a machine. Consider the problem of finding, without vision, a part for an assembly in an environment that is not well structured for that assembly task. If the part were not in the immediate vicinity where it was expected, the system could fail. This is similar to the experience of a blind individual who requires some consistency of structure in the environment to function autonomously. Given a reasonably structured environment, a blind person can easily perform complicated assembly tasks very efficiently. In robotics, the attention to date has been focused on vision, and little work on other sensors has been accomplished. The motivation for work on these other sensors is obvious when we recall the type and extent of computation necessary to perform vision tasks as opposed to the computational requirements for other sensors.

Sensors can be classified into two generic types [20], contact and noncontact; clearly, vision is a noncontact sensor. Sensors can also be grouped into two functional classes, coarse sensing and fine sensing. Vision is fine sensing, whereas limit switches are coarse sensing.

Contact sensors imply that the arm or hand is in physical contact with the object being moved or manipulated or with some other element in the environment. With contact sensors, the part of the robot that is making contact is usually a compliant structure, so that sensing can take place without bending, scratching, or breaking something not intended to be bent, scratched, or broken. For example, the gripper may be spring-loaded or coated with a compliant material such as rubber. Contact sensors can perform the following functions in basic material handling and assembly operations [21, 22, 23]:

1. Searching—Using sensitive touch sensors on the hand's exterior to detect a part without moving the part.
2. Recognition—After searching, determining the identity, position, and orientation of a part without moving it. This is accomplished by touch sensors with high spatial resolution.
3. Grasping—Acquiring the part by deformable fingers with surface-mounted sensors.
4. Moving, placing, joining, or inserting—Using force sensors to determine the extent of acquisition, the degree of contact, or the extent of insertion.

Contact sensors are divided into the major categories of force (or torque) and touch. Force can be measured either indirectly or directly. For example, the force exerted by a joint can be measured indirectly by determining the power being applied to the actuator of that joint. In an electrical servo, the motor current can be measured directly. There are two means of measuring force directly: force sensors in the joints, usually in the wrist or hand, and force sensors mounted on the work surface that measure the force applied by the robot on the work space.

Indirect sensing is simpler than direct sensing, but it does not always accurately reflect the force between the hand and an object in the environment. Consequently, force sensors in the wrist are often used to get a more accurate measure of the forces excited. Wrist sensors consist of transducers mounted in a compliant structure such that force is measured in three orthogonal directions. The sensors themselves can be piezoelectric, magnetostrictive, or solid state. Similar devices can be used in systems for measuring force on the work space.

Touch sensors are used to measure the actual contact between the hand and the desired object or an unexpected object in the work environment. Desired objects are sensed by sensors on the inside surfaces of the gripper, and other objects or potential hazards are sensed by sensors on the outside surfaces of the grippers. The two categories of touch sensors are binary and analog. Binary touch sensors are simple contact devices such as microswitches or flexible conductive rubber material mounted on the gripper. More than one sensor is often used on a single contacting surface to sense motion—for example, in grasping and slippage. Analog touch sensors sense the motion of the compliant surface as it succumbs to the applied forces. Potentiometers have been adapted to this environment, as have photodiode and light sources at the ends of a compliant light channel that restricts light transmission as the compliant surface is compressed. Generally, however, contact sensors specifically designed and marketed for robots are not yet available, and most of the work reported here is in the laboratory stage.

Noncontact sensors are divided into three classes: proximity, electro-optical imaging, and range imaging. Proximity sensors are probably the most common noncontact sensors found in both fixed and programmable automation. They sense the presence or absence of an object without physically contacting it. The simplest of proximity devices is the magnetic switch that responds to changes in its magnetic field. Other techniques—such as radio frequency (RF) field change detectors and ultrasonic, photoelectric, and Hall effect devices—are also useful as noncontact sensors. Noncontact sensors can be used when the robot is approaching the limit of travel or before it encounters an obstacle. Since the noncontact sensor can detect the obstacle before it makes contact, there is more time to slow the arm before it hits. This is especially useful for high inertia arms. The ultrasonic ranging mechanisms from Polaroid cameras have been used by Albus to detect objects in the range of the robot. Electro-optical imaging systems, of course, utilize the vision techniques presented in Chapter 14. The physical devices used to create the image range from photodiode and charge-coupled device arrays to standard television cameras with vidicons, plumbicons, and silicon target vidicons with resolutions from 32×32 to 320×512. The simplest imaging system available uses a one-dimensional solid-state camera with from 16 to 1872 elements. This device can be used to view objects that are in motion relative to the camera, such as parts on a conveyor belt, as illustrated in Figure 15.16.

The final class of noncontact sensors is the range imaging sensor. These systems are used to determine the distance between an object and the robot. The two techniques reported for range imaging are triangulation and light or sound ranging based on the time of travel. Although range imaging

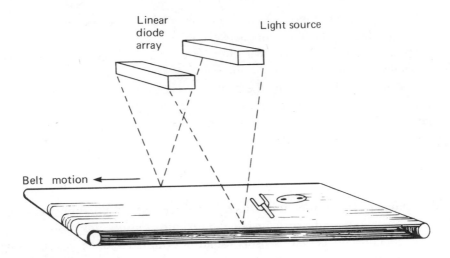

Figure 15.16. Linear imaging array, which uses the relative motion of the objects with respect to the camera to scan the scene.

has primarily been used to acquire and recognize objects, it has the potential to find a path through a factory, detect obstacles and pits, and inspect the presence or absence of parts in an assembly.

The sensors discussed here can be grouped into the taxonomy given in Figure 15.17. This type of classification can be used to determine the techniques required to handle a given problem.

Once a robot is equipped with vision and an assortment of contact and noncontact sensors, the next problem is orchestrating these devices into a complete system. At the highest level the robot system is driven by its goal-oriented sequencer as in Figure 15.14, and at lower levels the sensor data are integrated by the local equipment and joint controllers. One problem that occurs in both of the lower level controllers is the mapping of sensor data and joint control data into coordinate systems with different reference axes. For example, consider the system in Figure 15.18, which requires five different coordinate systems to describe all the elements in the environment. In order to convey the position of the object in the (X_5, Y_5, Z_5) system, to the gripper in the (X_3, Y_3, Z_3) system, the position must be referenced through the camera coordinate system (X_4, Y_4, Z_4) and the robot coordinate systems (X_1, Y_1, Z_1), (X_2, Y_2, Z_2), and (X_3, Y_3, Z_3). This problem, which

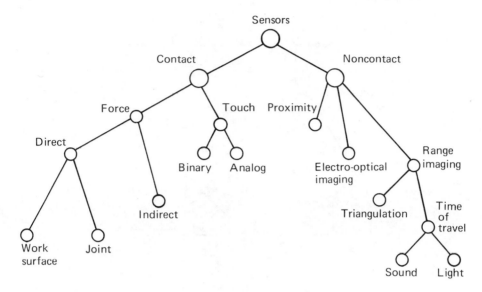

Figure 15.17.   Taxonomy of sensors for robotics.

limited the capabilities of early sensor-based robot research, was solved by Roberts [23] using a technique called homogenous transformations.

Homogenous transformations are based on the relative rotation and translation of one coordinate system with respect to another. Consider the problem of rotating one coordinate system (X_1, Y_1, Z_1) with respect to another coordinate system (X_2, Y_2, Z_2) as shown in Figure 15.19. Here, the relative angles between the various axes are α, β, and γ, respectively, and are called Euler angles. Thus, to go from the (X_2, Y_2, Z_2) system to the (X_1, Y_1, Z_1) system requires a rotation of $-\alpha$ about the Z_2 axis, $-\beta$ about the Y_2 axis and $-\gamma$ about the X_2 axis. Before we look at the solution to this general three-dimensional problem, consider the simple two-dimensional problem in Figure 15.20, where we are given the point P in (X_1, Y_1) space and want to refer to it in (X_2, Y_2) space. First, note that

$$X_2 = a + b \tag{15.1}$$

$$Y_2 = e \tag{15.2}$$

and then

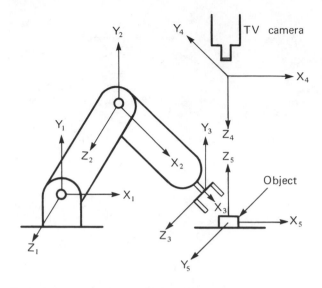

Figure 15.18. Robot system illustrating the several different coordinate systems needed to describe the environment.

$$a = \frac{X_1}{\cos \theta} \tag{15.3}$$

$$b = c \sin \theta \tag{15.4}$$

$$d = a \sin \theta \tag{15.5}$$

and

$$e = c \cos \theta \tag{15.6}$$

Also, from Figure 15.16,

$$c = Y_1 - d \tag{15.7}$$

and substituting Equation 15.5 for d and 15.3 for a,

$$c = Y_1 - \frac{X_1 \sin \theta}{\cos \theta}$$

Now, from Equation 15.6,

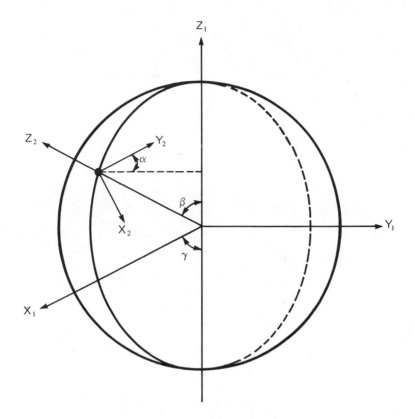

Figure 15.19.   Rotational relationship between two coordinate systems.

$$Y_2 = e = c \cos \theta = Y_1 \cos \theta - X_1 \sin \theta \qquad (15.8)$$

Similarly, using Equation 15.4,

$$b = Y_1 \sin \theta = X_1 \frac{\sin^2 \theta}{\cos \theta} \qquad (15.9)$$

and using a and b in Equation 15.1 and reducing gives

$$X_2 = X_1 \cos \theta + Y_1 \sin \theta \qquad (15.10)$$

This process can be represented more simply by the following matrix equation:

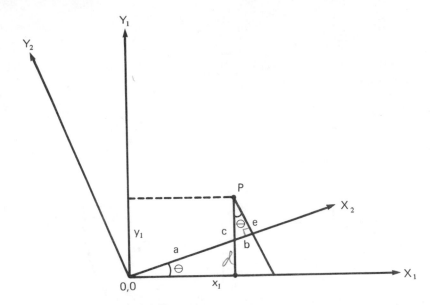

Figure 15.20. Transforming a point in the X_1, Y_1) coordinate space to a point in (X_2, Y_2) coordinate space.

$$\begin{array}{c} X_2 \\ Y_2 \end{array} = \left[\begin{array}{cc} \cos\theta & \sin\theta \\ -\sin\theta & \cos\theta \end{array} \right] \left[\begin{array}{c} X_1 \\ Y_1 \end{array} \right]$$ (15.11)

In a similar manner, the general solution to the rotation problem of Figure 15.14 can be found to be the product of rotations in each dimension of α, β, and γ, as shown in Equation 15.12. When multiplied out, is shown in Equation 15.13. This tool allows any two reference axes of any arbitrary rotational relationship to be related to one another. To relate two systems, one of which is translated from the other, requires that the appropriate axes be offset by the proper constants in the transformation. Thus, if the origin of the (X_1, Y_1) coordinate system in Figure 15.20 is displaced to the right n units, the n must be added to the computation of X_2. To do this in a matrix equation requires that another row and column be added, leaving a 4×4 matrix representation of a rotational plus translational homogeneous transformation. For rotation about the Z axis plus an offset of n in Z, this is given in Equation 15.13.

$$\begin{bmatrix} X_1 \\ Y_1 \\ Z_1 \end{bmatrix} = \begin{bmatrix} \cos\alpha & -\sin\alpha & 0 \\ \sin\alpha & \cos\alpha & 0 \\ 0 & 0 & 1 \end{bmatrix} \begin{bmatrix} \cos\beta & 0 & \sin\beta \\ 0 & 1 & 0 \\ -\sin\beta & 0 & \cos\beta \end{bmatrix} \begin{bmatrix} \cos\gamma & -\sin\gamma & 0 \\ \sin\gamma & \cos\gamma & 0 \\ 0 & 0 & 1 \end{bmatrix} \begin{bmatrix} X_2 \\ Y_2 \\ Z_2 \end{bmatrix}$$

(15.12)

$$\begin{bmatrix} X_1 \\ Y_1 \\ Z_1 \end{bmatrix} = \begin{bmatrix} \cos\alpha\cos\beta\cos\gamma - \sin\alpha\sin\alpha & -\cos\alpha\cos\beta\sin\gamma - \sin\alpha\cos\gamma & \cos\alpha\sin\beta \\ \sin\alpha\cos\beta\cos\gamma + \cos\alpha\sin\gamma & -\sin\alpha\cos\beta\sin\gamma + \cos\alpha\cos\gamma & \sin\alpha\sin\beta \\ -\sin\beta\cos\gamma & \sin\beta\sin\gamma & \cos\beta \end{bmatrix} \begin{bmatrix} X_2 \\ Y_2 \\ Z_2 \end{bmatrix}$$

(15.13)

$$\begin{bmatrix} X_1 \\ Y_1 \\ Z_1 \\ 1 \end{bmatrix} = \begin{bmatrix} \cos\alpha\cos\beta\cos\gamma - \sin\alpha\sin\gamma & -\cos\alpha\cos\beta\sin\gamma - \sin\alpha\cos\gamma & \cos\alpha\sin\beta \\ \sin\alpha\cos\beta\cos\gamma + \cos\alpha\sin\gamma & -\sin\alpha\cos\beta\sin\gamma + \cos\alpha\cos\gamma & \sin\alpha\sin\beta \\ -\sin\beta\cos\gamma & \sin\beta\sin\gamma & \cos\beta \\ 0 & 0 & 0 \end{bmatrix} \begin{bmatrix} X_2 \\ Y_2 \\ Z_2 \\ 1 \end{bmatrix}$$

(15.15)

$$\begin{bmatrix} X_1 \\ Y_1 \\ Z_1 \\ 1 \end{bmatrix} = \begin{bmatrix} \cos\theta & \sin\theta & 0 & 0 \\ -\sin\theta & \cos\theta & 0 & 0 \\ 0 & 0 & 1 & n \\ 0 & 0 & 0 & 1 \end{bmatrix} \begin{bmatrix} X_2 \\ Y_2 \\ Z_2 \\ 1 \end{bmatrix} \qquad (15.14)$$

And the generalized homogeneous transformation matrix with translation is shown in Equation 15.15.

The tools are thus at hand to transform coordinate systems from one reference coordinate system to another. However, before using the transformation, one must examine its computational requirements [22]. For example, consider the robot system in Figure 15.18. Here, four transformation or matrix multiplications are required. A brute force approach would take $[4 \times 4 \times 4] \times 3 + 4 \times 4 = 208$ multiplications and $[4 \times 4 \times 3] \times 3 + 3 \times 4 = 156$ additions. This process can be simplified by noting that the bottom row of each matrix is $(0, 0, 0, 1)$—there is no need to actually multiply every time. This reduces the computation to $[3 \times 4 \times 3] \times 3 + 4 \times 4 = 124$ multiplications and $[3 \times 4 \times 2] \times 3 + 4 \times 4 = 88$ additions. The characteristics of the problem can also be used to reduce the computational load by recognizing aligned axes, similar rotations, and so forth.

APPLICATIONS

As stated earlier, the state of the art of robotics has reached the point where application space has expanded beyond the generally hazardous environments of the early industrial robots. Today, robots are working in assembly environments side-by-side with the more conventional human work force, some members of which they have replaced at more tedious tasks. Let us now examine the use of robots in pick-and-place and assembly operations.

The first problem in both pick-and-place and assembly operations is the acquisition and orientation of parts by the robot. In many cases, conventional orientation techniques such as vibratory bowl feeders can be used to orient and move parts to within easy grasp of the robot. However, this is more specifically designed to suit a particular task than is the robot itself, and more sophisticated and general techniques have been reported [25, 26]. The common problem to be solved is removing parts from a bin into which they have been dumped. Robot-based approaches to this problem fall into two general categories—specialized picking tools and vision-based approaches.

Specialized tools can use jaws, fingers, magnets, vacuum cups as the pick-up mechanism, with the choice depending on the application. However, a University of Rhode Island research team [25] has suggested that a vacuum cup is a good choice for acquiring a large variety of randomly oriented workpieces based on the following requirements:

1. During visual inspection of the workpiece by the gripper, minimal occlusion is preferred for subsequent orientation. Therefore, the holdsite should be a single surface.
2. The grasping mechanism must handle workpieces weighing from a few ounces to five pounds.
3. The gripping mechanism must not be significantly hampered by the workpiece material.

To acquire an object, a vacuum cup must be parallel to a flat surface and in contact with it. Thus, the objects to be picked up must have one or more flat surfaces and the vacuum cup must be placed in the region of a flat surface. In a bin, the parts are randomly stacked up and around each other. Therefore, a vision system can be used to locate an apparent flat surface as a potential holdsite. The problem of placing the cup in parallel with a surface was solved quite elegantly by the Rhode Island research team [25] by employing a spring-loaded vacuum cup called the Surface Adapting Vacuum Gripper (SAVG) and shown in Figure 15.21. The SAVG also has a built-in switch used to sense when contact with the object has been made so that the air flow can be started. After contact, the SAVG is pushed onto the potential holdsite. The compliance of the spring allows the vacuum cup to conform to a surface that is not initially parallel to it. A sensor in the vacuum line signals the robot when the level of vacuum is sufficient to lift the workpiece. The vacuum can be locked and the object lifted. The workpiece can then be presented to a vision system to determine its orientation. Finally, the workpiece can be placed in the desired location with the proper orientation. The sequence of photographs in Figure 15.22 illustrates the operation of the SAVG.

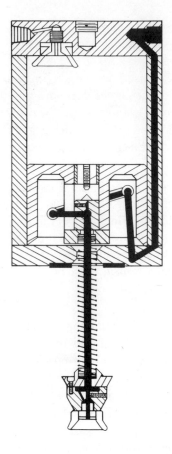

Figure 15.21. Drawing of the Surface Adapting Vacuum Gripper. The cup can be changed to suit the workpiece size, shape, and weight.

Since not all objects have a flat surface of sufficient extent to be picked up by a vacuum cup, methods for using more conventional jaws or fingers are needed for acquiring workpieces. Methods that use vision to locate a workpiece and the sites on it suitable for gripping have been reported by Birk, Kelley, and Wilson [26]. They proposed three approaches, each of which utilizes two distinct phases called the instruction phase and the execution phase. These are similar to the training and operating modes of the TLP in Chapter 8.

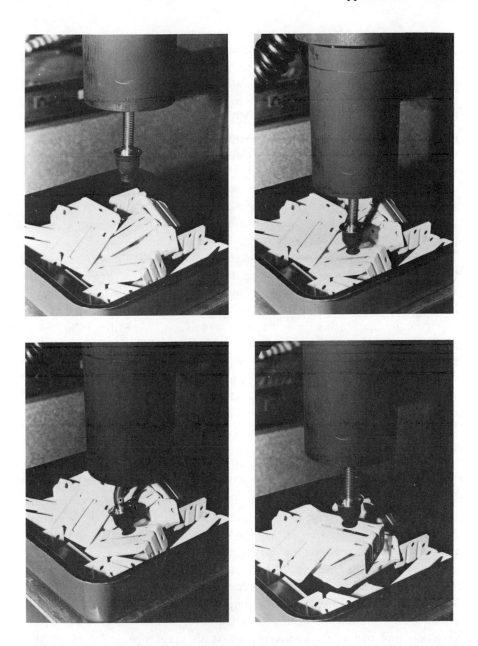

Figure 15.22.   Bin picking using the Surface Adapting Vacuum Gripper.

The first approach, called appearance acquisition, uses an instruction phase to calibrate the system to the appearance of the workpiece. The robot reorients the workpiece by rotating it in two dimensions while keeping the origin of the workpiece coordinate system constant. As the part is rotated in pitch and roll, sample observations are made. Proper grip sites are taught by placing the part in its final position, moving the robot to the end position, and having it grip in the copying mode. The robot's arm joint positions are recorded, and the relation between the gripper and the workpiece coordinate system is computed. When this relationship is reestablished, the system knows that the part is being grasped properly.

In the execution phase workpieces in the supply bin are viewed by the vision system, which looks for the features sampled during the instruction phase. In particular, a part within a given range in pitch and roll is sought. The difference in spin orientation and translation between this position and the final position obtained from the instruction phase is then computed, and the robot system reduces the differences to zero. At this point, the part has been acquired, oriented, and placed.

Another approach called "heuristic acquistion" uses rules based on a priori knowledge of the workpiece and its hold sites. Here, the instruction phase consists of testing different heuristics for acquiring a part, such as "look for the hole that is large enough to insert a finger into" or "find a flat surface large enough to accommodate the cup on a SAVG." During execution, the image of the workpiece is examined to satisfy the heuristics for that part, and the robot proceeds. Since a heuristic does not guarantee that there is a solution, safety mechanisms such as contact sensors must be included to protect both the robot and the part from damage.

Having explored techniques for acquiring parts, let us examine a fundamental problem of automatic assembly. Most assembly situations require that parts be mated, as, for example, in the insertion of a rivet or bolt into a hole in a casting. In this task, the object being inserted must be accurately positioned over the hole. In fixed automation, a great deal of attention is paid to ensure accurate positioning.

The consequences of improper positioning are illustrated in Figure 15.23. The insertion process can be improved by chamfering the hole, the object being inserted, or both. The chamfering assists in centering if the insertion tool can move to accommodate the guidance provided by the chamfer.

Figure 15.23 shows a peg being inserted into a hole at an angle and making contact with one side of the hole. If the insertion process continues at the same angle, two-point contact as shown in Figure 15.23b will take place before the peg reaches the bottom of the hole. This situation, which leads to "jamming" or "wedging," may halt the assembly process.

This problem has been studied extensively by a team at Draper Laboratory [27] that has invented a unique solution. A simple analysis of the process is illustrated in Figure 15.23c, which shows the sequence for

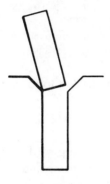

(a) Peg in contact with one
     point of the hole.

(b) Peg in contact with two
    points of the hole before
    the peg reaches the bottom
    of the hole.

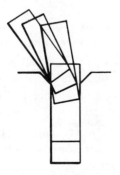

(c) Path for the peg to achieve
    insertion after two-point con-
    tact is made.

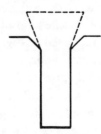

(d) Insertion funnel, which de-
    scribes the path the top of the
    peg must follow for proper
    insertion.

**Figure 15.23.   Insertion of a peg into a hole with an initial angle not parallel
to the center of the hole.**

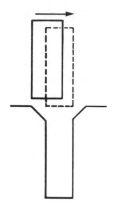 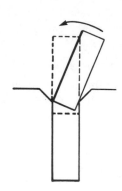

(a) Correction of translation error in initial peg position.

(b) Correction of approach angle error in initial peg position.

Figure 15.24. Initial position error and correction needed for proper insertion of the peg in the hole.

proper insertion after two-point contact is made. The top of the peg must fall within the funnel in Figure 15.23d for proper insertion into the hole. Note that the size of the funnel depends on the diameters of the peg and the hole. The other possible problem in locating a peg over a hole is translating the peg with respect to the hole.

These problems require that (1) sensors be available to determine the extent of the error and actively correct the robot gripper angle and/or position, or (2) some kind of compliance be included in the gripper to allow the actions indicated in Figure 15.24 to occur. The solution invented by the team at Draper Laboratory, called Remote Center Compliance (RCC), is illustrated in Figure 15.25; a version is shown in action in Figure 15.26. RCC is a passive solution to the positioning problem for parts insertion position correction. It reduces the requirements for initial positioning accuracy and the need for active position correction.

The applications we have examined thus far are particular subsets of general manufacturing and assembly problems. Let us now consider recent work on building complete automatic systems for future factories.

Two approaches have been used to incorporate robots into manufacturing processes. In the first, there is an attempt to employ robots as direct

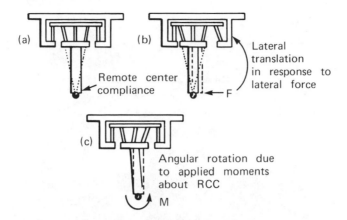

Figure 15.25. Remote centering compliance which allows parts to be inserted into holes without precise positioning or active correction.

replacements for people on an assembly line and was used by a team at General Motors Research Laboratories [28]. The second is a semihard automation approach that uses the robot's flexibility to accommodate a variety of parts on a line which was designed from the outset for robots.

The task that concerned the General Motors team was removal and orientation of parts that had been randomly placed on a conveyor belt. As shown in Figure 15.27, the system uses a robot and a clever vision system. The objects on the belt first pass under the camera of the vision system. They then pass the robot, which picks an object off the belt, orients it, and places it on an assembly.

The vision system uses a linear sensor array of 128 elements. The motion of the belt is used to create the scanning. A problem of vision systems in industrial environments is that sooner or later everything looks black or at least gray. The contrast achieved is thus low as well as variable. The GM system solves this problem by lighting the object from each side with narrow slits of light generated by slender tungsten filament lamps focused by a cylindrical lens. This is illustrated in Figure 15.28a. The combination of the two lamps eliminates shadows and maintains contrast as shown in Figure 15.28b and c. The result is that any object whose height is above the plane of the conveyor belt appears to the camera as a dark object with sharp external edges on a light background. Although the

Figure 15.26.   A version of the RCC performing a parts insertion task.

shadows cast by the lights may make some of the internal features such as holes appear fuzzy, the outlines and some internal features are usually more than adequate for most parts. Each part has a component descriptor associated with it to define the part. The descriptor contains data such as color (black or white), sum of the x-coordinates of the object, sum of the y-coordinates of the object, and area of the largest hole. On each pass of an object under the vision system, the descriptor is updated; only the descriptor gathered, not the pixel map of the object, is stored. Thus, like other systems discussed previously, the system has two modes, a training mode and an operating mode. The training mode is used to calibrate the object in the vision system and to train the robot on its grip sites.

This relatively straightforward approach to a complicated pick-and-place problem is now being "field" tested in a general manufacturing

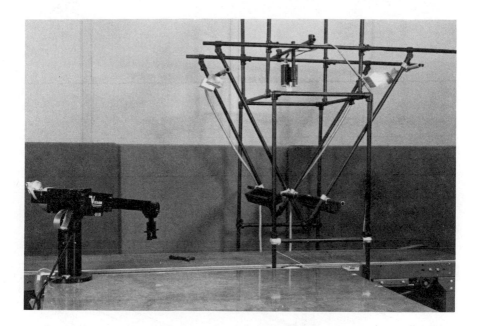

Figure 15.27. Photograph of the GM Vision Robot system.

environment. It represents one of the first uses of vision and robots in a general manufacturing environment.

The second approach, designing an assembly specifically to use robots, is illustrated by the Westinghouse system [29] called APAS (Adaptable Programmable Assembly System). This effort, which has not yet been fully implemented, is a long-term project to increase the productivity of batch assembly operations. The project focuses on the assembly of small motors. Westinghouse makes 450 motor styles, manufacturing them in relatively small average batches of 600 units. There is an average of 13 style changes per day—an ideal application for easily programmed automation.

The APAS combines the techniques discussed here to perform the motor inspection and assembly task. The complete system is shown schematically in Figure 15.29. The first task is assembling the end bell housings of the motor. The basic assembly shown in Figure 15.30 requires two arms, A1 and A2, and two vision systems, V1 and V2. Arms A3 and A4 and their associated vision systems, V3 and V4, inspect the basic

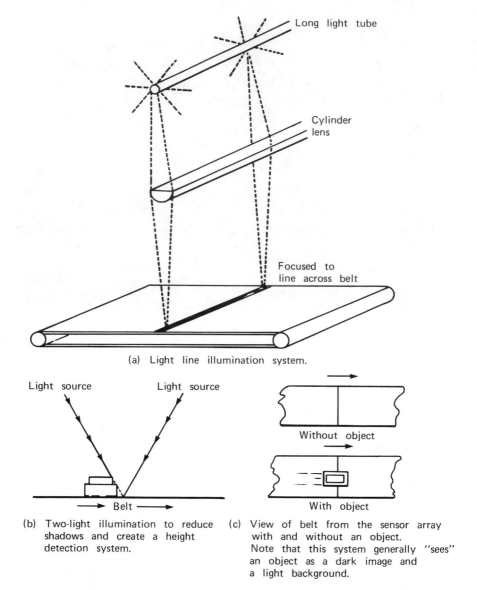

(a) Light line illumination system.

(b) Two-light illumination to reduce
shadows and create a height
detection system.

(c) View of belt from the sensor array
with and without an object.
Note that this system generally "sees"
an object as a dark image and
a light background.

Figure 15.28.   The illumination system and its characteristics as used in the GM Vision Robot system.

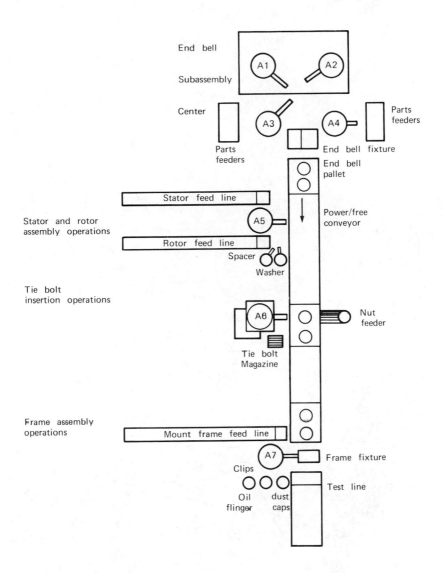

Figure 15.29. Schematic diagram of the APAS for electric motor assembly.

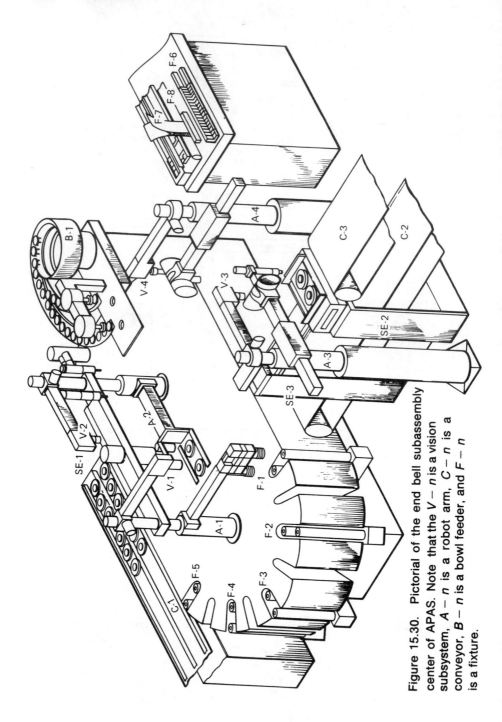

Figure 15.30. Pictorial of the end bell subassembly center of APAS. Note that the $V - n$ is a vision subsystem, $A - n$ is a robot arm, $C - n$ is a conveyor, $B - n$ is a bowl feeder, and $F - n$ is a fixture.

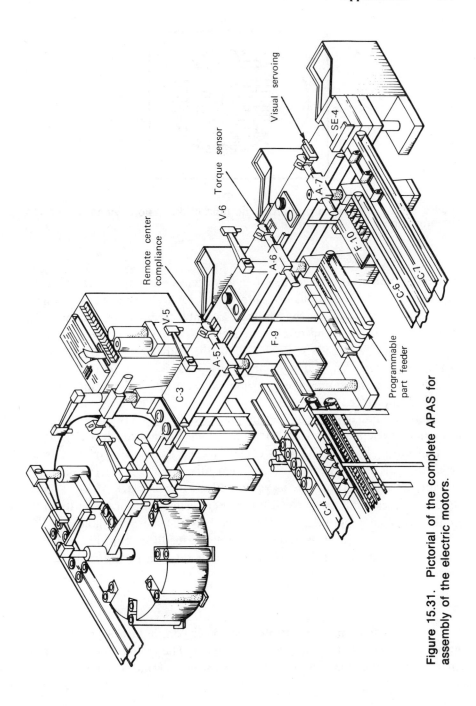

Visual servoing

SE-4

A-7

Torque sensor

V-6

F-10

A-6

C-7

C-6

Remote center
compliance

V-5

F-9

A-5

C-3

Programmable
part feeder

C-4

Figure 15.31. Pictorial of the complete APAS for
assembly of the electric motors.

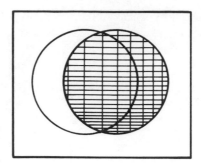

Figure 15.32.   The white portion of the hole in the vision system generates the error signal for visual servicing.

assemblies and add parts such as toggle switches and capacitors. Arm A4 also assembles finished housings onto pallets for transfer to the main line. Note that parts feed to the end-bell-assembly robots by conventional conveyors such as C1 and bowl feeders such as B1. The complete APAS is shown pictorially in Figure 15.31. Again, there are multiple arms labeled An, vision systems Vn, and associated conveyors, Cn, and fixtures, Fn. The assembly process requires the insertion of parts into holes using Remote Center Compliance.

One additional centering technique used here is visual servoing, a technique developed by researchers at SRI [30]. The approach is elegant in its simplicity. It uses a CCD array camera placed strategically over parts to be aligned, as in the peg-in-hole problem discussed earlier. The lighting provides an image of the hole as white and the peg as black. If we assume that the peg can only be grasped for proper vertical insertion and the task limited to positioning, then the difference between the white hole and the black peg can be treated as an error signal in a feedback control system. A simple representation of this technique is illustrated in Figure 15.32.

SUMMARY

The emphasis in this chapter has been on industrial robots and techniques currently used in that environment. The reader who leaves this chapter with the impression that the problems of industrial robots are varied and multidisciplinary has gained some understanding of the scope of the problem. The future of robotics depends on improvements in many technologies to reduce cost and increase the range of performance so that robots become effective in more environments. These technologies include motors, actuators, contact sensors, noncontact sensors, mechanisms, lubrication, electronics, computers, and artificial intelligence.

The history of robotics has shown us a world toward which we seem to be slowly evolving. Early in the history of robotics, Rossum's terrible robots took over the world, and Asimov has described situations in which his laws of robotics lead to contradictions. Thus, although we are beginning to see technology evolve to the point that a robot is an effective manufacturing tool, we must bear in mind how close we still are to the time of *R.U.R.* The models of control introduced in the chapter indicate that we are on the threshold of developing some rather intelligent robots. Yet when we examine the specific techniques of modern robots, such as control and sensor problems, we admit that we are still far from a coordinated factory robot with a good universal sensor system.

EXERCISES

1. Read one of Asimov's books such as *I, Robot* [15] or *Eight Stories from the Rest of the Robots* [6] or both.

2. Discuss the ways the three laws of robotics would affect your approach to robot design.

3. How many degrees of freedom are there in:

   (a) A bicycle?
   (b) The human forefinger?
   (c) The human arm?

4. Is the robot arm in Figure 15.9 adequate if the object being picked up contains nitroglycerine? If not, why not? Also, if not, design an arm that would be adequate and safe.

5. Does a conventional autopilot system for an airplane, using the on-board instruments as sensors, fit into any of the robot control models in Figure 15.14?

6. What constraints do the environmental hazards for industrial robots listed in Table 15.1 place on the power supply and actuators for an industrial robot?

7. Given a robot gripper with two fingers, three switches in each finger, and a compliant surface over each finger, and assuming that the fingers are hinged from a single point as shown below, create a heuristic device that will allow the fingers and their associated robot to pick up an object without using more force between the fingers than is absolutely necessary. What are the crucial design parameters of the fingers?

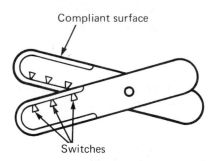

Compliant surface

Switches

8. Given the following robot arm and object, find the position of each joint required to pick up the object by placing the gripper over the object if the position of the object is $X_1 = 1$, $Y_1 = -2$, $Z = 0$.

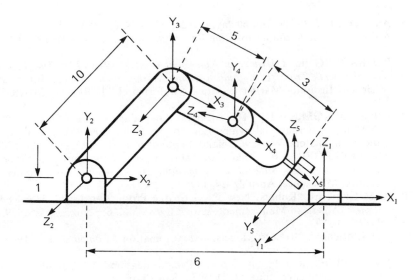

9. Lay out a robot assembly system that will pick up the two parts
    of a felt-tip pen with a push-on cap, and then push on the cap.
    The caps, with steel pocket clips already in place, are in bins and
    the other portion of the pen is on a conveyor belt. The assembled
    pens are to be dropped into a box. (Hint: Start by writing a
    detailed description of the assembly process.)

REFERENCES

1. CAPEK, Karel, *R.U.R.* (Rossum's Universal Robots), Samuel French, London,
   1923.
2. WILLIAMS, James M., "Antique Mechanical Computers, Part 1: Early
   Automation," *Byte*, July 1978, pp. 48–58.
3. WILLIAMS, James M., "Antique Mechanical Computers, Part 2: 18th and
   19th Century Mechanical Marvels," *Byte*, August 1978, pp. 96–107.
4. PENNIMAN, Charles F., "Philadelphia's 179 Year Old Android," *Byte*,
   August 1978, pp. 90–94.

5. ASIMOV, I., *I, Robot*, Doubleday, Garden City, N.Y, 1950.
6. ASIMOV, I., *Eight Stories from the Rest of the Robots*, Jove/HBJ Books, N.Y., 1978.
7. ROSENBERG, J., *A History of Numerical Control 1949-1972: The Technical Development, Transfer to Industry, and Assimilation*, U.S.C. Information Sciences Institute, Marina del Ray, California, I.S.I. Report ISI-RR-72-3, 1972.
8. ENGELBERGER, J. F., "The Artificial Appendage Game," Second CISM/INTOMM International Symposium on the Theory and Practice of Robots and Manipulators, Warsaw, Poland, September 14–17, 1976, pp. 517–530.
9. ENGELBERGER, J. F., "That's No Robot, That's Just Automation," *Proceedings of the IEEE Milwaukee Symposium on Automatic Computation and Control*, Milwaukee, April 22–24, 1976.
10. REMICK, Carl, "Robots: New Faces on the Production Line," *Management Review* (American Management Associations), Vol. 68, No. 5, May 1979, pp. 24–28, 38, 39.
11. PAUL, Richard, "Robots, Models, and Automation," *Computer*, July 1979, pp. 19–27.
12. ENGELBERGER, J. F., "A Robotics Prognostication," 1977, Joint Automatic Control Conference, June 22–24, 1977, San Francisco.
13. LISTON, R. A., "Walking Machines," *Journal of Terramechanics*, Vol. 1, No. 3, 1964, pp. 18–31.
14. MCGHEE, R. B., "Future Prospects for Sensor-Based Robots," *Proceedings of the Symposium on Computer Vision and Sensor-Based Robots*, General Motors Research Laboratories, September 1978.
15. MUNSON, John H., "Robot Planning, Execution, and Monitoring in an Uncertain Environment," Proceedings Second IJCAI, London, England, September 1–3, 1971 also SRI Artificial Intelligence Group Technical note 59, SRI Project 8259, May 1971.
16. NILSSON, N. J., *Principles of Artificial Intelligence*, Tioga Publishing Co., Palo Alto, Ca. 1980
17. TANNER, William R., "Basics of Robotics," Technical Paper MS77-734 presented at Autofact I, Robots II Conference, October 31–November 3, 1977, Society of Manufacturing Engineers.
18. NILSSON, N. J., "A Mobile Automaton: An Application of Artificial Intelligence Techniques," Proceedings First IJCAI, May 1969, pp. 509–515.
19. ENGELBERGER, J. F., "Designing Robots for Industrial Environments," *Mechanism and Machine Theory*, Vol. 12, No. 5, Pergamon, 1977, pp. 403–412.
20. ROSEN, Charles A., and David NITZAN, "Use of Sensors in Programmable Automation," SRI Artificial Intelligence Center Technical Note 122, April 1976.
21. BINFORD, T. D., "Sensor Systems for Manipulation," *Proceedings of the First Conference on Remotely Manned Systems (RMS), Exploration, and Operations in Space,*, E. HEER, ed., 1973, 283–291.
22. GOTO, T., "Compact Packaging by Robot with Tactile Sensors," *Proceedings of the Second International Symposium on Industrial Robots*, IIT Research Institute, Chicago, 1972.

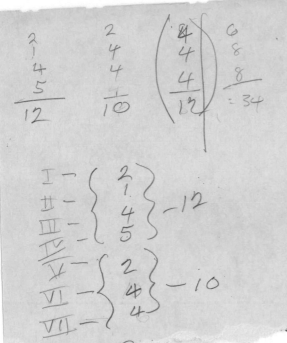

Three-Dimensional Solids," in
...ing, J. T. TIPPETT, et al., eds.,
. 159–197, M.I.T. Lincoln Lab

, "Kinematics of the MIT-AL-
rking Paper 69, May 1974.
lable Robots with Vision to
Fourth Report on NSF Grant
ngston, R.I., July 1978.
ON, "Acquiring Workpieces:
Eighth International Sympo-
May 30–June 1, 1978.
Y, et al., "Robot Assembly
IR Symposium on Computer
ptors Research Laboratories,

Mitchel R. WARD, "CON-
for Transferring Parts from
omputer Vision and Sensor-
atories, Warren, Mich., Sep-

ogrammable Assembly Sys-
n and Sensor-Based Robots,
arren, Mich., September 25–26,

30. ROSEN, Charles A., "Machine Intelligence Applied to Industrial Automation," Proceedings from the Fourth NSF/RANN Grantees Conference on Production Research and Technology, November 30, December 1–2, 1976, IIT Research Institute, Chicago.

Credits

Figure 10.20   Figure 10, W. N. Toy, "Fault Tolerant Design of Local EES Processor," © 1978 IEEE. Reprinted with permission, from *Proceedings of the IEEE,* October 1978, Vol. 66, No. 10.

Table 10.1   Table VIII from D. Siewiorek et al., "A Study of C.mmp, Cm*, and C.vmp: Part I—Experiences with Fault Tolerance in Multiprocessor Systems," © 1978 IEEE. Reprinted with permission, from *Proceedings of the IEEE,* October 1978, Vol. 66, No. 10.

Table 10.2   Table IX from D. Siewiorek et al., "A Study of C.mmp, Cm*, and C.vmp: Part I—Experiences with Fault Tolerance in Multiprocessor Systems," © 1978 IEEE. Reprinted with permission, from *Proceedings of the IEEE,* October 1978,Vol. 66, No. 10.

Figure 14.2   Courtesy Dr. R. L. Gregory, University of Bristol, Bristol, England.

Figure 14.8   Figure 3 from A. Hanson and E. Riseman, "Segmentation of Natural Scenes," in A. Hanson and E. Riseman, eds., *Computer Vision Systems,* Academic Press, 1978.

Figure 14.9   Figures 1 and 2 from S. Zucker, "Relaxation Labelling, Local Ambiguity, and Low-level Vision," in C. H. Chen, ed., *Pattern Recognition and Artificial Intelligence,* Academic Press, 1976.

Figure 14.10   Figure 3 from S. Zucker, "Relaxation Labelling, Local Ambiguity, and Low-level Vision," in C. H. Chen, ed., *Pattern Recognition and Artificial Intelligence,* Academic Press, 1976.

Figure 14.11   Figures 2 and 3 from R. Ehrich and J. Foith, "Topology and Semantics of Intensity Arrays," in A. Hanson and E. Riseman, eds., *Computer Vision Systems,* Academic Press, 1978.

Figure 14.13   From A. Hanson, E. Riseman, and F. Glazer, "Edge Relaxation and Boundary Continuity," in R. M. Harlick, ed., *Consistent Labeling Problems in Pattern Recognition,* Plenum Press.

Figure 14.14   Figure 3 from A. Hanson and E. Riseman, "Visions: A Computer System for Interpreting Scenes," in A. Hanson and E. Riseman, eds., *Computer Vision Systems,* Academic Press, 1978.

Figure 14.15   Figure 2 from C. A. Rosen, "Machine Vision and Robotics: Industrial Requirements," reprinted with permission, from SRI Technical Note 174, SRI Project 6284, November 1978.

Figure 14.16   Figure 3 from C. A. Rosen, "Machine Vision and Robotics: Industrial Requirements," reprinted with permission, from SRI Technical Note 174, SRI Project 6284, November 1978.

Page 413   Figure 4 from S. Zucker, "Relaxation Labelling, Local Ambiguity, and Low-level Vision," in C. H. Chen, ed., *Pattern Recognition and Artificial Intelligence,* Academic Press, 1976.

Figure 15.1   Courtesy Lucas Films Limited, North Hollywood, California.

Figure 15.2   Courtesy The Franklin Institute, Philadelphia, Pennsylvania.

Figure 15.3 Courtesy The Franklin Institute, Philadelphia, Pennsylvania.

Figure 15.4 Courtesy Brookhaven National Laboratory, Upton, New York.

Figure 15.5 Courtesy Joseph Engelberger, Unimation, Inc., Danbury, Connecticut.

Figure 15.6 Courtesy Digital Equipment Corporation.

Figure 15.7 Courtesy National Aeronautics and Space Administration, Viking News Center, Pasadena, California.

Figure 15.9 Courtesy Cincinnati Milacron, Cincinnati, Ohio.

Figure 15.13 Courtesy Cincinnati Milacron, Cincinnati, Ohio.

Figure 15.15 Courtesy Binks Manufacturing Company, Franklin Park, Illinois.

Figure 15.16 Figure 4 from S. Holland et al., "Consight-1: A Vision-Controlled Robot for Transferring Parts from a Belt Conveyor," in *Computer Vision Sensor-Based Robots,* Plenum Press, 1978.

Figure 15.21 From J. Birk et al., "General Methods to Enable Robots with Vision to Acquire, Orient, and Transport Workpieces," *Fourth Report,* National Science Foundation Grant APR74-13935, 1978.

Figure 15.22 From J. Birk et al., "General Methods to Enable Robots with Vision to Acquire, Orient, and Transport Workpieces," *Fourth Report,* National Science Foundation Grant APR74-13935, 1978.

Figure 15.25 Figure 13 from J. L. Nevins and D. E. Whitney, et al., "Research Issues for Automatic Assembly," The Charles Stark Draper Laboratory, Cambridge, Massachusetts.

Figure 15.26 Figure 15 from J. L. Nevins and D. E. Whitney, et al., "Research Issues for Automatic Assembly," The Charles Stark Draper Laboratory, Cambridge, Massachusetts.

Figure 15.27 Figure 1 from S. Holland et al., "Consight-1: A Vision-Controlled Robot for Transferring Parts from a Belt Conveyor," in *Computer Vision Sensor-Based Robots,* Plenum Press, 1978.

Figure 15.28 Figures 6 and 7 from S. Holland et al., "Consight-1: A Vision-Controlled Robot for Transferring Parts from a Belt Conveyor," in *Computer Vision Sensor-Based Robots,* Plenum Press, 1978.

Figure 15.29 Figure 4 from R. G. Abraham, "APAS: Adaptable Programmable Assembly System," Westinghouse Research and Development Center, National Science Foundation Grant ISP76-24164.

Figure 15.30 Figure 5 from R. G. Abraham, "APAS: Adaptable Programmable Assembly System," .Westinghouse Research and Development Center, National Science Foundation Grant ISP76-24164.

Figure 15.31 Figure 6 from R. G. Abraham, "APAS: Adaptable Programmable Assembly System," Westinghouse Research and Development Center, National Science Foundation Grant ISP76-24164.

Index